We Are All Poets Here
Thomas Merton's 1968 journey to Alaska,
a shared story about spiritual seeking

Kathleen Witkowska Tarr

We Are All Poets Here— Copyright © 2017 by Kathleen Witkowska Tarr. All Rights Reserved. This book may not be reproduced in whole or in part, by any means, mechanical or digital, without the written permission from the author or publisher, except for small excerpts used for instructional or education purposes.

ISBN: 978-57833-691-3

Library of Congress Control Number: 2017918027

First Printing January 2018
Printed in the U.S.A.

Editing:	Michael Burwell
	Vered R. Mares
Editorial Assistance:	Jonathan Montaldo
Cover:	Malaspina Glacier & Mount Saint Elias, USGS (used by permission)
Photos:	All photos from the author's personal collection, unless otherwise noted and credited. Epigraphs used by permission with special thanks to the Thomas Merton Center, at Bellarmine University, New Directions, and Harper Collins.
Map:	Map of Alaska, edited by Vered R. Mares
Published by:	VP&D House, Inc. 1352 W. 25th Ave. Anchorage, AK 99503 www.vpdhouse.com • www.facebook/vpdhouse 907-720-7559 • info@vpdhouse.com

Distributed in part by:
𝕿𝖔𝖉𝖉 𝕮𝖔𝖒𝖒𝖚𝖓𝖎𝖈𝖆𝖙𝖎𝖔𝖓𝖘
611 E. 12th Ave.
Anchorage, Alaska 99501-4603
Phone: (907) 274-TODD (8633) • Fax (907) 929-5550
www.alaskabooksandcalendars.com • sales@toddcom.com
with other offices in Juneau and Fairbanks, Alaska

For my sons, Banan and Derek,
and for seekers everywhere

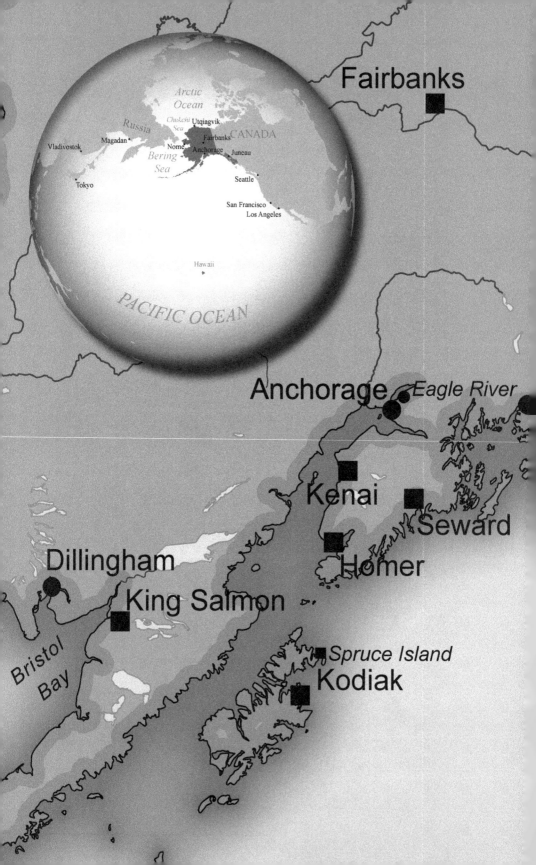

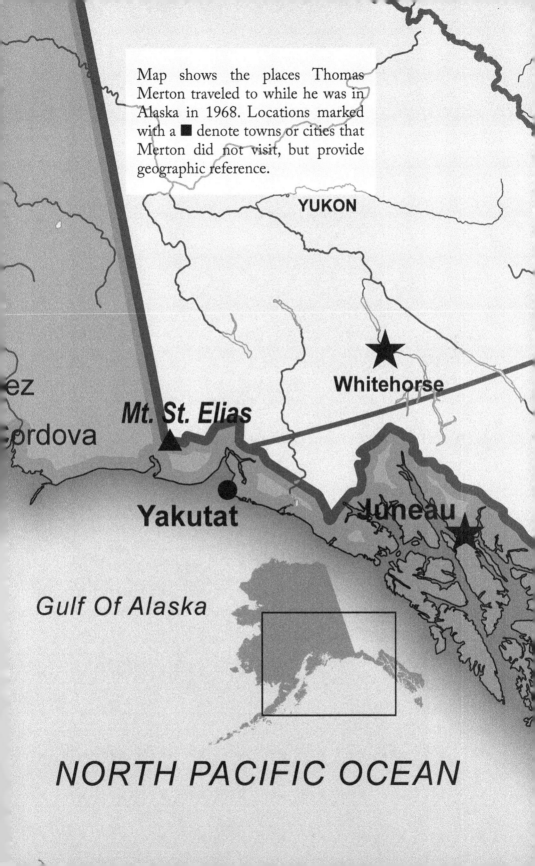

Contents

Alaska Map 4
Preface 9
1 The Golden Triangle 19
2 Migration to Alaska 33
3 Coming into Yakutat 53
4 Abyss of Solitude 63
5 Spirit of the Tlingits 75
6 Mr. Pavlik & the Silver Chalice 87
7 The Inner Ordeal 111
8 Retreat to Kentucky 133
9 Solitary Mountain 157
10 Burial at Ankau Lagoon 173
11 Merciful Sea 199
12 Pasternak's Tree 211
13 Prelude to Merton's Alaska Journey 227
14 Igor and the Holy Mountain 249
15 Retracing Merton's Journey — 1968 269
16 The Monk Flies North 283
17 Merton's Alaska Journal 297
18 Dillingham 309

19 The Russian Icon......................321
20 In the Land of Old Russian America..............331
21 The Mad Woman Runs to the Dark..............345
22 Contemplations From a Cabin...................357
23 Ocean Cape............................377
    Thomas Merton's 1968 Alaska Itinerary............392
    Bibliography...................................394
    Acknowledgements..............................397
    Publisher's Note...............................400

I have the immense joy of being man, a member of a race in which God himself became incarnate. As if the sorrows and stupidities of the human condition could overwhelm me, now I realize what we all are. And if only everybody could realize this! But it cannot be explained. There is no way of telling people that they are all walking around shining like the sun.

Thomas Merton,
Conjectures of a Guilty Bystander

Preface

I had my first real look at the scale and grandeur of Alaska from inside a single engine Cessna 180 flown, to my delight, by a female bush pilot. I climbed into the back seat and strapped on the clunky green headset. With no experience flight seeing before, my stomach tightened with nerves. Once airborne, I pressed my forehead against the window. Yakutat and its surrounding region were something beyond imagination. As my eyes beheld the scale of the landscape, I knew my life would never be the same. Boundless mountains and beauty extended in all directions. This was a piece of earth that rendered the talkative, speechless. The arrogant, meek. The powerful, humble.

Once the fishing village of Yakutat (population 350) left our view, I didn't spot another settlement, man-made structure or road anywhere beneath us as we flew over thickly forested islands on our way toward Hubbard Glacier. It was 1979 and having just relocated myself from the flatlands of Florida, all I could do was gape at the endless ice fields and glacial lobes reaching into Disenchantment Bay. I counted at least six other glaciers close by. The pilot's enthusiastic voice crackled in and out of the mic. The coastal St. Elias Range reached higher and was more impressive than the Rockies, she said. Due west was a sprawling piedmont glacier as big as Rhode Island—the Malaspina—bulging with rocks and zigzagging torrents of water that emptied into Yakutat Bay and the Gulf of Alaska.

I wondered what kind of quiet and isolated existence I had gotten myself into. Living near glaciers and wilderness did not match the role or life I had previously imagined for myself.

At the start of my junior year of high school, in 1971, my mother announced that my four siblings and I were moving from our birthplace of Pennsylvania to a rental in the subtropics. We needed a fresh start, she said. Only I didn't agree. I hadn't seen my biological father for years and wanted to stay in Pittsburgh where, one day, I might see him again.

With the move to Florida's west coast, and my pale, freckled, often sun-burned skin, I tried to adjust. When I reached college age, with no family financial support or savings, I received government assistance and continued working minimum wage jobs as a food server to make ends meet. Eventually, I finished a communications and journalism degree at a small public university in Pensacola. In the late 1970s, to my young eyes, St. Petersburg, Florida was dull, overrun with tacky tourist shops, a slack economy, and too many boring, gray-haired beachcombers.

With all my worldly ambitions, I clearly didn't belong to the Sunshine State. I deeply connected with the female lead on the popular Mary Tyler Moore television show. Unhappy with my lot in life, I wanted to break out of the standard secretarial pool. I'd be nothing like my mother stuck in dead-end jobs with no formal education raising five kids as a single parent for large parts of her life. I pictured myself as an independent, unmarried, modern-day career woman exactly like Mary Tyler Moore. Dressed in a smart suit, swinging a briefcase, I could walk down a busy Manhattan avenue, young, pretty, and practically carefree.

Instead, I wound up in bush Alaska.

I was a bundle of contradictions and harbored a restless temperament with a lot of confusion about female self-identity. On May 6, 1978, fleeing from everything I thought I knew and understood, I said goodbye to everyone and everything, the suffocating humidity and the neatly planted rows of palm trees. I arrived in Anchorage shortly after the pipeline boom times believing it might be easier to break into journalism. I landed an entry-level job at the local NBC television affiliate like my

Preface

heroine, Mary Tyler Moore, and planned my ascent from writing public service announcements to writing Emmy Award winning copy and sitting in the news anchor's chair one day.

But, to my surprise and contrary to my own goals of independence, I was reacquainted with a man named Michael, and eight months later we were married.

I agreed to follow my new husband as he pursued a promising aviation job as a flight service specialist working for the Federal Aviation Administration. Yakutat was a remote Tlingit Indian village on the north Pacific coast with no roads in or out, no radio, newspapers, shopping malls, and with more bears and bald eagles than humans.

For the next four years, as we settled into that speck of a place in the middle of the Tongass National Forest, I had to learn from others much wiser than me how to be Alaskan. For the sake of Michael's career advancement, we were forced to move frequently to other parts of the state including the former Russian-American capital of Sitka. I gave birth to two sons and as the years passed, everyday life grew intensely more complicated. With a family to raise in one of America's most expensive states, both of us were consumed with full-time jobs and the typical familial pressures mounted.

By the mid-to-late 1990s, I joined the staff of the Alaska State Chamber of Commerce managing their statewide communications and regional office. Russian current events entered my life, front and center, in the dramatically changing political atmosphere. Under Mikhail Gorbachev, the new *glasnost* policies and *perestroika* reforms led to optimism and cultural euphoria in former Russian-America. Alaskans and Russians rekindled their close historical links and unparalleled cultural exchanges unfolded—a kind of grassroots, international diplomacy unseen in the Lower 48.

I was thrust into exciting roles and projects in my new job and helped organize high level business programs, including ground-breaking trade missions to cities throughout the Russian Far East in Magadan, Irkutsk, Khabarovsk, and Vladivostok. Communism in the USSR, and the Soviet Union itself, bureaucratically collapsed a few years later. All the goodwill about Russia's New Economy and its move toward more honest and open politics dwindled in time for complicated reasons. Widespread business and educational programs between Alaska and Russia began drying up. Russians were basically left to figure out their own best strategies of economic survival.

We kept making more household moves around the state. On the Kenai Peninsula, I took a full-time job working at the Kenai Visitors and Cultural Center, down the street from a Russian Orthodox Church. Five more years raced by. Youthful dreams and desires long-buried from college days, returned. I wanted to study writing more seriously and to take leave, at least temporarily, of the daily grind. With an offer for a competitive teaching fellowship, with full spousal encouragement, and both sons raised, I departed for graduate school. It was "mom's time" to get back to her roots. When I arrived for my MFA studies at the University of Pittsburgh as a "mature" non-traditional graduate student in 2002, it was the first time I saw my birth city in twenty-nine years—not since my mother had abruptly uprooted us with the move south to Florida.

In the last semester of my three-year program, while under immense pressure to finish classes and return to my regular domestic life, I discovered Thomas Merton.

Thomas Merton was apparently the most famous monk in American history, a religious celebrity, especially among Catholics, and a leading spiritual thinker in the English-speaking world. A Trappist monk from the austere religious order, Cistercians of the Strict Observance, he was also an international bestselling writer and called the "master of mysticism" by some.

But I'd never heard of him. I considered myself irreligious and secular. I hadn't belonged to any church nor read much of anything by way of great religious writings. I didn't own a Bible and had not read from a Bible to my children as they grew up.

Preface

As a graduate student, I kept seeing Thomas Merton's acclaimed autobiography, *The Seven Storey Mountain* (1948), on various book lists as a must-read, and my literary curiosity was piqued. Upon its release, *The Seven Storey Mountain* quickly became a bestseller among the religious and secular alike, and was translated into over twenty languages. Ever since, it has been ranked as a classic in world literature. Merton told an intimate and compelling story about his religious awakening in a twentieth century world seemingly gone mad with destruction, barbarism, and mass killings. Years later, editor Robert Giroux, said Merton's book was the "right subject, told at the right time, in the right way." People were still grappling with the psychological trauma and spiritual emptiness following the devastation and shocking atrocities witnessed during World War II with atomic bombs being dropped over Japan and Jews being gassed to death in concentration camps.

In February 2005, I decided to find out what this esteemed memoirist, Thomas Merton, was all about. What kind of writer was he and what made him so good? Overloaded with academic work, teaching freshman composition and in tears about how I was going to finish my creative thesis given all the pending deadlines, I nevertheless picked up *The Seven Storey Mountain*. Merton's memoir had nothing to do with the subjects I was writing about and most concerned with—Alaskan and Russian history, human migrations, and nature. The only spiritual book I had ever bothered to read was Herman Hesse's *Siddhartha* and that was long ago.

I delved into Merton's writing.

Spellbound by his lyricism and his warm and engaging narrative voice, I found my interest went beyond an appreciation for eloquence and intellect.

When I read him, I naturally looked back on my own life. I related to his stupid younger self (mentioned frequently), to his pride, arrogance and drive to be a big somebody.

Most of *The Seven Storey Mountain* centered on Merton's early years in France and England—the son of an American mother and New Zealander father, both artists—and his gradual spiritual awakening. Right out of Columbia, Tom Merton received an impressive first teaching position at St. Bonaventure's College in Olean, New York, in the same town where his best friend from Columbia University, Robert Lax, had come from.

And just as Tom Merton seemed to have his career in academia all figured out as a literature professor, he walked away from it, took a train to rural Kentucky, and vowed to be a penniless monk.

Why did a twenty-something sophisticated, well-traveled man from New York City, at the peak of his youth and sexuality, choose such a drastic lifestyle change? Why did the young Merton give up bars, jazz clubs, women and sex? Why forego a chance to earn money, to romp around the world as a bachelor, or to become a husband or parent?

I admired his convictions and his deep faith, which seemed in dire contrast to my chaotic frame of mind at the moment—a constant dividing of self and family, a life fraught with interior tensions. A product of the times, I was spiritually lost and confused.

Merton's autobiography captivated me on many levels, but I quit reading him after that.

I needed to get back to real life, give up the fantasy of living as an older graduate student away from daily marital responsibilities. It was time to help pay the bills again. I finished my three-year program, returned to Alaska, and looked for another job as I promised I would.

I might never have thought about the monk again, except that one day, I checked out a book from the Anchorage library—*A Republic of Rivers: Three Centuries of Nature Writing from Alaska and the Yukon* (Oxford University Press, 1990). As a long-time Alaskan, I was interested in nature writing and had started to sporadically publish a few essays of my own.

As I thumbed through the table of contents, in utter astonishment, I saw Thomas Merton's name. What was that monk doing in an anthology about far north nature writing?

Preface

I flipped to the editor's note and found a brief and startling explanation. After 27 years in the monastery, Merton left Kentucky and made a surprise trip to Alaska for seventeen days in September 1968.

I had assumed that after the success of *The Seven Storey Mountain* Merton remained safely tucked behind monastery walls praying from dusk to dawn until the day he died. What drove him to leave the Abbey of Gethsemani and make a trip to the wilds of Alaska in 1968? What kind of life had he been leading for two decades? And why in 1968, in that particularly tumultuous year, did he make his first extensive trips outside the Abbey and to Alaska?

As I read further into the nature anthology, there was more of a reason to be flabbergasted.

One of the excerpted passages taken from Merton's 1968 Alaskan journal read, "September 27/Yakutat."

I wanted to fling the book across the room! Eleven years before I got to Yakutat, Thomas Merton had apparently flown in a bush plane over the very same glacial landscape near the Saint Elias Mountains and Hubbard Glacier as I had. In all my years in Alaska, no one I knew, writers and Catholics included, ever mentioned his name.

As was his compulsive practice, the monk kept a journal while traveling. Merton's notes mentioned the torrential rains he experienced in Southeast Alaska and the "snowy nails" of mountains he saw.

Step by step, I immersed myself in his life story and writings, and I eventually bought the Alaska Journal. At first, Merton was the spiritual spackling, he wasn't the wall. Without knowing anything about it, though, I became a Merton pilgrim. He became my alter ego. He began following me around, inhabiting my consciousness, and appearing in my dreams. Uncanny synchronicities cropped up between us; the coincidences multiplied. Over a period of years, I slowly started to retrace his physical steps in Kentucky, New York City, northern California, at City Lights bookstore in San Francisco, and especially in Alaska locales. Ten years later, the charismatic monk is still by my side.

Thomas Merton has not delivered any foot-stomping sermons. I do not light incense or hear a chorus of angels singing sweet hallelujahs whenever I think of him. He has not offered me any Twelve Step Program to Spiritual Wholeness. He simply wasn't that kind of monk.

Many things have gone wrong in my life, and much has changed since my first discovery of Merton. Deep losses. Heartaches. False starts. Eternal self-doubts. Emotional fault lines that widened with time.

But through Merton, I have gained a few rays of inner clarity. I learned that to know my true self, the core of who I really am, more drastic measures were often needed. A complete change of scenery was called for.

Once more, I was reminded to step away from the noise—all the shaky foundations, media-driven images, ready-made social expectations, and the surreal politics. The time came when I had to face the naked truth about the illusions and falsehoods I continued living under and hiding behind for too long.

This is the story about my spiritual odyssey with Alaska, Russia, and with the beautiful, towering, and flawed human being—Thomas Merton. It's also the story about the monk's little-known and under-told trek to Alaska in 1968, one of the last pieces of earth he saw, and a story that needs telling in Merton's biography.

Merton wrote, "I'm here in answer to somebody's prayers."

An obsessive note taker, the monk recorded those hurried, but prescient words on the pages of his thin, half-forgotten Alaskan journal.

It was he, Thomas Merton, who applied the salve to my half-wrecked soul.

17

So now, when the time came for me to take spiritual stock of myself, it was natural that I should do so by projecting my whole spiritual condition into the sphere of economic history and the class struggle.

In other words, the conclusion I came to was that it was not so much I myself that was to blame for my unhappiness, but the society in which I lived…

—Thomas Merton,
The Seven Storey Mountain

1 The Golden Triangle

The past doesn't come to haunt you; it comes to wake you up. It disappears some fathoms under the sea, but there are moments when the past surfaces, breaches like a whale, and you gasp to behold its power before it crashes back to the depths and disappears again.

I thank God I was born in Pittsburgh, under the sign of the water bearer, in the smoky city of bridges and rust, the city of steel mills bellowing over sad, murky rivers. Pittsburgh, the birthplace of my father and mother, Louis and Margie Witkowski, children of immigrants in a patchwork of immigrants—Italians, Slovaks, Germans, Jews, Irish, Polaks—everyone struggling alongside everyone else, riding crowded public transit buses and streetcars, electric sparks flying from metal wheels screeching down metal tracks. The iron city, the steel city, the symbol of the Great American Worker city, where proletarians in factories, laborers of all creeds and colors with little education, carried aluminum lunch pails packed with chipped ham and bologna sandwiches and punched time clocks and sweated through long shifts to keep the industrial furnaces firing at Jones & Laughlin Steel Co. Generations of anonymous white and black faces helped build America through their toil. My people filled the commercial bakeries, mom-and-pop upholstery shops, small ethnic groceries, brick warehouses, steel mills, and the Heinz ketchup factory.

It's the city where *babushkas* like Julia Vachie, my paternal grandmother, found occasional work as public school janitors, and where women of little means could work as seamstresses or shout orders across the lunch counter at the downtown McCrory's Five & Dime. They took minimum wage jobs without guarantees to help feed their families. This is how you made it in the "new country." You earned your way. You tried to learn English and recited the Pledge of Allegiance and sang America the Beautiful. You taught your kids to work hard at public school memorizing multiplication tables and practicing reading. You saved for years and bought your first car with cash. You took one family vacation by driving to Lake Erie. For something more extravagant you headed with the masses for a cheap motel or cottage on the Jersey shore.

Many families felt connected through their shared common stories, at least I thought of them this way. We were all in this Pittsburgh riverboat together. In my youth, I heard stories about how families had drastically uprooted themselves from their homelands to migrate across the Atlantic Ocean looking for work. Immigrants helped build many of the city's Catholic and Byzantine Churches. Somehow, the "displaced" persons managed to keep some semblance of their pre-America cultural history, religious rituals and traditions intact. Descendants of African-American slaves had fled the Deep South for what they dreamed would be a better life in the prospering urban north. In fifth grade at my public school, I was taught old Negro spirituals and no one thought it was culturally inappropriate. I saw how people of all colors and backgrounds held onto one another through the pain and sufferings of racial and ethnic hardships. These Pittsburghers I remember were living proof of humanity's ability to fight hunger, alienation and despair.

During much of the twentieth century Pittsburgh was nationally mocked and defamed as "hell with the lid off." But as I recollect my origins, as I try to coax shaky memory into the more solid form of story, I view it a little differently now. And maybe that's what the passage of time does; it heals. I understand that a certain part of my character was formed in the palette of its polluted, run down, bankrupted existence.

The Golden Triangle

Years later—and many lifetimes since I played hopscotch on its street corners and carried around a transistor radio—I still regard the city through this colorful lens. By some strange grace, a spiritual vitality and energy had seeped into the place. On an elemental level, grit and tenacity lay beneath the industrial soot. Looking back at its littered enclaves and amid its many old churches and synagogues, I came to believe that a purifying spirit, some cleansing power must have been at work helping the spectrum of people I saw struggle to make it better for their children.

For much of my life, I created a self-image, forged from the inner city as Steel Town Girl. I liked to think she was tough, endowed with inner fortitude and tenacity enough to withstand any tempest. Steel Town Girl didn't grow up in the suburbs with a mommy and daddy, a shiny family car, Holy Communions, dance lessons, and summer camps. That's not the somewhere I was from. I wasn't sure where I belonged exactly, but it wasn't to that.

With every streetcar ride I took as a kid, a sense of possibility and adventure unfolded. On many Saturdays in fifth and six grades, I hopped on streetcars because the fares were cheap and mother usually slept during the day after working night shifts. They took me downtown or as locals would say, *dahntahn*. I roamed beneath skyscrapers and cathedral spires, and rode the escalators up and down Gimbels Department Store, the only department store I knew of. I pretended to have more than measly quarters in my pocket and tried on cosmopolitan clothes in the dressing rooms, then put everything back on the rack. Sometimes, I had enough baby-sitting money to rent ice skates at the new Civic Arena. I aimlessly wandered the streets. The noise and bustle of the city were a sanctuary away from the tensions at home.

My little brother Richy and I collected pop bottles. We were poor and understood that this was how we could get spare change. We hung around the train trestles and scoured through playgrounds and parking lots looking for stuff we could cash in on. In sixth grade, Richy grew more resourceful. He got himself into a new line of income-producing work as a petty shoplifter, but he always shared whatever he stole from the convenience stores.

One of Pittsburgh's most recognizable landmarks was the cable car known as the "Incline." It still carries riders up the hillside to Grandview Avenue on the top of Mt. Washington, a much glitzier skyline today than it was during my childhood. To my young girl's eyes, Mt. *Warsh*ington was a bona fide mountain, bigger than any hills I'd seen—until time and fate took me to Alaska.

If the Carnegie Library book mobile van rounded the corner and entered our block, I ran from our apartment to the curb to meet it. The library's special mission was to bring books to under-privileged, low-income kids. I was drawn to stories featuring daring female protagonists, whether in film or books, but they were hard to come by in those years. I got my hands on a book about Nellie Bly and her exploits as a muckraking reporter. I read a story about Amelia Earhart's courageous feats in early aviation. Another girl of my dreams was Jo the tomboy character in Louisa May Alcott's *Little Women*, the one who also liked to write. My imagination lived in the pages of books—*Black Beauty*, the *Bobbsey Twins*, Greek mythology, and children's rhymes.

After my parents had been divorced for three years, mother rented a two-story wooden house about 100 years old and in need of major repairs. It was located in an alleyway off Cedarhurst Street within the Beltzhoover section of the city. At age ten, I was the oldest of four kids in a single parent household. My biological father was long gone, out at sea somewhere in the Pacific on a merchant marine vessel. I would only see him once between the ages of twelve and seventeen. Our 'hood, Beltzhoover, was falling into further economic decline similar to other poor neighborhoods suffering from "urban blight." The Italian grocer a few streets away closed up shop and nothing else was commercially happening.

To earn some ice cream and pop money, Mrs. Everett, a friend of my mother's, recruited me to be her kitchen helper. Mrs. Everett, an enterprising black woman, was raising three sons alone and running a part-time catering business out of her house across the alleyway from us. She sat me at her table, tied a half apron around my waist, and shoved bushels of apples and potatoes next to my wooden chair. When I finished peeling the potatoes and apples, she showed me how to use a special tool to carve melon balls out of cantaloupes. Since I was also a good reader, she paid me to tutor her son Charles, who was two grades below me in my brother's class at Beltzhoover Elementary School.

I will be forever grateful to Mrs. Everett for introducing me to jazz. She insisted I learn about her favorite singer, Ella Fitzgerald. While we worked together in the kitchen, she played her scratchy vinyl records.

"Child, you've got to hear what real music sounds like," she said. And another Ella Fitzgerald, Duke Ellington or Louie Armstrong record would come on. Ella became one of my favorite female singers. I tried to emulate her creamy smooth voice, her sophistication, the way she perfectly enunciated every word. I listened to how she transformed her voice into a unique musical instrument. "Nobody could scat like her," Mrs. Everett said. "Aint' nothin' wrong with Motown, but I want you to listen to Lady Ella." She taught me about the variations of words, the many intonations, and diction. I was also infatuated with the Beatles and liked to dance to James Brown with my playmates at school.

One thing culturally hard to understand while growing up was why so many Pittsburghers skipped eating meat on Fridays. We were told the ritual was supposed to be something respectful and connected to church. But we didn't go to any church and lived in a secular household. No matter what religious group a family belonged to, locals still ate a lot of fried fish sandwiches on Fridays.

For Richy and I, it meant our tired and dragged out mother would send us walking to the closest sandwich shop. We'd come back loaded with paper bags of tasteless fried cod cut into perfect squares on white buns slathered in tartar sauce with sides of greasy French fries and cans of pop. This supplemented our diet of potato chips, root beer, hot dogs and beans, Reeses's peanut butter cups and Kellogg's Frosted Flakes.

Things in Beltzhoover seemed alright for a while. Mother met and married her second husband, Bill, and gave birth to a fifth child, my sister, Beth. Bill owned a gas station but problems with alcoholism led him to lose his business. We continued living in the alleyway in the old house with the mice. Mother worked night shifts as a hospital admissions clerk. We got by fending for ourselves much of the time.

America was changing only we didn't understand how strong the undercurrents of change were. The myth of freedom for all, that blacks were living "free" since Emancipation, that we had somehow in the twentieth century moved beyond racism, that ours was the proven land of equal opportunity—this myth was lacerated. We were still divided into blacks and whites as the television news showed every night, though in my neighborhood we played together. A disproportionate number of urban black youth were being sent to detention centers, jails, and prisons. Mrs. Everett's son, Charles was my brother's best elementary school playmate. Before his sixteenth birthday, after we had moved away to the suburbs with my mother's new boyfriend, Charles was senselessly killed by a policeman. It all happened during some kind of robbery mix-up at a convenience store where blacks didn't normally go. Richy sobbed when he learned about Charles' death. Years later, whenever my brother spoke of it, in sadness and grief, he said, "Beltzhoover was a good neighborhood, if you lived through it."

Andy Warhol, Pittsburgh's most famous visual artist, said something like your own life, while it's happening to you, never has any atmosphere. Not until it's a memory.

America was fighting a war with itself. As a young person, I tried to make sense of happenings around me. Bits and piece of garbled rhetoric and sound bites rang in my ear from television, radio, music, and the streets. I could push a button and a continuous soundtrack of random noise played. It was a mixture of defiant political speech, startling images, violent acts, and powerful song lyrics jumbled into a Sixties phantasmagoria:

Cities burning. Civil rights. Tet Offensive.
Women's liberation.
Counter culture exhilaration.
Boys in 'Nam. Boys in body bags.

Silence like a cancer grows.

Police brutality. Mother fucking, racist, Gestapo pigs.
Commie bastards. *I ain't your nigger.*
Nike missiles and nukes.

Just put a little love in your heart.
We're Sgt. Pepper's Lonely Hearts Club Band.
We hope you will enjoy the show.

Oppression. Black liberation.
All the world over, people got to be free.
Breakdown. Meltdown. Lock-down.
Peace, man.
No way to Yahweh.
See the My Lai photos.

What is a man, what has he got, if not himself, than he has not.
I did it my way.
It's a ball of confusion.
Right on! Restless, young Americans.

California Dreamin' on such a winter's day.
The words of the prophets
are written on the subway walls.
Some joker left the cake out in the rain.

Hey, Jude, where's my solitude?

It was impossible to tune out the flood of words, song fragments, political diatribes, and poetry. I was a television child. Bloody newspaper photos, stark headlines and disturbing magazine images appeared everywhere. From prejudice and deep-seated fears, toxic fumes of hatred spread across the country.

April 4, 1968. The Reverend Martin Luther King, Jr. was shot and killed in Memphis. Riots broke out nationwide in the days following Dr. King's death. At my school, which was almost evenly divided between blacks and whites, bands of students tore through the hallways. They kicked in rows of lockers, screamed, cursed, hurled rocks against the windows, smashed bottles. The sirens blared.

Our eighth-grade teacher did her best to create more calm, but we read the fear and panic on her face as she locked the classroom door. "Everyone back to your seats!" she yelled. "Get away from the windows!"

I rushed to my desk, heart pounding and waited for the frightening moments to pass. Sirens only grew louder. More glass shattered. As the harsh reality of Dr. King's murder set in, rage and violence swept from coast to coast. The deep emotional wounds from the gunning down of Martin Luther King resulted in arson, looting, and a need for people to recklessly cry out.

Robert Kennedy condemned the lawlessness and lamented the sorry direction in which America was heading. And a few months later, he too, would be assassinated.

An editorial in the *Pittsburgh Post-Gazette* (April 7, 1968) said:

> The U.S. is close to being a hate society, not a Great Society. What's the matter with us anyhow? Why do we insist on wasting so much energy fighting against each other instead of harnessing our energies to work *with* each other? And the irony of it all!

> Here we are blessed with more material wealth and greater physical health than at any time in our history, yet spiritually, we are poorer than ever, and morally we are sicker than ever....

Whether I liked it or not, the psychological angst and turmoil of the day followed me around—fears about nuclear war and giant mushroom clouds, fears about more race riots, and fears that the USSR was going to launch an attack. Everything in my surroundings was suddenly thrown into a state of flux and radical readjustment—same as my family.

As a by-product of those fractured times, I was guaranteed a lifetime supply of restlessness and a longing for some Disneyesque place with castles and rainbows. Even the safe public school erupted into violence.

I wanted to feel as though something grounded me, but where was the sense of security or unity to be found? Pittsburgh as a northern city with a heavy black population was in turmoil, the same as Cleveland and Baltimore. My family, broken by divorce and alcoholism, would be broken time and time again. In the instability and uncertainties of the times, there were no answers, only more questions about where my real future lay.

Organized religion was part of the overall social malaise, losing its controlling powers and influences over the "good Christians." Half the country seemed to be suffering from some form of spiritual neurosis or malady. *God was dead*, according to the cover of a popular news magazine. What did people mean that *God was dead*? I didn't know. I was too young to understand. John Lennon declared in 1966 that the Beatles were more popular than Jesus. All I knew was that religion per se had no place in our family. We didn't own a Bible nor display any religious items in the house. Yet, the utterance of those three words—*God was dead*—chilled me to the bone, though I had no concept of any God except to believe that somewhere up in the cloud formations, if I stared long enough, I could make out a bearded face.

My mother did not offer religious guidance or mentoring to her children and neither did any grandparent. "I have bills to pay and mouths to feed," she continuously reminded us. What she said, more or less, is that churches expected too much with their rules and commands. She couldn't wake up on Sunday mornings after working all week long and rush to feed and dress four sleepy kids to go and hear a priest. What for? To listen to a choir? To say some routine *amens*? To give an offering when money was so tight?

Although once a more important part of her life, religion was reduced to basic practicalities—on the same level, perhaps, as choosing a car. What kind of real personal mileage would she get out of being a regular churchgoer? None at all, she said. How reliable was organized religion? It did nothing for her and would do nothing for us kids. Did she really need the Catholic Church to get to where she needed to go in this life? No, she did not. She needed a man with a steady job. And as far as she was concerned, the Catholic Church didn't welcome women like her, or women impregnated out of wedlock, women who drank, cussed and swore, and who wanted go on birth control pills. More and more women in the Sixties were coming to my mother's same conclusions about the Catholic Church.

We lived on government food stamps. She had no family for financial or moral support—no mother, father, brother or sister. She gave the impression this was her lot in life, that you had to buck up and do it all on your own. No pretending everything was fine, that the Almighty loved us, or that the Lord God would provide.

"Grin and bear it," she said. "Do you think my childhood was a bed of roses? You at least have a mother and a bed to sleep on. Remember, my father stuck me in an orphanage." Prayers were not going to change anything. Prayers did not put meatloaf on the table. But I knew she hadn't always thought about her faith that way.

Truth was, my official affiliation with the Catholic Church began and ended on March 27, 1955 in Pittsburgh. Margie, age 20, took me, her six-week old infant, to be baptized at St. Valentine's Church in the coal mining hills south of the city close to where we lived at the time. Margaret Marcella Armstead Witkowski, after two miscarriages, gave birth to me, her first child, on February 4. In rapid succession, three more children followed: a son, Richard, and two more daughters—Patty and my deaf sister Donna—all by our father, Louis. (Our sister, Beth, was born ten years later to second husband, Bill.)

The priest who baptized me as an infant at St. Valentine's warned my mother that according to church rules, he could baptize only *one* of her children, no matter how many others might be born after me. She didn't relay this story to me until I was in my forties. The way she remembered it, the priest was very cold and matter-of-fact in his explanation. Though my mother was raised Catholic, she was clearly a fallen, non-practicing one, as the priest reminded her. She didn't belong to any parish and she and my father Louis had never been properly married in the sacraments of the Roman Catholic Church. They had defied church rules and customs and eloped in 1952 to marry in a West Virginia courthouse.

Margie admitted there was no point in asking the priest for any special dispensations to try and make up for her religious apathy and disobedience. She was never going to properly marry my father in another, pre-approved ceremony in the eyes of the church. She confessed to me that her marriage to my father was probably doomed anyway, though she bore him four children. Our family's Catholic line was apparently severed at St. Valentine's. She remained outside of the church for the rest of her days.

The smoky city of Pittsburgh was in dire need of a facelift while I was growing up. Its business elite and political leaders cooked up a way to improve its depressing urban plight, lift its woeful reputation, and restore a sense of civic pride.

Geographically, the city occupied the confluence of the Allegheny, Monongahela, and Ohio Rivers. In their marketing genius—though I don't know in what year this happened—city leaders bestowed the mystical name of the *Golden Triangle* on this precise piece of land where the three rivers met. People bought into the idea and promoted the new public relations moniker. A bright future and renaissance awaited the Steel City. Less soot, more culture!

I didn't quite understand that the Golden Triangle wasn't real; it was nothing more than an advertising slogan. I believed in its literal and material existence. All I had to do was travel downtown by streetcar, I thought, and look for the sign: "Walk This Way to the Golden Triangle."

I vividly recall riding in the backseat of my mother's Buick on a Sunday afternoon. We were transporting Donna, age 6, back to her boarding school at the Western Pennsylvania School for the Deaf across the city in Edgewood. As we emerged from the Liberty Tunnel off Route 51, we turned right and drove parallel to the crowded Southside and again, I'd search for the mysterious Golden Triangle.

In the haze and smog, I caught sight of a shimmering object. Flashes of light. Pieces of turquoise and gold. Whatever the edifice was, its glow cut through the layers of gray. I couldn't contain my curiosity. I had to know what it was. As we passed the silhouettes of narrow row houses and dilapidated warehouses, I called from the back seat.

"Mom, look over there! See that shining thing?"

"Kathy, can't you see I'm driving? I don't know what you're pointing to," she said with irritation.

I turned to my little sister Donna seated next to me and gave crude hand signals for her to look across the Monongahela River. But I was impatient and didn't want to keep pointing and using my made-up sign language. I stopped trying to communicate with Donna and fixed my eyes on the gold, onion-shaped domes and cupolas.

With mother, I tried again.

"It's something sparkly like from a fairy tale," I said. "Can't you tell me what it is, Mom?"

But in her distraction and stress, my questions from the back seat of the car went unanswered. Each time we drove Donna to her school for the deaf, we took the same route. I searched again through the distant haze and smoke for reflections of light across the contaminated river. In the great Pittsburgh elegy, with those onion-shaped domes, some kind of symbolic power and indescribable longing were planted in my imagination.

I have become convinced that the very contradictions in my life are in some ways signs of God's mercy to me: if only because someone so complicated and so prone to confusion and self-defeat could hardly survive for long without special mercy.

—Thomas Merton,
A Thomas Merton Reader
"First and Last Thoughts: An Author's Preface"

2 Migration to Alaska

Abruptly, we left the pallor of the industrial north. Mother divorced her second husband, married a third, and decided we needed a fresh start. We moved to the west coast of Florida. Pinellas County was cleaner and cheaper and seemed booming with economic opportunities, she said. We pulled out of Pittsburgh in an old Chrysler Imperial and U-Haul truck in the fall of 1971 and joined the masses in search of paradise.

I wore the face of a disgruntled, miserable teenager. I didn't want anything to do with the subtropics and starting over in a new school.

We squeezed into an apartment above a Laundromat in Redington Beach adjacent to a tourist attraction called Tiki Gardens. Peacocks often escaped from Tiki Gardens through the front gate. If Richy and I saw them from our window, we ran outside and made a game out of chasing the slow-moving birds back to safety before they got hit by cars full of tourists driving down Gulf Boulevard.

I finished my last two years of high school and dreamed about the colossal impact I would likely make upon the world as a future journalist. I was all wrapped up in these professional dreams and need to prove to my family that I could achieve more than they thought possible. I planned to reconnect to my urban past imagining that after college I would one day travel to New York or Washington, D.C. or possibly an international city, except I had no money to pay for any of it. What was my inner nature? What about my self-image of Steel Town Girl? My true self? What lurked underneath the surface? I didn't have answers for these questions.

The only voice I heard was the one that told me I was in total control of my destiny. It was *my* future. By the sheer force of *my* will, I'd gladly enter the rat race, take my lumps, and external rewards—money, fame, applause—would naturally follow. I didn't have to resort to being a man's secretary. Or an elementary school teacher. Or a nurse. Or a minimum-wage hospital worker as my mother had been. I vowed to rise above the drudgery of her nondescript life. I didn't openly say these things to her, but in my prideful youth, I lived by those intentions. She read Barbara Cartland romance novels. I read Betty Friedan and Gloria Steinem. I was part of a new generation of women and we were smarter and dreamed bigger than our reserved and abiding mothers.

In my half-formed social awareness, I wanted to do my part to help stamp out the injustices and evils committed by mankind. Underneath the bravado of socially concerned activism, however, I had to admit I was as self-absorbed as everyone else my age. Who hasn't at one time or another dreamed of being famous for *something*? For starring on Broadway, for pitching in the World Series, for winning an Olympic gold medal, or for being discovered as a great beauty while you stood in a drug store line, as happened to Marilyn Monroe?

Some days I aspired to be Janis Joplin; other days, it was just the opposite. For a long time in pre-adolescence, and embarrassing now to admit, I wanted to be one of the Lennon Sisters on the *Lawrence Welk Show*. His show was a mainstay of Pittsburgh public television and frequently featured the Lennon Sisters. I tuned in all through my childhood even though I didn't exactly fit the demographics of the show's viewership—Polident users—but I watched the maestro because it was one of my grandmother Julia's favorites, mainly because it was filmed right in Pittsburgh and she liked that the host was an immigrant who spoke with an accent.

Naturally, I paid closest attention to my namesake Lennon sister—Kathy. With baton in hand, the conductor faced his orchestra. "And now, ladies and gentlemen, to entertain you, I present the lovely Lennon Sisters!" Lawrence Welk said.

The four of them emerged on stage in front of stupid, fake-looking sets, but they were poised, smiling, and wholesome. They exuded a formulaic, girl-next-door charm—the requisite image of chastity, sugar coated to please the older, conservative audiences. Because at least when you heard the Lennon Sisters, you could forget all about the chaos and social change running rampant through society in the 1960s, how the damn hippies destroyed basic decency with all their long hair, dope smoking, and sleeping half-naked in the parks.

Each time the Lennon Sisters sang, my Nana knew that everything was fine and the country wasn't going totally to hell in a hand basket. People could wipe their minds clean from politics. They could forget the threats of nuclear war, the growing involvement in Vietnam, the increasing social unrest over the struggle for civil rights, and the Red Menace facing us every day from the Russians.

Kathy Lennon dressed in full cut skirts with a wide, patent leather belt pulled tightly around her nonexistent waist, Audrey Hepburn style. Her silky brown hair, whether loose in soft curls over her shoulder, or swept up in a ten-inch high beehive, seemed to be held in place with a full can of Aquanet.

Everything about the Lennon Sisters appeared perfect. Every moment in front of the appreciative live TV audience—*perfect*. How did they all get on TV like that? Who believed in them and paid for all those private music lessons? Who bought them so many nice, identical clothes? What kind of parents did they have?

As young girl, I watched the television screen and pretended I could be one of the Lennon Sisters. I sang along to the television, preparing for my inevitable forays on the New York City theatre scene, where, as a Polish-Russian-Irish prodigy from Pittsburgh, I was truly destined to be a singular sensation on Broadway with every move that I made, though I had never been taken to any live theatrical productions. Or perhaps I'd rise clear to the top and be a diva at the Metropolitan Opera.

We Are All Poets Here

But as the social unrest and rebellion of the 1960s blasted to the forefront, my self-identity changed, too. I recalled how much pre-teen admiration I innocently felt for the singing Lennon Sisters, how I had pretended to be Kathy Number Two on the variety show. But by the time I finished high school, I cringed to think of it. *Are you crazy? The rosy-cheeked Lennon Sisters? Oh, yeah, sweet as lollipops. Regular Pollyannas.*

But Janis Joplin, born Janis Lyn Joplin in a very Christian family in Texas, well, she was something else. Joplin had soul—the kind that truly spoke to me. She was a misfit, and rejected the conventional standards of her time. She was a bluesy singer people would never forget—a woman with vocal firepower, like Liza Minelli and Barbra Streisand and Ella Fitzgerald, only rougher—without stupid poodle skirts and bobby socks.

Whenever I heard Janis—the Cosmic Witch, the White Lady of Blues—sing "Piece of My Heart" or saw one of those unflattering pictures of her in a magazine, she looked hungover, reckless, ragged, and more like the kind of women I saw in real life. She wasn't simply going through the motions memorizing somebody else's music and lyrics. She *lived* all the heartache she sang about and unleashed wild, female energy; she was no obedient housewife, no prim and proper churchgoer who prayed to Jesus every day.

Born between the illusion of the squeaky-clean Lennon Sisters and racy 1960s rock and roll stars, I searched for an acceptable feminine identity, but the world was giving me far too many confusing signals. I faced relentless historical and social paradoxes having to do with how to be a woman.

At least my family could have bestowed a more exotic moniker upon me, something more musical, and preferably Polish or Russian-sounding, like Alexandra, Sophia, Ekaterina.

But no, I was called *Kathy*, one of gazillions, and no one batted an eye. And my name, Kathleen, meant "the pure one." Though inside, I knew I was more connected to Joplin's sharp edges. She had ratty hair, she wore layers of bangles, and she draped a feathery pink boa around her neck and over her shoulders. She made a statement, not about purity, but about being true to yourself, even when you couldn't be a fashion model and received no marriage proposals.

The post-Watergate era of the 1970s brought terrible gas shortages, skyrocketing inflation, and high unemployment. Janis Joplin died from a heroin overdose, as did many 1960s rock stars I loved. Family variety shows like *Red Skeleton* and *Ed Sullivan* left the airwaves.

The clarion calls to *be* somebody still rattled around in my head. And I was in a hurry. Steel Town Girl didn't daydream a wink about marrying or someday having kids. To give up and became a housewife or a mother would have been copping out, a backwards turn of the clock. By the time I edged closer to college, I was consumed with fervor, swept up in the media's idea and definition of the new successful career woman—more liberated and enlightened who, through sheer willpower and a few lucky breaks, could escape her working class limitations.

I wince about it now. Nevertheless, back in the day, through the endless self-interrogations and comparisons, I also knew how lucky I was to be born in the middle of the twentieth century, a grateful beneficiary of the determined American suffragettes who fought for the right to vote and finally won it in 1921. I wasn't about to let all their dedication and hard work and passion go to waste.

Dreams to fulfill some Grand Female Plan continued beyond high school. I graduated in Pinellas County and later attended the University of West Florida, an inexpensive state university near the Alabama border in Pensacola. I came into my fledging womanhood committed and conditioned to feminist causes I supported. How could any church authority intervene with how women used their bodies? Why were priests and popes trying to control a women's right to have an abortion if it was an unwanted pregnancy or the woman was alone and in trouble? Why did the Catholic Church oppose the use of birth control? My mother had five kids because the pill wasn't yet invented or not readily available—not because she wanted to act on her maternal instincts and give birth to five children.

I frequently found myself in arguments with male friends and boyfriends while I smoked Virginia Slims and drank Tequila Sunrises and glasses of Lambrusco and Blue Nun.

Certainly, after college, I would follow the articles in the popular women's magazines and wear perfectly matched suits, carry an expensive leather briefcase, and cover my ears in chunky gold, being sure the jewelry wasn't too flashy, and the skirt not too short, the suit, muted, no prints, something corporately tasteful, almost masculine, in pin stripes, maybe.

Gloria Steinem was my hero. I knew all about Steinem's famous undercover journalism work posing as a Playboy Bunny and how she wrote scathing stories about women who got stuck in sexist jobs, dull and tedious, and how she championed women to use their brains above their bodies.

At the same time, I, the young "intellectual" who faithfully read *Ms. Magazine* would also buy taboo fashion magazines. I lay on my bed with thick issues of *Cosmopolitan*, excited for tips on how to dress more provocatively and for information about how I could achieve and enjoy more orgasms, once I accumulated some first-hand knowledge about what they were.

But all the while, as I combed through page after page of glossy ads with free perfume samples attached, and blonde-haired Swedish models, I worried about my "no more than a mouthful" breasts and my plaster white, sandpiper legs.

How was a woman supposed to be a woman in this looser, freer world that was drastically different from my mother's experience? This question gnawed at me. I raced back and forth between wanting men to take me seriously as an intellectual, and wanting to be drooled over for sexual attractiveness.

Now, as I write these words today from my home in Anchorage, I'm not sure why I let myself be so blinded and brainwashed by advertising messages telling me how young women could or should behave. I was on the way to leading a life imposed on me by others, with no real sense of who I was inside or what my supposed, God-given gifts really were.

Somehow, mother managed to physically keep our family together. I was grateful we maintained a shred of family life, and that we weren't sent away to an orphanage, as she had been. But I didn't plan to stick around the adopted, subtropical home front once I finished university.

The clock was definitely running, and if I didn't get going *somewhere*, if I didn't start something new and exciting, I might be stuck working as a food server in Florida's tourism sector. Mother found a job tending bar and cooking hamburgers at a local tavern after we moved to Pinellas County. Later, she took a full-time job with benefits at the Publix Supermarket, a job she held for the next 20 years. My mother worked in the refrigerated meat processing rooms wrapping and labeling packages of meat for the butchers.

As I struggled to figure out my role and direction, I couldn't speak intelligently about my spiritual state of mind at the time, except I recognized that same restlessness that shadowed me around since childhood. There were other, more subtle forces at work in my innermost self.

It was like a dream where I was in a great symphony hall and was invited on stage with the world's best, most talented musicians. And just as the performance was about to begin, I was immobilized, unable to play a note. All I could hear were a few faint musical bars. A part of me was missing, but I didn't know what.

On my bookshelf today, I still treasure a hardbound copy of John McPhee's *Coming into the Country*. Funny thing is, that book was not written by some hell- raising feminist author, but by an old white guy—East Coast born and bred, Ivy League educated, son of a physician, product of a happy and together family under the single roof of their New Jersey home.

I found McPhee's celebrated *Coming into the Country* while working my day job in a B. Dalton's chain bookstore at a St. Petersburg, Florida mall. The nation was in the middle of a recession and an energy crisis. At twenty-two years old, eager to break into journalism, I lived by the words I recalled from the Crosby, Stills, Nash & Young song, "Chicago" which the band had originally dedicated to Mayor Daley: "…We can change the world, re-arrange the world. It's dying to get better….Politicians sit yourselves down, there's nothing for you here…"

But job markets were tight. After my shift at the bookstore was over, to earn money, I drove to my night job as a food server and cocktail waitress.

McPhee's book got me thinking. What would it be like to be a more courageous and stereotype-denying woman and live in the remote, oddball Alaskan towns he described, places like Chicken, Eagle, Dead Horse, and Circle—where women my age didn't spend their time in shopping malls and baking in the sun? In all of Alaska the only department stores were found in Anchorage or Fairbanks, hundreds of miles away and apart.

As a staff writer for the *New Yorker*, McPhee had spent part of several summers in the 49th state and a few weeks of winter, mostly east of Fairbanks in Interior Alaska.

His vivid descriptions brought eccentric bush characters to life for me, people like Ed Gelvin, a man described as a "trapper, sawyer, pilot, plumber, licensed big-game guide, welder, iron-worker, mechanic, carpenter, and builder of boats and sleds" from Central, Alaska, population: 16. Gelvin's wife hunted with him and helped run the trap lines—not that I fancied myself as a future, northern huntress, but this was a woman *Ms. Magazine* should know about!

Maybe that's another reason why Alaska crept into my imagination.

I didn't know much, but I knew Alaska, of all places, was surely a man's world because men hunted wolves and bears and traveled by dog sled in arctic blizzards and the whole state was cold beyond belief. Not one of my girlfriends ever breathed a word that she was dreaming about moving away from the swaying palm trees to some freezing paper birch forest for personal fulfillment.

I questioned my life. When it came to necessary, practical living, to possessing a basic understanding of outdoor survival skills or anything mechanical, I knew about as much as my mother knew—nothing. I couldn't bake a cake, sew, change an oil filter, drive a stick shift, or pitch a tent. I had more education than anyone in my immediate family, the first and only one to finish college, but all I really had was a lot of book knowledge that seemed less and less relevant.

Compared to the Alaskans McPhee described, I had zilch survival experience in the outdoors. The sum total of my "nature experiences" consisted of a few vague childhood memories, where I played under towering oak trees lining the Pittsburgh streets. We visited the city zoo once on a field trip, and I noticed how purple morning glories twisted around chain link fences. There were no walks to the playground with my mother and father. As children, we didn't take family trips to the state parks, nor have a yard to keep a garden.

As McPhee showed, Alaskans lived in the wilderness and faced it head on. They fixed airplane engines and boat motors, and were content in the middle of nowhere near the Chuchki Sea without movie theatres, McDonald's, and swimming pools. They ate grizzly bear roasts, caribou, muktuk, and ptarmigan.

Most people I encountered in my day-to-day life in the subtropics existed pleasantly enough in their routine surroundings. (In the 1960s, Florida's Cuban population boomed after the onset of the Cuban Revolution.) But on the surface, as I looked back, most of the northern transplants seemed they had no deep connection to where they were, no sense that their spirits and souls truly belonged and thrived there. Unlike the Cubans, they didn't migrate to Florida because of political strife. Florida was like a smooth gliding ointment people applied to cover up their cares, troubles, and failures. The Sunshine State's new arrivals were merely warming up their bones, escaping higher state income taxes, taking leisurely golf cart drives, and dining on stuffed flounder at the early bird specials.

In the land of the "newlyweds and nearly deads" as the St. Petersburg, Florida area was often described, people were kicking back and enjoying their golden retirement years by surf fishing, taking cheap Bahama cruises, and drinking margaritas and Captain Morgan's and Coke every day at five o'clock. They weren't living as McPhee's characters were—physically, emotionally, and spiritually immersed in the land, a land they subsisted on and defended—their beloved Alaska.

I couldn't help but make comparisons. I was living in a miasma of materialism and creature comforts—living the quintessential, insular suburban life, more or less, but in a warm climate. For the people around me in Pinellas County, everything essential to daily survival had either been provided in the form of paid services (electricity for air conditioning came from some utility somewhere) or made so convenient (the local mall or Publix Store had whatever you needed), they hardly had to think of it at all. And neither did I.

In my narrow vision at the time, for someone to become a Floridian, little seemed to be required psychologically or spiritually to adjust. You simply relocated yourself farther south, planted a hibiscus or potted an orchid, you bought flip-flops and lots of new sunglasses, seven tee-shirts, seven pairs of shorts, and changed your voter registration card. Chances were, your neighbors were transplants, too, and they didn't know much about the real history of their newly adopted homeland, who or what Indian tribes first settled its rivers, swamps and coastal marshes, or how the railroad and fruit and citrus industries had built Florida's economy.

To become Alaskan, as McPhee well illustrated, took something more—more mindfulness, more spunk and direct involvement with the details of the actual land and indigenous cultures around you. And a lot more socks.

From what I discerned, living in Alaska was like pushing heavy loads every day, as a friend had put it. You had to expend great amounts of physical energy to get through all the seasons, especially the six-month-long winters in much of the state. I imagined it took immense amounts of psychological stamina to survive its physical challenges, the sheer geographic distance from the rest of the country, its steep prices, and all the ways its land and climate could kill you.

The Alaska McPhee wrote about and the Sunshine State I temporarily inhabited were extreme opposites. According to McPhee, Alaskans knew *how* to do things. Women of the far north possessed a kind of earthy smarts I sorely lacked and deeply respected because their kind of survival knowledge wasn't anything I had come in contact with before.

Alaska ladies did not appear on the pages of women's publications like *Cosmopolitan* or *Ms. Magazine*. Women out in the Alaska bush did not collect Estée Lauder perfume samples and gift bags. They didn't glue on fake eyelashes.

The longer I stayed in the south, the hot sticky weather and intense sun sucked something vital out of me. The southern sun became a bore.

Before I left for Alaska, I struck out on a big career opportunity. I blew my chance to land an entry level journalism job at the *St. Petersburg Times* at one of the paper's small news bureaus. With my two years of practical experience working on the University of West Florida's student newspaper in Pensacola, and after finishing a student internship at the *Pensacola News Journal*, I looked forward to impressing the *St. Petersburg Times*.

On the day of my job interview, I strolled in confident, well informed, eager to please.

"So, Kathleen, how do you feel about covering local community news, including the churches in our area?" the bureau chief asked. "The job entails assembling the calendars for the Sunday section and any news from local churches. You know, community things."

It wasn't what I expected the job to be—anything concerning churches—but I quickly recovered from my shock and disappointment. I zoomed right in to the real subject at hand—my perceptive smarts and my vast understanding of the religious landscape of America in the late 1970s.

"Well, sure, I'd be very interested in that, sir," I said.

And then to demonstrate that I was "up" on religion, I said, "As you probably know, Pensacola, where I went to college, is in the middle of the Bible Belt. There are churches everywhere, practically on every corner. In fact, I've never seen so many churches," I said. The editor looked up from under his pile of papers and files, and shifted his black framed glasses around on his nose.

"Oh, really, you don't say?" he asked. "Well, why don't you tell me more about your impressions of this Bible Belt?"

To further display my erudition and depth of understanding about organized religion, I put on my best reporter's voice.

"It's true that pockets of the Far Right occupy the Florida-Alabama border. These people are quite vocal about their faith and religious beliefs. The Far Right, many of them Southern Baptists, but really I'm not quite sure what the difference is between a Southern Baptist and a Presbyterian, though, thankfully, *none* of my friends called themselves *Baptist*....anyway, I do know that Southern Baptists were definitely more on the holy roller side. Not that they don't have a right to be that way, I mean it's a free country, and I understand that."

And I blabbed on about political conservatives who made up the Bible Belt, how they believed God was on their side for everything. Yes, it was all a rather fascinating lesson in human dynamics living so close to the Florida-Alabama border.

The editor kept writing with his pencil, and he let me talk at him.

I said, "I could see how strong the political influences were from the conservative Christians since they were always fighting against abortion rights. You see, I *do* understand why it's important for newspapers to cover churches and how they really operate in our community." And then I paused.

Migration to Alaska

The spectacled gentleman graciously allowed me to offer a few more promulgations before he put his pencil down. As he started to stand up, he closed his file, shook my hand, and thanked me for my interest in the newspaper.

And there went my first big chance to break into print journalism.

I was nobody's child, except the media's, stuck in my own commonplace judgements of the world and religion.

Months later, I was still searching for a newspaper job, realizing how I had blown the interview with my politicizing. I continued to work nights serving lots of "surf and turf" at the Red Cavalier restaurant on the inner coastal waterway, the same restaurant where I worked in high school and on college breaks.

I learned the ropes in the restaurant business from Edna and the other waitresses—chain smoking, no nonsense, middle aged women in black polyester pants and white blouses. They treated their assigned tables—the best in the Red Cavalier—and their regular customers as personal property. None of us young punks had better lay a mitt on them, not even to refill coffee cups.

Edna and Emmie were the soft-shoed veterans of the beach waitress corps; they were in their seventies and had earned the right to serve shrimp scampi and rock lobster tails to the higher spending clientele, while we youngsters got stuck serving early bird specials to the folks on pensions.

Edna and Emmie worked through one crowded winter tourism season after another, bent their backs waiting on beach loving vacationers and those "cheapskate Canucks." Along the way, they saved their hard-earned tips to spoil their grandchildren, or to occasionally escape the south's dreadful summers on jaunts north of the Florida-Georgia border. They worked their shifts, took care of their families, and devoured stacks of cheap and musty Harlequin romance novels.

One day, while standing in my waitress uniform—a puffy sleeved, short, black polyester dress covered in a white, ruffled apron—I was gabbing to Edna. I told her I was restless and felt stirrings to migrate away from the lazy, beach lifestyle to a more rugged landscape with cooler air.

It had been six years since we had left Pittsburgh, and I was eager to return to the north. And to experience, once again, elevations higher than a causeway or a fire ant hill.

"I really don't think I want to live here anymore," I said. "I know I sound insane but I might buy a ticket to Alaska."

Edna poured herself another cup of coffee and shook her stiffly sprayed head of hair, and spoke with traces of her rural Kentucky accent.

"Darlin', I can't believe what I'm hearing. *Alaska?* Don't you see how lucky we are?

People in Minnesota would give their right arms to live like we do in this kind of wonderful weather! And you want to go where, *A-las-ka*? Is there somethin' else going on you wanna tell me about? Are you havin' any kind of family troubles?"

I didn't want to bring up all the usual strife in my home life. The sorrow I still felt about being separated for so long from my biological father and the Witkowski side of the family. That my brother, so inventive, determined and full of dreams was forced to join the U.S. Air Force because there wasn't enough money to help him with college. Donna attended the boarding school for the deaf in St. Augustine, Florida from age ten until eighteen. We saw her only a few times a year. With her disability, we worried about how Donna would ever find a decent enough paying job to be independent.

"I've made up my mind," I told Edna. I planned to leave the dive bombing pelicans and sunbathing alligators.

I had to ignore her, and almost everyone else in my life who asked, "Alaska? Why Alaska? What on earth will you do there?" always in alarmed tones, as if I had said I was moving to McMurdo Station in Antarctica. All their stunned reactions only reinforced what McPhee wrote about, and made the primitive, faraway land sound even more enticing.

Young single women didn't make such rash decisions, to pick up and move themselves alone to Alaska, leaving all their relatives and friends behind. Saying I was going to leave warm, sandy beaches for ice cold fjords didn't sound like a sensible plan. I did have fears about the cold climate and the geographic distance, but it wasn't enough to change my plans. Within a few weeks of my surprise announcement to Edna, June, Emmie, and the rest of the hard-working restaurant crew, I bought a full-sized Rand McNally map of Alaska and pinned it to my lilac-colored bedroom wall.

In most maps I had ever seen, Alaska looked like a walnut floating off the West Coast, a little northwest of the State of Washington. Or else it was squeezed into the lower left corner of newspaper and television weather maps somewhere near Baja, with Hawaii practically joined to it. Rarely did anyone get its scale right. Often much of the Southeast Alaska Panhandle and half of the Aleutian Islands were arbitrarily cut off; at a quick glance no one could really decipher how close Russia was geographically, and I didn't realize it either. Back then, before reality television shows and cruise ship lines had discovered Alaska, it was mostly a social and cultural backwater, best left to fishermen, crabbers, the military, and a multitude of oil workers who eventually poured into the state.

I started squirreling away tip money to pay for the plane fare from Tampa to Chicago to Anchorage. Jan and Emmie gave me a farewell gift: a pair of handmade, loosely knitted, unlined, baby blue mittens, the kind no Alaskan in her right mind would ever wear for real winter protection. My coworkers presented them to me as we gathered around the dual burner coffee-makers, with everyone laughing and teasing me mercilessly about being Nanook of the North all over again.

"Honey, you're gonna need a lot more than baby blue mittens once you get to that cold damn state," Emmie said.

"At your age," Edna advised, "I understand you crazy young girls today have to do what you got to do. I'm pretty sure you'll be back within a few short months, soon as Father Frost comes around. And when you do, don't forget June will still have a job for you, so don't you worry, ya hear? Honey, you can live with me for a while if you have to, to get back on your feet. And I got contacts in Kentucky, too."

From my bedroom wall, I studied Alaska's shape and tried to memorize a few of the strange sounding names, many of them Russian-derived, as my literary hero McPhee, had done:

Ninilchik, Shelikof Strait, Baranof Island, Mt. Veniaminof.

Alaska rested on the northern edge of the Pacific Rim, connected to a string of volcanos exotically named the Pacific Ring of Fire. From what I could tell, it was practically on top of the earth, about as far as I could possibly travel—more than 6,000 land miles, I figured—and still be an American patriot.

And there were mountains! Oh, were there ever mountains! Swarms of mountains. Cathedrals of mountains. Really tall ones. Supposedly Florida's highest geographic point, not counting any of its causeways, was something like 700 feet.

I liked the idea that Alaska, as a gigantic open space, was still in transition, not yet categorized or defined, not yet cemented over, and that maybe I could help define it. But what did I know of tundra and taiga? I'd never visited real wilderness in my entire life. I remembered how, back home, Pittsburgh public school teachers taught us about the history of "Penn's woods" and what the Quaker State once looked like before the Industrial Revolution. In the beginning, before steel mills and factories, Pittsburgh once stood as nothing but a French fort surrounded by deep green woodlands at the intersection of three winding, wild and clean rivers.

By happenstance, and against my teenaged will, I had inherited a place full of shell filled beaches with Gulf of Mexico waves and flocks of terribly spoiled seagulls demanding to be fed. But in temperament, I was still very much a northerner masquerading as another nameless, sunburned Florida transient. And worst of all, I was cursed with red hair and pale, pinkish skin, blotched by infinite dots of freckles and who probably had no business living in so much clear, bright sunshine anyway.

I was living on the tail end of the American cultural idea about youth rebellion. From the Beat Generation to the rock and roll generation, sworn to stay free, we lived for individual rights and desires, to satisfy our egos as long as we weren't causing harm to others. And as long as we didn't sell out to all the cultural norms and conventions of our parents' generation, we could leave our homes, the pedestrian and mundane families, pack up, and head out. As Woody Guthrie once sang, we could "blow down the dusty road" to make it in whatever form of freedom we imagined. Better to burn out than fade away was the youthful motto.

Shortly after talking to Edna and the girls, I went shopping and made a major purchase of my first pair of hiking boots for a whopping fifty dollars. Vasques, in sturdy brown leather with red laces. Today, I still have them in my Anchorage garage as a keepsake.

As for other necessary outdoor gear, it was close to impossible to find in Florida, and I didn't have the money or the knowledge about how to outfit myself for the remote reaches of North America. Along with my still unworn hiking boots as heavy as bowling balls, my manifest also included, *Coming into the Country*, filled with pencil marks, and a blank journal made out of Italian Florentine leather, a gift from a college girlfriend.

I packed my 35-millimeter camera, the one I used throughout my college newspaper days, and a suitcase full of climatically incorrect clothes. I bid quick farewells to my family and flew out of Tampa wearing the worst outfit I could have worn to Alaska—a below-the-knees coral skirt, a long sleeved, silky blouse with delicate, pale yellow flowers, large pearl earrings, pantyhose, and smart black pumps. All that I owned was stuffed into my wheelless, hard shelled, fluorescent pink, Samsonite luggage that Richy bought for me as a college graduation present. Overall, I looked as though I was on my way to an Easter brunch.

Just in case Edna was right, I traveled with a roundtrip plane ticket.

I arrived in Anchorage on May 6, 1978, with the tired hungry shorebirds, waterfowl and raptors from every continent.

Spring had barely arrived in Southcentral Alaska. I noticed the resident birds right away, the intimidating, loud magpies and gangs of ravens as big as Pennsylvania's wild turkeys with bellies that seemed to drag on the ground.

Birch and cottonwood trees had yet to break out in full foliage; only small buds of leaves were showing. The tops of the Chugach Mountains were still blanketed in snow, but I didn't care. Coming from the south, the explosion of cool, clean air, bright and fresh, energized me at once.

Female moose were tending their calves and teaching them how to pilfer tasty lilac buds from shrubs right in the middle of city neighborhoods. The *Anchorage Daily News* reported Eskimo whaling crews in Barrow had successfully landed three bowhead whales to help feed their community. People trailered boats to Resurrection Bay and the Kenai Peninsula in preparation for the upcoming commercial and sport fishing salmon seasons. Every living creature was alive with hyperactivity, energy, and non-stop motion.

From those first few weeks, as daylight lingered past 10:00 p.m., Edna's voice rang in my ears, and I pretended she said, "*Honey, put down your shopping bags and mint juleps, this isn't the Kentucky Derby for genteel ladies. This is Alaska. And you better buckle in your fanny.*"

The spring days ticked by during those first few weeks. Temperatures climbed to 50 degrees and the daylight kept increasing. There wasn't a single minute for me to waste lounging around being idle while all that precious northern sun was shining.

51

Contradictions have always existed in the soul of individuals. But it is only when we prefer analysis to silence that they become a constant and insoluble problem. We are not meant to resolve all contradictions but live with them and rise above them and see them in the light of exterior and objective values which make them trivial by comparison.

— Thomas Merton,
Thoughts in Solitude

The freedom that is in our nature is our ability to love something, someone besides ourselves, and for the sake, not of ourselves, but of the one we love... This power to love another for his own sake is one of the things that makes us like God, because this power is the one thing in us that is free from all determination. It is a power which transcends and escapes the inevitability of self-love.

Thomas Merton,
Unpublished, from the original manuscript of
The Seven Storey Mountain

3 Coming into Yakutat

I was married at 10:00 a.m. on a Monday morning in late January inside a courthouse. Michael and I met at a campus party at the University of West Florida in Pensacola. He was from south New Jersey, not far from Ocean City, a handsome, well-built rugby player and former surfer who also studied philosophy, had read the *Tao Te Ching*, and published poems in the university's small literary journal, the *Nautilus*. His parents had relocated for job reasons to the 49th state while he was away at college. That's how he ended up in Anchorage—on a summer holiday to visit his family. But the chance to experience living in raw, rugged wilderness had gotten into his blood and he remained.

Who gets married in the middle of an Alaskan winter inside a drab courthouse on a Monday morning? It wasn't your typical wedding, and I wasn't crying for the usual reasons. Mine involved hypothermia. It was bitterly cold, less than ten degrees, and since I was so new to Anchorage—this being my first long, dark winter—I didn't have good Sorrel boots, a down parka or a decent pair of gloves. While the Justice of the Peace administered our perfunctory marriage vows, I stood shivering. Dressed in the same long, plaid skirt and brown corduroy blazer I wore as a college student in Pensacola, my face was red and flushed with tears. I had been in Alaska for less than eight months.

Michael's parents and his brother and sister smiled sweetly in the corner. Overcome with emotion, I cried through most of the civil ceremony thinking about the special moment I was now passing through. This was my wedding day, except there were no bridesmaids or groomsmen, no hired photographer, no cake, no romantic music, no invited guests, no priest or minister to lead us through the vows, and no honeymoon to Hawaii. I had no circulation in my fingertips and had started my period.

I, Kathleen Witkowski, was literally following my man into a new life because in exactly ten days, we would fly out to what residents called the "bush." We were moving to a tiny village called Yakutat that I knew almost nothing about except it was the only region in the USA located in the Yukon Time Zone. It was inhabited by Tlingit Indians, there were no connecting roads in or out, and rain fell constantly. It was in the middle of muskeg with no newspapers, radio stations, clothing or shoe stores, no friends, no family, but I willingly chose to go, because, well because, *I was in love*. And being in love with all my heart meant I could endure the temporary bout of solitary confinement and social backwardness I was about to enter.

How fitting it was to learn that my new, much blander last name—*Tarr*—held maritime connotations. I understood that "Tar" or a "Jack Tar" was old British slang for a sailor. It alluded to the abundant use of tar onboard ships to caulk the seams and combat against corrosion; tar was derived from coal residue. Yes, this surname was a good fit for Steel Town Girl and the daughter of a former World War II Navy man and merchant mariner.

We arrived in Yakutat on a dark February day in 1979 on Alaska Airlines Flight #66 with everything we owned: Michael's prized beer can collection, some Beatles, Jimmy Buffet and Allman Brothers albums, an assortment of paperbacks—his favorite science fiction by Frank Herbert and Theodore Sturgeon. I brought along my Iron City beer can featuring the 1975 Pittsburgh Steelers Super Bowl champions. My collection also included *Time-Life* photography books, new Nikon 35-millimeter camera, a large cast iron skillet, hardbound copies of Barry Lopez's *Of Wolves and Men*.

We also had a small hardcover book of poetry, one that Michael never returned to his Mainland High School library in south New Jersey. The Viking portable library edition, as it was called, plain brown cover, originally published in 1946, featured selections of the 18th Century English poet, William Blake. I had vaguely heard of him, but not read him. Why steal a library book on Blake? All I remember Michael saying at the time was that Blake possessed a vivid imagination and that he liked his rhymes.

For precautionary measures and to save money, we packed extra coolers of food, articles of clothing described as "foul weather gear especially recommended for Alaska," a 25 pound bag of rice, jars of creamy Jiffy peanut butter, extra fishing rods and reels, rubber boots, pistols, rifles, and boxes of bullets. Our 1968 Ford truck was delivered later by a C-121 cargo plane.

Upon landing in Yakutat, we walked across the tarmac and entered the smallest, most spartan airport terminal I'd ever seen. Jim Jensen, a man in his mid-fifties and Michael's new boss in the Federal Aviation Administration, was the FAA "chief," as managers were called then. He greeted us inside the blue sheet metal building. One room contained it all—a single ticket counter, about ten yellow, plastic chairs for all arrivals and departures, and the spot where the one "ramp rat" or baggage handler could be seen manually throwing the bags through a chute with a few hanging rubber strips that resembled a pet door opening.

After collecting our suitcases and few boxes of household goods strapped together with duct tape, Jim said he wanted us to feel welcome, so he walked us straight over to the bar. The bar was part of a small establishment known as the Airport Lodge, which stood adjacent to the sheet metal "terminal."

This moving to Yakutat was a great grace, only I didn't see it that way back then. It felt like career purgatory, a temporary way-station before I could get myself reoriented on the right worldly path.

I stepped into the dark, cold February night without streetlights, lines of blinking cars, or a single traffic light. If there was a real town of Yakutat, I couldn't see it. Few buildings existed in the area—a dilapidated, World War II airplane hangar, a two-story flight service building which also housed the U.S. Forest

Service office, and the one story structure of the Airport Lodge. A pair of aircraft refueling pumps stood next to it. Across the road was a small row of rooms, at that time all empty and locked, reserved for visiting hunters and sport fishermen.

Many years later I would learn that on a rainy, overcast day in September 1968—Thomas Merton stepped out of his plane and after seeing some of the village, he ate one of his meals inside the same lodge. The world famous Trappist monk and writer from Kentucky was hosted by Frank Ryman and his wife, the owners of the small establishment in 1968. But in February 1979, I hadn't yet befriended the Ryman family. And the names of Thomas Merton or any other Catholic thinkers or writers meant nothing to me.

The winter weather had been particularly bad when we arrived; massive snow piles reached the roofs of abandoned pickup trucks.

"Hey give us a couple of Buds," Jim Jensen yelled to the bearded man behind the counter, as we found some open bar stools.

As we took our seats at the smoky bar, I reached for Michael's hand, digging my nails into his palm, while we watched the lights of Alaska Airlines Flight #66 stream down the runway until it disappeared into the night sky on its way south to Juneau.

"Wonder how many times we'll be hearing that sound?" I said, gripping Michael's hand ever more tightly.

"Better get used to it," he said. "Alaska Airlines will be our lifeline from now on. It's the only way we have to get out of here."

While he talked, Jim smoked one Camel cigarette after another and fidgeted incessantly with the coins in front of him. Sprawled across the back of his nylon windbreaker blazed the words: *Evinrude Motors*. Jim didn't look like a federal aviation man; it had been days since he'd shaved. I detected a slight odor of burnt wood on him from a woodstove, perhaps. His brown polyester high water pants hung over his skinny frame. His mis-fitted pants and his heavy-duty BF Goodrich rubber boots suggested that this man cared nothing whatsoever about the first impression he made on newcomers.

All the men in the bar knew him. Every time the sturdy door swung open and another diesel stained logger or fisherman walked in, they gravitated to Jim's friendliness and energy. As they brushed by, they gently slapped him on his upper shoulder.

"Hiya, Jim."

"Hey, good to see ya. Where've you been? Working on that sorry-ass boat of yours?"

Whenever Jim laughed, his deep cut wrinkles reflected the face of someone who battled cold, chiseling winds and stormy seas every day of his life. Yet, he was a man who sat on a comfortable leather chair peering at a runway through the flight service station window while speaking into a microphone and taking flight plans mostly from private pilots. He clearly enjoyed telling stories and explained how he came north to the Territory of Alaska in 1949 with the U.S. military in the days when "Alaska would eat women alive."

By the time we met Jim Jensen, he had spent fifteen years in Yakutat working as manager of the FAA's small flight service facility where Michael was now assigned to. Jim met his Yup'ik, wife, Sue, in Kotzebue, in the far northwest part of the state on the Chukchi Sea above the Arctic Circle. They had fourteen children together, and eventually transferred the whole Jensen brood to the much milder, but rainier climate of Yakutat, between Cordova and Juneau, on what's considered the northernmost limit of Southeast Alaska.

As he took another drink from his can of Bud, Jim paused for a moment to speak directly to Michael, his newest employee to transfer in, and now one of the current crop of five flight service specialists to man the 24/7 station, all of whom had come from somewhere else.

"Think you'll like it here? If you don't like to hunt or fish, chances are you won't. Air traffic's pretty damn slow this time of year, but it's hoppin' in the summertime."

"Yeah, I've heard this place can have some really good fishing," Michael answered without probing for too many details. He purposely wanted to sound like more of a novice about fishing, although he already knew about the local prized runs of steelhead trout and salmon. He couldn't wait to cast his line into the Situk River, which he reminded me about constantly. It was good to see him revert to what he called his sponge mode so that Jim clearly had the authority and pleasure in telling us about the town.

Michael sat there in his jeans and hiking boots, a strongly built 25-year-old, and not what you'd call a very excitable guy, more analytical than spontaneous, a quiet one and a good and necessary complement to my hyperactivity. The last thing Michael wanted to do was to insert his own personality or knowledge into Jim's moment. He wanted to learn as much as he could from this long timer while he remained calm and attentive.

I felt uneasy especially when I looked up at the framed sign above the bar's dirty windowsill: *Wanted. A good woman who can clean, cook, fish, dig worms, clams, sew, and owns a good fishing boat and motor.*

I sat at the bar smiling and listening intently to the men talk about Gulf Air Taxi—the town's small air taxi service, and what kinds of private aircraft depended upon the FAA's flight service specialists. Small talk was about some of the other families we would now be based with, including the National Weather Service employees living adjacent to the other three aviation families. More beers were plopped down in front of us. The men's conversation soon drifted away from floatplanes, and which pilot flew under which call letters, to facts about when king salmon season would start. Jim was telling Michael what he would need to run a trap line for marten and mink, and asked whether or not we intended to buy a skiff to pull our own crab pots in Yakutat Bay.

I felt left out until the topic turned once again to something I needed to know about: the weather. From Jim, we found out the climate could be worse than some of the other soggy fishing villages and towns of Southeast Alaska, such as Ketchikan or Metlakatla. The number of days officially classified as "clear and sunny" averaged fewer than 40 per year. The rain didn't pitter patter; it assaulted you. During one November alone in Yakutat, it would rain 47 inches, but we had not yet experienced that deluge and had no concept of this kind of rain when we came into the country that first winter night. All that wetness would come later. Merton, too, would come to experience the deluge.

"Hell, you'll get used to the rain, I guarantee it," Jim said. Then he laughed and coughed hard a few times. "No one bothers with umbrellas—what would be the point?"

It didn't take long to learn that Southeast Alaska rain is not something you duck away from; it's something you experience full force from under an infinite array of leak proof, Gortex hoods. That night, being so new and inexperienced on outdoor matters—especially anything concerning hunting, fishing, and trapping—I found myself staring at layers of grungy dollar bills thumbtacked to the bar's walls and eavesdropping on the rambunctious conversations from the other male patrons.

In the next breath, the chief leaned over the bar, turned his head, and looked me right in the eye.

"We want you women to like it here, too. We really do. I know it's a big change, especially since you just got married. But you don't need to worry—best to listen to my wife Sue. I damn well guarantee you she's gonna teach you a lot."

He laughed loudly, hacked, then took another toke from his Camel. "So, Michael, what guns you plan on using for bears?"

Michael went back to talking about how he planned to reload his own ammunition for his Smith & Wesson 44-magnum revolver with an extended nine-inch barrel and his Remington .338 shot gun. He had already lived in the state long enough to know how to talk bear and all about proper firearm protection and bear spray and bullets.

Here we go again, I thought, the women are relegated to the sidelines while the men discuss their important business. I was a wife now, and that probably meant I was supposed to sit quietly and bat my green eyes and not say too much. I'd have to seek out some other wives to learn the ways of Yakutat, but my first impressions told me this place was caught in a worse time warp than I was led to believe. Alaskans, men in particular, prided themselves on living in a freewill paradise.

My older, more mature self can look back now and see where all my trepidation came from.

As a newcomer first exposed to the wilderness and to people like Jim Jensen and eventually to a family known as the Pavliks, I was convinced I'd be out of the bush in no time. I wasn't meant for their kind of quiet isolated life. What about all those times I imitated Barbra Streisand and stood before my college roommate and belted out "I'm gonna live and live now, get what I want, I know how…"

Well, who was raining on my parade now? It was me! I had let this big move out to the bush happen. I was a new wife in the middle of a rain forest with no job prospects and no friends and as far away as I could be from my family and still be in America.

Now it was Frank Sinatra's song that ran through my head: "Wake up and kiss the good life goodbye!"

I was taking temporary leave of the world, disappearing into the backwoods of nowhere, and for how long I didn't know. Though I was happy to be with Michael as he started the first position in his new professional life, I waded through a pool of self-doubts and contradictions about my personal decision. Pre-Yakutat, my dreams and goals had been all figured out. *All figured out.*

I lived and strived for the future applause and approval of others—an echo of what I later came to know about Thomas Merton in his younger days. Merton led a kind of itinerant, bohemian existence in his youth, crisscrossing the Atlantic nine times. After his American mother died when he was very young, his New Zealander artist father subsequently dragged him from place to place—Bermuda, New York, England and back to the countryside of France, near the Pyrenees, not far from the same place he was born on January 31, 1915. As a college student, he tried to be hip and frequented jazz clubs, smoked, and drank. Merton wrote poetry and fashioned himself as the next Great American Novelist, but he never got anywhere significant with his fiction writing. None of his four draft novels were ever accepted for publication during his lifetime. Like me, he was no stranger to failure.

I related to how Merton had tried on several "self-identities" in his early twenties. Along with many of his fellow young intellectuals, he decided to become a Communist. The Communists were making sense about man's sense of alienation in an overly-materialistic, profit-driven world. Merton attended a few meetings, but realized that he had a mistaken impression about the Soviets. They were not the true friends of all the arts, as the history about Stalin's purges later proved. Under the totalitarian system, they had silenced, exiled, and murdered members of the intelligentsia—writers, professors, and poets.

I didn't read Karl Marx, nor did I ever become a Communist, but I went through my radical feminist phase, living for some made-up mystique about how I should live, what causes I should care about, and what identity I could try on as mine. Venturing into a God-forsaken wilderness, even for a brief interlude, was at the very least, an unconventional choice. After this challenging detour, I was convinced the excitement and stimulation of the *real* world would later open its coffers to me.

Michael's new boss detected my nervousness as we drank another beer. I imagined how Jim Jensen was sizing me up. *Yeah, all this peace and quiet, it's gonna be tough on this broad. She may be book smart, but she's pretty stupid, alright. Doesn't have a damn clue what she's in for.*

Jim advised me not to worry. His Yup'ik wife was going to "take me under her wings." But what did that mean?

"Oh, thanks, Jim. Yes, you're right. That will be very nice," I muttered politely as the men talked some more.

The truest solitude is not something outside you, not an absence of men or sound around you; it is an abyss opening up in the center of your own soul.

— Thomas Merton, *Seeds of Contemplation*

…If I trust You, everything else will become, for me strength, health, and support. Everything will bring me to heaven. If I do not trust You, everything will be my destruction…

—Thomas Merton, *Thoughts in Solitude*

4 Abyss of Solitude

Jim drove us to our FAA government housing five minutes from the Airport Lodge. Our second floor apartment was practically on the direct flight path of Alaska Airlines, not far from the runway.

"Every day, you'll be able to see the jet on its final approach, and right from your picture window, you'll have a good view of Mount Saint Elias, *if* and *when* it's clear," Jim said with a grin as he turned the key to open the door.

The one-bedroom apartment came with an orange, yellow, and brown plaid couch, scratched up pine end tables, two oversized olive green lamps, a bed, and a chest of drawers. We didn't own a single piece of furniture and had nothing to supplement the décor except one dried up African violet. Michael also brought a piece of wood with strange Chinese symbols he had carved into it. For a long time, he had a fascination with Lao Tzu whom I had not heard of before and said the carving was supposed to represent the *Tao Te Ching*. I feigned understanding who and what he was talking about.

Time passed slowly over the next few months, especially in the days before satellite television, computers, and Internet. Through the mail, I ordered a copy of a thick hardcover book, *The Norton Anthology of Literature by Women,* to entertain myself during the monotony of staying in the apartment alone while Michael worked shifts at his aviation job filing pilot flight plans and learning about weather systems.

To force myself outdoors, I wandered around the small boat harbor with my camera, often loaded with Infrared film, to take pictures of aging fishing boats and the piles of empty, rusted crab pots strewn on the gravel bank. (Thomas Merton stood on this very same spot in 1968 with his camera. He couldn't resist taking a black and white photo of an old fishing boat named Tommy Boy.)

Lots of new words filled my head. *Muskeg*—something Yakutat was full of—a bog of organic material in poorly drained areas. *Moiety* (moy-uh-tee), a word meaning one of two equal parts, two Tlingit social groups, either Raven or Eagle. And "toion," a word of Russian innovation that translated to Tlingit "chief."

My life had become so different from what I dreamed, that all I could do for the first six months was cry and feel sorry for myself. I had really gone and done it. I'd be forgotten before I was ever discovered and die a slow death in obscurity.

I wasn't someone who knew what to do with real solitude—the kind of solitude you have to face day in and day out, solitude born in geographic isolation you can't run from, solitude that forces you to take a good, hard look at yourself. But for all the serenity and inner stillness my new quiet wilderness surroundings might possibly bring, I wasn't the least bit grateful. I fought against it. Striving for this or that, to get ahead, setting goals, making money, building careers and reputation—I bought in to the predefined picture of what success should be.

Even after I had met Jim's wife, Sue, and she shared some much appreciated household advice, I moped around the apartment and wallowed in self-pity. The days dragged on.

I stared at the cardboard boxes of personal belongings but couldn't bring myself to unpack them. Relocating as we did in the dead of winter made it far worse. Fast food restaurants, video rental places, ski trails, movie theatres, or medical offices were nonexistent. Isolation suffocated me.

It was winter and it was dark, or it was dark and it was pouring rain, or it was dark and spitting snow.

A few months passed, and we still didn't know very many people. I can't remember the precise moment when my friendship with Jennie Pavlik and her family began. She was the daughter of a Tlingit woman and white father. They were a large, eccentric family and the subject of much local gossip. Every now and then, one of the Pavliks would show up at our apartment with Rudy Pavlik's famous canned, smoked king salmon or fresh caught Dungeness crab. Everyone, including the Pavliks heard we were the *cheechakos,* newcomers in Alaska, and people felt a little sorry for us.

Rudy was one of Jennie's five brothers, a friendly guy who whenever we bumped into him even when the rain was battering every square inch of Yakutat, never wore any kind of rain jacket or hat.

I wondered about this awe-inspiring mountain view Jim had told us about. Because of the mountain's trickery, the downpours and the gloomy days, I had not yet seen any full views of Mount Saint Elias. Though Mount Saint Elias supposedly dominated the horizon, most of the time, the peak remained cloaked in clouds or was only partially visible.

Some days were better than others during my self-imposed wilderness exile. Eventually, I set up a darkroom in the basement of our building. On April days when conditions slightly improved, I drove down to the small boat harbor to shoot photos and kept trying to capture Mount Saint Elias, but no matter what I did, the pictures I produced were always lacking.

The Jensens lived directly behind our apartment in a modest ranch house, one of the privileges of being aviation chief. This made it easy for me to show up unannounced in Sue's kitchen after Michael left on his one-mile walk to work. I'd stand near her crowded pantry full of jarred salmon, 25-pound bags of flour and sugar, boxes of powdered milk, case lots of mayonnaise, tomato sauce, and Pilot Bread that had all been delivered via barge from Seattle. Sometimes I'd watch her prepare moose meat. She and some of the wives of the U.S. Weather Service employees showed me how to make bread, how to roll and stretch the dough and pound it into the counter a few times until it was elastic and smooth enough to be covered for its first rise.

It was odd that I should meet my first Yup'ik woman in the midst of a Tlingit Indian village so far from the treeless, northwest arctic coast in Kotzebue where Sue Jensen had spent most of her life. All I knew about Alaska Natives was what I'd seen on television growing up. Eskimos dressed in real fur parkas and lived in igloos surrounded by polar bears and they traveled by dog sled pulled by huskies. Public school didn't teach details about the 49th state; there were no lessons about Aleuts, Athabascans, Eskimos (Iñupiaq and Yup'ik), Tlingits, Haida, and Tsimpshians, not when there were so many other Indian tribes in the Lower 48 and closer to home.

It didn't matter when I showed up at Sue's. She always welcomed me with my lists of culinary questions about how people usually cooked sockeyes and kings, which became our primary food sources, along with moose, and how to make "Poor Man's Lobster" by dropping halibut chunks into boiling water sweetened with a little sugar. Sue answered my nagging questions so cheerfully that I thought all locals must be as good natured, and generous about whatever they knew.

But Mr. Pavlik shattered that initial impression. The notorious patriarch of the Pavliks, Jennie's father, Mike Pavlik, kept a wealth of trade secrets about how to live off the land. He believed his knowledge and wisdom should be guarded like a rare family heirloom and not shared, especially not with anyone outside of his immediate family and never with those "bastards who don't give a damn about the land."

Alaska existed as an icon of untouchable wilderness, a vast land of impenetrable ice. The superficial view of history mostly revolved around its boom-and-bust days in gold mining, fish processing, military expansion, oil exploration and drilling. Alaska was a detached mountainous enigma. The state was not really thought of as a state, but as a gigantic piece of tundra way up there on the top of the globe, a whopping cold wasteland even though *less* than 20 percent of it actually sits *above* the Arctic Circle. In contrast, Alaska also attracted young backpackers, adventurers, loner artists and wandering monks who wanted to lose themselves in the Land of the Midnight Sun.

Days for Sue Jensen centered around cooking, cleaning, or washing clothes even though most of their brood of fourteen children had left the roost. For a little fun, she went to the Alaska Native Brotherhood Hall to play bingo on Friday nights. Occasionally, we'd see one another at the Glacier Bear Lodge. Sometimes, when she had a few beers, she would repeat the same old lines about her marriage to Jim.

"Kathy, you know what's funny? I've spent twelve years of my life pregnant! You can count it up yourself. You will never pass me in this with your man," she'd say. And we'd both burst into laughter.

We ate a lot of frozen hamburger and jarred spaghetti sauce procured from Mallott's General Store since the summer salmon season was months away, and I didn't yet know how to cook. Part of what held me together was driving down the one-and-only paved road to the post office daily. I was desperate for packages and letters and mail order deliveries from Outside. Michael started playing basketball at the elementary school gym. He befriended George "Chunky" Henninger and Jimmy Bremner, both Tlingits who had grown up in Yakutat, and both performers with the St. Elias Dancers.

Yakutat is an ocean town, a forest town, a glacier town, a rain town. It's north of Juneau and situated 220 air miles southwest of Cordova on latitude 59'61' N, along the north Pacific coast, or on the shores of the Gulf of Alaska. The northernmost border of the Tongass National Forest reaches Yakutat, part of the world's largest temperate rain forest, comprised of the greenest, tallest, thickest Sitka spruce and hemlock you've ever seen. The Tongass National Forest covers 16.9 million acres and stretches almost 600 miles south, to below Ketchikan.

Except for those few, hardy steelheaders, most people bypassed the town altogether. The reason was simple: weather. Yakutat's average precipitation was over 130 inches per year compared to Anchorage's 15 inches. The tedious rain kept people out. And that's the way Mr. Pavlik and his whole family liked it.

Approximately 70 miles northwest of town stands Mount Saint Elias, the third highest mountain in North America. Imagine a peak dramatically rising out of the ice and snow like a gleaming all-white Egyptian pyramid. From sea-level, it shoots up to 18,008 feet, higher than any peak in the Rockies. As mountains go, it doesn't quite look like any other precisely because of its singular, dominating appearance. Mount Saint Elias stands alone and aloof from its many glacier covered brothers and sisters. Technically, the border splits this triangular, trowel-shaped mountain down the middle—half of it lies in Canada, and half within Alaska's legal boundary.

Two things happened when summer finally arrived. First, we bought an all-terrain vehicle, a Honda three-wheeler to ride the backcountry logging roads and down the shoreline and out to Ocean Cape—it was delivered as airfreight aboard Alaska Airlines.

And I finally landed a job to make Gloria Steinem proud: I became a fish slimer.

When the commercial fishing season began in June, I reported for duty down at the docks at 8:00 a.m. to work in the fish cannery.

Six or seven days a week, from early-to-mid-summer, cannery workers stood in an assembly line against a long, plastic counter to gut and clean salmon. The whole place reeked of raw fish and entrails. Thousands of pounds of salmon were piled high in white plastic fish totes that looked like garbage dumpsters. If I arrived at the cannery for the morning shift on an empty stomach or with the slightest feeling of a hangover from being out with Michael the night before at the Native-owned Glass Door Bar, the overpowering odor of fish waste would make me gag.

Once the morning shift began, those totes had to be emptied, every one of them, and quickly. Scraps of fish intestines, fish scales, salmon eggs, and streaks of blood splattered everything, even forklift blades, and the unformed cardboard boxes stacked high in nearby flats. Fish scraps stuck in between the wooden planks of the floor.

Large, steel freezer doors continually slammed shut and hundreds of pounds of crushed ice went tinkling and pelting like a waterfall. Manual labor stretched for eight or ten hours at a time. Sometimes we traded stations on the slime line to relieve the drudgery of standing in the same place. Within a few weeks, a fish slime camaraderie developed as I got to know some of my fellow workers. Nikko, a Japanese man, gave the white glove treatment to salmon eggs, handling each sac as if it were a crystal vase. All the salmon eggs were saved for export to Japanese seafood markets.

One by one, the salmon were beheaded, their organs stripped, and the main artery which runs along the fish's spine scraped clean. Carcass after carcass slid down the assembly line. I firmly gripped a metal tablespoon and scraped out any remaining blood or slime, then heaved the red salmon, often weighing up to ten pounds, down to the next group of workers who would then give it a quick rinse and toss the sockeye into its holding container. There were no conveyor belts; everything was done by hand.

Most of the cannery workers showed up from the Lower 48 either as lost souls bumming around the Pacific Northwest, as college students who hoped to make fast cash, or as perpetual seasonals who migrated around wherever they could find work.

But not Barbie. She was a veteran, one of the regular cannery workers, a local who had grown up in town. Barbie seemed to enjoy her role as one of the strongest and most dependable fish handlers. I knew her only casually as the sister of someone else I knew in the village. I watched her wield a knife with the speed and agility that won her the first position on the assembly line. Her shoulders and biceps bulged; she was firmly sculpted, as if she built houses for a living. Barbie spent all day cutting off salmon heads, and she was proud of it. She had never married, never even had a boyfriend that I knew about, and didn't order any pretty clothes from the Sears & Roebuck catalogues. Although she was my age, it was hard to talk to her because Barbie didn't like "girl talk" like my pre-Alaska girlfriends did. During her off time, she hung around anything with motors: rusty pickup trucks, ATVs she could race down the beach, skiffs, Zodiacs, and even her brother's dirt bike. Whenever I saw her at the Glass Door, she sat at the far end of the bar and rarely spoke more than four or five words in an evening. She stayed to herself and sipped her drink.

At the morning break from the slime line, or when it was quitting time, we all ran to the hoses to wash off the salmon blood and guts from our massive, army green bib overalls and brown rubber XTRATUF boots. A stream of ice cold water mixed with fish blood swirled to the floor; rivulets of maroon waste flooded the drain. But Barbie was apparently in no hurry to rinse off. At the end of the shift, she hung back from the hoses for a few minutes, grabbed a pack of smokes, and smirked at the rest of us who jetted to the hose and sprayed a full blast of water down our front sides. I started wondering if life in the bush had put that hard, smelly crust on Barbie, and if that kind of hardening up would happen to me in this surreal and primitive place the world had forgotten.

Generations of Tlingits had built their Southeast Alaska culture in the fjords and bays and rivers next to the North Pacific Ocean, subsisting on salmon for their very survival for thousands of years. One of the Tlingits' early fishing methods involved trapping fish in tidal estuaries, or in small ponds called *ishes*, where salmon would rest after their tremendous migrations. Once the salmon collected in their tidal paradise, clever Tlingit fishermen would direct them into their nets. Tlingits caught and hand-processed and smoked the salmon into dried strips, each family in their own way and for their own tribal and family needs, without the benefit of modern canning machinery, vacuum sealers, or Ziploc bags.

Abyss of Solitude

The Libby Packing Company opened Yakutat's first salmon cannery in 1905. Half a world away in bustling New York City or London restaurants, customers dined on salmon cakes from fish caught and canned in places like Yakutat.

Six weeks passed on the slime line. It was the most physically grueling, smelliest, most unconventional job of my life. I tried to console myself. I'm not some wayward city woman who's simply biding her time in this male-dominated fishing town until her husband saves her and they transfer out. Steel Town Girl wanted to show how tough she was. She wanted to be liked and to fit in.

But for the time being, feminist fish slimer or not, I still cared about *appearing* feminine, about being sensual and sexy. I complained to Michael about the stench in my hair—it smelled like dead fish. And how much my wrists and lower back ached—as if I had been lifting spruce logs all day. How I never dressed in anything nice anymore—except in Yakutat tennis shoes, BF Goodrich, XTRATUF knee-high rubber boots and in dirty, red bandanas. I wore baggy sweatshirts that advertised the "Yakutat Rain Festival from Jan. 1 to Dec. 31."

I stopped wearing mascara, eye shadow, skirts, or anything remotely feminine, as none of it worked anymore. In less than six months, I had become a parody of the self I had been striving to be. From every angle, my current situation was full of paradoxes that I didn't quite understand.

In the beginning, I never considered where the salmon I was gutting had migrated from. Nor who the men were who risked their lives season after season out in the dangerous breakers in small skiffs to haul in those thousands of pounds of sockeyes. Or why the bay outside the cannery, Monti Bay, and the beaches beyond, the Ankau Lagoon system, and Ocean Cape, and the great fanfare of mountains—too numerous to name—were so much in the blood of these Yakutat Tlingits. For millennia, they nourished themselves with fish and kelp covered in herring roe and with all the delicious edibles the sea provided.

I knew nothing about wild salmon as a species, or about fishing as a means of food gathering. I knew nothing about beach rye grass and skunk cabbage, that the blueberry bloomed in August, or that pink salmon fed the bears, or that ravens were among some of the smartest birds alive. Of bald eagles that scavenged for fingerlings, I knew nothing. Nor of potlatch, pewter skies, Disenchantment Bay, seal hunting, glacial moraines, plate tectonics, coho, brown bear, Devil's Club, salmonberry, williwaws, moieties, or the *teet kwanni*—spirits of the sea in Tlingit.

"Being Tlingit is *knowing who you are*. Being Tlingit is living in partnership with the land." I heard these words spoken, but I had no real concept of what a close relationship to the land really meant.

I had little direct, in-depth knowledge of mountains, streams, forests or the natural world from anywhere I had lived before. Not in the close physical and spiritual sense that the Yakutat people had. The Tlingits—they weren't merely subsisting on the land. They were embodied and *enspirited* by it.

I grew more interested in my own ancestry. The indigenous peoples of Alaska had lived for 10,000 years without Western products and religion. They lived in deep awareness of the sacred landscape surrounding them, and they did it without a church or book. What sacred rituals and traditions had been passed down to me? What traditional clothing or dress to mark my family's heritage? What prayers, stories, or songs had my family ever shared?

I recalled how a few longtime Alaskans had erroneously warned us as we prepared to move to the village: "Remember, don't ever shoot a raven, or say anything negative about those noisy, black birds, either. That would be a very offensive thing to do…because to the Tlingit Indians, ravens are like God…they hold the spirit of their ancestors."

What city people often repeated about the "*Click-it*" Indians was often nothing but pure speculation and stereotype. It's not that the Tlingits perceived Raven as God, or as a special deity to be worshipped. Tlingits saw ravens as creatures to be greatly respected. They believed in One Spirit Above, without written doctrines, syllogisms, theology books, or Scriptural references.

The spirit of their ancestors…the spirit of their ancestors. Those words repeated through the drooping vine of my soul. I was a drifting boat, unsure of where my moorings were, and could not speak with any authority or conviction about my ancestors.

The relentless gray of winter came around again and we weren't going anywhere. It was time I had a heart-to-heart talk with myself, a clearing of the mind. Maybe there was a Creator at work in the universe.

Finally, I caught my first unobstructed views of Mount Saint Elias from our living room window near the FAA and airfield, and again from the boat harbor. The mountain appeared as white as a piece of paper— the whitest white triangle dominating the horizon. I took out the blank leather journal I had packed in with our meager belongings and for the first time in a quiet moment, I sat down to scribble a few quick words.

I wrote, "Mount Saint Elias is the most beautiful mountain I have ever seen. Petty ambitions will die on mountainsides."

...It was a bright day and the sea was calm, and I looked out over the glittering blue water, realizing more and more that this was where I really belonged. I shall never forget it. I need the sound of those waves, that desolation, that emptiness.

—Thomas Merton
Notes from *The Intimate Merton*, 1968

5 Spirit of the Tlingits

In trying to get more acquainted with my new home, I studied maps and realized the Pacific was one mother of a big damn ocean. Everyone knows it's the biggest body of water on earth. I knew this much at least, but I hadn't thought about its actual scale or dimension until I moved to Alaska. I first laid eyes on the Pacific Ocean, not from sunny Santa Monica or Hawaii, but from the uninhabited, cold, and blustery beaches of Yakutat. I wondered how many Gulfs of Mexico would fit into it, and why we rarely saw vessels on the cloudy horizon.

The northern rim of the Pacific—the open Gulf of Alaska—is an 850-mile arc extending from the Kodiak archipelago south to Ketchikan near British Columbia's border. It was fun to imagine that if I had a sailboat, and if I could sail it straight out into the horizon and head due west from Yakutat and south without ever changing longitudinal direction, I wouldn't see a trace of land again until I reached the Marquesas Islands over 4,000 nautical miles away, below the equator and deep into the South Pacific. In equatorial climes, we tend to associate the ocean with turquoise seas, sparkling sunshine, coconut palms, and bronzed women walking through warm sands in yellow strapless sundresses. But in those early years, from where I first saw the Pacific, every nuance of its tropical, *pacific* persona was cast away. I stood chilled to the bone, covered head to unpolished toes in drab olive green rain gear and pants three sizes too big, without a Tiki hut or garden in sight.

The Yakutat people deal in everything that is wet or about to become so. Historically, Tlingits are ocean-going people—*low tide people*—a name that suits them well. Harvesting marine resources remains a central part of their culture. "When the tide goes out, the table is set," as the old Tlingit expression goes. An estimated 16,000 to 20,000 Tlingits live in Southeast Alaska, with five Eagle and Raven clans calling Yakutat home—Yakutat being the northernmost territory in the Tlingit region.

For centuries, Tlingits constructed sturdy canoes out of spruce and hemlock logs and became experts at handling them. To save their rowing muscles, they often improvised by turning their canoes into prototype sail boats and attached canvas material to poles and paddles to increase propulsion across bays and fjords. In more modern times, Tlingits became adept at launching and running skiffs as set-net fishermen in the choppy seas, as all five of the Pavlik sons had learned to do as commercial and subsistence fishermen.

I spent as much time as I could investigating the beaches on my ATV. I rode with Michael from our apartment down the gravel road to Canon Beach and hugged the shoreline for miles until we reached Ocean Cape. The name refers both to the beach and to the bluff above it where the long expanse of natural beach temporarily halts, and the indentation that forms the mouth of Yakutat Bay begins. From our apartment the whole one-way trip by three wheeler to Ocean Cape took about thirty minutes, depending upon how fast we zipped through the pebbly sand, and how many times we stopped along the way. On most days, especially in the fall, I donned full rain suit regalia and wore gloves to cut the chill.

At Ocean Cape, the surf was loud and booming. Swells could reach twenty feet. The Pacific whirled up, converged with the twenty-mile-wide mouth of Yakutat Bay, and relentlessly broke over boulders as it pummeled the shore. Ocean Cape was, and is, spectacular. More so than the great Gulf Island National Seashore near Pensacola.

The memories I had of north Florida beaches all seemed like another life after I moved to Alaska. My college girlfriends and I hung out on those hot, sugar white beaches, and as the Jimmy Buffet song went, we saw tourists covered with oil, living on sponge cakes, watching the sun bake. We wore bikinis and slathered on baby oil mixed with iodine and enjoyed the gentle, blue-green waters. Sprawled on frayed blankets with our portable radios blasting Lynyrd Skynyrd, we baked, too, under an intense, glaring sun. I lived under the hopeful delusion that fair, freckled skin like mine might actually darken to another tint besides pinkish-ivory.

At Ocean Cape there could be snow pellets in early September, and if I saw anyone at all at the beach on a fairly decent day—one with periodic drizzle instead of rain that fell by the barge load—it would be the Tlingit kids on their ATVs with an uncle or auntie, zipping down the shore. It was mostly about the thrill of the ride, but the kids, too, inspected the wrack line for whatever marine treasures washed up. A few of them were bundled in hooded sweatshirts and gathered around a small fire made from the sticks and driftwood scattered across the sands. By the sheer force of nature, the Gulf of Alaska would deposit whole spruce trees, 30 to 40 feet long, onto the beach, as if they were nothing but large Tinker Toys wedged in the sand.

Less than 20 miles north, the world's largest piedmont glacier, the Malaspina, extends its lobe down to the Gulf of Alaska between Icy Bay and Yakutat Bay. The Malaspina completely dominates the western side of Yakutat Bay, an area known as the Grand Wash where the ever resourceful Mr. Pavlik and his sons frequently explored. If this were southern California, every sliver of this virgin beach and waterfront would be clogged with pricey condominiums, crowded boardwalks, and seafood restaurants. But in the isolated North Pacific, Yakutat's coast is a lonely place.

From this vantage point, the ocean rolls into an unbroken shore, part of an undisturbed strip of rain forest and coast that could technically extend uniformly without interruption for almost 200 miles, except for the mouths of streams and rivers that empty into the sea, and a few scattered fish camps near those rivers.

A dense, but narrow, band of tall Sitka spruce mixed with western hemlock and thick underbrush grows parallel to the Gulf of Alaska beach. Brown bears of all ages and sizes roam these pristine shores. Sandhill cranes and trumpeter swans fly overhead on their annual spring and fall migrations along the Pacific Flyway. Bonaparte's gulls and Great Blue Herons search the shallow waters and tidal outwash. Harbor seals occasionally bask on one of the large boulders. Succulent wild strawberries and purple lupine grow in sandy margins along the open greenbelt before dense Sitka spruce and hemlock forest begins. In a matter of minutes, you can walk from the waves straight into the shadows of the rain forest, thick with salmonberry, lily-of-the-valley, twin flowers, ferns, lichen, and green walls of extra-thorny Devil's Club that only a bear can move through. The shrub thrives in Yakutat's fertile coastal environment growing well over 12-feet tall.

In this most tumultuous region of the North Pacific, a 60-foot wave is often a ripple.

From Cape Fairweather 130 miles to the southeast, to Cape Yakataga due northwest from Ocean Cape, the sea is often driven by over 100 mile per hour winds. The wind battered the shore and boulders carried downward by glaciers could be reduced to grit in no time.

Tumultuous. Fleeting. Dramatic. Seismically off the charts. A good place for restless women. The "turbulent crescent," the geologists called it, a land of widespread metamorphism. When it came down to it, Ocean Cape was not a beach to dabble your toes in. Instead of striped beach towels and coolers of chilled iced tea and sodas, you might see a rotting salmon, pieces of fishing net, a trail of bear footprints in the sand—or a brown bear ambling toward you. The north Gulf of Alaska coast is where other Alaska Native people—the Eyak—from Copper River in the north near Cordova had settled. The Eyak would portage across ice fields and streams to make their passage southward into Yakutat. The Tlingits who lived closer to Sitka ventured north to Yakutat in their canoes for trading.

Frederica de Laguna, was a well-respected Bryn Mawr anthropologist who spent much time in the Yakutat region during the 1940s and 50s. She believed that *Yakutat* was likely derived from an Eyak Indian word meaning "the place where the lagoon is forming."

Tlingits sometimes interpret its name to mean "the place where the canoe rests or bounces."

The Russians, European explorers, and other traders made initial contact in the region over two centuries ago. The explorations of Cook, Lapérouse, Malaspina, and Vancouver drew new nautical charts of the Southeast Alaska coastline. The ships' naturalists studied the inlets, coves and islands, recorded the abundant wildlife they saw, and collected botanical specimens. They made sketches of Tlingit women adorned in labrets—dramatic piercings of their lower lips where pieces of bone were inserted.

At the start of the twentieth century, the lands which the Tlingits and Eyaks had called home would be "discovered" by gold panners, drifters, East Coast museum collectors searching for finely woven Native spruce root baskets and Chilkat blankets.

Swedish missionaries bent on introducing God to the frontier's Godless tribes with their devil dancing and totem painting followed. The zealous Christians, the ones with the "million dollar missionary smiles" as some Natives later described them, came to evangelize *the heathens* who must be converted to the way of The Word. The Tlingits did not possess any guides to "Godly Living" and didn't keep Bibles around.

I wondered how they knew what they knew, if not from words printed in a book. In the Yup'ik culture, they spoke of "*ella*," a deep awareness of the world, and a more selfless way of living. With the Pavliks, and with other Tlingits I befriended, they said the land itself was their Holy Prayer and Holy Spirit. They were grateful for the raven, the salmon, and for the mighty forces of the glacier. They felt a presence of a unifying creative spirit, perhaps, in the rains that endlessly fell on their heads and in the challenges forever thrown their way by Nature in this land of metamorphosis.

The human voice speaking to you, especially by an Elder, was a consecrated act. This was also stressed as something to pay close attention to. And in the Tlingits' way of life and cultural values, it meant you obeyed the traditions of your ancestors when they spoke to you individually or in a group. You showed respect for self and for elders. You were to be strong in mind, body, and spirit. You were to listen well and always try to hold each other up. These were fundamental Tlingit values passed down from one generation to the next. Put another way, as Native people believed, it was important to "stay inside the drum" in language and culture.

Compared to my family upbringing—so much of my youthful cultural awakening had been dependent upon what I heard and learned from the media—all of this sounded completely foreign. In my first few years of living in Yakutat, I was reminded daily about how disconnected I was to the natural environment, to my family, and to my own ancestry.

At the Carnegie Museum once, I came across a poem displayed as part of an exhibit in the American Hall of the Indian. I recognized the name of its author, Walter Soboleff, a well-known Tlingit elder with a Russian last name. I once him heard speak in Juneau. Soboleff's untitled poem reads:

> Nature is like people.
> Nature is alive.
> Mountains are like people.
> Trees are like people.
> Fish are like people.
>
> If my mother were to meet a brown bear in the woods, she would say:
>
> My father's people, don't harm me.
> My father's people, peace, peace, peace.

Historians began making films and researchers took down oral histories as the twentieth century wore on. Nora Marks Dauenhauer and Richard Dauenhauer, both linguists and historians, referenced Andrew P. Johnson, a Tlingit language teacher and minister from Sitka. In a 1971 recording, Johnson explained,

A person will say 'I am going to speak to you.' Public speaking is like a man walking along a river with a gaff hook.

Spirit of the Tlingits

He lets his gaff hook drift over a salmon swimming at the edge of the river. When he hooks on it, the salmon way over there becomes one with him.

This is the way oratory is. Even speech delivered at a distance becomes one with someone.

I started taking more of an interest in Tlingit practices and beliefs. They adapted the potlatch tradition from their contact with Russians. When any member of a clan dies, it is the opposite clan who makes all the funeral arrangements and assists the grieving family. At the end of forty days of mourning, the grieving family thanks everyone by organizing a potlatch, a large community gathering, where speeches honoring the deceased member and some of the deceased ancestors are made, and people share local foods and come together to support one another after the sadness of death.

Meanwhile, Michael stayed busy further refining his wildlife viewing skills. He learned to set traps for mink and marten and spent most of his free time steelhead fishing. From a small bridge over the Situk River, he taught me how to spot the elusive steelhead near log jams. He insisted I don hip boots to hike through the brush to his favorite trout holes. Some days he took me practice shooting so I could learn to fire a Smith & Wesson .357 revolver on the side of the road near Harlequin Lake. He had no real adjustment period. Other than learning his FAA job, everything about the lifestyle seemed to bring out the best in his primordial, masculine nature.

Never agitated or second-guessing himself, he didn't question what tomorrow would bring, but was content to be who he was, where he was, carrying his fishing rod like a torch as he moved down trails through thick alder and over massive spruce tree roots.

I started to write a different story and pictured myself as the migratory woman, the woman who was not Tlingit or Eyak, who was not of this place, who had no tribal clan, no tribal mask, no Eagle or Raven name.

As often as I could, I rode up and down the shore in my three-wheeler to where the wind meets the Pacific at Ocean Cape.

With each passing day, I started to lose part of myself in its dampness and beauty. Pieces of my external self slowly emptied in the rain-washed air.

Everywhere I turned, I saw water—water frozen, water free running. Water seeped and spilled into a pattern of glacial streams, rivers, saltwater lagoons, wetlands, bogs, and sloughs. On the forest floor, I felt spongy layers of moss under my feet.

The weather was miserable. Rains fell hard. Gales blew. Storms swept in. Winds battered. It's rough out there, fishermen said. And then the North Pacific would hurl a few more hemlock logs ashore and the currents would pound and hammer the boulders to bits.

Long ago, in another life, as another self, my toes curled in fine, hot sand and touched pretty pink seashells. No more.

Rain beat against my heavy, yellow rain jacket. Every day, the same old weather story:

Today: rain. Rain likely again in the evening. Then a chance of rain, late. Southeast winds 15 to 25 miles per hour. Chance of rain: 70 percent.

Tomorrow: rain likely. Windy. More rain.

I sulked and skulked. Every day, I waited for better weather, for the sun to please stay. Come back, sun!

But my friend, Jennie Pavlik, scolded me. "We don't wait," Jennie said. "Grab your jacket! We go anyway! Come on! Who cares about dumb old rain?"

And so I went with Jennie and with her Tlingit mother, Genevieve. Sometimes, we picked blueberries. Sometimes we walked in silence beneath Sitka spruce trees. On the beach, we usually found something interesting poking out of the sand—bald eagle feathers, frayed rope. Jennie stuffed her pockets with pieces of this or that, some smooth, white rocks, maybe a razor clam shell. She was always collecting objects for her children and for her arts and crafts.

Everyone hunted glass balls. I tried to find them, too. Best to go after storms, locals said. They came from Japanese fishing boats used long ago in the Pacific. Some glass floats looked like rolling pins, some like blue-green beach balls. The Pavliks had glass balls hanging everywhere to catch light.

But me, the migratory woman, I never found a single one. Michael, he found many.

He had a well-thought out glass ball strategy, a rational method for finding them, a sixth sense about it, as he did with fishing and wildlife.

"Ocean and glacial winds bury the glass balls inside sand dunes," he said. "Storms blow them out again." Glass balls looked like big green eggs tucked in the sands and scrub. When my husband hunted, he left the open beach and patiently searched the margins between sand and coastal forest.

"You are always in too much of a hurry," he said. "You need patience when hunting for glass balls. Search wherever others easily overlook." And then he grew quiet again.

"Okay," I said, "I will try that, except…except, I don't like moving slow. You know it's not my nature to sit still and just be. To wait in one place. And not talk. It's hard to not talk."

"You see, I have no patience," I said. But with my Tlingit companions, I did take time to listen. For a long time, we women did not seem to be doing much of anything but looking at the beach and waves. They shared stories with me. They told me about Knight Island and how they lived in Yakutat Bay. Jennie spoke about her father and the important knowledge he taught his children about how to live.

We enjoyed each other's company. We listened to many squawking ravens. Bald eagles swooped right by them and flew low over the surf.

The black birds never shut up. "Too noisy! Go away, you stupid ravens!" I said.

But the ravens only laughed and paid no mind.

We sat near the surf in unzipped jackets. No hats. The cold Pacific winds blew down our necks. Jennie and her mother made me smile. So many family stories! Her brother Rudy was always chasing or running from brown bears. All of her brothers hunted seals and otters. Her father cooked with seal oil and made her taste porpoise meat and drink rose hip tea.

I liked these Pavlik women. Gentle, quiet women. Women in repose. Women spiritually whole and well-grounded. They knew how to live in wild and free places. They made me feel calmer inside.

"Look, tide's in!" Jennie only said what needed to be said, nothing more, nothing less.

No *talk-talk-talk*. It was enough.

More often, at my favorite place in the world—Ocean Cape—I was with Michael. We traveled on the old dirt logging roads, past lagoons with muskeg and with yellow pond lilies, only occasionally seeing someone else pass by. Along the creeks and estuaries of the foreland, wherever we rode or walked, it was important to check for fresh, brown bear sign. If out on the clear open beach, I always made sure to check. Brown bears also roamed the sands and sniffed the tides.

We climbed the bluff and explored the area where the old World War II radar equipment and bunkers used to be—the White Alice communications site. From there, we paused to look down at the scrolls of waves rumbling to shore. The surf boomed, and the water splashed with immense power, as if a great force was purposely announcing its presence.

Wind blew my copper-red hair. I daydreamed. On my three-wheeler, I spun and swerved around, made figure eights in the sand, and made sure Michael was close by on his machine. We circled amber pieces of kelp, tangled clumps of seaweed, and washed-up sculpin bones. With the engine switched off, I listened to rain pelt my jacket. My mind opened to the sand, the nettles, the sweetgrass, the chocolate lilies, and the heavy, steel gray clouds dancing above.

I rode in rain and felt a rawness that soaked right through to my breasts. As time passed, I didn't mind the mizzling weather so much. I stooped down low to pick flowering beach pea and inspect the wrack line. A wave broke across the beach and I dragged my hand through the bubbles left in the fine gravel and through the swirls of sea foam as Michael approached.

"Michael, Mount Saint Elias—it looks like a seagull on the water," I said.

"Where did you come up with that? It hasn't been out yet."

"I read it. A Tlingit elder once said that about the whiteness of the mountain."

I probably repeated that gorgeous metaphor one too many times when we were out in the elements three-wheeling, but it's a description that runs through my mind to this day. There was something mystical about the sharp pure air, the steady winds blowing across the mouth of Yakutat Bay, and the fact we were all alone at Ocean Cape without human intrusions. In my imagination, this swath of pristine land and the Pacific Ocean were mine; the wonderful open space and perfection of nature before me, inseparable from my very breath.

But I felt fear. To be in such sublime beauty overwhelmed me as if I was shown a glimpse of some hidden reality that I couldn't begin to articulate. I didn't know where the fear was coming from, but I felt a pang of terror. I looked up and searched gray skies for the great white mountain but was disappointed. The alabaster pyramid was there, but it was not going to show itself for my benefit and pleasure. I looked up two or three more times. No behemoth of a mountain to feast my eyes upon.

Under the imaginary gaze of Elias, my throat tightened and my stomach churned. "Why did you bring me here? What is it you are trying to teach me? Have I not opened my eyes wide enough?" I said. But I wasn't speaking to Michael who was driving fast, weaving his ATV in and out of driftwood piles.

I was dumbfounded. What was I doing talking to a mountain I couldn't even see?

I addressed Elias again, my wet fingers growing numb on the handlebars. "Why wait this long to show me such magnificence? What is it I should do with all this whiteness?"

From the rain and crashing sea, and from the Pavlik women, I was learning how to live in this world.

...Now my whole life is this—to keep unencumbered. The wind owns the field where I walk, and I own nothing and am owned by nothing, and I shall never even be forgotten because no one will ever discover me. This is to me an immense source of great confidence. My Mass this morning was transfigured by this independence...

—Thomas Merton,
December 22, 1949, *The Sign of Jonas*

Dear Pat,

I just tried to notarize this but it's nearly impossible with the present form. It has to be signed by someone in Kentucky. I suggest you contact John Ford and... More later.
I'm writing this at the Post Office. Alaska—*terrific*.

Best to all,
Louie

—Thomas Merton letter from Alaska to
Br. Patrick Hart, Abbey of Gethsemani
September 18, 1968
previously unpublished

6 Mr. Pavlik & the Silver Chalice

As autumn approached, my life changed again. I gladly gave up my spot on the slime line and became the sole librarian for Yakutat's only school, grades kindergarten through twelve. That's about the time I befriended long-time residents Skip and Rose Mary Ryman. Rose Mary was born in Guam and worked as the school secretary. Her husband, Skip was the station manager for Alaska Airlines at the town's small airport. The Rymans belonged to the tiny Catholic parish of St. Anne's and it was Skip's father, Frank Ryman, who had invited Thomas Merton to Yakutat in September 1968. But I didn't know anything about this when we began married life in Yakutat.

I was happy to be hired for the school job. The principal overlooked the fact I had no real training or credentials. In the Yakutat School District, where the entire student population was less than 100, he entrusted me to my new part-time job and said to "have at it." The library was a neglected classroom with a few metal shelves of random books and there was no budget. The first thing I did was to write a grant. Within a few months, funds came in for me to assemble an Alaska history section with as many materials as I could find about the area.

In Hardy Trefzger's 1963 memoir *My Fifty Years in Alaska*, he relates the story about how, before World War II, he leased land and lived on Knight Island in Yakutat Bay not far from Hubbard Glacier. (Merton noted the "small lost islands that dotted the bay" in the pages of his journal.) Hardy tried to make a go of mink farming on the island, but in 1944 Trefzger's sold his lease to a young and cocky Wisconsin transplant, a former farm boy, Catholic altar boy, and high school dropout—to Jennie's father, Mike Pavlik.

On many afternoons, after Mr. Pavlik was forced for health reasons to vacate his homestead on Knight Island, I visited him at his cabin on the mainland. He often dug out his special, autographed copy of *My Fifty Years in Alaska* forgetting that he had shown it to me on prior visits.

Mike Pavlik considered himself religious, but he was no saint, and he'd be the first one to tell that to Merton had the two of them ever met. But when the famous monk slipped into town as the special guest of Frank Ryman and his family, the Pavliks were living in seclusion on their island homestead.

Father Merton was in Yakutat for one day and night on September 27, 1968—but he might have heard about the Pavliks, as they, along with the Rymans, were part of a handful of living, breathing, practicing Catholics residing in the Tlingit community. The Pavliks were cut from a different religious cloth than all the other life-long Catholics with whom Merton was acquainted. Pavlik, his Tlingit wife Genevieve, and their eight children practiced a kind of do-it-yourself Catholicism. The closest Catholic church was about 300 miles away in the state capital of Juneau, reachable only by air or by sea.

Merton, though apprehensive about seeing so many guns and knives around the Pavliks, would have appreciated hearing the details about Mr. Pavlik's more unfettered life. Mike Pavlik had always lived as his own "free bird"—exactly the kind of man the learned monk feared was disappearing from society, a man purposefully living on the margins, away from the dehumanizing forces of the modern age. The Pavliks, lifelong Catholics, were "solid and simple Catholics," as Merton himself described some of the Alaskans he bumped into.

Rudy Pavlik and his four brothers could not care less about a wimpy, poetry scribbling monk born in France to artist parents. He would have had a field day with Merton, especially when Merton was a young man, before he learned to appreciate the fruits of hard manual labor at the Abbey. The wilds of Alaska were far too much for someone as naïve and spoiled as Merton, Rudy would say. "Merton might be a Trappist monk, but he don't know a damn thing about trapping."

Once, when I stopped to visit Rudy and were standing together in the rain in front of his place, he admitted he only completed school up to the second grade, and then he lifted his arms in the air.

"Everything I am is right here," Rudy said. "*This* is my book."

In the Pavliks' point of view, you are a real man, *if* you are a survivor—*period*. If what you know about how things work in the world tends toward the more abstract side of things, based on your having read a few nature guide books at the monastery, well, Mr. Pavlik and his boys wouldn't give you the time of day. You were a *man's man* if you forged your own way by *living and breathing* off the land, doing all that's required, no matter how physically challenging and dangerous, to be a true subsistence hunter and fisherman.

And you did it all without throwing out a lot of what Rudy called high powered words to people. He didn't see a reason to put on airs or to show off or prove you had gone to college. Rudy Pavlik detested high powered words.

It was in the summer of 2006 that I was seriously starting to take spiritual stock of myself. I wanted to see if Mr. Pavlik would be gracious enough to share his thoughts, but he was aging and time was running out.

In the years after we moved away from Yakutat, I had been having too many sleepless nights. Maybe I could distill some of his insights about how to live, similar to the way those old Russian *staretsy*, the Orthodox monks and hermits from the thick northern forests were respected as wise spiritual fathers. Those old monks would provide advice and counsel to any Russian pilgrims or curious peasants who showed up at their door.

But Jennie's father was no quiet, empathetic Slav. He often growled at visitors. He liked to shout anti-government epithets to anyone who came to his door, cussing and swearing and sounding as if he didn't have one compassionate Christian bone in his body.

Mr. Pavlik was one of the area's most talked about residents, respected for his longevity, practical know-how, willpower, and vast wilderness experience, but disliked for his sometimes blatant disregard for government rules and regulations that his fellow good citizens were obliged to operate under.

Many accusations, true, false and wildly exaggerated, were repeated about him by friends and enemies: He's difficult to get along with; he's an old geezer sourdough who doesn't trust anyone; he's a jack-of-all-trades; and he's a troublemaker who thinks he has *carte blanche* to do whatever the hell he wants around here. People liked to gossip about the town's hermit so much, you'd think the Pavliks had been hiding skiffs of gold at Knight Island.

In town you had people called Muskeg Johnnie and Kayak Tom and Chief Paul Henry, and any one of them might say Mike Pavlik was a conniving son-of-a-bitch, a little too quick tempered, and too proud for his white britches.

He had enjoyed his fair share of fights and squabbles in his younger days, but with all the Pavlik men, the more important measure of manhood had nothing to do with who bloodied the most noses, but rather who had the most mink and marten. And who had successfully hunted seals and sea otter in Disenchantment Bay. Who had run into their share of bears on Knight Island and around Esker Creek across Yakutat Bay. And who had been forced over the years to kill bears in self-defense. Who was the most skilled hunter, and who could gulp down mugs of tasty duck blood soup.

During the last few years of his life, age had softened him somewhat, made the old man more introspective.

"If there was *no* life after death," he said, "why be fair and square in your life? You could get away with whatever the hell you can."

Mr. Pavlik & the Silver Chalice

His story—I always called him Mister Pavlik out of respect, never Mike—will sound familiar. It's a tale of a bygone era, an America of the 1930s and 40s when earning a college English degree, especially from an impressive institution like Columbia, wasn't at all available or considered a young man's ticket to success. Among the less privileged classes, for people like Mr. Pavlik and my father, young men were expected to search for physical work to support themselves. They did not have any trust funds or inheritances to fall back on as Merton did in his student days.

You could better yourself by dropping out of high school to work on the farm, in the factories and steel mills, in the mines, or join the military. My father went only as far as the eighth grade in Pittsburgh and ran off and joined the U.S. Navy at age 17 during World War II as the lowest ranking sailor. Mr. Pavlik would have had a hard time understanding why any young man would waste his time hanging out with his male friends in posh summer cabins to try and write novels or poems, as Merton did with his closest friends in Olean, New York. In Pavlik's eyes, this was not what real men did.

Jennie told him I'd be dropping by his cabin. Her father was cranky and in a lot of pain and Jennie warned me not to expect much in the way of conversation. He allowed family to visit, but wasn't very friendly to anybody else.

"Don't be surprised if he's forgotten all about you," she said. "Chances are he'll either be too ill or too ornery for Sunday afternoon company."

"You know how he is," Jennie stressed again. "He'll make an exception because it's you and you once lived here, but I'm not sure how much he'll feel like talking today, or if he'll be nice enough to even let you in the door."

I looked forward to any time we might have together knowing he had a lot to say about his faith and not in the more detached terms like someone who had taken formal classes. Mr. Pavlik relayed to his eight children the importance of praising God, something we never discussed in our family growing up, nor when I became a mother of two sons.

"There *is* a hell," he told Jennie. "Live the way God wants you to live. If not, that is hell."

The June day was partly overcast, the temperature in the mid-60s, much warmer than usual and Mass at St. Anne's should have ended. In 1972, a small two story, beige, wood-framed house with T1-11 siding was built on top of a sloped gravel lot a short distance from Yakutat School. This structure became St. Anne's—the town's first and only Catholic Church which didn't look anything like a real church.

If it weren't for the involvement and devotion of the Pavlik and Ryman families in the tiny parish, St. Anne's would have been boarded up soon after its construction, or turned into a bingo hall.

I parked my borrowed Ford pickup next to a rectangular plywood shack that looked like it had never seen a coat of paint. Mr. Pavlik built hunting cabins more structurally inviting than this neglected and rundown looking place.

If you didn't know someone lived in it, you might think Mr. Pavlik's cabin was merely a storage shed for old boat parts, carpentry tools, and commercial fishing gear. Some of the brush was cleared away, making it possible to walk on the narrow gravel footpath. The small dwelling had no porch, only two wooden steps, and its garage-type windows were smudged and streaked with dirt. Wood ferns and tall ostrich ferns, salmonberry shrubs not yet ripe with berries, and a patch of Devil's Club surrounded it. Most of the junk lying about—concrete blocks, half-coiled rusted chains, a dented plastic bucket, and an old axe—looked as though it had been dumped on the ground years ago.

Yakutat's year-round population had grown to almost 700 people by the early 2000s. After the introduction of the Internet, an espresso machine at the general store, and with satellite dishes on the rooftops, calling it a fishing "village" no longer seemed accurate.

But whether it was 700 locals or only 70, that was still too many people in rain forest country for Mike Pavlik, and everyone in town knew it.

If you talked to a few locals and the professional fish and game managers, they'd tell you the Pavliks brought much of the organizational trouble upon themselves. It was known that over the years, the family often did whatever it took to engage in basic survival activity, sometimes without regard to what season it technically was, and what the latest federal, state, and local resource laws dictated.

The type of nature experiences the Pavliks traditionally enjoyed had nothing to do with those—as Rudy would say—tree-hugging, flower-sniffing, little pansy earth-kissers with their Gortex jackets, GPS systems, digital cameras, and expensive hiking boots.

The Pavlik men were akin to the Vikings in temperament. As one of the local men joked, Rudy knew how to survive all winter long with nothing but a packet of sugar and salt. Rudy bragged that he could track a lizard over bare rocks. He and his brother could star in their own television survivor series and they wouldn't need a script.

But there would be no reality television show because he had been raised by a father who was guarded and stingy about his insider knowledge on how to live off the land.

At one time or another, Rudy's father repeated the following mantras to him and the rest of his siblings.

"Learn to think for yourself or else you're a poor excuse for a human being;" "Whatever you're doing and trying to figure out, you can get things done, if you set your mind to it;" "Yakutat will provide for you, if you know what you're doing, and *if* you don't give away your hard-earned knowledge about the land to people who don't care one stinking iota about it."

The Pavliks learned to hunt black bear for food and how to kill brown bears in defense of life and property. They hunted moose, wolves, otters, and coyotes, trapped mink and marten, raised 500 sheep on Knight Island, launched rickety skiffs into hairy breakers out in the Gulf of Alaska, "the meanest waters there are around here," as their father would say. They collected and ate seagull eggs and pulled dozens of Dungeness crab pots. Mr. Pavlik tried cross-breeding cockles and butter clams; gardened in the middle of a rain forest using salmon heads and starfish for fertilizer, prospected for gold, drank tea made from spruce tips he collected, and worked metal into his own tools and hunting knives. He used fiddlehead ferns and blueberry blossoms for salad fixings, melted animal fat to make soap, and after hunting and putting up a moose, he boiled the bones and made one of his favorite delicacies, jellied moose nose which I had always declined to sample.

Until Mike Pavlik reached his seventies, he lived without the need for television, radio, or telephones. With his five sons by his side—two of them would die in boating accidents at sea— he slowly and painstakingly built seven different hunting cabins on the Point Manby side of Yakutat Bay. There are no roads to haul in construction materials. Every plank, nail, and hammer had to be dragged, skiff load by skiff load, across the dangerous mouth of the bay, a construction process that took many years. Some of those cabins lasted a long time, some didn't.

He taught his sons and daughters to be close observers of the land, to predict weather by studying the light and cloud formations right over their heads. He was well acquainted with the extremely turbulent Grand Wash area across Yakutat Bay near the Malaspina Glacier. At the Grand Wash, he often witnessed glacier melt rivers storm down from Canadian ice fields and empty into the bay, only to vanish a few weeks later, the currents and debris all lost or absorbed in some other water drama involving flooding glacial rivers and bursting ice dams.

I hoped he'd throw some mercy on me, the obvious Outsider from Anchorage, and let me visit him after so many years away. He had always disliked senseless intrusions, meaning from anyone not in his extended family circle.

Mr. Pavlik thought anyone remotely affiliated with any branch of government was a blood-sucking parasite. For ten, maybe twenty years, he'd squabbled with assorted agencies and "money-grubbing attorneys" over what his fair and proper lease payment and taxes should be today for his beloved Knight Island parcel, and these financial and legal disputes had greatly intensified. He showed me a copy of an old U.S. Forest Service letter he safeguards in his files. The official wrote a letter back in the 1970s to his regional supervisor complaining about Mike Pavlik. He reported that Pavlik was interested in only one thing—to build his own private game reserve. Once his wife passed on, the senior Pavlik had to be physically dragged off his island hermitage to live in town, in the middle of booming civilization.

But I really wasn't interested in rehashing all the inside details on why his federal lease increased from about $5 per year in 1944 to the $1,650 he must pay now. No reason to make him any testier than he already was, especially since his health had been deteriorating.

For a long time, I had romanticized the more solitary kind of life Mr. Pavlik and other pioneering Alaskans like him had carved out on their large tract homesteads and in remote cabins off the road system. These rugged Alaskans became ingrained in our mythology. People like the Pavliks and all the practical experience they had gained the hard way had intrigued me since the day I left Pinellas County, Florida.

But the years had ticked by, and after more than 20 years, I was finally an Alaskan. On every visit back to Yakutat we made, Jennie shared family stories. I coveted their cache of memories and found many elements that resonated, if only to show me what was missing in my own upbringing.

After all these years of solitude and more quiet living on Knight Island, I wondered if Mr. Pavlik felt any closer to God. He had a life of prayer and solitude with Genevieve and his eight children by his side. He didn't buy into the life and mystique of the hardy, solitary man of the wilderness without female companionship and family. That wasn't right, Mr. Pavlik said. It was abnormal to him, maybe okay for priests and monks, but not for him or his boys. He wanted to live in solitude, happy and huddled in the rain, but with the everyday closeness of his family.

When I think about it now, I can understand how I projected my own unfulfilled needs upon Mr. Pavlik. I went to him as if he were some kind of spiritual master, like a Tibetan lama imparting scraps of long, lost wisdom. I started thinking about him as a kind of surrogate father, too, as someone who might care enough to share a family expression, a half-formulated value statement, a tip about how the world worked according to his eyes, a word about God or faith—anything I might store for future reference and contemplation.

With my biological father, we simply ran out of time. I don't remember any moments that ever came close to that kind of familial sharing.

Jennie and her family were everything the family I grew up in was not. They were fully aware of their surroundings, they were closely in tune with nature and with one another, and they were as sure about their faith in God as they were about the rain that would fall tomorrow.

I, in turn, carried a trunk full of doubts about who I was and what I believed in. With a restless impatient disposition, I continued to shape my identity according to the expectations of others.

In the 1940s and 50s, when anthropologist Fredericka de Laguna was traipsing through this volatile, soggy terrain, she mentioned seeing a white man and his Native Alaskan wife on their remote Knight Island homestead in the early 50s—those were Jennie's parents.

De Laguna rode a skiff 13 miles northeast of town to Knight Island to excavate a site near Strawberry Point finding artifacts like fish hooks, stone picks, knife blades, iron objects that would help de Laguna catalogue and preserve the historical memories of this little known place.

Although she had known of Mike Pavlik, de Laguna avoided him and never conducted any research directly with him for her seminal, three-volume study, *Under Mount Saint Elias: The History and Culture of the Tlingit Indian* (1972). When I was new to town and working as the school's librarian and trying to learn as much as I could about Tlingit culture, de Laguna's work provided crucial perspective on the area's history and culture, a perspective I as a newcomer sorely needed. My guess is the locals must have cautioned her to keep a safe distance from the ornery Mike Pavlik, and she gladly followed their advice.

I will have to remind Mr. Pavlik that I do not represent the U.S. Forest Service, those "dirty bastards" about whom he says he has run out of swear words to describe. And I will have to reassure him that I have nothing to do with the IRS or Homeland Security.

Approaching his cabin's door, I heard voices. I knocked, but nothing happened. I knocked again, a little harder. More voices, and the crack of what sounded like rifle shots echoed from a television. Mr. Pavlik still didn't answer.

I turned the doorknob and entered the small vestibule, a little afraid of what I might find.

It was dimly lit and smelled as if it had been awhile since any fresh Alaska air had blown inside. Tang, his mangy orange cat with clumps of missing hair, leapt off a table onto the torn linoleum, slinked past my legs, and bolted outside. The oil stove was cranked so high it must have been almost 80 degrees in the dark entryway. Instantly the heat suffocated me. I wanted to go back to the truck and forget this stupid idea of visiting the old man. What Alaskan in his right mind burns an oil stove piping hot on a warm June day?

I left the outside cabin door ajar to increase the circulation, and in case his sickly orange cat wanted to come back in.

"Hey, Mr. Pavlik. You there?"

"Yeah, yeah, you can come in," he said with irritation.

I slowly opened another door and tip-toed into the main cabin where I found Mr. Pavlik slouched on an old recliner watching "Gunsmoke."

A rope dangled in midair over his right side. As he reached for it to try and switch on the light bulb, he also began to slowly hoist himself out of his chair. For a moment he stood with the help of a rubber tipped cane, but he was so severely hunched over that I felt six feet tall next to him.

He was dressed in baggy, wrinkled jeans that had a bleached out square of denim awkwardly located right on top of his crotch, the same outfit I'd seen him in before. A big ace bandage was wrapped around his lower back for extra support. His slippers looked like two blue, velour boxes covering his feet. They were crimped together with black document binder clips.

Water continuously trickled in the tiny, trailer-type kitchen, possibly from the cabin's leaky gaskets and faulty pipes. From the extra loud television came more gunshot noise and the sounds of whinnying horses. He fell back into his threadbare recliner.

"Hello, Mr. Pavlik. Hope you remembered I'd be coming by."

"*Who?* Who did you say you were? Oh, yeah, okay, well…I feel lousy," he said while casting me a disgruntled look and stealing glances at "Gunsmoke."

"I've got this headache, right here on the top of my head. It starts from the neck up, you see. I've had it for two weeks now without letting up. And towards evening, it builds, you know, like in a daze. I can't do much but sit here.

"I mean, I feel, you know, my mind is okay," he continued as if not really addressing anyone in particular. "Sometimes it does start to go out, like last night when my granddaughter Lily was here. I start talkin' like a drunk where you don't make any sense. I don't know. What the hell, it's hard to explain.

"I don't drink or nothing like 'dat anyway, you know. Booze won't work with my pills.

Same as smoking. I used to smoke like hell, and I still sneak one in now and then. Christ Almighty, a man needs to do something."

He immediately told me if I came back for a visit again, I had better plan to come *after* 4:00 p.m. when the double episode of *Gunsmoke* was over and not smack in the middle of it. Every day at 3:00 p.m., without fail, Mr. Pavlik watched *Gunsmoke* reruns on his new satellite television channel.

My father loved that western, too. When I was five or six years old, before my parents divorced, I used to sit on the couch with my father and little brother to watch *Gunsmoke* in the

1960s. It was the only program I can recall we ever watched together.

I never wanted to be the Ms. Kitty character. I wanted to be the heroic sheriff who tracked down renegades and outlaws. With my dad and Richy sitting beside me, it was like we were a normal and secure family who would always be together.

My eyes were automatically drawn to the large plastic crucifix hanging on Mr. Pavlik's cabin wall. He might think of himself as a model Catholic, but he still wanted to kick the government types to kingdom come. Near the crucifix, he kept a cracked statue of the Virgin Mary, a cherished possession he rescued from Knight Island after a terrible fire had destroyed much of the family's original homestead.

The cabin walls were filled with photographs of his deceased wife and his eight kids, and what were, then, his 47 grandchildren and great-grandchildren. Three more grandchildren were soon to be born.

I knew I wouldn't be long for the wretchedly hot and congested cabin, and I wondered how to make the afternoon more pleasant for both of us.

"Holy Christ Almighty, I don't care where you sit," he said as I grabbed a brown metal folding chair and placed it directly in front of him so he could better hear. I peeled off my nylon windbreaker, took out a plastic bottle of water to quench my growing thirst, and tried to act as natural and as relaxed as possible.

I presented him with some chocolates and his favorite Limburger cheese—which I had brought for him on my trip down from Anchorage. It was a gesture that pleased him. I tried to figure out how to start a conversation. I knew he didn't know a thing about Thomas Merton, and I wanted to be the first person to tell him the story of how Merton had visited Yakutat back in the day when hardly a soul made it to the place.

I didn't want to spend too much time listening to his bloodcurdling bear stories or hearing again how he had to make his own hunting knives and cigarette rolling contraptions. Maybe he could enlighten me about why he was a Catholic instead of a

Methodist, say, and why it had been so important to recreate the sacraments all these years on Knight Island, especially while the whole family led a subsistence life with no Catholic priest, nun or cultural milieu in sight.

I guessed our casual talk would soon drift to the oft-repeated folklore of how Rudy at age 12 once killed a bear in self-defense with nothing but a homemade spear. Or he'd jabber on about how the Pavlik boys skipped protective raingear, and used their bare hands to handle fish.

Mr. Pavlik sat the same way he stood, all hunched over, a bottle of Pepto Bismol and a drawer overflowing with 40 or more amber plastic pill containers close by his side. Far back on his wrinkled forehead, tufts of thin, gray-white hair were pushed down on his scalp. A kind of English-Irish ruddiness had washed over his skin though his ancestry was 100 percent Slovakian. His ice blue eyes watered heavily; he had to dab them constantly with tissue. Although they were small, with no detectable lashes, his eyes were not in the least bit elderly. They still projected spitfire, and this surprised and attracted me. I'd seen eyes like his before somewhere, maybe on my father's face long ago. Pavlik was a man with bite left in him, a livewire inside a shrinking, frail body.

"Well, I got a lot of stuff we could talk about, and I'm not makin' it up. I'm not kiddin' you on this, I don't need to make it up."

His words seemed to form only on the right side of his mouth and were laced with a Slovakian accent. When he spoke, he reminded me of voices I once heard long ago in Pittsburgh.

"Hey, wait a minute," he said with the trace of a smile.

"You had these pictures once of bears or *somethink*, didn't you?"

This he suddenly blurted out while taking a swig of tea from a plastic coffee mug that looked as though a squirrel had gnawed all over it.

"Well, yeah, it was my bear photograph. I used to have my own darkroom when I lived here. I was really into photography. But how did you possibly remember that photo of mine?" I asked.

No response.

"Mr. Pavlik," I said again, but much louder, "How did you possibly remember that photograph? I took it such a long time ago when I first moved here."

He started searching for his cane, wanted to try and get up again to find the framed black and white bear photo, one I originally gave to Jennie over 20 years earlier.

"Oh yeah, heck yeah. I got 'em over here," he said. "What was it again you called it?

Five is too many bears or *somethink* like that?"

He tried to shuffle toward the bookcase filled with all the videos he'd watched a thousand times about Annie Oakley, Calamity Jane, and the building of the Alaska Railroad. Before he could get to the crowded shelves, though, he had to maneuver around loads of boxes crammed full of U.S. Forest Service documents, attorney papers, bills, and stacks of old *Juneau Empire* and *Inside Passage* newspapers. The effort to leave his chair quickly drained his energy and he gave up the search and fell, pissed and sighing, back into the recliner.

"Close," I said. "I called the photo, Eight is Enough. Yeah, I was lucky that day, that's all. Michael and I used to go there all the time, to the garbage dump to watch the bears. Not much else for us to do when we lived here and didn't have any kids, yet, right?"

Most of the time, Mr. Pavlik slept right where I found him in his lumpy and torn recliner beneath yellow patches of insulation poking through the cabin's unfinished walls. He wore the same clothes he slept in—a gray, long-sleeved thermal undershirt covered by a frayed, blue plaid flannel shirt with a row of safety pins clipped onto the outside pocket, topped by red and black Harley Davidson suspenders.

Our conversation resumed, and he acted a bit perkier.

He wanted to brag about the old days and to talk about his membership in the National Rifle Association, and I let him. One subject near and dear to him was trains. In 1937, when America was still recovering from the Great Depression, John

Michael Pavlik, 15, left his family's farm in Cudahy, Wisconsin, certain that the wide, open road—not some boring school building—was his ticket to what really mattered.

John Michael started illegally hopping freight trains traveling back and forth by riding the rails. For two years he worked the harvest fields in the Dakotas and Montana, bucking hay, wheat, and barley into horse-drawn wagons from sunrise to sunset for what was then a lucrative $4.50 per day.

Whatever money he had left, he sent home to his parents on the farm. He lived like a hobo, eager to soak up real life experience, even if it meant an empty stomach and no idea where he'd toss his bedroll next. Once he made it to the West Coast, to earn his keep, he picked cherries on one of the country's largest cherry farms owned by Sam Goldman, a Seattle fruit grower. For shelter during that summer picking season, he slept in a junk station wagon with a friend.

One day, he spotted a train chugging through the Seattle train yards. It was full of Army tanks, which intrigued him, especially because of the markings on one of the cars: "Womens Bay, Kodiak Island." He asked his co-workers where those tanks were headed after they were reloaded onto ships.

"Way up north to Alaska," came the reply. The rough old timers who hung out near the tracks were always trying to help him out.

Well, there must be a lot of girls in Alaska, he thought, if there's such a place called *Womens* Bay. That one idea, and the peculiar geographic names, piqued his imagination.

"Hey kid, the U.S. Department of Engineers—they're hiring. You should go down to the recruiting office, but first shave off some of that peach fuzz. Try and make it *look* like you shave, I mean. And for Christ's sake, John-Michael, you better change your name. It's the damn truth, kid. You gotta lie. You gotta sound older or they might not take you. Remember, try to be more *mannish*."

The U.S. Department of Engineers, later named the Army Corps of Engineers, was urgently building runways and airfields and Army quonset hut barracks throughout the Alaska Territory. At that time, prior to the Japanese attack on Pearl Harbor, Germany was thought to be the biggest aggressor facing the world. The government's original goal was to secure America's far northwestern front against the advancing Germans, briefly allied with the Russians. It was speculated that the Germans and their Russian allies might march across Siberia and into North America through the Territory of Alaska. But Stalin was betrayed by Hitler and the whole war picture changed.

The young John Michael Pavlik hung out at the Seattle docks and he listened to the older men's advice to adopt the blander name of "Mike." Next thing he knew, he boarded the Alaska Steamship Company steamer sailing north, and was hired as a civilian food server for a new U.S. Army mess hall somewhere in *Yak-oo-tat*.

His military-related service in World War II would provide him with important mechanical training and education, as it had my father Louis (Lychie) Witkowski.

The Yakutat airfield, the one we once lived beside, was originally established to help service and refuel planes between the continental U.S. and Fairbanks, a distance of 1,500 air miles.

After Germany invaded Russia, the Soviet Union was suddenly allied with the United States. Boeing aircraft would be shuttled from Seattle through Alaska and across the Bering Sea to help the Russians in the famous airplane Lend Lease program. Hundreds of soldiers from the Lower 48 began arriving in the remote community to help build the staging area and auxiliary airfield.

The local Tlingit Indians mostly kept to themselves in the village center, separate from all the strange talking white people who were flooding into the area preparing for war, and living practically on top of the airfield with the other white families in the U.S. Weather Service, the U.S. Forest Service, and in the FAA.

"Where is it you live around here?" Mr. Pavlik asked.

"I don't live here anymore, Mr. Pavlik. Remember, I live in Anchorage now."

"Oh, yeah, Anchorage. *Why Anchorage?* What can you do in the city? I go to see my doctor there, but I'd just as soon skip seeing that sonofabitchin' city. Guess you know, I don't like noisy, goddamn crowded cities."

I swallowed another big gulp of water and tried to cool off. The hair around my temples and forehead were soaked in sweat.

*Sonofabitchin'….Goddamn….*Mr. Pavlik hurled cuss words the way my dad did.

I wondered why no one had ever bothered to do anything with all the yellow pieces of insulation poking out from the cabin's unfinished walls.

"Remind me later to show you my steel bear trap," he said. "I hate brown bear, you know. Black bear, I could eat, but I'm not too crazy about it. My son, Rudy, he loves black bear meat. You know he smokes it. My wife, Genny, she was a real good cook, too. My mother came up here for a while, stayed with us from Wisconsin. I got pictures somewhere… ."

"No, no, it's okay, Mr. Pavlik. You don't need to get up to find the family pictures right now."

The afternoon wore on. And the old man grew more nostalgic. In the same year, 1941, that Merton gave up his material possessions and boarded a train from New York to the Trappist monastery, Mike Pavlik, age 17, boarded a steamship and sailed north up the Inside Passage. Every day on the steamship, he played poker and chewed tobacco, and took out his Rosary beads and said his prayers.

The young man pictured what it would be like when he finally got to Latitude 59°, how the steamship would probably have to pull right alongside a giant glacier to dock—that was his impression. Then the U.S. Army men would have to throw out some kind of metal skyhook and clamps for the ship to attach to the glacier's face. Someone would shout an order and he'd have to shimmy up a thick, slippery rope, until he got to the top of the towering ice field before he could slide down.

He told me he imagined Yakutat to be a non-stop mountain of snow, with avalanches rumbling all over the place, with sheets of ice the size of Iowa cornfields. This wasn't going to be any ordinary port and docking, no siree ma'am, for in his estimation, this was like the Arctic, after all, and Holy Christ, he'd better figure out how to get off the ship and act normal because he was no sissy. How the Jesus could he stay warm in the icebox Uncle Sam was sending him to with his thin, crummy jacket and wearing uninsulated, cherry-picker's boots?

Three years after his arrival in the Tlingit community, Mike Pavlik was introduced to Hardy Trefzger, the mink farmer who had leased a parcel of property from the U.S. Forest Service on an island three-miles in diameter. Mike Pavlik fell in love with Knight Island and negotiated a lease transfer from old man Hardy, not an outright purchase of the six-acre parcel from the federal government, but a lease on the improvements—the house, the mink farm pens, and the other amenities.

After working in the 714th Special Battalion building railroad tracks in northwest Canada and Alaska, he returned from Seattle and met Genevieve, Jennie's mother. Genny was born and raised in the village of Klukwan and was the first Tlingit woman he'd ever spoken to. He met her in Juneau where she was working as a bus girl in a restaurant. Mike proposed with a ring he'd gotten through the Sears & Roebuck catalogue.

For the next 45 years, they shared their trade secrets with one another—Mr. Pavlik's words for it—every resourceful fact they knew about how to survive off the land with God's help.

After his story ended, I wiped the sweat off my brow again, and started, subtly, to prepare to leave, but Mr. Pavlik wouldn't have it.

"Well, see, what I wanted to tell you is that my sister and my brother they all lived in Wisconsin, but they really liked how we lived. Before they came up here, they all thought I was a crazy lunatic and said, 'What the hell do you want to live on an island for?' and 'What are you gonna do when you get old and you live all secluded in the boondocks with the glaciers and bears?

It's not good for your kids to grow up so secluded and isolated this way.'

"But when they got to Knight Island, and they saw where I come from, and all the wildlife, all the food we got on that island, and they seen what kind of peaceful, quiet life Genny and me had… and we were only starting in 'dem days…but by then they realized, hell yeah, we're pretty well off. You can't starve to death here. I don't see how in the hell anybody could starve to death in this country. God provides.

"Southeast Alaskans had plenty of moose to kill and eat. We had five different kinds of salmon to catch, lots of herring eggs and halibut to live off of. Remember, we got only a tiny population depending on what's here to feed ourselves.

"No such thing as a Yakutat down there in America. Unless you have military survival training or you're a farmer and know something about growing your own food.

"During the Depression, if you were lucky to be raised on a Midwest farm like me, maybe you got what you needed, but if you lived in a city, the land belonged to somebody, and all the trees belonged to somebody, and you was a screwed monkey during those years."

I was relieved. He seemed to be finding some reserves of energy. By all his chatter, I guessed he was over being mad at me for interrupting his precious *Gunsmoke*. He smiled a lot and seemed grateful that I was still sitting there, but we still hadn't gotten into anything remotely related to his Catholic faith and why he used to invite priests from Juneau to fly to Yakutat and hop in a skiff to come to Knight Island to say Mass every couple of years.

Mr. Pavlik offered to make me some hot tea on his oil stove, but I declined politely and took another huge swig of the water that had turned as warm as tea in my plastic bottle. Perhaps it was an opportune time to mention the cabin's unbearable temperature, but I chose not to say anything. I needed air, though, and stood up and cracked the vestibule's door a little wider while he kept talking.

"If you wanna come back tomorrow," he said with another big smile on his face, "I could give you my secret recipe for clam balls."

"Oh, Mr. Pavlik, I'd really like that. I love clams, too."

He stopped talking and we sat alone in our first truly quiet moment together.

I had come to Alaska in my early adulthood, same as he. Our real initiation was right here, in this land studded with lakes and islands, alluvial gravels, seals, lynx, marten, and fat and bossy ravens. But he became a much more intimate part of it, given his family's upbringing and their long, unbroken history. Yakutat was the literal source of his food and shelter; whatever economic ups and downs and cultural fads were sweeping the country, it mattered not to him.

As a young wife, I stayed there for four years before life went once more in a drastically different direction. We no longer made our livelihood there, and our two sons, though they feel deeply connected and often visit Yakutat, mostly grew up in Soldotna, south of Anchorage in a subdivision where they walked on sidewalks to get to school and played Little League baseball and took piano lessons.

At some point, Jennie's father might have pulled up his family stakes, too, but his deep faith and close connection to the land had somehow merged in this rain-filled landscape.

For 67 consecutive years, he lived under the eye of Mount Saint Elias.

Maybe he wasn't the world's most neighborly guy during this long span of time. Maybe he wasn't an exemplary Alaskan citizen, but in this irascible, hunched-over man, I saw something else. Physically and spiritually, he had found an *inner alignment*, a wholeness, and a grounding and unity that felt right, something I had only experienced traces of.

He freely belonged to Yakutat and it to him. It was his *rodina*—his motherland, as the Russians call it. He was who he was, and that was that, and that was more than enough.

Mr. Pavlik broke the silence and resumed speaking, but this

time he used a different tone, softer, more somber, with less sense of his usual shenanigans behind what he was saying.

"Hey, you wanna know where you can see the dandiest sunsets?" he asked. "Well, I'll let you in on a little secret. See, I used to spend a lot of time hunting near the Grand Wash…"

Again, to be polite, I leaned forward, being careful to keep that "you don't say" look on my face and prepared myself to hear still another death defying, titillating bear survival story.

"Well, when the water was calm in front of my hunting camp, with lots of ducks flying around, with certain types of light that came in. I don't know how the hell to explain the quality of the light over there in the Grand Wash, but I would see a beautiful reflection of Mount Saint Elias upside down on the water."

He looked at me and paused, as if he wanted to describe the memory of this particular alpine image perfectly.

"Oh boy, there was some dandy sunsets over Mount Saint Elias. Dandy, alright," he said. "If a man never stops to look at a sunset, if he never cares enough to do that, I mean, then what kind of a man would he be?"

I lightly wiped my face and sat quietly until he completed his thought.

"Yeah, that's God's country over there. Yes it is."

Mr. Pavlik seemed to forget I was in the room after a few minutes as he spoke in a kind of trance-like way, stuck in a memory about the Grand Wash and the colors and the mystical atmosphere he remembered.

"Here's another important thing I'm telling you. If you *want* to know God and to be in God's country, you will be in it then. Simple as that. You'd have to be an idiot not to open your eyes to God's presence."

I could tell the old man was getting weary after several hours. I slowly got up to signal it was time for me to go, though I wished we could keep talking.

"Mr. Pavlik, I'll try and come back tomorrow, if that's okay with you and after *Gunsmoke*, of course. I really have to return the pickup I borrowed today." I cast him a big smile, but he was still lost in his thoughts and memories with his arms resting on his recliner.

He started speaking again, as if he never heard me say I was leaving, "Oh yes, I'd look at them sunsets and think a lot about things whenever that special kind of light happened on Mount Saint Elias. And you know what? That reflection of Mount Saint Elias, well, it looked like a silver chalice. That's all I'm trying to say. To my eyes, the mountain looked like a *silver chalice*. That damn mountain is watching us. And I'm not kidding you on that."

…Every minute life begins all over again. Amen.

—Thomas Merton, *The Sign of Jonas*

7 The Inner Ordeal

The years following Yakutat gave way to the preoccupations of raising a family, working various jobs in nonprofits, maintaining a household, saving for the future. I wasn't much of a hot tub and hammock kind of person. I was more skittish. Like the shorebirds, I was prone to a scurrying, frantic existence. I was bowled over with activities like everyone else I knew—trying to juggle the demands of modern life with mounting family concerns. I had not yet begun that hard walk into solitude.

A lot of the busyness, I brought upon myself. When I thought about it all—who had become estranged from whom, how this sister didn't talk to that one, how no one really knew what to do about my brother's mental illness and his never-ending visits to the VA Hospital—my answer was to stay occupied and check out. Busyness equated to escape, a temporary immunity of sorts.

Only by compartmentalizing my life could I shield myself enough from family let downs and pain to keep myself from unraveling. And it worked for a while. But to quote John Haines, "Listening, I could hear within myself the snow that was coming, the sound of a loud, cold trumpet."

My mother was battling a rare form of liver cancer. Her prognosis was three to five years. At the same time, my teenage niece in Indiana faced an onslaught of serious medical challenges. Doctors discovered an inoperable brain tumor on Daisylee's brain stem when she was five years old, and now at age fifteen, she was developing a host of associated problems, particularly with her neuromuscular coordination. She was under the care of a neurosurgeon at the Riley Clinic in Indianapolis, not far from her hometown of Fortville. My sister Donna told me Daisylee was taking a treatment called B-proton therapy, but she was losing her sense of balance, and her long-term health was uncertain. Donna and her husband, also deaf, meant the geographic distance and expense from Alaska made it more difficult to stay connected and prevented more regular visits. If I wanted to hear directly about Daisylee's latest medical report, my only option was to speak to Donna through the assistance of special telephone relay operators for the deaf. This heartache and physical separation was our family's long-time reality.

Meanwhile, my mother still lived in Pinellas County, Florida, and I lived half a planet away. I rarely saw my mother or siblings, and instead, relied on frequent phone calls and emails now that my mother had her first computer.

Younger brother Richy, gifted with a sharp scientific and technical mind, was diagnosed in his mid-twenties as a paranoid schizophrenic. Richy got arrested frequently and spent time in and out of jails and mental hospitals. He was in his fifties now and still lived on government disability in Pinellas Country with his cherished cat Buddy. Mood stabilizing anti-psychotic drugs kept him in check, but the medications created unwanted physical side effects.

What I didn't know then, was that Richy invited an unemployed ex-convict and his girlfriend to live with him. She had a criminal record and was a drug addict. The couple took Richy's bed in the dilapidated trailer, leaving my brother to sleep on his own couch covered with a filthy sheet and tattered blanket.

Once I learned about his living situation, I harangued him to please give up the cigarettes and to get rid of those parasites he had for roommates. As long he heard my voice regularly, he was happy even if I was not.

"I know you don't approve," he said during a more lucid conversion, "but you're wrong. Well maybe you are right about some things. They don't look like much, that part you know. And Denise is fat and maybe lazy and watching television all day.

That part is true. But Ron and his girlfriend, well they don't have anything, but they'd give you the shirt off their backs if you needed it. People living in my trailer court have more kindness than anybody you'll ever meet. How do you think I got the ambulance last time? They saved me. Picked me right up off the floor when I passed out. They're my friends, Kathy. They care about me."

Due to the pattern of Richard's hallucinations and conspiracy theories, he became estranged from everyone in our family, except me. I called him regularly. Three or four times a week, he rang or left me voicemails about a scientific patent he wanted to work on, or how sick he was of mankind's absurdities, or how he believed the Mayans traveled the universe ages ago, or that Jesus was the alpha and omega who told off the Devil.

Richy had a knack for calling me in the middle of quiet Sunday mornings when I was trying to concentrate on something or write in my journal. I'd curse him for doing this, for causing me to be so distracted all the time. He interrupted to explain his spiritual dilemma this way, "The devil wants me. The government wants me. And God wants me. Who do you think I should go to? You know I have more money than God. God doesn't have any."

He swore he saw Jesus in his jail cell. How could I speak to him about such visions? Yes, he was often delusional, but sometimes he made complete sense.

"Sis, you *do* have a lot of energy, and *sometimes* that can be a good thing," he once stated over the phone. It was just the sort of backhanded compliment I'd come to expect from him, and I laughed.

Then one day, out of the blue, it seemed he became disenchanted and left this two-sentence voicemail, "Hey Kathy, I have some really good advice for you. No matter what, don't ever live in a trailer court."

Along with all the chaos of my family, I was diagnosed with malignant melanoma resulting in surgery on my leg. I stopped to consider my next moves. We had left Yakutat, and were living on the Kenai Peninsula. After working five years managing the cultural center in Kenai, my desire to write returned. With full spousal support, and our kids grown, I applied and was accepted to the University of Pittsburgh's MFA program. Before I started school in 2002, we moved to Anchorage, and I left for the University of Pittsburgh.

I was no longer in the rat race. I was simply an older student from the freezing tundra. No one cared about my resume, what kind of neighborhood I lived in, the model car I drove, or how much money I had in the bank. Being in graduate school was a drastic change from my other life as a mother, wife and working woman. Grateful for this gift of time and space at the University, I didn't want to squander any of it.

Three academic years passed, and at the start of my last semester I was winding up my teaching assistantship, finalizing my creative thesis, and looking forward to slipping back into regular domestic life with Michael in Anchorage.

The year 2005 began with optimism. In late January, I strolled into a small bookshop near Pitt's campus a few blocks from the Cathedral of Learning and bought a copy of Thomas Merton's *The Seven Storey Mountain*. This wasn't assigned reading. None of my professors mentioned the celebrated religious writer and thinker. I bought the book strictly out of literary curiosity. I kept seeing Merton's name mentioned on lists highlighting the "Best Books of the 20th Century" or "Best Memoirs."

When Merton's memoir hit bookstands in 1948, it became an instant phenomenon. Americans felt a spiritual hunger after the devastation and atrocities of World War II. Critics said it was written in the tradition of St. Augustine's masterpiece from the fourth century, *The Confessions*, considered to be one of Western civilization's most important books and the first written in the genre of autobiography.

I imagined a few literary wisdoms might be revealed through some sort of osmosis. After all, this monk penned more than 40 books. But the image I had in my mind of what a monk's life was like didn't match Merton's. I wondered how a monk could be so prolific if he had to spend half his day in prayer cycles and the other half mopping the monastery's hallways? How did Merton manage to write so much? I figured he must've been one of the busiest monks in world history. When did he have any time to pray in the chapel, for God's sake?

As I dug in to this new and foreign category of reading spiritual writing, my academic work lapsed. Completing my thesis was difficult enough, and I didn't need any dead Catholic monks to further distract me.

The Seven Storey Mountain seized my imagination. Over the course of one February week, I read it in fits and starts, sneaking it in between everything else I was supposed to be doing, including teaching freshman composition.

Thomas Merton oozed literary charisma and possessed a capacious intellect. Merton's pedigree afforded him plenty of professional choices. He could have been a career diplomat, a journalist, a tenured literature professor, or an art critic for a major publication. All of those professions perfectly fit his natural gifts.

On one level, I was simply enthralled with the artistry of his prose and with his warm, self-deprecating narrative voice as when he admitted, "…If what most people take for granted were really true—if all you needed to be happy was to grab everything and see everything and investigate every experience and then talk about it, I should have been a very happy person, a spiritual millionaire, from the cradle even until now."

With this passage, I held the mirror up to myself. He could have been describing me and my internal vow to seize the day, to soak up as much experience as I could, preferably as far outside the norm of my family's upbringing as possible.

"If happiness were merely a matter of natural gifts," Merton said, " I would have never entered a Trappist monastery when I came to the age of a man."

Merton reflected about his carefree youth in New York City, waking up on Sundays after being out all night partying. It brought back memories of being an under-grad in Florida, working the evening shifts at the beachside restaurant with Edna and Emmie and then running off to drink gin fizzes and dance in the discos until my legs gave out at 2:00 a.m.

Merton loved New York City and I always had, too. Though I never had the chance to live there, I used to dream of it, that one day I'd pull out of Pittsburgh and work in a skyscraper, and ride the subway all over Manhattan, and buy my lunch from a street vendor in Central Park.

"God made it a very beautiful Sunday," Merton wrote in his autobiography. "And since it was the first time I had ever really spent a sober Sunday in New York, I was surprised at the clean, quiet atmosphere of the empty streets uptown. The sun was blazing bright. At the end of the street, as I came out the front door, I could see a burst of green, and the blue river and the hills of Jersey on the other side."

One Sunday morning—February 20, 2005—I awoke in my studio apartment on Oak Hill about a mile from campus and turned on American Public Media's radio program called St. Paul Sunday. String quartets played Brahms and Haydn. I made my usual pot of strong black coffee, consumed two cups quickly, and sat down to resume reading this very strange book.

I don't know exactly what came over me, but after about twenty minutes, I suddenly put *The Seven Storey Mountain* down, got up off the couch, and walked to my desk—a plastic, card table where I kept my laptop.

A very peculiar notion entered my mind. I decided to check the web site for St. Paul's Cathedral, the imposing Catholic Church close to the Heinz Chapel, at the center of the University of Pittsburgh. St. Paul's Cathedral was an impressive Gothic-style building I passed on my walks around campus, though I'd never set foot inside. Distinctive, with large stained-glass windows, arches, and flights of concrete steps leading up to its massive and ornate wooden doors, it was a big church fit for fine, upper class weddings.

The Internet listed a noon Mass, and right then and there, while sitting at my laptop, I made up my mind to go to Mass at

St. Paul's Cathedral. Before that moment, I had not felt an impulse to attend any Mass in my whole life.

I slumped onto the couch with another cup of coffee and went back to reading Merton's memoir.

Merton began relaying the story of what happened to him while a college student at Columbia University: how a flash or drive began to assert itself, and for inexplicable reasons he felt a strong urge to stop time and everything he was doing that minute.

"It was something quite new and strange," Merton wrote, "this voice that seemed to prompt me, this firm, growing interior conviction of what I needed to do. It had a suavity, a simplicity about it that I could not easily account for. And when I gave in to it, it did not exult over me, and trample me down with its raging haste to land on its prey, but it carried me forward serenely and with purposeful direction."

Merton recalled how he phoned his sweetheart who lived outside the Manhattan Borough and said he wouldn't be on the train to visit her that quiet Sunday morning because he was going to Mass. Merton went to find the little brick church, Corpus Christi, on 121st Street near Columbia, not far from Harlem. He was going to go to the first Mass of his life.

And there I was doing the same incomprehensible thing on a Sunday morning! Letting some unknown force, some unexplained longing, carry me to St. Paul's Cathedral.

My hands started shaking. With the classical music softly playing, I thought about what had happened for a good long while. Coincidence? I didn't think so. Mysterious synchronicity?

More like that, as if I had been given an omen or sign to pick myself up and go. I concluded there was nothing to do except carry out my spontaneous desire to see what Mass was all about.

I put on my black hooded coat, grabbed my gloves, took the elevator down two floors, and briskly walked along Allequippa Street. A light snow fell like dust and stuck to my wool coat. I reached Fifth Avenue Boulevard, stopped for a moment or two to admire the church's Gothic spires, and the well-dressed pedestrians and jeans-wearing college students filing through the tall doors. It was one of the city's oldest churches, built in 1905. By comparison, so many of Alaska's bland churches reminded me of empty airplane hangars.

I meekly entered a side door and sat in the back pews of the cathedral where no one would notice me as a religious impersonator.

The missal contained the Scriptural readings, and I tried following along the best I could, but I was only pretending to be liturgically experienced. My lips moved slightly, but no real words came out because I had no idea what these Catholics were reciting.

Many details about the Mass and the words spoken that day are now lost to me, except for one phrase I recall from the homily.

"Let us each climb our mountains of change," the bishop said, as he talked about Jesus and his disciples at Mount Tabor. As an Alaskan who constantly gazed at mountainous landscapes, those words meant something.

The congregants in my row stood up, stepped around and over me, and humbly moved toward the center aisle. They lined up, took their places in the fast-paced, very orderly Holy Communion lane. I was flustered and stayed frozen in the wooden pew. Was I supposed to stand up and join them in the line? What do people like me do who stumble into a Mass without any in-the-flesh Catholic guides, like Jennie Pavlik? Should I swallow the cracker or whatever they were given, cross myself, and sip the wine anyway? No one would know the difference. Did they have some alternative, express lane for lost souls like me who were still under consideration, the ones who had never quite been sure about their spiritual bearings?

The best course of action was to split, which is exactly what the young Merton, age 23, did at Corpus Christi Church near Columbia University in 1938 the first time he attended.

I ran out of St. Paul's feigning some dire personal emergency. To reach Allequippa Street, I cut through the medical district again and huffed up a very steep hill—Cardiac Hill, as it was known—and back to the psychological safety of my apartment.

Gasping for air, heart pounding, I went back to the rest of my day wondering what kind of religious nonsense had gotten into me. First reading Merton, and now this! Being intellectually curious was one thing, but sitting in a church and witnessing the diversity of strangers and how they stopped talking and kneeled quietly in prayer was another. Hearing fragments of Latin, seeing ornate gold candlesticks, the purple drapery covering the walls, and women with triangular pieces of white lace on their heads fascinated me.

Later that same Sunday, I couldn't wait to phone Michael in Anchorage. He was four time zones away, still working full-time, holding down the home front while I was at the other end of the country enjoying my fantasy bohemian life.

I related the bizarre sequence of events, how I had spontaneously decided to attend my first Catholic Mass all alone for a worship service unrelated to a funeral, baptism, or any special community event. Though he had wholeheartedly supported my decision to attend an out-of-state school, the developing marital strain was often hard to hide, especially if my voice was overly enthusiastic, making it sound as if everything I was doing—attending poetry readings and workshops—was wondrous and exciting.

"You are really going off the deep end down there with this Catholic thing," he said.

"You'll not get any sympathy from me on any of this. I don't want anything to do with the Catholics, their controlling agendas and brainwashing. Now, you're looking at organized religion? *Now?* Why, *now?* Have you been listening to what's going on in the news lately with the church and all its pedophile priests? Are you seriously thinking about what you're doing? Do you really think this is a good time to be examining any organized religion?"

"No, probably not," I demurely said. "Don't worry, I won't be going back to St. Paul's next Sunday. Really, it was only an experiment. It's nothing to seriously worry about."

But Merton was subtly working on my subconscious. Bit by bit, his shadowy presence started to settle me down. I needed to unclench my fists, to stop the white-knuckling, to sit in quiet long enough and think.

April came and it was time to pack up after graduation. I vacated my studio, returned to Anchorage and began searching for another job as I promised Michael I would.

I had three job interviews and was hanging around waiting to see if anything would happen. One day while walking through the book stacks at the Anchorage public library I came across an anthology of Alaska nature writings. There was no special reason why I should have wanted the book—*A Republic of Rivers: Three Centuries of Nature Writing from Alaska and the Yukon* (Oxford University Press, 1990)—other than general interest. The title wasn't at all familiar to me, but it should have been since I had recently begun writing and publishing essays with nature themes.

I took the anthology home, and that night while I lay in bed to read, my eyes fell to the table of contents and to the list of contributors. And there was Thomas Merton's name! How this could possibly be, I didn't know. Quickly, I flipped through the pages and read the brief and startling biographical note supplied by the editor stating that Merton was in Alaska during 1968 for 17 days, and the anthology featured a few short excerpts from part of his journal.

The journal entry, dated September 27, 1968, was the one that stopped me cold.

It had been penned from *Yakutat, Alaska.*

I let out a scream and nearly threw the book on the floor in a mixture of shock, amazement, and exasperation.

"Michael, you won't believe this. Merton was once in Yakutat! How come we never knew this? Why didn't anyone like the Rymans or Pavliks ever say a word about it? This is unbelievable. Merton in an Alaska nature writing book? I've got to get on the Internet and find a copy of his Alaska journal right now."

"Well, it couldn't have been that big of a deal to the people of Yakutat if no one ever mentioned this historical detail to us," Michael said.

"But this *is* a big deal, don't you see? Famous people like Merton didn't pop in to visit a remote and isolated place like Yakutat. Not in 1968. They didn't have regular ferry service.

Cruise ships weren't coming into Yakutat Bay, remember? *No one* ever went to Yakutat."

"But we did," he said with a smile.

The next order of business was to locate Merton's little-known Alaska journal—*Thomas Merton in Alaska—The Alaskan Conferences, Journals and Letters*—and read it cover to cover. The journal was a working notebook, different from his others because it was not edited by Merton as were *Sign of Jonas* and *The Secular Journal*. The cover featured one of Merton's snapshots, a black and white, blurry photo of mountains obviously taken from the window of small plane flying around somewhere in the Last Frontier. It wasn't until 2015, after much alpine sleuthing, and asking many Alaskans to make guesses, including people in Southeast and Southwest Alaska, that I finally confirmed its identity. One summer evening as I was exiting a restaurant in south Anchorage and walking to my car across the parking lot, I looked up in the direction of Flattop, and there it was! Part of the skyline that was practically under my nose every single day, but I that failed to connect with Merton's blurry image—O'Malley Peak in the Chugach Mountains right here in Anchorage. We see what we want to see.

I was like an unfinished, unglazed piece of pottery sitting on a dusty shelf, waiting to be placed in the spiritual kiln. And it was Merton, apparently, the expert potter in his monk's robe who was going to work on me.

What began as pure literary fascination turned into love. Being introduced to Merton's life story made me realize I had to face my own emptiness, ruin, and confusion. I had to open things up and say what really needed to be said about the flotsam of bad memories still floating inside me.

I could no longer brush Merton off as a writer's crush.

For the next decade, and from nothing I could have preconceived, I was on a parallel road with a fast-talking, jazz-loving, poetry-worshipping, Trappist monk.

It went on in a bewildering, manic, time-jumping, unpredictable, crazy-assed, disturbing way, that at times, reminded me of Jack Kerouac's novel *On the Road*.

From inside the monastery in the 1950s, Merton, voracious reader that he was, must have read *On the Road* because Jack Kerouac had also gone to Columbia University a few years after Merton was there as a student in the English Department. Kerouac and Allen Ginsberg both studied poetry at Columbia under Mark Van Doren, the same gifted professor who taught Tom Merton, though Kerouac never completed his Columbia degree. Kerouac met Lax around 1953 and contributed two poems to Merton's *Monk's Pond* in 1967-68.

Merton turned into my perfect companion. And as many have said, he was a monk who felt a special kinship to the Beats and the Hippies and poets in general, in particular the Latin American ones. To me, he was a bit of a monastic hipster, always trying to stay out front culturally, to be tuned into the literary trends, and he had to keep up with everything by writing old-fashioned letters to his inordinate number of correspondents.

He was a Cistercian with spiritual swag, more independent-minded than other monks around him. He made music with words and he also displayed a biting wit as a word master. He was a man who appreciated having a good time and a few laughs with all kinds of eccentrics. Half the time, he didn't act or speak or write like a religious person at all.

As a modern-day, spiritually dislocated woman, full of self-doubt, conflicted and hyper, we spoke the same language. We both got by with a little help from our friends.

It helped to remember that in Kerouac's *On the Road*, Dean Moriarty and his pals were depicted as being out there searching for something, the real America, their *real*, true selves, that real something they knew was missing from their lives, but which couldn't quite be defined.

During another one of Dean Moriarty's breathless emotional outbursts, after hundreds of miles of aimless, often drug-induced drifting, driving around, and living entirely in the rhythm of the present moment, he addressed his close friend, Sal Paradise.

"Troubles, you see, is the generalization word for what God exists in. The thing is *not* to get hung-up."

Inner troubles, I had galore, and Merton had them, too. Even though he lived in a protected monastery, and even though he had become a big-name writer, he wasn't satisfied. Too many paradoxes, contradictions and tensions needed to be sorted out.

In my catch-and-release moments of solitude, on the weekends, I often woke before dawn, always before Michael, and as a way to connect to some much-needed serenity. I read from Merton's *The Sign of Jonas* with my coffee. *The Sign of Jonas*, Merton's spiritual journal, is a compendium of entries recorded from 1946 to 1952. He supplied many impressions of daily monastic life at the Abbey of Gethsemani. For a time, my daily practice involved beginning each day without checking emails, without listening to NPR. Only Merton and me on the couch.

I felt about Merton as he had felt about William Blake—the subject of Merton's Master's thesis at Columbia. Merton believed the poet, and graphic artist Blake, was, in his day, the most important religious artist in England. Blake, in his devotion, chose to make great financial sacrifices for the sake of his art rather than succumb to the artistic tastes and styles of his times to stay out of poverty. Blake symbolized a new way of looking at the world, one that de-emphasized precision, dexterity, imitation, and facility in artistic technique. What Blake cared about, as Merton saw it, was the virtue of the artist himself, how his imagination and intellect could be transformed by or through nature, not from mere attempts to imitate nature's beauty or to delight the senses. Blake taught Merton that a true artist has an ability or intuition to see beyond what the eye sees, to see into the very essence of things, without ideation and logical concepts to obscure the vision.

This is the way Merton interpreted Blake, and this was the way I started to interpret Merton, without having read a word of Merton's thesis.

Merton's writings were becoming the light beam to my dark, inmost self. Merton questioned and grappled with many more things than he ever supplied answers on. Merton was easy to listen to, a far cry from being extremist, fundamentalist or self-righteous in his views. In *The Seven Storey Mountain*, which he composed in the zeal and fervor of becoming a new Trappist, he did come across as biased against Protestants, something he later openly regretted and remained embarrassed by.

He expressed his dissatisfaction with preachiness.

"If we find God in our souls and want to stay there with Him, it is disastrous to think of trying to communicate Him to others as we find Him there. We can preach Him later on with the grace He gives us in silence. We need not upset the silence with language" (May 17, 1947).

We seemed to be living in an era when no one in public life could be trusted, not even men of God, and I wrestled with this dilemma, too. For the American Catholic Church, in particular, these were not exactly shining cultural and religious moments, as Michael had repeatedly reminded me.

The shocking truths about priests and sexual abuse made it into the national news and into the headlines in Alaska. The Fairbanks Catholic diocese filed for Chapter 11 bankruptcy after 292 people, mostly Alaska Natives from remote villages, had filed claims they were sexually abused by Catholic clergy and church volunteers from the 1950s through the 1980s. The diocese was forced to sell many of their key properties to settle lawsuits totaling $11 million according to a newspaper article I read.

I had to agree it was an odd time to be so interested in the life of a Catholic convert and priest when so many independently-minded people were fleeing from the controlling and out-of-date Catholic Church.

In *The Seven Storey Mountain*, Merton mentioned the fear Americans had of the Catholic Church in general, and he said he shared that fear, too. His American grandfather on his mother's side helped to instill the hatred and suspicions of Catholics in his grandson. As Merton remembered it, "In Pop's mind there was a certain sinister note of malice connected with the profession of anything like the Catholic faith. The Catholic Church was the only one against which I ever heard him speak with bitterness or animosity."

Merton said he lived with this vague and evil thing called Catholicism in the back of his mind when he was coming of age.

My personal experience verified that the numbers of checked-out Catholics far exceeded the pocket full of faithful, still-practicing ones such as the Pavliks and Rymans of Yakutat.

Writers are often formed out of deep experiences with tragedy, devastation, loneliness, loss, childhood traumas. Writers and poets often live in the margins, clinging to the places where the push and pull between scientific determinism and the values of the human imagination meet. If it's true artists, poets, and writers exist in a state of eternal anxiety, disequilibrium, and self-doubt, then Merton and I could compare notes.

For a brief time as I considered aspects of Merton's enthralling life story, I thought I might be on the cusp of some great personal change. Maybe it was possible for someone like me to will herself into more spiritual alignment. Maybe I could stop all the internal jabbering and move into a new phase—a philosophical centering—without all the spinning and thrashing around between acceptance and belief in the historical force of scientific knowledge and progress, and the need for another part of myself to be answered unscientifically.

Like the Barrow sun that sinks below the horizon for a long stretch of time in winter, the marital spark and excitement had also been slipping away, and this only compounded my internal torment. Our communication styles were sharply different; we were fighting more often, mainly due to my dissatisfaction with myself, which I often took out on my husband.

We had been married for over twenty years, and like most couples, had faced the typical cycles of highs and lows. But lately, after so many years of routine and long periods of time spent apart, an overall sense of ennui had set in, and I wasn't sure where my lack of spousal attention would lead. We had never been one of the clinging, smothering kind of couples who couldn't trust one another to spend a weekend separated. We had agreed since the very beginning that this was the best thing to do to maintain a semblance of personal growth for each of us.

But maybe it had been too much time apart. We both paid a price for it, a high emotional cost for those long absences away from one another, me going to graduate school, and all his male-bonding fishing trips that he insisted he take without me, year after year after year.

Not only were we drifting toward opposite spiritual poles, we were often physically out of sync. "You run on some kind of warped sense of time," Michael joked. "It's way too fast for most people to even try and keep up with you. You should slow down."

We tried to keep the conversation light-hearted, but then I'd remind him that aging was slowing him down too much. "I think you're in a holding pattern," I said, "and maybe you needed to speed up your living. I swear there must be such a thing as male menopause."

We had different personalities and came from drastically different family backgrounds, but none of that ever mattered. His introverted self was what I needed to temper my peripatetic nature. He was my life raft, the one sure thing I could count on. My husband who took care of things, who fixed things, who always came home for dinner, who was a wonderful father, who pitched in equally around the house. Who put up with me. I thought of myself as an interesting partner, a great conversationalist like Merton, a woman who promoted his intellectual life and also his independence and need to retain his self-identity outside of being a husband, a father and an aviation manager.

I tried to articulate the underlying spiritual dimension of my life, but the earnestness with which I began the start of this new internal dialogue was going nowhere.

My eye was constantly on the clock. The next deadline. The next project. The next family blow-up.

He mostly looked at life through a rational, scientific lens. He spoke of biological and chemical organization, genetics, quantum mechanics, logical and informational processes. To him, there was, perhaps, a Supreme Being or force, but he didn't think of God as having taken on a distinct, physical body and entering history in the form of a man, as in Christianity. His God was the biological and mechanical genius behind the workings of the universe.

His God was a concept that he couldn't prove, nor dispute. God was the Master Craftsman and Master Commander. He existed in an abstract realm beyond our comprehension. Organized religion was mainly invented for human control and consolation.

All of this confounded me. As humans on God's green earth, was it enough to admire God's handiwork, and speculate that there was some great force at work, without doing more of the hard work of faith? The idea that there was a resurrected Christ and that there are such persons as prophets and a Holy Spirit floating around—these sounded far-fetched. Michael didn't buy any of it except he did say that "Jesus of Nazareth was a wise philosopher teacher, nothing more."

We kept our "God thoughts" more private between us, as we had done with our children.

Too many of the world's serious conflicts and problems were born in the "junk room of religion," as Richard Rodriguez phrased it. Nobody around us ever said much about the positive outcomes. A heavy negative pall hung over religious topics.

"There is no mystical component to our existence," Michael said during one of our many heated discussions, "only limits to our understanding of our existence and our ability to describe it or communicate." I admired his intellect though I often disagreed with him.

Not everything should be made accessible or perceived through cool edged rationality. I understood how the world had greatly changed after the Enlightenment, the Industrial Revolution, and humankind entered the Age of Reason. I read Richard Dawkins' works and admired and respected his scientific mind. But atheism left me in a crevasse. It didn't offer me any satisfying response about how to crawl out of the spiritual emptiness.

"C'mon," I'd argue, "there must be more to understanding life than unscrambling genes, and figuring out chemical reactions, discovering ever-smaller particles, and speaking about metabolisms, mathematical circuits, and algorithms."

Sometimes I'd continue, "I mean, you're the one who stole and kept the William Blake poetry book, remember! Didn't Blake rebel against scientism and materialism? Wasn't he a man who trusted passion and the mystery and longing for all that's invisible and hidden?"

"But human beings are self-deluded," he replied, "especially when it comes to religion, and confused if they think they're having a mystical experience."

"Well, Merton never thought of himself as a misty-eyed mystic," I said. Michael listened while I continued, "Though he read and understood much about it, especially the early Christian and Asian mystics. Who knows? Maybe while walking under a full moon at the monastery, or some other silent time, he might have admitted he experienced a fleeting, mystical feeling. In any case, you should try and read some Merton. You might like him."

Once I discovered Thomas Merton, it made for interesting domestic conversations. We'd go back and forth and I was amazed, relieved, and happy that we related to one another on this intellectual level, and how my husband could enlighten me with his probing insights, even if it meant we had some real differences in perspectives. His quiet stoicism could drive me mad.

"If everything was accessible to the intellect, then maybe God *is* the intellect," he said.

"Michael, that's a really good point."

What exactly was missing from my life? What was I looking for? I had a solid marriage of over 25 years, two healthy, wonderful sons, more formal education than anyone in my family, and I had beaten malignant melanoma.

Did a sense of well-being flow like a wave over you when it came, if it ever did?

Or was it supposed to feel more like a mist that stealthily creeps into your being?

A little W.S. Merwin poem summed it up:

Life.
Candle Flame.
Wind coming.

Why was it always calm and storm, calm, and then *bigger* storm? Why were we never completely satisfied, even when we were blessed? Why did we call someone "our rock," yet go on hurting them?

Did you have to be a cloistered nun, a fasting yogi, a roaming Russian monk, or a desert hermit to be more contemplative? What did a monk like Merton do in his bleakest hours? Contemplate? Pray? Will himself into being more like a desert father? Or did he scribble another note on his tablet and trust in God that the frustration and emotional pain would simply melt away?

Why was there no solution in migrating and no solution in staying put? These were the questions racing through my mind.

"You need to chill out," my sister Patty, advised. "Just *chill*, big sister." This was my hyper-talking, chain-smoking, Lottery-playing, divorced sister in Florida giving me advice. Her idea of peace was to be left alone in her chosen solitude of a Las Vegas or Biloxi casino away from her two grown kids and insurance job. She hadn't ever stopped long enough for anything remotely related to meditation or a spiritual retreat. Spending a half-day in serious reflection or introspection was out of the question. Religion, to her, held no value. Her life was consumed with her non-salaried job, the commissions she had to earn, watching the Miami Dolphins, and cooking in whatever free time she had with her live-in boyfriend of many years.

"What do you mean, Patty? You think I should watch more television, get a massage? Take more herbal supplements?"

"Well, I do know a lot of people on Prozac," she replied.

My inner predicament was hard to explain.

"I'm not saying I need longer doses of relaxation in a bathing suit on a packed Florida beach," I said. "I don't think I need cannabis to watch more HBO or start golfing to take my mind off things. Yes, pedicures and facials sound good. Sure, the Caribbean cruises are cheap these days, but, it's the…"

"Yeah, I know, I know," she said. "You don't like the idea of all those men in God-awful Speedos running to the buffet line. But these cruises are so cheap and you can really, truly get your mind off all the shit."

The joking went on but I didn't bring up Merton's name. My literary communion and infatuation with him was fine, but what was I learning on a more practical level? As my family and the Pavliks had attested over and over again, books might be nice, but they don't solve anything.

Theodore Roethke, a poet and contemporary of Merton's said in his poem *In a Dark Time*, that "in a dark time, the eyes begin to see…A man goes far to find out what he is—death of the self in a long, tearless night…"

The poet asked, "Which I is I?" We are always dying into ourselves, then renewing ourselves.

In the depth of his soul, Merton desired to draw closer to God and live for God alone. But wasn't he already doing that as a monk living behind monastery walls doing God's work?

Wasn't twenty-seven years of monastic celibacy enough quiet time for God?

How was it, I wanted to know, that a Cistercian monk's life could grow so complex, so full of external noise, that he would feel a great need to re-calibrate his well-ordered, well-structured monastic life? That as a deeply religious man, he would still be searching for something.

To put it the way Canadian scholar, Angus F. Stuart, so aptly asked, "What was Merton looking for that he could not have gained simply by moving a couple of miles further out from the monastery in the Kentucky backwoods?"

Merton was no more God's answer to the perfect model of a monk than I was God's answer to the perfect wife and daughter. Or that Old Man Pavlik was the perfect, law abiding, man and subsistence hunter. And what is it about these Catholics anyway? Why are they so mixed up and paradoxical? And why can't they seem to keep their flocks together?

I was a manic trying to be more meditative and I had failed every time. I had no desire to seek a therapist or counselor.

About this time, I saw an Internet ad for a program on "contemplative living" in the far off land of Kentucky. Maybe this is what I needed. Something completely unconventional, a more drastic option. The retreat on contemplative living was being held close to the Abbey of Gethsemani, Merton's monastery.

...I think that unless something very definite comes up to change things, this (Alaska) would be the obvious place to settle for real solitude in the U.S. Also, apart from that, I think that it is a place where God is calling some to solitude...

—Thomas Merton, in a
letter from Alaska to Father Flavian Burns,
September 26, 1968
The School of Charity

...It would be folly for me not to consider Alaska as one of the best possibilities for a true solitary life and I hope I can return here when I am through with Asia... You ought to see this country some time!

—Thomas Merton, in a letter
from Alaska to Father Flavian Burns,
October 1, 1968
The School of Charity

8 Retreat to Kentucky

I got lost driving a rental car on the back roads of Kentucky trying to locate Thomas Merton's famed monastery. Markers for the various junctions confused me, and without any customary mountain ranges to rely on for directional clues, I took many wrong turns. I had my window open the whole time I drove south of Louisville on Highway 65. What a luxury! On typical March days in Anchorage, spring doesn't simply arrive; it's willed into existence. Glacier-sized ice sheets still cover north-facing driveways. At this moment, our subdivision neighbors were probably outside slamming shovels, loudly cracking and chipping away at the ice, a ritual and therapy I've seen Alaskans perform for hours—anything to speed up the melting process in early spring. No one loves the sight of slush more than we do. When Alaskans think of spring and the joyful Easter holiday, we don't think about creamy yellow daffodils and siren red tulips adorning our yards—we think about seeing bare asphalt again and that's joy enough.

After two hours of driving, I finally figured out the map to the Bethany Spring retreat house where I'd be staying, less than two miles away from the Abbey of Gethsemani. On the way, I pulled into the monastery's new welcome center to browse their souvenirs and library of religious books and DVDs. I purchased a guardian angel pendant in sterling silver for my teenage niece, Daisylee.

It was late on Wednesday afternoon by the time I arrived at my first-ever, non-writing related retreat on the subject of "Bridges to Contemplative Living." The program wasn't slated to begin until the weekend. I relished the idea of being there all alone in the extra solitude without the need to keep checking my clock.

According to the brochure I received, "Contemplative living is living a life of right relationships, with ourselves, God, and others, that produces the ultimate sense of purpose, wellbeing, and appreciation for life."

Right relationships and a sense of well-being. This described exactly what I needed. I didn't know anything about the facilitator, Jonathan Montaldo, and didn't bother to read up on him in advance, preferring to learn about his biography once the retreat began.

The day was piping hot, about 70 degrees. It felt liberating to walk outdoors jacket free in the Bluegrass State with so many different kinds of birds (other than our resident winter chickadees and redpolls) chirping and zipping from one branch to another. Dogwoods, redbuds, and Bradford pear trees were lush in pink and white blossoms. The southern sun shone over nearby glens and through sycamore, cedar and white pine. Sweat started to form on my brow. I was hungry and thirsty, had a slight headache, and wasn't sure what to do next.

I could have done what many sun deprived Alaskans do over their precious spring break—travel to Maui or Cabo San Lucas to lounge poolside, stretched out in my under-used bathing suit with the straps pulled down, and absorbed in a good book, drinking buckets of mango margaritas. I worked hard and deserved to be a lazy slob soaking up rays of valuable Vitamin D. The Alaskan winters often felt never-ending. The constant snow shoveling had definitely grown wearisome to Michael, and his dislike of the cold and long winter seasons only grew worse. "Well, why don't you take off and go to Hawaii for a little mini-vacation while I'm in Kentucky?" I said to try and sound more sympathetic. Practically every single couple in the state of Alaska—except for us—had at one time or another been to Oahu or Kaua'i to cure their seasonal affective disorder.

"You can take a solo trip to the sun and palm trees since I signed up for what will probably be a really dumb thing near Bardstown," I said. "I know this wouldn't be your cup of tea and nothing you would want to join with me on. Hawaii might be the medicine you need. I know how miserable you are."

He mulled it over briefly and then made arrangements to spend one week alone on the Big Island. I didn't think too much of it at the time, how stupid this decision would prove to be, sending my spouse to Hawaii while I went to the Bluegrass State to learn more about contemplative living. Without any umbrella drinks.

I like umbrella drinks very much and am definitely not the kind of person who runs off to alcohol-free gatherings for brotherly and sisterly dialoguing, or to hold hands with a group of strangers—Buddhists, Jews, Quakers, Unitarians, and all manner of Christians from the evangelicals to the Mennonites and the Episcopalians. I remembered that when Merton was a very small boy, his mother, Ruth, attended Quaker services. That meant that Ruth was an exceptionally good listener because that's what being a Quaker was all about. It's a lot of sitting in silence waiting and listening for what the Quakers call "the Divine Push." In the Quaker form of worship, there were no meddling priests, pastors, ministers or other earthly higher-ups. And there was no music or choral singing, either. Once I met a Jew-turned-Quaker (however that conversion happened), where we were seated next to one another at a luncheon. After some conversing, the older, lively man asked, "And of what faith tradition are you?"

The man's question made me uncomfortable.

"Well, I guess, no faith tradition in particular," I said. "I'm a seeker, seeking."

Merton would say I hadn't yet plumbed the most meaningful depths of my own being. For real understanding, more was required. As Simone Weil said, "The action of grace in our hearts is secret and silent." It has little to do with religious labeling.

Something inside me had really started clicking with Merton. I was at a crossroads of sorts and this was the first time I could openly say it out loud. The conflicts Merton was always wrestling with were my conflicts, too. How to scrap all the falsehoods and pretenses and try to live in a *simpler* fashion, with more contemplation and less continual striving and comparing yourself to others? How to really live as God wants you to live, as who you are *inside* and out; to live more contemplatively because you have figured out who that person inside really is?

Even as an obedient monk, he felt at times, that too many distractions were getting in the way between himself and God. Beginning in the 1950s, he fantasized about living in a less socially active place, with fewer of his brother monks in such close proximity. As one writer said of him, to be "nearer to his 'ordinary' self, more vulnerable to God's love."

It was historically interesting to see the Abbey of Gethsemani. The monastery, founded in 1868, had roots that reached all the way back to France in 1098 with the founding of the religious order, the Cistercians of the Strict Observance. I planned to visit Merton's grave.

I hoped the Kentucky experience might help me figure out my thoughts. I was aware, as Merton was, that removing myself, however temporary, from worldly attachments might lead to new perspectives. As Merton said, the real journey in life is interior. As I was aging, part of me wanted to be less encumbered, to be left alone to my solitude, tending my roses and vegetable gardens. The other part of me wanted to hang out in big cities, to be right in the thick of it, in the swirl of lights and action. If I was ever to understand anything and to love, I had to stay directly engaged in the world and not turn myself in a recluse. I had to pay attention to humanity and the times I lived in.

I didn't know any prayers by memory except the Lord's Prayer. On the flights from Anchorage to Louisville, in copying some of Merton's journal practices, I tried writing a prayer, and scratched out a few mostly cliché lines.

"Lord, help me mend my broken down soul. Bring me some of your sweet amazing grace…" But that's as far as I got.

Unlike me, all the Catholics I had ever known seemed to be quite good at recitation and kneeling in silent prayer.

Take Jessica for instance. I was grateful to have met her in graduate school. She was a young Catholic thinker and believer from Louisiana—tall, brunette, fresh-faced, and svelte—who was somehow able to quote memorable lines from papal encyclicals. She wore flat, pointy shoes and pink satin belts to our writers' workshops. Jessica's father quit the Catholic Church after her mother died an early death from cancer when Jessica was a teenager, and though Jessica never stopped considering herself a Catholic, after her mother's death, she found herself drifting away from church. Her father's new-found interest as an evangelical Christian, and his "brainwashing," as she called it, made her frightened of Christians in general. She soon grew disillusioned with organized religion after watching what was happening to her father and, thereafter, stopped attending church for several years. She left Louisiana for Pittsburgh and claimed to be a fallen Catholic when she arrived, but more recently had undergone a kind of spiritual metamorphosis.

One night Jessica and I were drinking some Yuengling beers at a bar in Squirrel Hill, a Jewish neighborhood near the university. "I knew if I was ever going to church it would have to be Catholic," she said. "And the more I read, the more I believed that was true. I read tons of skeptical books about Christianity, and they all ultimately led me back to the Catholic Church."

In her recent return to her Catholic roots, she was re-examining her faith from every possible historical, personal, and literary angle. I liked tormenting her by reciting a litany of papal atrocities dating back to the Crusades—all the corruption and killings which had been committed throughout Christendom in the name of God.

"Hey, it's a human institution, and humans make egregious mistakes," she said in response to my stinging criticisms. "It's the people who keep the church going, not the hierarchy. It's easy to forget amid scandal and shame that it's really all about Jesus. It's easy to lose faith if I become too dependent on the idea of the church as this noble and beautiful structure, but this structure can be easily overshadowed by sin and corruption."

I appreciated having a sophisticated and theologically informed friend like her, someone who freely and articulately shared her insights without proselytizing. The year before, we had formed part of a close-knit circle of women writers who dubbed ourselves, *The Loud Girls*. We came together, temporarily, in the Quaker State, but there wasn't a quiet one among us. We were vociferous about literature, about what great book or essay we were reading. We shared abiding passions for the poets of witness—like Czeslaw Milosz and Anna Akhmatova—the poets who lived through the hideous cauldrons of revolutions, oppression and wars, in Europe and in Soviet Russia.

We were loud, too, about our sometimes overly smug literary opinions. To borrow a line from the Sufi poet, Rumi, "We each strove to be a jar full of water whose rim was never dry, to be in touch with the vital forces of Life and Art." This was our Loud Girl credo. Faith discussions, Loud Girl style, meant we slipped into fascinating philosophical conversations about G.K. Chesterton's works and Amy's recent Catholic conversion. Her Catholic baptism was scheduled at St. Gregory's in Amy's hometown of Chicago within the next few months. And in the next breath, after I once again recommended they all read more Russian poetry, especially Pasternak and Akhmatova, I reminded everyone about the upcoming Steelers vs. Ravens football game, and that the game would be on in my studio and they should drop by.

Sometimes, a few of the Loud Girls (there were about six or seven of us) would hang out snacking on Pittsburgh's famous Ukrainian nutrolls or Polish pierogis, and I'd steal another opportunity to hurl religious questions at Jessica.

"What's the Community of Saints?" I asked.

And Jessica would correct me. "It's the *communion* of saints." A minute passed.

"How's that neoprene creed go again?" I asked.

"No, no, no. It's the *Niocene* Creed."

"Well, not in Alaska! We believe in Neoprene," I said.

And the barrage of questions continued. "Hey, Jess, why do you Catholics put ash on your foreheads?" An illuminating explanation would follow and I pretended I understood the nuances.

I confess these were loaded questions requiring many eye opening discussions and many ice cold beers to adequately answer. Jessica was saintly in her patience with my nagging interrogations. She filled my head with anecdotes about various saints. I think there must have been five hundred of them.

Occasionally, she would drop the names of her favorite writers—Patricia Hampl, Henri Nouwen, Richard Rodriguez, Brian Doyle, Dorothy Day (founder of the Catholic Worker movement and its newspaper), Annie Dillard, and Flannery O'Connor. It happened that some of them were my favorite writers, too, especially Richard Rodriguez whose book *Brown: The Last Discovery of America* I had recently read. The connection I failed to make was that all these writers were Catholic.

Rodriguez was openly gay, lived in San Francisco. The paradox was that he freely and unabashedly called himself Catholic, and this only made me question Catholicism even more. Did it really matter what the Vatican decrees about personal relationships? Can't people be people? Then again, how could a person still consider themselves a Catholic if they disagreed with the religious hierarchy about abortion or homosexuality? Rodriguez seemed to have figured this out while still remaining a Catholic.

"Flannery O'Connor said faith is not an electric blanket." Jessica repeated this often though I didn't quite grasp the meaning of it. I wasn't as familiar with Flannery O'Connor as she was, and hadn't researched how many of O'Connor's short stories were related to matters of faith.

"To be a Catholic is a long, drawn out process," Jessica admitted. "It's a mysterious life journey and it raises more questions than it answers."

She taught me it was possible to identify yourself with an organized religion and still remain intellectually open, as Merton had done, and to still harbor doubts.

"People crave a sacramental existence," she said.

I assumed a blank look again, pulled out my notebook, and made a quick note to myself to get further clarification. I wasn't sure what a *sacramental existence* looked like when you were working in life sucking jobs, raising five kids paycheck-to-paycheck as a single mother, dealing with economic downturns, a cancer diagnosis, struggling with teenagers hooked on heroin, taking care of a dying parent or a mentally ill sibling, or facing foreclosure on your home—the array of problems that came with emotional and economic survival in the richest and most powerful country in the world.

"Look, K.Tarr, doubts and worries were always a part of it. I am no closer to understanding how to live as a Christian in this world than I ever was, especially as a writer, which only seems to bring out the worst in me," Jessica said.

During our many *tête-à-têtes*, I would scribble notes about the Divine Office, the Liturgy of the Hours, the difficult-to-comprehend concept of transubstantiation, hoping I'd have a chance to mull over all these new concepts later. Eventually, though, her promulgations on the mysteries and beauty of Catholicism and the unfamiliar theological and scriptural references, mentally wore me out.

I wasn't attending the Kentucky retreat to weigh my Catholic options. I remained skeptical and realistic. Attending a three-day retreat on contemplative living would hardly solve the quandaries, but at least I could deal with a part of myself that didn't appear on a resume. This pale-faced Alaskan might return home, soul replenished, thinking and fretting a bit less around Michael, and being more pleasant and relaxed overall.

On the other hand, this was only a temporary fix. We can go to a lot of such retreats and conferences and gather up all the positive vibes and energy, and swear to keep in touch with our new acquaintances, and promise to remember the teachings our facilitator imparts until life intervenes again. I hoped mostly not to emotionally burden Michael so much and felt certain he'd feel rejuvenated, too, after his excursion to warm Pacific beaches.

Michael was reserved, sometimes almost laconic, steady-as-a-rock, level-headed, the way you'd want your neurosurgeon to be. He was a "I never get flustered, I am in control" type of person. When we were younger, he perceived me was as a go-getter, an over-achiever. As for himself, he didn't cling to any idea of who or what he should be one day, other than who he was in that particular moment. I was not the Yin to his Yang, but the high wire and spring that sometimes snapped him in two.

I was having a hard time sleeping, nothing unusual in that. I was out of sync with most people because my internal clock ran faster, brain and body chemistry all sped up, sense of time and of how fast things should have been done were skewed and abnormal. I couldn't relax. My mind jumped around, muscles don't want to stay put or reclined for long. And I wanted to do more, and see more. Michael liked to poke fun about my mental state of being, and how, one day, my epitaph would sum it up nicely.

"Here lies Kathleen Tarr, always on the go. We wonder where she went." But what *does* tend to slow me down is the act of writing.

Actually, writing doesn't slow me down—it grinds me to a halt.

No wonder I am a painfully slow writer. It's the one part of me that is supposed to be slow.

But not Merton. I don't know how he got all that work done without computers, without an office of his own before he moved full-time into the hermitage on August 25, 1965. He only had a few hours of uninterrupted space before it was time to attend None, Compline, and Vespers, or before he made notes on Zen Buddhism or the poems of Chuang Tzu, or as Master of Scholastics, preparing a lecture for his students on what made good art.

I was willing to listen to Jonathan Montaldo, the retreat facilitator. Montaldo, as I soon found out (and was stunned to learn) had for many years been the director of the Thomas Merton Center at Bellarmine University in Louisville. He sounded like a kind of spiritual master in his own right organizing and facilitating retreats nationally and internationally. As a well-known Merton scholar, he edited volume two of Merton's seven posthumously published journals. I couldn't believe my good fortune. For the entire weekend, I was going to hang out with a real Merton guru. Privately, I vowed not to talk too much, to control my Loud Girl self, and keep her under wraps.

An inkling of what Merton meant about the concepts of contemplation and centering prayer started forming in my head, but there wasn't much practical application. How does a person slow down long enough to pray regularly? What kind of life looks like that? I'd only be pretending. Patience was not my virtue. That contemplative frame of mind, the *no-mind*, and the notion of contemplation a pathway to your true self, which Merton spent so much time reflecting and writing about, the self that exists when you peel away the mask, rarely materialized except in brief intervals. Life stress and family problems made sure of that. Where was true contemplation to be found?

Merton reminded me, "We must first recover the possession of our own being."

But truth was, I seldom rested—truly rested—mind, heart, and body at once. A sense of inner unity remained an abstraction.

I couldn't rid myself of the guilt that sits and eats away at the gut because I had chosen to live so geographically removed from my immediate family. Alaska and Florida were at opposite poles. Children needed raised. Airplane tickets were expensive. Time was short. Years sped by.

The monk entered my life at the best possible time—when I needed to break down my own interior walls and illusions.

I never seemed to get enough shuteye; Merton suffered the same malady. But at Bethany Spring, a few days of authentic spring weather out of Alaska might bring some solid rest. It seemed like a good idea. The young Merton had first visited the Abbey of Gethsemani during Easter week, 1941, upon the recommendation of one of his former Columbia University professors and good friends, Dan Walsh. For Merton, it was a profound, life-changing experience. On December 10, 1941, age 26, after he quit his job as a college professor in Olean, New York,

Merton arrived by train to the monastery convinced his fate was to be a Trappist.

The front screen door to Bethany Spring retreat house was unlocked, allowing me to step inside an old-style Southern home with oak floors, antique dining room furniture, a reading parlor, and country style kitchen. The house, formerly part of a bourbon distillery, was owned by the Merton Institute for Contemplative Living, headquartered in Louisville.

I unloaded my luggage and stored it near the steps, put on a pair of comfortable shoes, and fell into the big front porch swing in the warmth of the late March afternoon. For a minute or two, I sat with pen and journal in hand. I thought about jotting down some first impressions: *Conjectures of a Confused Pilgrim*. But it was much too sunny and pleasant amid these welcoming, verdant Kentucky hills to think about writing.

Gray squirrels, much plumper and bushier than the far northern variety, scurried and scratched their way along the roofline, over and through the gutters. I dangled my legs over the porch swing, listening to the squirrels, and remembering what real heat felt like on my sun-deprived arms. I wondered if Michael found a place to cast a fishing rod in Hawaii, or whether he went swimming or surfing yet in the Pacific.

Nearby, loud power tools sawed away. Streams of school buses, and motorcycles, and trucks with loud engines roared by. The property was much noisier than I thought it would be. There were far quieter places in Alaska I could have gone—Yakutat for one—if being in quietude was all I sought.

Alaska always provided its own special form of solitude for those who dared to venture there. But most of the writers and artists who had deliberately chosen this path, to live a solitary life on a remote parcel, were in fact, men. Writers and artists like poet John Haines and the painter Rockwell Kent comprised part of this spiritual stampede. They had moved themselves to the far north—in Kent's case, only temporarily—to live closer to nature and to discover a deeper sense of contemplative solitude. They were seekers of a more unconventional existence and had challenged themselves to live more simply and primitively in cabins. Haines at his place about 70 miles south of Fairbanks, and Kent on Fox Island in Resurrection Bay near Seward. In their desires to embrace an all-encompassing solitude, they created portfolios of paintings, and filled notebooks with sketches, and poetry. As men, they needed breathing space and freedom to simply be who they were. Or maybe to discover *who* they really were.

We women have needed this, too. Although historians recorded the wagon trains carrying courageous women across Western plains, British ladies who traveled to Africa and rode camels, and the women of the Alaska gold rush who risked their lives to carve out new livelihoods, mainly there were always males nearby who traveled in their party to help them. Men served as mechanical helpers and porters, carried the rifles, and provided sheer physical strength and protection. I wanted to be more like Kent and Haines. Realistically, I knew I lacked the survival skills to live as a solitary in my own wilderness homestead without depending on human contact.

I knew the story of how, in the winter of 1917-1918, Rockwell Kent, a renowned visual artist and book illustrator from New England, ventured to live on Fox Island in the middle of Resurrection Bay with his ten-year old son. The painter and his boy arrived in the small port of Seward by steamship from Seattle, a grueling two-week trip through heavy seas. Fox Island was pure wilderness with only a handful of old prospectors, fishermen, and trappers in the area. In a journal entry, Kent exclaimed, "With less faith it might have seemed to us a hopeless thing exploring the unknown for what you've only dreamed was there. Doubt never crossed our minds.

To sail unchartered waters and follow virgin shores—what a life for men!"

"There are times in life—when nothing happens—but in quietness the soul expands," Kent said.

The wonder of the wilderness lay in its tranquility. "Nothing in all creation is so like God as stillness," Meister Eckhart said.

If I were truly living in the wilds of Alaska, I assumed I'd be with a man for these longer periods of stillness, and that I wouldn't be entirely alone in the wilderness for more than a week. In practice, I tended to live vicariously through the adventures of people like John Haines and Rockwell Kent.

In his notable memoir about his homestead years in Alaska, *The Stars, The Snow, The Fire* (1977), Haines, who in the early days had also intended to be a professional painter, asked, "Who comes here, to this whiteness, this far and frozen place, in search of something he cannot name?"

"There are silences so deep, you can hear the journeys of the soul, enormous footsteps downward in a freezing earth," he wrote in his poetry collection, *Winter News* (1966).

In another of his poems from *Winter News*, "Fairbanks Under the Solstice," he wrote:

"Slowly without the sun, the day sinks toward the close of December. It is minus sixty degrees."

Off and on, from 1946 until the late 1960s, Haines had lived at his homestead in the bitter cold of Interior Alaska. I was fortunate enough to meet him in Anchorage when he was around 84, during his last few years of life, long after he had regrettably sold his homestead property, and while he was living a meager existence in a rental apartment in Fairbanks. He was still writing still and teaching one class through the University of Alaska Fairbanks. Named to the American Academy of Poets in 1997, he nonetheless fell on tough financial times without a steady retirement income or guaranteed pension after so many years of interrupted, part-time teaching at various universities nationwide.

Since he didn't use email much, the two of us struck up a correspondence of old-fashioned letter writing after our initial meeting. Michael and I hosted him for an overnight visit. I cooked him a pot roast with mashed potatoes and bought him a bottle of Scotch. He came to the table leaning on his cane, couldn't stomach the beef, had trouble with meat digestion, he said, but appreciated the fine liquor and asked if I could ship a bottle to him in Fairbanks. As the son of a U.S. Navy officer, and himself having been a naval officer during World War II, we talked about the war years since my father, as I explained to John, fought in the Pacific Theatre as a sailor among the lowest-ranking enlisted men.

In his widely-published nonfiction, and in his short and spare lyric poems, Haines wrote about the stark, silent trees, the pebbled, icy rivers, the sub-arctic winds that pour like water through mountain passes, and an imagined frozen sea in which the moon is anchored like a ghost in heavy chains. Haines said he didn't consciously or deliberately intend to write poetry. Though he went to an East Coast art school and wanted to be a visual artist. However, at his cabin off the Richardson Highway, the constant cold kept freezing all his paints, so he turned to something far more manageable. He began writing poetry.

After 12 years in the wilderness, "I merely lived my life and, as the poems came to me, I did my best to give them the form and substance they seemed to want."

John Haines became a nationally recognized poet after the publication of *Winter News*, and one of the most famous and celebrated writers to have ever sprung from the great northern woods. I am convinced he would have made a strong and lasting impression on Merton, had they met. Russian poet, Yevgeny Yevtushenko said the only Alaskan poet he wanted to meet was Haines, when he paid an unexpected visit to Haines' homestead cabin in 1966.

When I returned to Haines' work, as I often did, I also came back to Merton, startled by the many ways these men were of the same poetic ilk.

The thrust of Haines' work was as a "solitary seer," as one writer observed in the many essays and tributes written about him after his death. Haines even wrote a poem called, "The Hermitage."

As a fairly new monk at the Abbey of Gethsemani, Merton still held dreams about carving out a more solitary life, to live far removed from his day-to-day obligations at the monastery. In Haines' "Poem of the Forgotten" I read it as if the speaker was Merton:

> I came to this place,
> a young man green and lonely.
> Well quit of the world,
> I framed a house of moss and timber,
> called it a home,
> and sat in the warm evenings
> singing to myself as a man sings
> when he knows there is no one to hear.
> I made my bed under the shadow
> of leaves, and awoke
> in the first snow of autumn,
> filled with silence.

At his 160-acre homestead, Haines learned what it meant to be *still like a stone in the sun*. He ran a trap line for marten and knew how to use moss to insulate his cabin from biting wind, how to hunt and butcher moose, how to read animal scat, how to improvise with the tools he had. Haines and Kent dropped out of the mainstream for a while to explore untrodden places. They each wanted to live away from the mire and muck of their former selves. They wanted to step outside the norm. The careful study of what was directly underfoot—this is what interested them most. Haines, Kent, Pavlik—all three of them were dreamers who had wandered off into the wilderness and found the wealth hidden in their own souls.

But even the kind of solitude Haines experienced at his homestead and the land Kent relished on Fox Island, and the solitude the whole Pavlik clan had laid claim to for years on their Knight Island paradise in Yakutat—this wasn't quite what the solitary explorer, Thomas Merton, had ultimately sought. In all those situations, certain family members also lived by the men's sides—wives, girlfriends, children. John Haines had married several times and often shared his homestead with female companions. Merton was surrounded by his fellow monks, lived on a road system, and had regular mail delivery, and had visitors who came and took him on picnics or drove him into Louisville to see doctors.

By the mid-1960s, Merton was a monk on the run from his monastic status quo and all his incessant writing and teaching. He dreamt of being more of a true, unaccompanied, hermit, as a monk who longed for an existence in almost total privacy. Possibly he wanted to live more like those reclusive Carthusians, who might see a fellow monk once per week or one hour a day. Merton couldn't stop thinking that ultimately this was where his life should go, into more profound silence, perhaps not as drastic as a Carthusian, but definitely as more of a hermit than he really was.

As I sat on the front porch swing of the Bethany Spring retreat house, I realized I wasn't supposed to drag my laptop, flash drive, cell phone, chargers, journal, file folders, and piles of books with me to the seminar. This experience was supposed to be about simplification.

I languished in the sun with my eyes closed, stealing a few minutes of silence, but footsteps broke my trance. A man in jeans and a short-sleeved shirt introduced himself as Father Richard Creason, an Irish Catholic priest from Holy Trinity, an inner city church in St. Louis with a K–8 parish school in a low income neighborhood that was "bereft of art."

"We're the only two guests here at the moment," said the priest in plain clothes. "All you have to do is go around back to the caretaker's cottage. Alida will help settle you in."

I thanked him and reluctantly gave up my quiet spot all alone in the sun. I hadn't expected to see any other retreatants yet, especially not a priest who needed a break from pastoral duties. Both of us were seated on the sunny porch, and I didn't quite know whether to converse or not. He asked me a few questions about my background and I mentioned how interested I had become in Merton. This opened up a conversation that continued over several shared meals, and at the end of the second day, we found ourselves seated in the parlor listening to a CD called, "Celtic Twilight." On the table next to the CD case was a brief directive for "Prayer of the Heart," with tips to help you be more mindful. "Be moderate in food, drink, and sleep. Learn to love silence. As much as possible, avoid distracting occupations."

I enjoyed getting to know the Irish priest. He told me about Daniel Berrigan, the Jesuit priest, and his brother Philip, also a priest, both peace activists, who were jailed for their anti-war protests in 1968. The Berrigans knew Merton personally. Daniel wrote many books, including an essay on Merton. The priest advised me to read the essay, "Thomas Merton, Friend and Monk." Father Creason explained that when he was a young seminarian, "it was during the milieu of the Sixties and an exhilarating time. We had more open-mindedness and freedom and this was changing the dynamics of the typical seminary education."

"It was very exciting," Creason continued, "the civil rights movement, the women's movement, the ecology movement, anti-war rallies—all the soundings, all happening at the same time—and theology with social thought and activism. The European theologians were stimulating American thought to be more engaged in the world around us, in more of a political theology."

"Interesting," I replied, "what about your family? Were they always Catholic?"

"My father's two favorite types of people in the world," the priest said, "were baseball players and priests. My older brother also joined the priesthood during the 1960s."

"My mother had me baptized as a baby, but that pretty much ended it until I discovered Thomas Merton," I mentioned.

"My dad lost many siblings while he was growing up. They were on the verge of destitution, and the Church helped him through those huge losses. You might find it interesting to know that Merton's books helped fill empty slots in the seminaries."

Vibrant yellow forsythia bordered one whole side of the Bethany Spring property. Cardinals, my mother's favorite, and definitely not an Alaskan bird, looked like red bouncing balls as they flitted about. So many elusive songbirds alive in their choral auditioning. It was as if Merton had ordained them to welcome me.

In February 1950 after watching a hawk prey upon a small bird, the ever curious monk made a nature observation on the pages of his journal, later included in his book, *The Sign of Jonas*.

> …The hawk, all alone in the pasture, possessed his prey. He did not fly away with it like a thief. He stayed in the field like a king with the killed bird, and nothing else came near him. He took his time.
>
> I tried to pray afterward. But the hawk was eating the bird. And I thought of that flight, coming down like a bullet from the sky behind me and over my roof, the sure aim with which he hit this one bird, as though he had picked it out a mile away. For a moment I envied the lords of the Middle Ages who had their falcons and I thought about the Arabs with their fast horses, hawking on the desert's edge, and I also understood the terrible fact that some men love war.
>
> But in the end, I think that hawk is to be studied by saints and contemplatives; because he knows his business. I wish I knew my business as well as he does.

Before Merton, I used to believe monks let their beards and hair grow into tangled bird's nests and that they didn't often bathe. Monks hid themselves away in cold and drafty places, in caves and forests, sometimes forever, to be in communion with God. Monks shunned the distractions and pettiness of the outside world, all the human-created things that could lead them astray. Monks didn't like to talk much, except occasionally to their brother monks and to Jesus statues. Monks drank a lot of herbal tea and subsisted on rice and boiled carrots. Monks lived more perfectly and intensely for God. Monks didn't watch network news and they didn't read newspapers, and they didn't like company—especially if it involved groups of loud women.

Merton didn't exactly fit monastic stereotypes. Throughout his life and after his death, people described him as a great talker. A real jabber mouth who loved conversing and corresponding with all sorts of intellectuals. From social activists, artists and writers, students, seminarians, nuns, to even with his monastic barber, in those rare moments when his nearly bald head needed a trim, Merton enjoyed the company of others.

Nuns who knew him, like the sisters at Our Lady of the Redwoods Monastery in northern California, recalled how upfront he was in his beliefs that women should live fully-realized lives, not beholden to how men defined them.

When he lived at the Abbey of Gethsemani, women were barred from going on retreats in the guest house on the monastery's grounds. That was one of the original reasons why the former bourbon distillery—Bethany Spring—opened down the road from the Abbey's main complex.

Merton had his own controversial history with women and one particular female entanglement from his youth still haunted him. The embarrassing details were never spelled out in *The Seven Storey Mountain*, only subtly alluded to. In his autobiography, Merton did make reference to his freewheeling, misdirected, morally debased ways, and the "concupiscence of the flesh."

At 16, following Owen Merton's untimely death from a brain tumor, Tom Merton continued living in Great Britain. In October of 1933, when he was 18 and attending Clare College at Cambridge, his father's close friends—a medical doctor, Dr. Bennet, and his wife—served as guardians, though not legally. It was during this time that Tom impregnated a young British girl. Apparently, the girl hailed from the working class, much to the consternation of Merton's more gentrified guardians and relatives. They were never a couple, had no real relationship, and didn't develop one after her pregnancy was revealed. It was suspected that Merton's grandfather on his mother's side had financially provided for the young woman. The story went that a few years later, she and the child may have died during Hitler's bombing raids on London. Since all contact with the young woman was severed immediately after her pregnancy became known, Merton never learned what really happened to them. He lived with this guilt the rest of his life. Not much beyond those few facts were ever elaborated on by Merton's biographers, Merton scholars, nor by Merton himself. The scant historical details were left as they were, buried in his "sinful" past.

Alida, the Bethany Spring caretaker, was not at her cottage, but I could see a woman across the yard wearing black, rubber boots, work jeans, and a loose fitting red plaid work shirt, tinkering in the flowerbeds. As soon as she saw me, we exchanged waves. She crossed the soft, muddy ground to introduce herself.

After 49 years as a cloistered nun, Alida, age 74, was more than satisfied to be laboring outside of a convent. My impression, besides noting her youthful and healthy appearance, was that she was the kind of woman who never complained about anything. She possessed the same calm and self-effacing disposition as Jennie Pavlik. Alida was a woman who was grateful and happy to be doing what she was doing in the solace of a welcome spring day.

"I'll be serving as your cook tonight," Alida said, "but the spaghetti sauce will come from a jar."

"That's fine with me," I replied. I wanted to inquire about the availability of red wine but managed to keep my mouth shut. She forewarned me about another retreatant sharing the house, a Missouri priest.

"Oh, I've already met Father Creason, and we've had a nice chat on the porch," I said.

Alida wore a white plastic bracelet on her wrist symbolizing support for Bono's African Relief program. She didn't volunteer anything else about her life. Thankfully, she didn't inquire about my religious affiliation or why I had chosen to live in the freezing state of Alaska.

"You'll be staying in the Pink Room," she said while leading me up the creaking, wooden steps to the second floor. And then she left me alone.

The Pink Room contained a twin bed, white furniture, a Laura Ashley-type quilt, lace curtains—everything in cheerful pink and white, including the towels and dresser lamp, but without a radio, clock, television, Internet capability, or free electrical outlet. I would have to go down the hall to use the one shared bath designated for the five guest bedrooms. There was no air conditioning. I knew this pre-menopausal Alaskan woman who fluctuated from night chills to night sweats would need to plead for a fan. From the open window, frogs and crickets chirped outside, and those sounds filled me with joy.

Everyone in the weekend retreat group said the same thing: the time for silence is hard.

Johnny was a deacon-in-training at a Baptist church in a small Kentucky town who wore a "Save Darfur" tee-shirt. One participant was a theology grad student. Roger was a Mennonite, and Wendy and Tom were a warm and friendly couple about to become grandparents again. Denise first introduced herself by telling how she had witnessed her husband's death—he drowned in front of her—and her sense of hope had turned to deep despair. The well-dressed, blonde haired Maggie from Tennessee, said it had taken her "so long to be quiet." Maggie said, "you don't have to buy anything," that superficial, needless stimulations were interfering with her spiritual formation.

"Taking intentional solitude and time for meditation," Maggie said, "was something I didn't think I could do since I didn't like all that quiet before. And I didn't want to over extend myself by trying all these new things. But you can't be on fire with God all the time. It's more like a constant simmer, a gift."

I could have listened to Montaldo's mesmerizing voice for hours, laced as it was with New Orleans musicality. Well-groomed in his neatly pressed gray slacks and black turtleneck, he reminded me of a young Al Pacino, but more soft spoken and never gruff or pushy. He was a big admirer of Mary Oliver's poetry and shunned putting on any scholarly or academic airs.

"I've been reading Merton since I was thirteen years old," Montaldo admitted in an almost whisper. In the snapshot I formed of him, he seemed the consummate expert on calmer living with his non-anxious, non-flashy presence. Though he was a Merton expert with his vast knowledge of Merton's Cistercian life and writings, he spoke almost nothing about his own accomplishments and remained tuned in to others. He knew how to draw stories out of people, how to help them speak directly and openly from their heart. I pictured him as a kind of backup singer to Merton, yet as someone completely comfortable in his own shoes, a man with compassion and sensitivity, a person with humility who didn't flash his credentials at others.

"Merton sailed his inner seas while a monk at Gethsemani. The Abbey had been the monk's life raft. But by his 50s, Merton wanted to explore other waters," Montaldo said.

As retreatants, we shared our reactions to the various readings and poems Jonathan had included in the booklet on contemplative living he designed and wrote. And in his soothing speech, he often repeated, "I hear you. I hear you," and no one seemed the least bit nervous vocalizing to the suave facilitator where they were on their spiritual roads—except me.

Each time I exited the Pink Room over those few days, I saw Merton's face in a portrait that hung in the hallway. It depicted the contented, smiling monk dressed in white habit and black scapular, his bald head uncovered, his arms and hands tucked within the folds of his black over-garment. I couldn't help but stop several times to admire his handsome face—the same black and white photograph I'd seen reproduced on countless book jackets. I stared into the warmth of his eyes, which I knew to be blue, his friendly, serene expression—as if he had invited someone to pull up a chair and throw another log on the campfire.

Well, Tom, I made it, I joked to myself as I stood eyeing his portrait. *Believe it or not, I'm here from Alaska. Can we talk?*

On a short break, I took a stroll through a meadow across from the Abby. The sound of my phone surprised me. It was Michael calling from Hawaii.

"Hey, how's it going there?" He sounded relaxed.

"It's great! I'm walking in a meadow right the second across from the abbey. Everything's in bloom."

"Well, you'd really like the flowers in Hawaii."

"Are you having a good time?" I asked. It was his first trip to Hawaii, but he seemed to be more reserved than I expect. Maybe the vacation was a good thing, and he missed me.

I wished Merton were alive. We could talk up a flirtatious storm together. Or begin by sharing the frustrations and self-doubts of the writer's life. For Merton, as tremendously successful as he was, he was also very much conflicted about his literary skills and successes. He was either deeply grateful for the nourishment provided through the act of writing or else he was full of doubt and frustration that God had seen fit to make him a writer at all.

I wanted to tell him out right, "Look, Mr. Merton, I'm not very good at this contemplative-state-of-being-thing. You know, it doesn't run in my family. Remember those brown bears in Alaska you were so damn afraid of? Well, sometimes biologists in Yakutat have to move threatening bears so they'll be less dangerous to people. To do that, they use a dart gun to tranquilize the bears. That's exactly what I think I need sometimes—to be shot in the hip with a tranquilizer dart."

The retreat weekend drew to a close at 3:00 p.m. on Sunday after the session, Compassion: Prayer in Action. All the Midwesterners simply climbed in their sedans and drove home, and I went upstairs to pack my belongings in the Pink Room and to fill out postcards addressed to friends and family.

I left Bethany Spring thinking about Montaldo's words to me.

"You have to be comfortable to live inside the question mark," he said when we were alone in the dining room after the others had left the premises.

"Yes, that's exactly where I exist, in peaceful uncertainty," I said. I wasn't going to be marching down the road to a religious conversion anytime soon. Of this I was certain. But inside, I was starting to see some light.

The clouds opened over Mount Saint Elias and after that I was overwhelmed by the vastness, the patterns of glaciers, the burnished copper sheen of the sun on the bright blue sea...

—Thomas Merton's Alaska Journal,
September 19, 1968

9 Solitary Mountain

Jennie Pavlik called me from Yakutat with bad news, just three days after I returned from Kentucky. She found her father collapsed, face down on the floor of his tiny cabin, the fingers from one swollen, calloused hand still curled around the edge of his coffee table. Jennie guessed he died from a burst artery. Yakutat didn't have any medical doctors when we lived there as newlyweds and still doesn't. During the last year of his life, physicians at the Alaska Native Medical Center in Anchorage recommended amputation of both legs due to severely clogged arteries and veins.

Although the surgery would improve his chances, Mr. Pavlik adamantly refused to go through with the amputation. At age 82, he was not going to leave Yakutat to fly to any more city hospitals. When death came, he was still going to be right there, in his place of refuge surrounded by his large extended family, with love in his heart, on the land that had both burdened and consoled him for sixty-seven years.

Jennie had been taking very good care of her father, checking in on him several times a day, hand carrying meals she fixed for him—the salmon chowder, the halibut cheeks. She easily walked from her place overlooking Monti Bay down the dirt road to his cabin. She soaked his feet, changed his bloody bandages, and made sure one of his more than 50 grandchildren occasionally visited. It fell upon her, as one of his two remaining daughters, to round up family members from Alaska and the Lower 48 for his funeral. For the Pavliks, that was practically an empire.

Mr. Pavlik's death hit me hard.

I was still trying to sort out my thoughts about my experiences in Kentucky. For a brief time, I felt the recent bouts of self-questioning were getting me somewhere. That I was unbinding my inner self, learning how to drop the preoccupations that led to feelings of spiritual dryness. I had been wandering around this wilderness of faith for a long time, journaling, reading Russian literature, dabbling more and more in Merton, but I hadn't really gotten to the crux of the matter.

Was I, or was I not, a person of faith? If I wanted to be in a quiet place for meaningful solitude, it wasn't because I needed to pray or to converse with a Higher Reality. It was usually because I desired more privacy and quiet time to read or write, or reconnect with Alaska's bounty of wildlife and nature. Was all that communing with Nature making me more "spiritual?" Or was I simply cramming more facts into my head about the birds I saw, the rock formations I drove by, the sub-alpine wildflowers I was checking off in my nature guide book?

I went into solitude for self-gratification. To get away. To rejuvenate. I didn't put any "I'm contemplating God" spins on it. About faith, I was ambiguous and full of doubt.

Yet during the Kentucky weekend, as I listened to my fellow retreatants and their stories, I started to see the paradoxes about my own life more clearly. When it came to God, about the only thing I considered was "God was God. He/She/The Spirit existed." I believed in the concept of God and His or Her magnificence. But why go any further? Wasn't that enough? Enough to say I believed the universe was governed by a Higher Power. And that it lay beyond my comprehension. Therefore since I didn't know, couldn't confirm, couldn't prove, that it was enough to leave it at that? Everything was one big, unsolvable mystery. I didn't need to plunge into prayer or contemplation to arrive at that conclusion. Did I need to declare myself Protestant, Russian Orthodox, Buddhist, Catholic—*anything*?

Except for watching movies with Biblical themes, I hadn't studied the names or stories of the disciples and apostles, or who went to their deaths as Christian martyrs.

Alaska's frontier ethos was alive and well within me. I went my own way—independent, tough-minded. No need for therapists, counselors, mood-altering medications, cannabis or spiritual directors to increase my attempts at consciousness-raising.

Maybe the trip to Kentucky was too much, especially since it was spring break and I wasn't traveling with my husband to Hawaii. Maybe I had reached the limit with reflections from Trappist writers and their medieval stances on solitude and contemplation. I had slept but not rested, had eaten but not felt satiated. I had sat alone in quiet, but not been stilled.

Before I could even unpack my bags or process the retreat, I was back on a plane heading to Yakutat to attend Mr. Pavlik's funeral. As much as I cared about Jennie and her family, I failed to keep in regular contact the last few years, and this neglect weighed on me. I was hung up with my own worries and problems, and what could I do? Kick myself. That's what. The self-criticisms would inevitably follow: the *could-haves*, the *should-haves*, and the *it's-too-lates*.

My mind raced back and forth. No more fatherly counsel from Mr. Pavlik. He was dead and gone. I could no longer sit with him and covet his heirloom of memories.

Jennie phoned a second time sounding even more run down, her voice more mono-toned than usual. "Kathy.... Jennie. Lucy's gonna meet you at the airport."

"Lucy? Who's Lucy?" I asked.

"She was born here. But she's in Wasilla. She's got the hinges for dad's casket."

"What? You're making your dad's casket?" I shouldn't have been surprised—of course they were building their dad's casket, a typical Pavlik thing to do.

"Andy's building it out of plywood. Lucy's also got a blanket and pillow for dad. And an old photograph of him with Mom and Lucy's mom all together. Lucy framed it."

It wasn't hard to find Lucy at the airport. She stood near the security entrance line talking on her cell phone wearing jeans and a denim jacket that immediately signaled her clan affiliation. Embroidered beads in bright yellow, red, black and white covered the back of her jacket in a stunning eagle motif. When I complimented her, she proudly stated she had worn it at Celebration 2006. Celebration is a biannual gathering in Juneau honoring Native traditions and culture.

"I bet Jennie will be at the next one teaching beading and sewing," I said.

"It's cool the St. Elias Dancers will be honored as the leaders at the next Celebration," Lucy said.

The first time I saw the Wrangell-Saint Elias Dancers was in 1979 on stage at the Alaska Native Brotherhood Hall in Yakutat shortly after we moved into the community. I had my camera with me to photograph Chunky and Jimmy, the two Tlingit dancers Michael and I met.

On stage were about 30 Tlingit dancers of all ages dressed in robes of black, red and white, with colorful beads and buttons sewn into patterns, with symbols of ravens and eagles. Tlingit men beat sealskin drums, knelt down low, and swayed their arms as if they paddled canoes. The women gracefully reached over their heads and sang, *haya..ya...ya. haya..ya...ya*, about the land and the water and the salmon and the birds. I was transfixed by the rhythms of their voices, the way their arms bent like eagle's wings each time they stomped their feet across the wooden stage. I remembered Chunky in his tribal regalia, his beaded felt headdress with eagle feathers, how handsome he looked with his black hair, eyes shining as he danced. He sang as if a spirit guided him. I'd never seen such an expression on anyone's face before, trans-like, in unity with his place. The Tlingit elders among them, Chief Paul Henry, gray and hunched over, moved alongside the little ones, some only three or four years old, and the generations came together in unison. I dreamed what it must be like to be among these people, a member of Eagle or Raven clan dancing and singing, telling stories, and re-telling stories, to know and to remember your origins and values. I tapped my feet to the sound of the drums and felt my spirit lifted by the steady beat.

At the airport security line, Lucy handed me several packages.

"I just ran into Home Depot and grabbed some metal handles and hinges for the coffin. I hope they're okay," she said. "Hey, maybe you'll see one of the grandkids, Samantha, on the flight. I heard she was coming in from Hawaii."

I thanked her and then hurried through the checkpoint, with more carry-ons than were permissible, and hoped I wouldn't get stopped.

As I fell into my seat for Alaska Airlines Flight #66, my mind drifted back to the warmth of Kentucky, to the sunny, pleasant days above fifty degrees, to the green meadows, and the purple crocuses and daffodils around Thomas Merton's monastery. According to the calendar, it was the first week of April, but looking around the Ted Stevens International Airport, there were few signs of spring. Snowplows still lined the runways. I wore boots and a Polarfleece vest, was run down and harried.

I knew which side of the plane might offer the best views of Mount Saint Elias, provided the north Gulf coast of Alaska wasn't too socked in with low ceilings. I took a window seat on the left side of the plane, and hoped the usual stubborn and consistent cloud cover would be gone.

The southbound jet was only half full, but an excited and boisterous bunch of passengers boarded, mostly college kids out for spring break skiing in Cordova, clad in expensive North Face jackets, and tasseled, Norwegian type wool caps. Overhead bins were crammed to the brim with their gear, and as the skiers and snowboarders took their seats and buckled in, they carried on their lively conversations oblivious to the rest of the passengers. As soon as the jet zoomed down the runway and headed west over the silty waters of Turnagain Arm, it changed direction and began the steep climb over the snow-capped Chugach Mountains.

The north Gulf Coast of Alaska boasts the highest, most dramatic coastal mountains on earth. If mountains could go on retreat, this is where they'd go, to the Wrangell-Saint Elias Range. Outside of Greenland and Antarctica, this is the most glaciated region on the planet. Glaciers and great ice fields spread out from the mountains like endless rolls of cotton batting. What place could be quieter, or more full of solitude than the 13.2 million acre Wrangell-St. Elias National Park and Preserve?

Whenever I fly anywhere near these great white sharks of mountains, it's as if I'm looking at a different planetary surface altogether, irresistibly beautiful, harsh, foreboding, and peak after peak, inaccessible to humans by any means of ordinary travel.

There's enough solitude in these plenteous mountains to last a person ten ice ages. If Thomas Merton had ever seen this lonely coastline at its best on a rare, clear day, as I have been graced to see it, he would have parachuted right out of the plane.

Mountains make me grateful there are still places of purifying quiet left in this frenzied world. The Saint Elias Range exerts profound effects on the area's weather patterns. Be it from changing winds, temperatures, or collecting massive amounts of precipitation, the Saint Elias mountains have a hand in it all. Some peaks accumulate up to 400 inches of snow or rain per year feeding massive icefields and glaciers. Despite their awesome natural power, that is not what impresses me most. It's that in their grand and silent presence, mountains *can* and *do* speak to you.

When it's fully visible, Mount Saint Elias isn't some fuzzy, ghosted image on a distant, hazy horizon. It's the mountain I *have* shared, and still *do* share my life with—which is to say, it's the one I came to know first. Never having lived near or under any towering mountains before, I was more attached to Mount Saint Elias than to any other peak, including the higher, more legendary Denali, at 20,320 feet. But you have to be more patient for Yakutat's mountain. Elias rarely unveils itself fully, in its most glistening countenance, as it rises three miles straight up from sea level.

I have stared at this mountain in many different manifestations of weather, cloud formations, and times of year. In each instance, my mind clears.

I didn't know anything about the peak's connection to Russia and Russian exploration back in 1979 when I was bemoaning my fate as a newlywed living in exile in a godforsaken fishing village.

Its "discovery" by Vitus Bering's expedition led me to wonder about my forgotten Slavic past, which led to more questions which, believe it or not, decades later, led me closer to Merton.

Sometimes life takes you to places and in directions you couldn't possibly dream up. In my case, a solitary mountain seized my imagination and snapped me out of myself.

The first thing the mountain did was rekindle my abiding childhood interest in explorers and sailing ships—the intrepid adventurers who crossed dangerous, uncharted seas. And through a young and lonely girl's imagination, the mountain reminded me of how magnificent and enchanting those old and ancient tales of wanderlust could be. These were the stories I liked to read as a kid, about marine explorers, the adventurous men who left, time and time again, on their next expedition. Girls were invisible much of the time. The forlorn and forsaken females stood on the quay and waved goodbye with a baby suckling at their breast.

As time went on in Yakutat, and Mount Saint Elias dared to show itself from the steely-gray horizon, I grew more bewitched by it and by its strange twist of seafaring history.

Mount Saint Elias, part of the United States and Canada, was originally named *Yasetaca* by the Tlingits and later renamed and claimed by the Imperial Russian empire. Russian maritime influence in the North Pacific has not been greatly acknowledged.

In the 1700s, the Danish sea captain, Vitus Bering and his men, in service to the czar, trekked across the vast reaches of Siberia by foot, by horse, and by river from St. Petersburg to the Kamchatka peninsula, a distance of roughly 4,000 miles and 9 time zones to the east.

Once Vitus Bering reached Kamchatka on the far Pacific coastline, he and his men had to wait *several more years* before ships could be constructed on site from the ground up. Finally, under orders from Czar Peter the Great, they hoisted sail and took off in three ships for the Great Unknown. They sailed around the treacherous and uncharted waters of the Aleutian Islands, and further east into the stormy bowels of the North Pacific. Naturalists, scientists, and map makers were part of their crew.

From their vantage point in the in the Pacific's icy-cold northern arc, the Gulf of Alaska, the Russians spotted a single, all-white peak dominating the horizon. Not unlike myself or Thomas Merton, the Russian explorers were awestruck by the powerful presence of this *gora*—mountain.

Vitus Bering's perilous voyage would ultimately go down in history as the official "discovery" of Alaska. The Russian Empire secured its imperial claim to the new land and this "ownership" lasted from 1741 until 1867.

Russian Orthodox Christianity and its part of the story was completely out of my zone of understanding. At the time, I had no idea about the Russians' early adoption of Christianity in 988 CE. And without any knowledge of whose Bible was translated from whom, I glossed over the religious details when I was a brand new arrival in Yakutat. I had little familiarity with prophets or saints, other than St. Francis.

But as the Mount Saint Elias story went, Bering's sailors, after spotting this tremendous triangular peak, consulted their Orthodox calendar for that particular day—July 16, 1741. It was near the feast day honoring the Old Testament prophet, Elias, also known as Elijah.

I was relieved to be on such a short flight from Anchorage. It was under thirty minutes until touchdown in Cordova. We landed in the commercial fishing town, and the exuberant skiers deplaned.

A few Cordova based passengers in Carhartt jackets and hiking boots shuffled out onto the tarmac to board the plane, the only daily southbound flight connecting Cordova to Yakutat, Juneau, and Ketchikan before reaching its final destination in Seattle. Pilots called Flight #66 the "milk run" because it was the slowest way you could get from Anchorage to Seattle via commercial airline due to the many scenic stops it made along the way.

Merton stopped in the small town of Cordova on September 23, 1968 noting that he landed at the "cool, lovely airfield shortly after dawn." Cordova, much like Yakutat, was (and remains) disconnected from the road system.

"Still freezing," he said, "I rode into town on the airport bus—a school bus—with a bunch of duck hunters very voluble about their luck and about the good weather which is bad for them as the ducks and geese have not begun to move south."

Merton saw flocks of wild geese feeding near beautiful Eyak Lake and said in many ways it seemed a perfect place to live. "The quiet end of it is several miles back in the mountains, completely isolated, silent....bears would be the only problem," he wrote.

But Fr. Llorente (the Cordova priest who hosted him) assured the fearful monk that the Cordova bears were not as big as the Kodiak grizzlies.

As the Boeing 737 sped down the runway, we were soon off into thick clouds the same color as the airplane's wings, flying over infinite ribbons of streams, estuaries, and glacial runoffs, with everything below a diffused gray-green.

For Mr. Pavlik's sake, I wanted to pay homage to the mountain. For the next 35 minutes, I stayed glued to the jet's window, making sure I would not miss seeing any part of Mount Saint Elias, when and *if*, it came into view.

What was it about these forbidding, snow-covered peaks, and the desolate north Pacific coast, that brought such a smile to my face? It was that these mountains made me forget about everything else.

After Cordova, except for a sprinkle of seasonal dwellings in Cape Yakataga and Icy Bay, there were no real settlements along this section of coast to speak of until the plane reached Yakutat. This stretch had no visible signs of human habitation—networks of interstates, squares of farmland, man-made reservoirs, and obtrusive water tanks, towers, and powerlines. There was virtually nothing, except icy, snowy, mountainous wilderness.

At that moment in time, the contours of my innermost self were a lot like the geography I was flying over—full of sharp edges, craggy lines, dangerous precipices with barreling alpine winds. A lot of internal scree was blowing around, but that was nothing new. Jennie Pavlik and her family were always a calming influence on me whenever I was around them; they radiated a sense of groundedness and rootedness.

Flying over this panorama of mountains reminded me again that I could never revert to being a flatlander, no matter how mild and pleasant the climate. The gentle Kentucky hills where Merton loved to wander, or the heavily treed ridges of my childhood home of Pennsylvania with its softly sculpted hills—could not sustain me. I had been in Alaska far too long.

While all the heart-stopping geography floated by, the couple seated in front of me, heads down, stayed absorbed in their crossword puzzles. Jaded passengers, maybe, not at all impressed when another scenic mountain range appeared before them.

The Pavliks, too, knew that the world's truly spectacular peaks such as St. Elias ran on their own clock. They didn't magically show themselves because you yearned for an alpine fix from your jet window or from the deck of your Princess cruise ship or for that matter from the back of a skiff because you needed to have a brief but reassuring connection to The Mountain.

People longed to be reminded of Mother Nature's more permanent existence, but most of the time, you had to accept knowing that the great geometric peak loomed over you though you hadn't seen a single speck of it for weeks on end.

Yakutat's environment, its mountains, fjords, glaciers, rain forest, islands, and its connection to the bay and to the Pacific Ocean itself, seemed caught in a kind of geologic *pas de deux*; with movement all around in land and in sea that you could bear witness to. There, it was as if you could detect the ticking of a geologic clock. The earth surged forth, it ruptured and eroded. Ice stepped forward, retreated and calved.

With its frequent earthquakes, this land was still under volatile construction—unpredictable and ever-changing, one that directed its own special drama, and announced its own idiosyncrasies. A perfectly suitable place for someone like Mike Pavlik, a man who handled almost anything nature threw his way. But maybe a little too geologically challenging for the inexperienced-in-the-wilderness-Merton.

Mr. Pavlik's voice echoed in my head. *Yeah, yeah, yeah, it's miserable outside, and it's pouring like hell, and the rain won't quit until it turns to snow. It is what it is. You can't be whining about it. Learn to live with it.*

Big mountains made the boldest among us want to climb them. But St. Elias, one of the least climbed of the high peaks in Alaska, had something else that made it distinct. A small band of brave but ill-equipped mountaineers first tried to scale Mount Saint Elias in 1886, under the direction of a retired and decorated U.S. Army officer from back East, Lt. Frederick Schwatka.

Schwatka and his men ultimately failed in their Yankee attempt, reaching only 5,800 feet due to a lack of stamina, supplies, and of tolerable weather. When the peak burst into Lt. Schwatka's view, he saw "one of the most glorious alpine spectacles one could possibly imagine, with Mount Saint Elias in the central background, covered to the very base with ice and snow, and raising its glistening head for nearly 20,000 feet into the light steel blue sky."

In the days before movies and television and the Internet, harrowing adventures from courageous mountain climbers or sea voyagers sold newspapers and magazines.

The New York Times helped sponsor Schwatka's expedition and in return, the military man wrote and filed five front page dispatches for an eager adventure starved public to read.

Lt. Schwatka relied upon the stronger males and a few hand-picked Tlingit men from Yakutat to be his guides and porters. Without their expertise and involvement, Schwatka's high priced adventure would never have been realized.

Yet when it was all over, despite the fact he needed the Tlingit men just to have a chance at a successful expedition, the "superior" and arrogant Schwatka in his lengthy *New York Times* stories, went on to describe Native Alaskans as selfish extortionists, hagglers, and lazy vagabonds. He referred to the Tlingit men of Yakutat as *aquatic savages*.

In 1891, several more attempts to scale the mountain were made by a United States Geological Survey team. Hostile conditions forced the USGS expedition to give up and turn back.

Mild turbulence struck before we approached the landing in Yakutat. I drifted back into my earlier days in Alaska, remembering how at first, when I was an Alaskan novice, I associated the fortress of impenetrable mountains with a rock solid, stable, undisturbed landscape, symbolic of a geologic age or epoch that had long since passed.

However, in the time it took a puddle to form, the entire landscape could tremble and quake so that whole islands in Yakutat Bay might rise or sink, and rivers might completely change course or disappear altogether under a great seismic event, as Mike Pavlik and I had witnessed at different times. At any moment, earth's subterranean forces and grinding tectonic plates could unleash unfathomable energy. Subduction zones, three within close proximity, came together not far from Yakutat.

On a seismic scale from one to ten, with ten being the most dangerous, the village's surrounding area, located directly on the famous Pacific Rim of Fire, was rated a ten. From 1893 to 1974, at least six earthquakes ranging in magnitude from 7.0 to 9.2 occurred within a 250-mile radius of Yakutat.

I received my first real geology lesson during one of those cataclysmic moments of churning earth—a massive 7.9 earthquake in February 1979 in an earthy drama that happened under the alabaster eye of Mount Saint Elias.

I had been in Yakutat for less than one month, and was home alone in our small, apartment near Jim Jensen's house, while Michael was at work in the flight service station.

The wooden structure began shaking back and forth violently, the glasses and dishes slid off the shelves, and when I realized what was happening, I did what any *cheechako,* or new Alaskan, might do—I screamed in terror.

I ran outside on that wintry morning in my terrycloth bathrobe and slippers and stood on the frozen ground in the wide open space which was moving like an amusement park ride. The telephone poles and Sitka spruce trees bent like plastic straws while shock wave after shock wave rolled beneath my slippered feet.

As it was happening, I thought a giant hole would surely open up, and down into the frigid abyss I would fall. I knew I'd be trapped and buried instantly, swallowed into the darkness of the earth's crust, like the famous Bible story about Jonah being sucked into the belly of a whale, but unlike Jonah, I would not be saved by the Lord in a miraculous rescue. No, I would never come back.

God had decided my end was right there in that very moment, under Mount Saint Elias, in the middle of a horrible earthquake, in a place where everything was in some peculiar state of motion and flux, where I didn't belong. And that seemed about right. To die when the whole center of everything was crumbling and collapsing, and the exterior self I thought I knew was shaking loose from its flimsy foundation.

Before landing in Yakutat, I dug through my carry-on bag, and pulled out *The Seven Storey Mountain*. It was a book more dog-eared and annotated than John McPhee's, *Coming into the Country* or any poetry book I owned. But it wasn't long before I gave it up, all concentration was lost, and I stuffed Merton back in my bag.

Though my stomach was empty, I passed on the in-flight food offerings of three-ounces of orange juice and a tablespoon of peanuts. What would the next few days bring? All those crazy Pavliks would be running around setting up for the memorial service and burial. I planned to stay at Skip Ryman's cabin on Monti Bay a few doors down from Jennie's place and would do anything I could to help her out, but I felt inadequate. And so far, my "Bridges of Contemplative Living" retreat had left me indifferent, as there wasn't much time for serious deliberation.

Maybe I'd catch a good view of Mount Saint Elias as the jet approached the runway and this would be the alpine medicine my restless soul needed.

The *waterwheel of thought*, as the poet Antonio Machado had described it, did not slow down. But, as Machado asked, "was that waterwheel going around now, cups empty, carrying only shadows? Had the inner beehives that work in the night stopped?"

I didn't think so; my inner bees buzzed louder than ever. Without much warning or preparation, I was grateful to be going back in St. Elias Country, as the Tlingit people liked to call it.

And the mountain, solitary and everlasting, did not show its face.

…It's quite possible that if and whenever I get back from Asia, I may end up here (Alaska). Local bishops extremely friendly and generous and everybody very helpful.

Lots of little lost islands and spots like fishing villages with two 'Catlick' families who'd be glad to have Mass on Sundays, wonderful lost towns with no road to them only reachable by plane or boat, places turned upside down by tidal wave and earthquake and moved to another spot, etc.

The mountains are the finest I have seen anywhere. It is a GREAT land. Today off to Juneau and SE Alaska and then back to Anchorage for the nunnies…"

— Thomas Merton's letter to friend,
Wilbur H. "Ping" Ferry,
Anchorage, September 26, 1968,
The Hidden Ground of Love

10 Burial at Ankau Lagoon

After my spring escape to Kentucky to learn about the benefits of contemplative living, I found little time for quiet reflection. My mother was growing weaker from her liver cancer treatments. Family stress was high as we discussed options. We decided to move her out of her own home in Florida and into my sister Beth's place nearby. My brother had taken to walking with a cane and after his stroke, lived on meager disability checks. Guilt ate me up inside. The trip to Kentucky was selfish.

In hindsight, I wasn't being much of a wife, either. More like an explosive that could detonate at any given moment. Our intimate moments were rare. I had to write, I said, and my energy had to go there. How could I expect to write anything worthwhile if I didn't stay focused? Maybe later, I said. Oh, we were invited out dinner? Go without me, I said, because I want to read this other Merton book. Michael, please, I can't be bothered with phone calls right now. Tell so-and-so I'll have to call them back. No, I can't go to lunch today. I don't do lunch. Why is this so hard for people to understand? Because I'm not commuting on a freeway or driving myself to an office? I need the solitude and concentration. It would be nice to sit and relax, but I can't right now. I haven't written in my journal for a long time.

As a wise Desert Father once said, "if you haven't first conducted yourself well among men, you won't conduct yourself well in solitude."

I felt ragged and used up in the spring of 2007. Hormonal changes started affecting my body and mind in odd ways. I developed frozen shoulder syndrome making my right arm immobile. I couldn't lift it above the waist. Me, the world's worst sleeper, slept even less.

Every time I got off the phone with a family member in the Lower 48, I tried to downplay the details and not talk about them with Michael too much. Why was it always on my side of the family? Why were they always the crazy ones who were having one streak of bad luck after another? Losing their incomes, having another mental collapse and breakdown. Drinking too much. Living in terrible marriages. Working in soul-sucking jobs. Dealing with teenage pregnancies. Serving jail sentences. Time in and out of state mental institutions.

One thing I knew for certain, and took some relief and comfort in, was knowing Mr. Pavlik's memorial service and burial in Yakutat would be pure, authentic, unadulterated *Alaskana*, unlike any burial of a loved one I'd ever experienced before. Or will likely witness again.

It fell to Jennie to coordinate and oversee most of the logistics. She first had to confer with Rudy Pavlik, and the rest of her siblings, Annie, Andy, and John about what Psalms should be included for the "Liturgy of the Word" in the funeral Mass and what song should be sung for the "Liturgy of the Eucharist" knowing it would have to be something special for her father.

As a musical accompaniment, she chose "On Eagle's Wings," though her father's favorite tune had nothing to do with sacred music or traditional hymns.

Mr. Pavlik's favorite piece of music was an old number called "Pistol Packin' Mama."

The burial plot near Ankau Lagoon needed preparing and the grave digging was strenuous even for the Pavlik brothers and each of their grown sons who were all as strong as bull moose. The old man was going to be laid to rest in the place which had been reserved for him, adjacent to his wife Genevieve's grave. Genevieve was buried next to the Pavliks' first daughter, Mary, who died giving birth in September 1980. Mary, Jennie's oldest sister, was pregnant with her fifth child. At the same time, I was pregnant with my first son, Banan.

Mary developed medical complications and had to be medevacked to an Anchorage hospital in her final weeks of pregnancy. Skip Ryman notified Alaska Airlines of the emergency and the company re-routed a jet that happened to be flying over Yakutat at the time. After giving birth to another girl, Mary died a few hours later from uncontrollable hemorrhaging. Jennie raised Mary's daughter as one of her own.

To prepare Mr. Pavlik's grave, it took hours and hours for his sons and grandsons to dig through the top eight inches of frozen ground and then to dig further until the proper depth and dimension of the hole was made. For tools, the men used sturdy red, yellow and blue "fish hole" shovels, the same kind alpinists and extreme skiers relied upon to dig their way out of avalanches. Rudy and his sons could really jam through the hard-packed ground with these. A wooden frame was constructed to fit partially inside the depression and over the hole to hold the casket in place during the graveside service. The wooden frame was also needed to support the layers of soil so that the temporary walls wouldn't collapse on all sides before the casket was finally lowered into the ground. The brass handles I had stuffed inside my carry-on bag were affixed to the plywood coffin by Andy Pavlik. The blankets and photos Lucy gave me in Anchorage lined the box along with other treasured items. Up until the last minute, Andy stayed busy finishing the carpentry work.

One part of the memorial service was not open for debate—the Pavliks planned to Pray the Rosary at a special gathering at St. Anne's on Sunday night, the day before the actual burial. The family well knew, Mr. Pavlik had recited prayers holding his rosary beads often. I had no idea what this would entail—how people prayed with rosary beads, or what they really muttered under their breath, but I told Jennie I'd attend.

The rosary beads brought back a vivid and recent memory of my mother on one of my visits to Florida. That trip, like so many others, was hurried. It had been 52 years since mother had stepped inside a Catholic Church. She was weak from doses of strong medication and had difficulty walking. But I offered to drive my 71-year-old mother to Mass at the Blessed Sacrament Church in Seminole where neither of us had been before.

"Mom, won't it make you feel better to be inside a church? I was thinking you might like to try it out again since it's Lent, after all," I said to cheer her, though I feared this might do the opposite.

"Okay, I'll go. I'm still a hospital Catholic, you know. God will probably strike me dead as soon as I go through the door," she said with a slight grin when we got to the church. Blessed Sacrament was another one of those architecturally drab, low-budget suburban churches with a big parking lot, yellow tinted windows, a few palms with brown fronds, and too much scorched lawn.

The whole idea of me accompanying her to church was awkward for both of us, as it was the first time we had felt any reason to go to church together, maybe not since my own infant baptism in 1955. I wasn't sure how it would go, or what the correct Catholic protocol was. We stepped into the foyer. No choir or organ. All was quiet. People, many of them well over sixty, were kneeling down, holding their foreheads in their hands, covering their eyes, or staring at the altar. Those damn Catholics, I thought. Why don't they sing more hymns and play foot-stomping Gospel music to welcome you? Or hang a few television monitors with words to clearly follow and get their congregations going? Was all this silent praying going to cheer mother up, or would it make her think even darker thoughts about God and death?

Margie stopped to dip her fingers into the font of holy water and then crossed herself before we made our way to the back pews. She wasn't able to kneel at the pew, and could only bow her head as we took our seats. She looked pale and nervous in her yellow polyester pants and wrinkled, long sleeved white blouse. Her black vinyl handbag was crammed as usual, bulging with old receipts, folded newspaper articles, grocery lists she didn't need anymore, medical notes, a flashlight, wads and wads of discount coupons held together by rubber bands. Her half-opened purse was hanging over her right arm as if it were a crutch. As the Mass began, I fumbled through the books and pamphlets in the seat pocket, not really concentrating.

She whispered the Hail Mary prayer and spoke softly in my ear, "Kathy, I can still remember some of this stuff. Guess once it's drilled into your head, you never lose it." She seemed to enjoy whatever memories the Lenten service was conjuring up as strangers kneeled and prayed earnestly and solemnly around us.

It really was a marvel that after so much time, my mother could still find a few minutes of solace attending Mass in a nearby Catholic church she had no social or personal connection to. Since it was Easter time, she told me the Stations of the Cross were being prayed, something that my graduate school friend, Jessica, once tried to explain to me. The problem was my mother was faint and couldn't stand up or move around the church for any of it. I sat next to her in complete silence and wondered whether we'd ever have another moment like this together again.

Jennie said she needed to put together some kind of printed program for her father's memorial service. This presented another challenge since Jennie and her siblings were uneasy with spelling and putting words on paper. I wasn't sure who among her sisters and brothers finished high school. In all likelihood, it would be left up to someone from within the younger generation of Pavliks to design a printed program from a home computer since Jennie didn't yet know how to use one.

Following the burial, a community potluck would be held at the Alaska Native Brotherhood Hall for anyone who wanted to come and pay their last respects to Mike Pavlik. That meant borrowing tables and chairs, serving bowls and chaffing dishes, extra coffee pots, cups, and all the kitchen utensils. Community members volunteered to bring most of the main dishes of seafood they caught themselves—shrimp, baked king salmon,

Dungeness crab, and halibut casseroles. Annie Pavlik made a living at times cooking her "firecracker salmon" recipe for sport fishermen and loggers; she was the family's most experienced cook when it came to feeding large groups. Annie baked the turkey and ham that I purchased at Costco and transported in my suitcase.

Jennie hoped a few of the Tlingit elders would drop by. A few of the elders were still around from the 1940s and 50s when Mike Pavlik, the Wisconsin farm boy, stepped off a steamship and into the rain forest, but for Jennie it was hard to know how many of the elders would actually attend. Who among the regular townspeople would even care enough to say their goodbyes to someone with such a mixed reputation as Mike Pavlik?

Once Mr. Pavlik's body was embalmed and returned from Anchorage, the funeral procession began from Yakutat's airfield. Along the one paved road leading to town, people followed the procession in their junky pickups, and old rusted cars. Jennie worried that the road crew from the State of Alaska Department of Transportation wouldn't be able to clear the tons of snow still blocking Ocean Cape road. Without the state's special help, the road would remain impassable. Early April temperatures had risen high enough for the snow to begin melting, but it would be several more weeks before breakup was over. It was nothing like the Kentucky sunshine I had recently experienced. But the state road crew had come through and the procession moved on.

Rosie, the town's police officer, and a lifelong resident, directed vehicles to drive slowly across the old narrow single-lane wooden bridge near Ankau Lagoon. Rosie was dressed in her police uniform with a pistol in her holster. After the bridge crossing, the cars and pickups needed to veer sharply right to drive down another normally unplowed, dirt lane to make it to the town's "cemetery." The lane was full of large ruts, heaps of snow, and deep slushy potholes, and had standing water everywhere.

Yakutat's designated cemetery didn't come into existence until the 20th century. Unlike standard Western cemeteries with their neat rows of tall granite tombstones enclosed by walls or fences, each grave was designed simply. There was not much in the way of artistic ornamentation or custom-engraved granite slabs; mostly, graves were marked with plastic flower bouquets that hadn't been destroyed by wind and rain. The graves were randomly scattered across a patch of sandy, spruce-covered wood, thick with moss and *usnea* lichen that dangled from tall trees like fish nets. The whole place gave off a feeling of being part of a dark enchanted forest where a witch or a goblin might jump out at any moment.

On funeral day, Bishop Michael Warfel, the visiting Juneau priest, held a traditional Catholic funeral Mass at St. Anne's. Jennie and her siblings had grown up with "hit-and-miss" priests who only occasionally flew to Yakutat, mostly at the behest of their dad who would plead with the Juneau Archdiocese through handwritten letters and word-of-mouth messages to please send in a priest. In those days, all clergy could fly for free, courtesy of the regional air carriers in Southeast Alaska. The Juneau Archdiocese covered 72,000 square miles, mostly over water, from Yakutat south to the Tsimpshian village of Metlatkatla near Ketchikan.

In years past, after the visiting priest arrived (almost always in summer), one of the Pavlik boys would escort him to the small boat harbor and transport the Most Reverend Father by open skiff up to the Pavliks' homestead, a bumpy, choppy, and wet 40-minute trip to Knight Island. The priest jumped out of the skiff in his rubber boots into the cold waters of Yakutat Bay since there were no docks or pilings to tie up to, before walking across a gravelly beach, past the rows of old, smelly mink pens, and up to the Pavliks' two-story wood house.

One day, I traveled in the back of Jennie's skiff while her husband, Matt, ran us out to Knight Island. We both had on our XTRATUFs making it easy to jump out of the skiff when we reached the beach. Jennie and I walked slowly, crunching through piles of razor clam shells and skirting around pieces of driftwood.

"I'll show you where we used to hold a private Mass outside," Jennie said as we walked through the trees, up to the old Pavlik homestead.

"Dad would sometimes have a priest come from Juneau and we'd all stand in the middle of the living room, but most of the time, we celebrated the Eucharist outdoors."

I moved into a thicket of wet alder and willow under a dense canopy of spruce and hemlocks where, as Jennie said, her father had ingeniously fashioned a homemade altar. Piles of unevenly stacked rocks formed a kind of semi-circle, which gave the makeshift structure the appearance of an Italian grotto. I didn't understand how the structure could still be standing since no one cared for it anymore. Why hadn't glacial winds and storms blown it to smithereens?

A worn gray and white statue of the Blessed Mother once sat tucked inside the rocky enclosure, protected from the elements. Jennie's father removed it and kept that statue in his cabin for the rest of his days. It was the same Virgin Mary he had on the shelf when I visited him.

"Jennie, I can see you and your family standing here on this squishy ground out in the pouring rain for Sunday service," I said. "Yep, you Pavliks, that's something I can easily picture."

While bald eagles, sea gulls, arctic terns, and ravens flew overhead, Jennie, her mom and dad, and seven siblings remembered their sacraments, recited their devotional prayers, listened to their father say a few Psalms, and together, every Sunday, they praised God.

As the time approached for the funeral Mass to begin, St. Anne's filled up with a large crowd of over 100 people. When Rudy saw the respectable turnout, he looked at me and said with good humor, "Wow! If Dad were here, he'd wonder where all these people came from. He never came to town so he'd be amazed."

Barbie, my old co-worker from my cannery days, sat directly in front of me. I spent only one summer season wallowing in fish-sliming misery, but Barbie had worked twelve summers beheading salmon and driving fork lifts. The slime line where I once worked proved too dull for her, she said. Recently, when the one paved road connecting the town to the airport needed resurfacing, Barbie joined the local road crew. She carried a few extra pounds but otherwise, looked like the same steely Barbie whose knife wielding skills on the slime line put me to shame.

The day before the St. Anne's service, I happened to be at the church with Jennie and some other Pavliks when folks were busy preparing the small entryway and moving brown, metal folding chairs around the room where Mass would be offered. Andy Pavlik the handyman went quietly about his carpenter's tasks, taking out his tape measure and drill, and not speaking to anyone unless he had to. He wanted to ensure the casket could be squeezed through the door for the open viewing of his father's body. The Pavlik women—the two remaining sisters, Jennie and Annie—plus Rose Mary Ryman and her daughters, and various daughters-in-law, nieces, and granddaughters were all there, scrambling to set up. Maxwell House coffee and Styrofoam coffee cups, a memory book, pencils, cookies for the kids, trays of light snacks, plastic dinnerware, and scrapbooks of family photos, were all put out.

Robert Johnson, the local sport fishery biologist, surprised Jennie and me with a framed, eight by ten color photo he took of Jennie, her father, and me inside Mr. Pavlik's cabin. In the photo, Jennie and I are kneeling next to her dad who's slouched in his brown recliner. His battered chair was covered with a colorful assortment of Afghans his daughters and granddaughters had crocheted for him. I remember that visit well. It was a happy moment for all three of us. Mr. Pavlik dragged out some of his old bear traps to show me, traps he had stored in the back of his cabin. He carefully placed his framed "Certificate of Appreciation" from the National Rifle Association in my lap. When I started to depart, he asked if I wanted to see how to roll cigarettes, and then he blew me a kiss goodbye, and admonished me again to give up Anchorage and move back to Yakutat where I belonged.

The Pavlik women and Rose Mary were quite pleased that Bishop Warfel would be offering Mass. Priests still didn't make it to the community on any kind of a regular schedule. Southeast Alaska's overall Catholic population was small, around 6,000, and concentrated mostly in the biggest population centers of Juneau and Ketchikan. When I later asked the bishop about it, he said that the vast majority of non-Native people in Southeast Alaska claimed no religious affiliation.

I felt a bit out of place since I didn't live in the community anymore, but still tried to make myself useful. Even without my help, the Pavlik women had everything well under control. It was a privilege and a grace to witness these women from all generations in action. They were the tradition-bearers, the calming presence, the herring egg harvesters, the moccasin beaders, the baby blanket quilters, the purse makers, the blueberry pickers, the jewelry designers, the basket weavers, but mostly I saw them as the real angels. I watched them step into their nurturing roles with such unassuming, natural ease many times before.

Remembering my younger self, I couldn't help but think how narrow minded I had been in my views, how I had railed against stifling, caretaking roles.

But now I didn't quite recognize that part of me. I was standing inside a nondescript church in bush Alaska in awe of women effortlessly and lovingly setting the tables and preparing the food for their community. In all the years I had known her, Jennie had done exactly that. She never questioned whether or not her life was fulfilling or conformed to anybody's contemporary expectations. I could see that in her heart she felt a genuine connection to others because she knew who she was; she felt no need to prove or defend anything about her position or rank in mainstream society. She sank into the rhythms of the present moment.

As for desiring more solitude, Jennie found it in prayer. She found it unnecessary to disappear from the obligations and routines of her everyday life, whether it was sewing otter pelts or pickling kelp. She didn't argue, insist, or clamor for more time alone without any family members; she lived surrounded by wilderness and couldn't care less about trekking in Nepal. Taking time solely for meditation would take her away from her kids and grandchildren. Her greatest adventure and her greatest spiritual expression was tending to her family.

Mayor Larry Powell stood up during the eulogy and said, "Mike Pavlik will be remembered most of all for the extended family he left behind. His many descendants and over 50 grandchildren are here today. Lots of them have remained in town opting out of a more urban existence in Sitka or Anchorage."

The Mayor continued, "His sons were more like rogues when they were younger, but they've since settled down and become quite respectable citizens." A lot of people sitting in their brown metal chairs chuckled. A Tlingit man wearing a beaded bolo tie came to the front of the room and said that old hatreds and rivalries were forgotten and we should "let bygones be bygones" and I wondered if in the future that would prove to be true. In any small town, but especially in one off the road system where everyone's business is everyone's business, much like it was in Merton's monastery, it would take a great providence to "bury the axes" and live in complete harmony and brotherhood.

It came my turn to speak, and as soon as I made my way to the front of the room clutching my notes, my eyes welled up.

"I don't live here anymore, but I've known the Pavlik family a long time," I said with a slight crack in my voice. I stopped to dab the corner of my eye.

"Mr. Pavlik made a strong impression on me, especially when I saw how unwavering his Catholic faith was, and how much he loved the land, as everyone in this room does," I said. "You may be surprised but I used to visit him at his cabin. But he would get really mad if I came during an episode of *Gunsmoke*. His granddaughter, Samantha, is right. He was a real problem-solver, a fix-it man, a survivor in the highest concept of the word. And you always knew where you stood with him. There was nothing artificial."

And then the really hard part. I could barely get any words out and couldn't look up.

"Mike Pavlik loved Mount Saint Elias," I said. "It is remarkable that he was able to stay connected to one place and one mountain for so long. For 67 years. Not many, not even in Alaska, could say that."

I returned to my seat but only a few more people publicly spoke that day. The whole Mass and memorial service lasted about an hour and a half, and when it was over, groups of mostly family members piled into cars and open bed pick-ups to drive to Ankau Lagoon.

Bishop Warfel zipped up his cherry red, Marmot ski jacket, put on his Notre Dame baseball hat, and headed out the door with Jennie and her family, while I walked with our friend, Robert to catch a ride.

Rudy left St. Anne's looking as he always did without a winter coat and dressed in his frayed blue and gray pinstriped shirt, like something old railroad workers might have worn, his top two or three buttons left open, his piebald chest hairs poking through and coated with frost. Whether he was logging, crabbing, hunting, or working on his boat, he wore that shirt. No matter how much rain fell, he wore that shirt.

The winter had been snowier than usual (over 120 inches had fallen) and although it was "spring," and changing from snow to the normal onslaught of plain old rain, dirty mounds of snow still lingered everywhere. Jennie always said about living in Yakutat that you do the best you could and enjoy the weather anyway.

"Wouldn't it be nice," Jennie confided to me, "if the rains and snow showers would hold off for once?"

"Yes, it would be good to have a rain interruption," I said. "Five or ten minutes of dryness. Maybe a double layer of thick clouds instead of this pummeling."

But everyone who knew Yakutat understood that the sun wasn't going to shine; no one expected the heavens to part. It was a muddy and snowy mess.

I wore my XTRATUFs and my warm Polarfleece hat to the burial site. If it didn't rain or snow, then it really was divinely ordered. It was about 35 degrees and my hands were freezing and so were my feet inside my uninsulated rubber boots. One week earlier, warm Kentucky sun caressed my face while walking around

Merton's monastery. Jennie's teenaged son, Lucas, rode to the cemetery on his snowmachine and a few non-Pavliks showed up to pay their respects. Everyone gathered closely around the grave to hear Bishop Warfel speak.

My mind drifted in and out of the moment. I was having a hard time of it, openly crying more than I thought I would, as if the death of Jennie's father had stirred up memories unleashing sad thoughts about my mother's illness, and my father's lonely death in San Francisco.

Standing in the damp chill with everyone circling the grave, the melancholy scene was reminiscent of the opening pages of *Doctor Zhivago*. Pasternak's novel began with a similar scene of people in heavy coats crying and sniffling and gathered in the cold gusts of wind and rain near a freshly dug gravesite under larch and birch trees. Yurii Zhivago was a young boy and his mother was being laid to rest in a village near the Urals on the Siberian steppe.

In that instant, I looked at the gray sky and at the snow. With the boots and dark and sorrowful faces, I half expected a biting wind, and for an Orthodox priest with a bird's nest for a beard in a long black robe to appear. It was as if we—all the Pavliks, their children, and their children's children and the smattering of townspeople present—were all closely joined, emotionally connected, in real togetherness, reminiscent of what the Russians call *sobornost*. And in that solemn moment near Ankau Lagoon, bells might chime from a monastery bell tower, as we the mourners moved slowly, arm-in-arm in a procession reciting *Holy God, Holy Mighty, Holy Immortal, have mercy on us*.

Through tears and whispers, coupled with the playful chatter of grandchildren scuffling over snow, Andy Pavlik's caulking gun made a great noise, going *tat-tattat*, as he sealed shut the plywood box containing Mike Pavlik's corpse.

Strangely, the normally boisterous ravens were silent and nowhere in sight. Rudy's youngest son, his sixth child, three-year-old Paul Calvin and his six-year old sister, Mikhala, were oblivious to the bishop's words who continued to read Scripture over the grave. The kids entertained one another by playing in the damp, heavy snow, though they weren't wearing any hats, gloves, or protective clothes.

To help prepare for the burial, Rudy took his skiff up to Knight Island a few days earlier and filled several fish buckets with soil and water from the family's vacant homestead. Various relatives reached into the buckets for handfuls of soil to throw into the grave.

Russian peasants and wanderers used to do the same thing in the old country, believing they should carry amulets of soil from their homeland with them always, and at death, no matter where they were, they should be buried with some soil—*zemlia*—from Mother Russia.

Not far from Jennie, I stood crying at the gravesite. She was with her husband and wiped her face frequently with a handkerchief as six of the Pavlik men began lowering the unpainted plywood box, now sealed up tight, down into the hole. Jennie had ordered fifty long stemmed red roses to be air-freighted in from Anchorage, and now, each one of Mr. Pavlik's grandchildren walked over one by one and tossed a red rose onto the casket.

Next, following a Tlingit tradition, which was carried over from their contact with the Russians, one of the granddaughters delicately lowered a black and white porcelain teapot into the grave so Mr. Pavlik's soul should not thirst.

And then the miracle happened!

Right after the plywood box was lowered into the ground and the muscular Pavlik men had half-covered the hole with dirt, a flock of honking Sandhill cranes flew overhead in V formation, part of their annual spring migration north to the Interior.

Then in an instant, the clouds parted, the sun flashed, and Jennie stopped and tilted her head towards the sky, glanced over at me, and started to wail even louder. I knew she believed God sent the cranes and the sunlight.

In the months following Mr. Pavlik's burial, my mother made an arduous trip to Anchorage, stricken with cancer and knowing her remaining days were growing short. It was her second visit to the state in thirty years. On her first visit, it was a happy time for my mother and me when she came to Yakutat to meet her newborn grandson, Banan. She took her first flightseeing trip. Together, we flew in a Cessna over Yakutat Bay and the erratic Hubbard Glacier, and though frightened by being in a small aircraft, she was awed.

Michael cooked her some steaks and a boiled heart from a moose he killed. After that short, early autumn visit, my mother wished us well in our peculiar but remote and solitary bush life.

Under the circumstances, we made the best of her return visit though her health and energy had greatly diminished. She experienced nausea and vomiting brought on by all her medications. From Anchorage, we drove her around as much as we could and tried to comfort her by creating a few more family memories. On the Kenai Peninsula, at the Exit Glacier visitor area, we sat down and rested on a bench.

"Mom, don't move," I said. "Stay completely still. *Listen to me*. Do *not* move."

A sow with two cubs came out from the brush and walked directly behind my mother not more than five feet away.

"Well, how do you like those cookies?" she said. "Ha! I don't need to pay any of those bear guiding services now, do I?"

She saw plenty of moose, too; usually the moose were dining in people's yards and along the roadsides. We went to the Eagle River Nature Center and witnessed a bird release party, which I knew would make her happy since she had a special affinity for birds. An injured bald eagle, now rehabilitated, was released from its cage to fly back to its wilderness home again. With all the little things we tried to do on her visit, we still couldn't quite make up for all the lost time.

One year later, the phone call came. Beth informed me it was time to move our mother Margie into a hospice care facility in St. Petersburg. She was slipping in and out of coherence and on morphine by the time I could physically reach her. In one of her waning moments of clarity, she kept asking for her damn purse and said she was "ready to get the hell out of here." She was frail, weighed less than 115 pounds, was unable to get out of bed any longer, and experienced increasingly more irregular breathing. The only food that satisfied her was vanilla ice cream, the kind that comes in little plastic Dixie cups with paper lids like we used to eat as kids in Pittsburgh. I fed it to her with a tiny, wood spoon.

"Mom, it's me, Kathy. I've come down from Alaska," I said holding the little ice cream cup. "I'm finally here now to be with you."

I repeated what I said, but it was not much use. I wasn't sure if anything I was saying was really registering. I stayed for a week visiting her at hospice, constantly in and out of the care facility. All the regrets and sadness about the distance between us—nothing to be done about it. I couldn't stay. I wouldn't be there for her when the time came because I had a new, full-time job, one I had waited a long time to get since my University of Pittsburgh program. I knew I couldn't be the kind of dedicated caregiver Jennie was. Time would run out and I would have to jump on an another airplane to return to the growing pile of projects and responsibilities.

In the last few days before our mother's death, Patty was by her side. My sister would sometimes drop in over her lunch break to stroke mother's hand, sneak her a taste of cold beer, and sometimes Patty slept on a cot in the hospice room. Patty says she remembers hearing my mother mumble about a lot of random subjects, asking about who the man in the white coat was, and saying how much she loved roses. *My girls, my four girls,* she'd say. And then she'd ask where her cell phone was because she insisted it was her turn to call Kathy. Patty would gently lean over her and repeat softly, "Let go, Mom. It's okay, you can let go."

Patty began to notice the changes, how mother's feet turned a bluish hue, the breathing became more sporadic, the mumbling was no longer heard. Margie lasted 51 days in the hospice center. My mother died at 12:54 p.m. on September 15, 2008. I was busy working at my desk in my windowless office answering emails when Patty called.

Medical personnel arrived at the hospice center to retrieve Margie's corpse. A mortician embalmed and dressed the body and covered up her face with the requisite amount of makeup. We held a very brief family viewing at the Garden Sanctuary Funeral Home in Seminole, less than two miles from my mother's home. A closed casket funeral followed with piped in CD music the funeral staff selected.

As a deaf person, Donna didn't fly often, but she flew in from Indiana with her daughter, Daisylee, who wanted very much to attend her grandmother's funeral. My niece was having trouble walking, as the symptoms from her brain tumor worsened.

During the short funeral service, the anonymous women from the VFW Ladies' Auxiliary, where our mother was a longtime volunteer, spoke about Marge's indomitable spirit, and her compassion for the military fighting men and women of our country. None of us had to worry about the costs for her burial, as years ago, she made all the arrangements herself and had scrimped and saved to pay for everything so as not to burden her busy children.

I choked up listening to the women from the VFW talk about mother's special concerns for those people in this world who had nothing, the failures, the wounded, the mentally ill, the orphans, the forgotten. My mother had grown up as one of those forgotten, unwanted people, sent to an orphanage by her father.

All the times I wished I had called her, all the letters I wished I'd written, the plane tickets I wished I bought, the laughs I wish we had shared. None of it mattered anymore. I couldn't take it back. I couldn't tell my mother how much I understood her, now that I had become a mother, too, and had by some grace successfully raised two sons. Unlike her, I did it with a husband by my side, a protector with a steady job. Unlike my dad, my husband was a man who didn't bash my head in or throw me against the wall and break my collarbone.

My mother often said she would have preferred to raise dogs instead of us five kids. I wanted tell her I knew she didn't mean it. That was her broken heart talking. That was Margie, the abandoned little girl talking. The courageous woman, who despite my protests, uprooted her family in search of a warmer life.

In Florida, Margie found her tender blue sky.

None of that past history mattered anymore because we had made it. Despite child neglect, domestic assault, cops at the door. We survived. Margie, through all the challenges, kept us together under one roof. She hung in there in her shit jobs. She didn't put herself first. Not the perfect role model by any means, but the lessons and values she passed on helped me gain fortitude. I wanted to say, *thanks, Mom, thanks for that fighting spirit you passed on to me.*

Margie Malesky's cremated ashes were moved into a gray cement crypt in the small cemetery across from Seminole High School where I attended my junior and senior years.

What a drastic contrast it was with Mr. Pavlik and his family. For a few minutes on that blistering hot September afternoon, my brother Richard and three sisters and I stood on the treeless area on the corner of the property. Few words were spoken between us, even though we hadn't all been in one place together for over twenty years.

Daisylee, her curly black hair covered in sweat, leaned in close to her mother for support. She was growing impatient and tired and needed to sit down. Donna signed to her that she needed to stop fussing and to be a good girl.

"Honey, we'll be leaving soon," I said to Daisylee. "A few more minutes to say goodbye, that's all, and we'll go have some snacks at Aunt Patty's."

"Okay, Aunt Kathy. I'm hot. It's too hot in Florida."

Richard's hair had grown long and unkempt. His white

tennis shoes were as scuffed and soiled as old work shoes, his fingers and nails tarred black from too much nicotine. He stared blankly at the crypt. He was nervous, disturbed, and kept checking to see if his checkbook was still stuffed into the rear pocket of his baggy jeans. I could tell that all my brother wanted to do in that moment was to escape to his dark and crappy trailer, sit under its crooked awning in his plastic lawn chair, smoke a pack of cigarettes, and drink cans of Coke.

Beth, in her mid-forties, was gaunt and frail from living too hard. Her legs were thin as rake handles, and although she had lived in the Sunshine State for decades, she was exhausted and pale. Beth stood with her husband trying to contain her emotions. They spoke nothing to anyone of us, but stood quietly in their grief.

Though Donna, Daisylee, and I had come from long distances, Beth chose not to spend any more time with the family. She gave us each a bag with a few of mother's belongings and left a short time later. The funeral home attached a gold plated nameplate to the outside of our mother's crypt to match the uniform rows of nameplates from the deceased others.

I said goodbye to my three sisters and brother, went back to Alaska a short time later, tried to resume my everyday life, learning my new job. I left the unfinished business of my soul unfinished. In the sorrow and futility of the moment, I once more cast Merton aside.

Daisylee's brain condition grew more serious. The following year Patty and I made a quick trip to Indiana over Thanksgiving to see her. I sat with Daisylee in the living room. She was bundled and wrapped in winter scarves and blankets while sitting on her soft recliner, listening to music on her MP3 player until she fell into a gentle sleep. Her German shepherd dog, Duke, lay by her feet. When she woke up, I gently moved her into the wheelchair and pushed her over to the dining room table where she wanted to do scrapbooking.

"Aunt Kathy, do you wanna see some poems I wrote at school?" she asked.

"Sure, honey, let's see them."

She asked her mother to get her writing tablet. While she was cutting out pieces of paper and pictures from magazines, I read aloud four of her handwritten poems and then asked if I could copy some down in my notebook. Daisylee wrote about her scary watchdog, the German shepherd, who runs and chases other dogs, and she had a poem about winter, "how the chilly air surrounds the earth and the snowman shivers as snowflakes fall." I came across another short poem, and copied it into my journal.

Daisylee read it aloud to me:

<u>Families</u>
Families.
Big, small.
Laughing, talking, sharing who love each other.
Families.

Doctors discovered other malignant tumors growing inside Daisylee. In her senior year of high school on New Year's Day 2009, one year after her grandmother's death, my sweet, most loving and caring, niece, Daisylee, age 17, died from cancer. I was sick with grief and anger.

Time, logistics, money, and jobs sadly prevented us from traveling to Indiana to attend Daisylee's funeral. My siblings and I put up our protective shields and made excuses why we couldn't be there. We left my sister Donna and her family alone to cope with the devastating loss of their child. All the cracks in our family unit showed.

Jennie said her dad wasn't afraid of dying. He'd grown spiritually in the last few years of his life. Mr. Pavlik had turned his whole life to God, she said, and he wasn't going to fight anymore to ask God for another day.

"The most important thing he taught me was prayer and to believe in the Lord and Faith, or else life will be miserable.

He drowned his sorrows in drink after my two brothers died at sea, and my sister, Mary, was dead, too. Watching him come back to his faith, he realized he should have treated my mother better. Whenever mom went to a Tlingit potlatch, dad got really mad."

"I never knew your dad was so negative about Tlingit customs, especially since your mom was half Tlingit," I said.

"He never understood potlatches," Jennie said. "Hours and hours mom would be gone to a potlatch. And when she died, as Eagles, we held a potlatch for the Ravens for payback and to honor her. Dad went and he couldn't believe it. He never understood the meaning behind it."

The gifting, the feasting, and the speaking and listening sessions of a potlatch can last for days and all through the night. Clans paid each other back for the help received for the burial of a loved one and for alleviating some of the pain and suffering after a family's loss.

Michael and I stayed at Ryman's cabin to be within walking distance of Jennie's house. She liked to wander over with a home-baked salmonberry cake, a present from her daughter, Justine, or to give us a few jars of her canned, smoked salmon and the seaweed she picked and dried herself. I pulled out a bottle of cabernet sauvignon and some artisan cheeses I brought down from the city.

After her father's passing, Jennie took a new summer job as a cultural presenter for a Miami-based cruise ship company that was making periodic stops in Yakutat Bay and taking tourists up past Knight Island to the active and advancing 76-mile-long Hubbard Glacier—a spectacular sight that everyone wanted to see. A few younger locals were transported by small boat to join Jennie on the decks of the cruise ships.

They wore traditional dress—red and black vestments, headbands with eagle feathers, loose pants, and everything finely decorated with intricate beadwork. The ship's captain made a loudspeaker announcement that the cultural attraction was about to begin. The Tlingits of Yakutat stood on-deck while the passengers sipped hot cocoa and coffee spiked with Bailey's Irish Crème as the ship approached the dramatic face of Hubbard Glacier.

Tlingits patiently answered the tourists' questions: *Are the Natives assimilated? Do you have a casino yet? Where exactly do you come from?* Jennie gave beading demonstrations and showed people how she used tanned moose skin and sea otter pelts to make moccasins, fur-trimmed leather gloves, and baby booties, made from seal caught by Rudy and her brothers who hunted them in Disenchantment Bay.

"The tourists ask me a lot of questions," Jennie said. "They say, 'why do you kill seals? I could never kill a seal', and I have to explain why Rudy does it, but they don't get what I say. Sometimes they want to know if I live in an igloo, and they ask me where the reservation is. They sound really dumb sometimes. Like when they say, if you've seen one glacier, you've seen them all, things like that." We both laughed.

Jennie and I made plans to take a walk around the salt marshes of Ankau Lagoon and visit her father's grave, though Jennie made her own regular pilgrimages. It was a half-pleasant day, with only an off-and-on drizzle. We didn't talk much, and I was used to Jennie's long pauses and clipped sentences. We ambled around the burial grounds, stopped to read the markers of the dead, many of them people I once knew or men Michael once played basketball with. On one grave sat a flattened basketball deflated long ago. It was under a broken cross marked with only the name, Chunky. On another grave, were some plastic Hawaiian leis and an Orthodox cross without a name. Some sites contained wooden plaques or framed photographs of the deceased covered by plastic protective sheets usually suffering some damage from the elements. The oldest grave dated back to 1871.

I liked seeing Mr. Pavlik's grave minus all the slushy spring snow and mud. Several concrete slabs, crooked and still half-sunk into the earth, were now visible. The sphagnum moss and lichen were thicker than ever, and hung in the deep shade. The squirrels planned for a nuclear winter, piling large middens of pinecones near Mr. Pavlik's grave. A hand-hewn cross already showing wear, seemed casually tacked on, along with a white-paper sign, drawn in crayon by a child's hand that read, "I gave Grandpa Pavlik a bear hug today."

"Do you know anything about the woman Indian saint?" Jennie asked, as she bent over to straighten the bouquet of plastic yellow daffodils on her father's grave. "Her name was Kateri Takakwitha, not sure how to say it right."

"No, I never heard of her, but then again I'm not really up on the millions of Catholic saints."

Jennie and I stood in silence, in the cool, fresh air, looking at the Pavlik family graves a little longer, taking in what surrounded us—alder leaves all wet and shiny in deep shades of green, and near the gravesite, enough fungi poking out from the musty earth to excite any mushroom-crazed Russian. Wild strawberries reproduced abundantly; their runners crisscrossed the ground and crept over the tops of the sandy grave mounds.

Jennie continued. "The woman was from a long time ago. Mohawk or something. She was mom's favorite. But the Pope, he hasn't said she's a real saint yet. Doesn't matter; she's still mom's favorite. That woman suffered, got smallpox, died really young. Never gave up her faith. She was the only one in her tribe to be Christian."

We each moved a few steps around the graves while boisterous squirrels chattered. It was strange to be standing over the graves of her parents and having this conversation.

And now both of my parents were dead, too. "When mom was ill," Jennie said, "and couldn't walk any longer, my brothers carried her into St. Anne's Church. One of the nuns from Juneau flew in to be here, too. On July 14, 1998, we all prayed with the nun in a special ceremony to the Indian saint Takakwitha. Exactly one year later, on July 14, mom died. And because of that, we put a picture of the Indian saint on mom's prayer cards."

A big, blue Steller's jay and a few Varied thrushes flew through low branches as we ambled about and talked. Curious and noisy ravens landed nearby, like they used to do long ago whenever Jennie and I sat on the beach. The ravens waddled toward us as if they had something important to say about our intrusion into their precious spot. I wanted to shoo them away, but changed my mind. Instead I chose to be in silence with my friend. The sound of the tides and surf from the bay and nearby Ocean Cape lightly echoed through the tall, thick forest. A summer mist began dampening our cheeks and as it turned to a soft rain, we both smiled.

...Maybe that was where my geography book came from—the favorite book of my childhood. I was so fond of playing prisoner's base all over those maps that I wanted to become a sailor. I was only too eager for the footloose and unstable life I was soon to get into.

—Thomas Merton, *The Seven Storey Mountain*

11 Merciful Sea

In *The Seven Storey Mountain,* Merton confessed that as a boy, he felt the only life for him was to be a sailor. Elena Mattis, one Merton's biographers, said Merton's life was one of continual discovery, of going beyond the frontiers. His life betokened a journey into the depths of human experience and a transcendence of the ordinary.

I was taught girls weren't sailors, but I was drawn to sea stories and to paintings featuring Greek explorer ships, three-masted sailing ships, like those I saw in the old movies about Jason and the Golden Fleece. And when I got older, and heard about the Spaniards, the Russians, and the British who sailed the North Pacific waters off the coast of Alaska, I found Harry A. Morton's *The Wind Commands: Sailors and Sailing Ships in the Pacific.* The names of ships conveyed special meanings and auras. In mythology, ships are symbolized great change.

I recently had a dream about a ship. I dreamt I was at Alaska Airlines sitting at a special arctic travel gate. The woman next to me was going to Greenland. But I said I wanted to go to Iceland. But it wasn't by jet at all—we were traveling by ship! I boarded the ship with a group of strangers. Seas were turbulent. The skies dark. I grew scared. We sailed around Yakutat Bay and I yelled, "Why are we going so fast? Boats aren't supposed to travel this fast!" The vessel missed hitting a giant boulder. The captain did not know what he was doing. I looked out the window—suddenly the dark, stormy seas vanished. The water smoothed out as if we had fallen down an unknown passageway or magic waterfall and out into a large, flat bay. The sun sparkled. It was beautiful and peaceful, with rays of sun on the water. I woke up.

The first time my father, Louis, set eyes on the Pacific Ocean was probably in San Francisco right before he boarded his ship as a new recruit in the U.S. Navy in the waning days of World War II, a scrawny, foul-mouthed 17-year-old from Pittsburgh. None of the Merchant Marine vessels my father served aboard much later in his life ever made it as far north as Alaska. This much I know.

He joined the Navy as a teenager to escape his troubled past and upsetting home life, and I'm sure out of his sense of patriotic duty—to fight the Japanese. But maybe there was something else to it— a curiosity about the rest of the world, an impulse that pointed him toward that unknown horizon, a desire to reach beyond the limits of his own misfortunes and poor economic station in life. Or as he might have put it, he needed to play with another deck of cards.

I have a favorite photograph of my father. It's a black and white snapshot that came tucked inside the personal effects box the U.S. Merchant Marines sent us a few weeks after he died. The telegram arrived in January 1973, informing us of his critical injuries and subsequent hospitalization. It took a lot of detective work by one of his sisters to locate us since we were estranged from his side of the family. When the news finally reached us, we were living in the apartment above the Laundromat in Redington Beach, Florida. It had been five years—since 1968 or so—when I had last seen my father.

Louis J. Witkowski died from injuries sustained in a bar fight somewhere in Hawaii.

It was unclear if he cracked his head on a sharp metal edge or got slammed too hard into the bar's floor or wall. We never got the full details from the Merchant Marines or from any of his shipmates about exactly where he was in Honolulu, or who he had been carrying on with at the time. The federal government covered the expenses to transfer his comatose body from Honolulu to a San Francisco military hospital where he died at age 46 two weeks later without a single family member or friend at his bedside.

Most of his belongings, including his clothes, had apparently been disposed of, or stolen from his ship's locker at the time of his death. Among his few possessions were a couple of childhood letters I had scribbled to him, some foreign coins, a few pages of miscellaneous government documents, and a few color snapshots of my father's many girlfriends. Richy described these women as his "Geisha Girlfriends." They were women sitting in bars, clinking glasses and puffing cigarettes, their eyes mostly covered under long, straight bangs and smudges of thick, black liner. We also received a notebook he kept about the boat's engine rooms and safety supplies, and a small card attesting to his Vietnam service.

But in this photo I like so much—I'm guessing it was taken in the late 1960s somewhere in Southeast Asia—he posed on the deck of his latest cargo vessel dressed in wide-cut dungarees. A rag hung from his belt. He leaned in close with his fellow seamen, their arms resting around each other. A cigarette barely touched his lips and dangled from the side of his mouth like a toothpick, the way Dean Martin used to smoke. He wore dog tags, a plain, light-colored, cotton shirt with sleeves rolled to the elbows, and a baseball cap with some kind of military insignia. His face was full of that *shit-eating grin*—words my mother used to describe his smirk.

All through my childhood, she complained about his intolerable cockiness, how one day the swagger would land him into big trouble, and she was right. Secretly, I admired him for it.

Isn't that what sailors were supposed to be like? To live at a higher, more spirited pitch than most? He hadn't yet figured things out, didn't yet know who he was, and perhaps that's why, internally, he was all wound up and his temper got the better of him. I wanted to believe in him.

In the moment the group photo was taken, my father appeared happy, content as can be in the midst of his fellow sailors. It must have been liberating for him to be at sea, no longer tied down by stifling domesticity with a young wife and four young kids—one of them deaf—and the grinding responsibilities that came with fatherhood. In the Merchant Marines, he had taken a less burdened course; he had his orders to obey, another voyage to take across the immense reaches of the Pacific, and the structure he needed to give him a sense of purpose and, most of all, to give him hope. On deck, I imagined he joked with his buddies. The escalating social and political problems of America, and his own family grief and bitterness were all but forgotten. Above him the clouds and winds shifted, the ocean spray salted his lips. And as his cargo ship pushed through the waters to Saigon or Da Nang, the drudgery and hardship of the coal miner's life was left far behind. Pittsburgh's smoggy skyline started to fade from his memory until it—and we—disappeared from his life altogether.

I know the other sailors in the photo were like him. They were men who didn't quite fit in, men who knew what they knew not from acquiring fancy college degrees at Columbia and a lot of useless abstract talk, but from the ability to get up and go where they needed to go, mustering whatever physical stamina and grit it took to get there.

After my parents divorced, my father took a job working as a garbage collector, and later, drove a cab. It was 1964-1965, just when the US presence increased in Vietnam, and when his lucky break came. A job suddenly opened up in the Merchant Marines.

I remember how my father's occasional postcards would fill me with dreams of my own oceanic journeys. I knew about the exotic places in Southeast Asia my dad had sailed to. When I was 10, one of his postcards arrived from some distant Pacific port. I snatched the card out of the stack of bills, and sat at the kitchen table reading it over and over until Richy popped in and took it from me.

"Does Daddy live in Japan now?" Richy asked.

"No, stupid! Don't you remember? He travels around a lot on those big boats," I retorted.

"When is Daddy coming home? Kathy, can we call him?"

"I don't know, Richy. Why do you always ask me? Ask Mummy."

I often lost patience with my brother's constant questioning about where our father was. I was two years older, but usually it was left up to me to explain all over again that no, our father didn't *live* in another country, but he visited which is why we sometimes got cool stuff in the mail like silk pajamas, strange coins, and postcards of ships. I was stingy with the postcards, especially since phone calls from him never came. I tromped upstairs to the room I shared with my three sisters and took out the gray shoebox where I placed his postcards for safekeeping. I stored a small stack of them held with a gum band in chronological order. On several he addressed me as "ace" or "kiddo" and wrote about how he had been low on funds lately.

Mother always complained if one of his postcards showed up because, although he remembered ten-cent postcards with photos of cherry blossoms and Buddhist temples, he frequently skipped sending the $80 in monthly child support he was legally required to pay for his four children. "He's spending your kids' food money on his damn Oriental girlfriends," is how she would usually respond in one of her tantrums, throwing our clothes down the stairs, and threatening to send us all to an orphanage.

Other girls had fathers who took them to Pittsburgh Pirates baseball games, to birthday parties, and to swimming lessons at the public pools. But he wasn't like the other dads who worked in the steel mills. My father was special, with bigger dreams than that. That's what I kept telling myself. He spent a lot of time in Asia and could be in the South China Sea or in the Philippines, and as I often bragged to my best friend in the sixth grade, "My father sent me a postcard from Pusan, that's in Korea." And, "Hey Penny, yesterday, I got a picture of the Golden Gate Bridge in San Francisco."

Truthfully, I didn't really know where he was. The Merchant Marine ships he worked on shuttled from one port to the next. One week he and his shipmates were in Hawaii, and a few weeks later they could be sailing stormy seas around a remote chain of Pacific atolls, or straight to the Saigon River. To my young ears, it all sounded adventurous.

Mother held no romantic notions about the sea or ocean exploration. How could she? She knew about my father's womanizing and she wasn't about to let me turn into some dreamy kid who believes in rainbows over the next horizon. "He thinks he's something pretty high and mighty over there," she said, "like he's some damn butterfly who can flit around from flower to flower. That, plus all his boozing."

I didn't know what to say when she went into a rage. He was my father, and I missed and longed for him, but we were barely surviving. "How am I supposed to do all this?" mother yelled while standing at the stove. " Go ahead, keep his lousy postcards, but that's not putting food in your mouth. Your father, the big world traveler. And a great bullshitter. Yeah, well, don't ever believe a word he says. Flat broke, my ass."

Important cargo containers needed to be hauled in and unloaded for classified, Merchant Marine missions, which involved a lot of risk in dangerous military zones. At least, that's what I chose to believe. I had a whole stockpile of necessary illusions.

One night, my father completely missed his ship's sailing, and he was left stranded in Korea. His cargo ship returned a few days later, and luckily, he was given a fairly lenient reprimand for his escapades and excessive drunkenness—ten days without pay. My father admitted this embarrassing detail in a letter he wrote to his sister, my Aunt Dorothy, a letter I saw for the first time in 2004. Aunt Dorothy sent me a few cards and letters she received from my father. I didn't see those letters written during the Vietnam War. In one of them, he admitted he needed to cut back on his drinking.

In another envelope was a color photograph of the merchant vessel, the *USNS General Edwin D. Patrick*. My father included a short note:

>Monday, 6 September 1965
>
>Out At Sea
>
>Hi, Pal. Happy Labor Day to you all. We just left Manila yesterday and I don't feel like no

champ, get the picture. We arrive in Viet-Nam tomorrow, first time the ship has gone there. It's a little different this time, because I'm a civilian in a combat zone. Tell Frank and the girls hello. See you later I hope.

Your brother, L.

In a later note to his sisters, from 1968, he wrote, "…Girls in the Far East are like streetcars. You miss one, you catch another one, if you have the fare, that is…"

Here are the ancestral bits and pieces I like telling about my father's people. My grandfather Ludwig (Louis) John Witkowski sailed across the Atlantic Ocean to Ellis Island aboard the steamship *Grosser Kurfürst* from the port city of Bremerhaven, Germany in November 1913. He was twelve years old when he sailed across the Atlantic bound for Ellis Island with his parents, two sisters, and brother.

His father, my great-grandfather, left what would today be part of Poland, part of the massive influx of over 40 million Europeans who migrated to America to fill mostly laborer's jobs. No one knows exactly what town or village they came from in the peasant heartland of Czarist Russia. (Poland had been split between Russia and Germany, and was no longer on European maps. It reappeared as its own country in 1920.)

My grandfather began working in the Coverdale coal mines at 13 years old and continued working in the mines until his lungs gave out. In the 1920s, miners were as expendable as the headlamps they wore on top of their hardhats. In many mines, especially during my grandfather's time, mules were often treated better than the immigrant miners who were forced to work in degrading, dangerous conditions in the black underground.

As a little girl, I remember a few visits to my grandparents' house. Louie and Julia heated their shanty with a coal-fired furnace and kept cabbages and potatoes in their root cellar.

They used an outhouse and never owned a car. From their front porch in Coverdale, they could see the mine's slag heaps, giant piles of dirt and gravel, horrible eyesores that defaced the landscape for decades.

When my grandfather was older, we called him Ta-ta, from the Polish word *tato* for father. My father's given name was also Louis, but the only name he ever went by in his personal circle was *Lychie (LIE-chee)*, the Hungarian affectionate nickname bestowed upon him by his mother. Through a clerical error at my father's birth, our ancestral name, "Witkowski," was mistakenly recorded as "Willowski" on his birth certificate.

Louis "Lychie" Willowski dropped out of public school in the eighth grade. He left rural Allegheny County about the time his Hungarian mother had run out of ideas about what to do with her trouble making son whom she worshipped and tried to protect. My grandmother Julia had three daughters to look after, and their family life had grown emotionally unbearable. My grandfather Louie fought constantly with his son. In his "old country" ways, Louie thought common sense and manhood could be beaten into him. But each time he struck his only son and called him worthless, Lychie grew more belligerent.

"Lychie, he no good," my grandfather would tell his drinking buddies at the Colonial Tavern. "Lychie, why he no want to work hard? Coal mines, no good for him? Only good for his old man?"

What choice did my father have but to despise the dismal shantytown? What did he want and dream about? Disillusioned with school, he dropped out same as Mr. Pavlik had done. My father rejected the idea of following in his family's tradition. He didn't want to carry a brown lunch pail into the black soot of Mine No. 8 six days a week like his father, grandfather, and uncles had done before him.

"No way I'm working down those crap holes," I can hear him saying. "I'll get my ass out of this little shit town. There's a war going on and Uncle Sam will take me. They need strong bodies like mine to fight those Japs."

On January 6, 1944, at age 17, Lychie's active commission began. He was ordered to San Francisco, the city which became his favorite of all. He weighed 135 pounds, swore like a boxer, and was ranked a seaman, third class. I'm sure he felt an Old World identity had also peeled off him as soon as he pinned on his U.S. Navy badge. He slipped on his bell-bottomed pants and headed out to the stormy Pacific on a brand new battleship, the USS *Wisconsin*.

Having survived World War II, he also served during the Korean Conflict. Shortly after Korea, one muggy summer day, Margaret Marcella Armstead, a 93-pound, recent vocational school graduate went walking near Forbes Avenue in downtown Pittsburgh. Lychie, twelve years her senior, fell in love with this skinny, pale brunette, age 17, who would become my mother three years later. Margie and Louis knew each other for exactly one week in 1952 before they were married by a Justice of the Peace in a West Virginia courthouse.

Margie remembered how much he liked to boast, especially about his exciting days in the Navy. "Lychie always had to remind me about his World War II service. He used to say things like, 'Well, babe, you were still a baby in diapers, when I was out risking my life in combat.'"

Mother continued, "I really can't remember specifics anymore, *except one thing*. Your father once told me some bullshit about his battleship, that it had been caught in a terrible typhoon or something. Your dad said a lot of guys died, but who knows? Half the time, he made things up. I never knew how much of what he told me was really true. He charmed me, that's all. I told you how good looking he was in his Navy uniform."

A man in a uniform was a man with a steady paycheck, government insurance, a possible way out of Margie's lonely life. She lost her birth mother before she was three years old, and had only a half-brother whom she never saw.

Soon after I was born, Lychie's attraction to the sailor's life returned. He used his past military service record in the U.S. Navy to transfer into the U.S. Coast Guard Reserves as a Boatswain's Mate, Second Class. As a young housewife, my mother spent hours pressing Lychie's uniforms being sure to iron his shirt collar and bib that hung over the back of his sailor's shirt.

That's when I first remember my dad wearing his bell-bottomed pants. I was only a toddler, but this image of him dressed up in his sailor whites when he left home for his duty weekends in the Great Lakes Region is one of my earliest memories. He always dressed immaculately, my mother recalled, in white pants, spit-shined black shoes, a white sailor's cap that sat on his head stylishly off-centered, a pack of Lucky Strikes snug in his hand.

I remember his heavily tattooed arms decorated in purple-blue paisley hearts and buxom female silhouettes, leftovers from his World War II days. Throughout childhood, I conjured up this carefree, bell-bottomed image of him whenever I saw those old MGM musicals with Gene Kelly and Frank Sinatra—the suave sailors who sang and danced their way into girls' hearts. I always thought my father possessed a little Frank Sinatra flair. But life wore my parents down, and my father's temper frequently exploded.

My brother and two sisters were born while my parents lived in Finleyville, outside of Pittsburgh. From my bedroom at night, I heard them fight, cursing and yelling. He threw my mother against bedroom walls. He threatened her with a knife. Her screams at sent me running and crying down the hallway. My father hung around Finleyville, and continued to drive cabs or to work on garbage trucks until the mid-1960s when he joined the Merchant fleet. That was the chance he had been waiting for, a way to return to the sea and to a ship—any ship.

For the rest of the 1960s, he remained employed as a seaman. Without much leave time and no means for travel, he had few opportunities to visit his family in Pittsburgh. For the rest of his short life, he crisscrossed the Pacific and never lived permanently on the ground again.

Louis and Margie, the author's parents pictured above. Kathleen Tarr's father Louis J "Lychie" Witkowski (Left) in his military uniform, circa 1955, and her mother, Margaret "Margie" Marcella Armstead, 1951 (right).

Photo of the author's family. From left to right: younger brother Richy, father Louis J. Witkowski, youngest sister Patricia, oldest sibling Kathleen W. Tarr, and middle sister Donna, Pittsburgh, Pennsylvania, circa 1962.

Jennie Pavlik Wheeler with blueberries, Yakutat, Alaska, approximately 2007. (Photo by Kathleen Tarr)

Panorama of Mount Saint Elias and Mount Logan. (Photo by Robert E. Johnson, and used by permission.)

Pavlik family annual gathering on Knight Island, in Yakutat Bay, for Mass, at their former homestead site, before the start of commercial fishing season Mike Pavlik, family patriarch, is pictured sitting (2006), a year before his death. (Photo courtesy of Jennie Pavlik Wheeler)

Mt. Saint Elias looms over Yakutat, 1979. (Photo by Kathleen Tarr)

Boat harbor Yakutat, Alaska with the boat "Tommy Boy." Merton walked out to the dock and discovered the boat bearing his name.

(Photographs by Thomas Merton and photographs of Thomas Merton by Sibylle Akers and John Howard Griffin used with permission of the Merton Legacy Trust and the Thomas Merton Center at Bellarmine University.)

The Lax family's cottage (2017) in Olean, New York near St. Bonaventure's College, is where Thomas Merton hung out in the summers of 1931 and 1932 with his best friend, Robert Lax, writing novel drafts, and having fun drinking beer and goofing off. (Photo by Kathleen Tarr)

Author at Thomas Merton's hermitage, Abbey of Our Lady of Gethsemani, Trappist, Kentucky, 2015. (Photo by Br. Paul Quenon)

One of Fr. Louis's favorite spots—reading in warmth before a fireplace, and inside his hermitage near the Abbey.

(Photographs by Thomas Merton and photographs of Thomas Merton by Sibylle Akers and John Howard Griffin used with permission of the Merton Legacy Trust and the Thomas Merton Center at Bellarmine University.)

Merton's reproduction of the icon of the Holy Prophet Elias (Elijah) being carried up to heaven in a chariot. The icon, gifted to Merton by a friend, hung on a wall inside his hermitage in the small room the monk used as a chapel. (Photo by Kathleen Tarr)

Merton as photographed by John Howard Griffin near Kentucky train tracks around April 1968.

In the 1960s, Merton developed a serious interest in photography and used the camera as a "contemplative instrument," according to Paul M. Pearson.

(Photographs by Thomas Merton and photographs of Thomas Merton by Sibylle Akers and John Howard Griffin used with permission of the Merton Legacy Trust and the Thomas Merton Center at Bellarmine University.)

Thomas Merton's personal Royal typewriter, nutcracker, and oil lamp on loan from the Collections of the Thomas Merton Center at Bellarmine University, and on display at a public exhibition in Louisville, Kentucky.
(Photo by Kathleen Tarr)

Fr. Merton writing in his journal at his hermitage near the Abbey of Gethsemani, date unknown.

(Photographs by Thomas Merton and photographs of Thomas Merton by Sibylle Akers and John Howard Griffin used with permission of the Merton Legacy Trust and the Thomas Merton Center at Bellarmine University.)

Thomas Merton looking relaxed outside of his hermitage and right before he traveled to Alaska, September 1968.

(Photographs by Thomas Merton and photographs of Thomas Merton by Sibylle Akers and John Howard Griffin used with permission of the Merton Legacy Trust and the Thomas Merton Center at Bellarmine University.)

(Photographs by Thomas Merton and photographs of Thomas Merton by Sibylle Akers and John Howard Griffin used with permission of the Merton Legacy Trust and the Thomas Merton Center at Bellarmine University.)

Wandering hermit hears call to solitude in Alaska

"THOMAS MERTON IN ALASKA: The Alaskan Conferences, Journals, and Letters." By Thomas Merton. New Directions, 1989. 162 pages. Illustrated. ISBN 0-8112-1048-0.

Thomas Merton, a Trappist monk and prolific author, came to Alaska in September, 1968, looking for a site for a new hermitage. He spent two weeks here, visiting Juneau, Cordova, Yakutat, Eagle River, and Dillingham.

Alaska thrilled him to the core: "This is a wild, grand and exciting country," he writes. He had lived in Gethsemani Abbey in Kentucky for 25 years, and very quickly realized that his growing desire for a change would be rewarded in Alaska: "Whatever else I may say—it is clear I like Alaska much better than Kentucky and it seems to me that if I am to be a hermit in the U.S., Alaska is probably the place for it."

Thomas Merton was already famous at this time. A very unusual hermit, he claimed that all hermits were unusual; that the objective of "the contemplative life" was to develop an unusual capacity for God's love, and that indeed, hermits and cloistered nuns were "specialists in inner peace and love," to which the rest of the world could look for solace, comfort and a reminder of God's presence.

As a hermit he retired from the active life only to experience life at its most intense: he wrote 60 books, including poetry, journals, an autobiography, a novel, books on mysticism and religious thought, and books in which he analyzed and criticized social problems. He made friends in all walks of life and maintained them with amazing ease. And, intellectually, he never restricted himself to the boundaries of his own Catholic faith. Merton read widely and opened himself to the teachings of other traditions, including American Indian, Jewish, Russian Orthodox, Greek Orthodox, Buddhist, Tibetan, and Sufi.

All of these traditions are mentioned in his Alaska journal. Merton traveled with a book, with many books. In between bloody Marys on the plane to Anchorage and describing the lakes of the Bristol Bay area ("like bits of broken glass"), he is quoting from his current reading.

There was definitely a rebel in Thomas Merton. After 25 years in Gethsemani, he reveled in the wanderlust that brought him to Alaska, and that was to take him on to Asia that same year. In his journal of the trip, which was not meant for publication, the compulsive writer is revealing a sense of wonder and delight, even amusement, at his new experiences. He notes Native place names; he records bits of conversation.

This is a slender notebook but it is supplemented with the letters he wrote from Alaska. He also gave several lectures on the contemplative life to religious communities here, and the lectures are included. They are a thoughtful and moving counterpart to the sketchy, spirited, notebook entries.

Mount Redoubt inspired his prose: "Redoubt (which surely has another name, a secret and true name) handsome and noble in the distance, but ugly, sinister as you get near it. A brute of a dirty busted mountain that has exploded too often. A bear of a mountain. A dog mountain with steam curling up out of the snow crater."

In Juneau, it seems, he didn't meet many people: "Bluegreen Juneau. The old cathedral. The deserted hospital. The deserted hotel. The deserted dock. The deserted school." But he ran into one well-known figure, whose reputation he knew as a protester against the Vietnam War. "We met Senator Gruening in the airport and shook his hand. Famous people are never as tall as you expect."

Merton died of accidental electrocution his hotel room in Bangkok in December, 1968. He never came back to the locations he picked out for a hermitage. We do know he might have, if he had lived:

"My feeling at present is that Alaska is certainly the ideal place for solitude and the hermit life. In fact it is full of people who are in reality living hermits. Men who have gone far out into wilderness with a stack of books and who get the selves a homestead, cut wood, read, and stay aw from everyone, living on moose, fish, caribou. . . . it is a place where God is calling some solitude."

Despite his own lapses in confidence, despite own continual searching for additional kno ledge, it seems clear that Merton was indee "specialist in inner peace and love." How inter ing it would have been to have him among us awhile.   —Marjorie C

Marjorie K. Cole is a Fairbanks writer and librarian wi background in Alaska studies. Several of her short stories been published.

Top Left: O'Malley Peak (far right frame) in the Chugach Range overlooking Anchorage. Merton's image of O'Malley peak would later appear on cover of "Thomas Merton in Alaska" posthumously published by New Directions in 1988. The mountain was identified in 2016 during the research for We Are All Poets Here. (Photo by Thomas Merton, courtesy Thomas Merton Studies Center, Bellarmine University)

Bottom Left: Book Review in the Fairbanks Daily News-Miner, September 24, 1989, by Marjorie Cole on Thomas Merton's posthumously-published Alaska journal.

Above: Former home of the contemplative nuns from the Convent of the Sisters of the Precious Blood, Eagle River, and building where Merton gave his talks to the Alaska clergy and nuns in September 1968. It is now part of St. John Orthodox Cathedral and its surrounding community.
(Photo by Kathleen Tarr)

Aerial view of Anchorage 1968 looking west from Merton's chartered aircraft. Downtown Anchorage is on the right portion of the photo, with Cook Inlet visible. (Photo by Thomas Merton)

(Photographs by Thomas Merton and photographs of Thomas Merton by Sibylle Akers and John Howard Griffin used with permission of the Merton Legacy Trust and the Thomas Merton Center at Bellarmine University.)

The sea of mountains and "snowy nails" Merton saw from his plane window while flying around Alaska. (Photo by Thomas Merton)

(Photographs by Thomas Merton and photographs of Thomas Merton by Sibylle Akers and John Howard Griffin used with permission of the Merton Legacy Trust and the Thomas Merton Center at Bellarmine University.)

A shorn-off, ominous Alaskan mountaintop with Mount Saint Augustine in the far distance as viewed from Thomas Merton's airplane window.
(Photo by Thomas Merton)

A skiff on the shores of Lake Aleknagik near Dillingham in southwestern Alaska. (2016) Merton flew over the lake on his way to Dillingham. (Photo by Kathleen Tarr)

Mt. Augustine, a volcano on the southern end of Cook Inlet is clearly visible from the window on one of the many charter flights Merton took while he was in Alaska, in 1968. (Photo by Thomas Merton)

Fr. Thomas Merton in Alaska, September 1968. Photo taken with Fr. Merton's camera by an unidentified Alaskan pilot or traveling escort.

(Photographs by Thomas Merton and photographs of Thomas Merton by Sibylle Akers and John Howard Griffin used with permission of the Merton Legacy Trust and the Thomas Merton Center at Bellarmine University.)

Left: Archimandrite Gerasim (Fr, Gerasim) in 1967, one year before Thomas Merton's visit to Alaska, and two years before Fr. Gerasim's repose. (Photo courtesy of St. Herman of Alaska Brotherhood and the New Valaam Monastery)

Right: The Russian Orthodox monk Fr. Gerasim (1888-1969) on Spruce Island near Kodiak Island, Alaska in 1938, age 50. (Photo courtesy of St. Herman of Alaska Brotherhood and the New Valaam Monastery)

Left: Reproduction of icon (owned by Kathleen Tarr) depicts the original group of eight Russian Orthodox monks, including the future patron saint of Alaska in the Russian Orthodox Church, Saint Herman, traveling to Kodiak in 1794. (Photo by Kathleen Tarr)

St. Nicholas Orthodox Church, Knik, Alaska. (Photo by Thomas Merton)

(Photographs by Thomas Merton and photographs of Thomas Merton by Sibylle Akers and John Howard Griffin used with permission of the Merton Legacy Trust and the Thomas Merton Center at Bellarmine University.)

Unidentified Alaskan nun from the Convent of the Precious Blood, Eagle River. (Photo by Thomas Merton)

Mount Redoubt, an active volcano, across Cook Inlet from Anchorage, taken from Merton's chartered aircraft in 1968. (Photo by Thomas Merton)

Thomas Merton took this photo of what is likely the Matanuska Glacier north of Anchorage, visible from the Glen Highway. (Photo by Thomas Merton)

(Photographs by Thomas Merton and photographs of Thomas Merton by Sibylle Akers and John Howard Griffin used with permission of the Merton Legacy Trust and the Thomas Merton Center at Bellarmine University.)

Fr. Thomas Merton (Center) with Archbishop Joseph T. Ryan (Right), Merton's Alaskan sponsor and first archbishop of Anchorage, along with Fr. Tom Connery (Left), assistant to Fr. Ryan, at dinner in downtown Anchorage, September 1968. (Photo courtesy of Fr. Tom Connery and the Archdiocese of Anchorage)

Above and Below: Aerial views of Eyak Lake, Cordova, Alaska—one of the sites Merton was considering for his future hermitage after his Asia travels were over. (Photos by Brian Coyle)

Unidentified Alaskan nun at Eklutna. The nun, holding the car door open, was from the Convent of the Precious Blood, Eagle River, September 1968, and likely drove Merton to visit Eklutna where the Orthodox church and cemetery were. (Photo by Thomas Merton)

One of Thomas Merton's up-close-and-personal photos of the Mendenhall Glacier near Juneau, Alaska. (Photo by Thomas Merton)

(Photographs by Thomas Merton and photographs of Thomas Merton by Sibylle Akers and John Howard Griffin used with permission of the Merton Legacy Trust and the Thomas Merton Center at Bellarmine University.)

The picturesque Saint Sergius Chapel situated on a small knoll is part of the present-day property belonging to St. John Orthodox Cathedral in Eagle River, Alaska, and was built with private donations by its church community. It was built long after Merton's visit.
(Photo by Kathleen Tarr)

Icon of Holy Mother of God, St. Nicholas Orthodox Church, Knik, Alaska.
(Photo by Thomas Mertony)

(Photographs by Thomas Merton and photographs of Thomas Merton by Sibylle Akers and John Howard Griffin used with permission of the Merton Legacy Trust and the Thomas Merton Center at Bellarmine University.)

Icons of Alaska's Russian Orthodox saints, including St. Peter the Aleut, on the wall at St. John Orthodox Cathedral in Eagle River, adjacent to the Big House and former convent where Merton gave his talks to nuns and priests.
(Photo by Kathleen Tarr)

Roshi Joan Halifax Ph.D., Zen Buddhist priest, makes a pilgrimage to Thomas Merton's grave at the Abbey of Gethsemani in 2015. (Photo by Kathleen Tarr)

A plain white cross marks Thomas Merton's grave on the monastery's grounds. (Photo by Kathleen Tarr)

Father Merton at the Abbey of Gethsemani wearing his traditional Trappist attire, a white robe and black scapular.

(Photographs by Thomas Merton and photographs of Thomas Merton by Sibylle Akers and John Howard Griffin used with permission of the Merton Legacy Trust and the Thomas Merton Center at Bellarmine University.)

...The solution of the problems of life, is life itself. Life is not attained by reasoning and analysis, but first of all by living. For until we have begun to live our prudence has no material to work on. And until we have begun to fail we have no way of working out our success.

—Thomas Merton, *Thoughts in Solitude*

...I continue to admire him (Pasternak) and revere him so much and never cease to feel close to him. I think it is terribly important today that we keep alive the sense and possibility of a strong communion of seemingly isolated individuals in various places and cultures: eventually the foundation of true human community is there and not in the big states and institutions...

—Thomas Merton's letter about Boris Pasternak to Helen Wolff, at Pantheon Books, which published *Doctor Zhivago*, (November 2, 1967)
The Courage for Truth

12 Pasternak's Tree

It was in Pittsburgh that my first vivid impressions of Russia were formed when by chance I saw a second run showing of *Doctor Zhivago* at a Saturday matinee. The film's sounds and images—the panorama of the snowy Ural Mountains, the crowded and whistling trains, the clanking streetcar Yurii rode at the end of the film (similar to the ones I always rode in Pittsburgh) and the mystery and scale of the wind-swept Siberian steppe with its fluttering birch trees—lodged into my subconscious. Like Russia herself, I could only understand the film emotionally because little about the plot, especially the reasons behind the cruelty, bloody fighting, and the confusing revolutionary politics in it, made much sense to me as a fourteen-year-old girl.

Russia—a country of great contrasts and contradictions—at once a cold cellar and a warm hearth. This was how it was artistically interpreted by the acclaimed British director David Lean. Lean, who also directed *Lawrence of Arabia* and *The Bridge on the River Kwai*, brought all his cinematic powers to bear in his 1965 treatment of Boris Pasternak's controversial novel. The American public was mesmerized by the film and equally captivated by Maurice Jarre's musical score. "Lara's Theme" played on American radio stations everywhere and the film's stars, Omar Sharif and Julie Christie were lauded. Though it received five Academy Awards, *Doctor Zhivago* lost the 1965 Best Picture Oscar to *The Sound of Music*.

Like other kids, I only understood the Russians as the Reds, in opposition to everything freedom-loving America stood for. Communist men and women were robots who marched in black boots and black hats with red stars, and they hated Americans. I was conditioned to believe that countries with stupid Communists running around couldn't possibly offer the world anything of material or cultural value.

As a schoolgirl I learned world history as a long unbroken timeline, notched and intersected by all the important discoveries and conflicts—a string of dates and conquests to memorize. Linear chalkboard history. Devoid of tone and short on meaning but an expedient way to introduce the subject of history to developing young minds until a university classroom might later offer more perspective and complexity.

The divisive, paranoid and absurd reality of the Cold War spanned my life from birth until well into adult life. Teaching the details behind the Russian Revolution or educating us about any of the USSR's greatest poets went well beyond the scope of public schools. Everything boiled down to the Soviet Union being our mortal enemy, not worth talking about, unless it was to vocalize the usual blanket criticisms.

But by the time I was twenty-two and holding my newly minted, official certificate of higher education, my curiosity about the Soviet Union had been dramatically re-awakened because I had moved to a place with direct Russian connections. When I arrived in Alaska, both America and Russia were still trapped in the chokehold of the Cold War. Military forces along the Russian Far East and Alaskan borders stood ready to launch weapons from secret missile silos. The geographic proximity of Alaska to our Soviet enemy drew my attention to all things Russian.

I now lived in a Russian-soaked land and heard Slavic names all around me: Shelikoff Strait, Baranof Island, Kalifornsky Road, Mt. Veniaminof, the Pribilof Islands, Nikolaevsk, Strogonof Point, the Samovar Hills, and many more from all corners of the state. Alaska, rich in marine resources, was claimed and occupied as a colony of the Russian Empire that fueled a productive and lucrative fur trade. Russians hunted sea otters and built trading posts along Alaska's coasts and rivers.

At the closest geographic point, along the International Date Line in the Bering Strait, a mere two and a half miles separates Russia's Big Diomede Island from Alaska's Little Diomede Island. Tourists from the Lower 48 who walk through Anchorage's downtown find a directional pole laden with wooden arrows touting the far north city as the "Crossroads to All Roads." One arrow designates the route to Moscow, eleven time zones west. Another arrow points to the town of Magadan on the Sea of Okhotsk, once an administrative center for the Soviet gulag system and today Anchorage's officially designated "sister city."

In the early 1990s, during Mikhail Gorbachev's era of glasnost and perestroika as the Soviet Union was falling apart, I held a full-time job that involved organizing several goodwill, high-level trade missions to the Russian Far East. Michael and I hosted exchange students from Magadan.

On a September day, while visiting Magadan with mining company CEOs and utility officials, I wandered into a group of school children and passed out bags of candies. Nadia—I remember her well—wore a red skirt, baggy tights, and had a yellow bow in her hair that covered half of her head. Nadia turned to me, and standing erect, folded her hands, cleared her throat, and began reciting lines from Alexander Pushkin's poem about autumn. It was Nadia's way of showing thanks.

My previous views about history were forever changed during those years. I became a Russified Alaskan-American.

Whether countries are closely connected or are military foes, whether our perceptions of each other are accurate or turn out to be mostly lies, these situations and assumptions expand and contract over time, like a cultural bellows. We don't really intuit history, *feel* history. We don't realize a whole era may be shifting and cracking like an Arctic ice sheet beneath our feet until we personally witness it, the way Boris Leonidovich Pasternak and Anna Akhmatova had.

Pasternak, born in pre-Revolutionary Russia, lived through the great turmoils and social upheaval of Communism. Many important literary figures—Blok, Gumilyov, Mandelstam, Yesenin, Tsvetaeva—had disappeared, been executed, or out of despair had committed suicide in the early years of Communism and during the Great Terror of Stalin's purges.

For unexplained reasons, Pasternak was spared the tragic fate of his literary comrades who were "ground up in the gigantic jaws of the gulag," as the poet Yevtushenko later described the silencing of those poetic voices. Why Pasternak had experienced such a stroke of luck has been speculated about ever since. For most of the 1930s he remained in the cultural shadows, working as a translator and scholar, translating the works of Shakespeare, Rilke, and Goethe, while maintaining his own publishing silence. It wasn't until after World War II that he began to work on his magnum opus, *Doctor Zhivago*.

In the second half of David Lean's film, Yurii Zhivago, in the midst of the civil war chaos and upheaval, sought refuge at his family's abandoned estate near the Urals to be with his lover, Lara, and her child. The country was being torn apart in civil war as the Reds and Whites fought for control of the provisional government.

I was young and absorbed very little about the film's chaotic political context and why Russians were fighting each other, or why people were freezing, going hungry and being forced to give up their belongings and their opulent Moscow apartments.

I was far more interested in the juicy love story unfolding between Yurii the physician and family man, and Lara the librarian and nurse whom he passionately loved. I eagerly awaited the kissing.

When Yurii and Lara arrived at the big country house in Varynkino, the severity of winter had transformed it into an ice palace, covered in the purest snow with hoarfrost that shone like diamonds. It was like a fairy tale. I wanted to pack my bags for Siberia and search for such a lustrous ice palace. It was so completely different from the gray-brown landscape where I lived amid billowing smokestacks and dirty rivers of Pittsburgh.

I loved all the romantic scenes from Varynkino—Zhivago riding fast on a horse-drawn sleigh, the joy and happiness he felt with Lara. But what struck me most about the scenes from Varynkino, was watching the film's "hero" Zhivago stay up all night to work on his poetry. Film heroes usually chased criminals, leapt off careening cars, or took up swords and guns to battle evil forces.

What movie had depicted a man who stayed up all night to write his highly individual, confessional poetry? Yurii Zhivago had no interest in ideology, no desire to be a heroic reformer or passionate revolutionary fighter. The protagonist was lost, distracted, and weak. And he wrote "useless" poetry.

How very strange! Here was Yurii Andreievich writing, hovered over a table in the middle of the night with a single candle burning. While his mistress slept, he wrote.

At any moment, they might have been captured by the Bolsheviks and arrested, yet he held fast to his creative vision and continued to work in a bitterly cold room. He wore threadbare gloves and a hand-me-down coat while he slowly dipped his pen into ink and painfully moved each sheaf of paper. From his blue-tinged lips, every breath froze and hung in the air. He scribbled in his notebook near a frosted window, oblivious to the harsh conditions and increasing dangers. Sounds of howling wolves grew louder as they moved closer to his door.

In a later scene, the doctor met the partisan commander, Strelnikov—Lara's estranged husband-turned-revolutionary. Strelnikov forcefully announces to Zhivago that the "personal life was dead in Russia."

Almost twenty-five years passed before any of this made sense to me: not until I finally read the novel *Doctor Zhivago*.

Yurii felt free when he wrote. Alone with his thoughts, in communion with his spirit, he dwelt in a place no regime could touch. He was being who he was, not defining himself according to the latest political structure and terminology. Yurii chose poetry as a means of renewing himself. I would one day choose writing for some of the same reasons.

As a poet, Pasternak knew he would have to write about the tenor and spirit of old Russia, before Communism, and the violence and bloodshed that followed after 1917. The reality of the zeitgeist, as he would admit after the novel was published, had grown too complicated and cumbersome. He felt it was his duty to re-create this epoch—to record the past and honor it—in *Doctor Zhivago*. He felt the need to resurrect the "beautiful and sensitive aspects of the Russia of those years."

Boris Pasternak felt he owed a great debt to Russia and its people. He lamented that his early poetry felt worthless to him since he was too preoccupied with stylistic experimentation over content.

"There would be no return to those pre-revolutionary years, or of those of our fathers and forefathers," he said during an interview with writer-editor Olga Andreyev Carlisle. "But in the great blossoming of the future," he told her, "I foresee their values will revive, I know."

In the winter of 1960, she visited Pasternak in Peredelkino on assignment for the *Paris Review*, at the writers' colony where he and his family had lived since 1937, about twenty miles outside Moscow. Olga Andreyev Carlisle, graduated from Bard College. She grew up in Paris in an elite family of Russian émigrés. Her father and grandfather were both well-known Russian poets and playwrights.

The ability to tap into and to express ourselves, regardless of the ideology of the day, is a human necessity. As Pasternak explained to Andreyev Carlisle, "a poem is never about the author's feelings alone, it is made by something immensely bigger than the poet himself or the ideas surrounding him." Life does not make sense if you choose to look at it and assign meaning through a fixed or conformist political party lens. Life makes sense, as Pasternak believed, only if you look at it as *mystery*, and not according to rigid doctrines and party platforms.

After the preeminent literary journal, *Novyi Mir*, refused to serialize any part of the novel, the manuscript for *Doctor Zhivago* was smuggled out of the Soviet Union and published first in Italy. An English translation appeared in late summer 1958, and on October 23 of that year, Boris Pasternak received the Nobel Prize in Literature—an honor also meant to recognize Pasternak for his lifetime achievement as a scholar, translator, and poet.

Four days after the Nobel Prize was announced, Pasternak was expelled from the Union of Soviet Writers. Without a membership in the writers' union, censored and controlled by the Communist Party, writers could not make a living by their literary skills.

An international furor quickly erupted and somehow Thomas Merton got wind of it (he read *Doctor Zhivago* in the monastery). The debate in the West focused on the Soviet regime's ongoing oppression and its severe stifling of artistic freedoms. The Soviet press called the novel a "squalid work," and Pasternak was rebuked by high-ranking party authorities and by a majority of his fellow writers. His novel didn't reaffirm Communism but harkened back to more of the spiritual values expressed by the people in pre-revolutionary times.

His novel echoed Christian symbolism and biblical passages, and therefore it was contrary to the atheistic tenets of Soviet Communism. *Doctor Zhivago* could not be tolerated in the USSR. Unless Pasternak publicly renounced the Nobel Prize, he would be forced by the Soviet government to live in exile.

For the beleaguered author and poet, the choice was clear. He refused the prize, and was unwilling to renounce his citizenship and live in exile from his homeland. On October 30, 1958, Pasternak wrote a letter to the Soviet authorities to try to correct any possible misinterpretations of the novel; his letter wasn't an outright apology but rather an attempt to quell the controversy. Regardless, attacks and harassments continued. Eight hundred members of the Union of Soviet Writers passed a resolution demanding the government strip him of his citizenship in the USSR.

From the abbey in the countryside, Merton exchanged a series of personal letters with Pasternak beginning in 1958. Merton had literary friends all over the northern and southern hemispheres, but his literary friendship with the Russian writer was especially moving and of lasting importance to Merton. All through his life, the monk felt a special solidarity with poets and with the "uselessness" of their art.

In Pasternak, Merton discovered a kindred spirit as a thinker, an artist, and defender of inner freedom. Both men belonged to the cultural intelligentsia. They were educated in prestigious universities, fluent in several languages, and enjoyed lives full of art, ideas, and travel. Pasternak spent time studying in Germany, Italy, and France. Both sought tranquility in nature; one strolled through the knobby woodlands of Kentucky, the other took walks under the linden trees of Peredelkino.

Both of their mothers were pianists, and their fathers professional artists who tutored their sons in the fine art of beholding—an intense and disciplined way of looking at life.

Merton, as a prodigious journal keeper, referred to the Russian several times: *How else shall I study Boris Pasternak, whose central idea is the sacredness of life?* From an entry on October 12, 1958, *before* the Nobel Prize announcement was made, Merton wrote, "Thursday afternoon Reverend Father gave me a letter from Pasternak inside an envelope from New Directions—air mail, registered, but unopened. I explained with vehemence to Reverend Father that Pasternak was a great and basically religious writer. I could see he did not believe me—or if he did, a little, it was against his will to do so."

On October 18, 1958, the Trappist monk noted receipt of two more letters from Russia. "I was very pleased. Will write him again. He keeps insisting that his early work is worthless." Merton continued, "This simple and human dialogue with Pasternak and a few others like him is to me worth thousands of sermons and radio speeches. It is to me the true Kingdom of God, which is still so clearly and evidently 'in the midst of us.'"

Despite his busy teaching schedule and the many literary projects he constantly juggled, Merton took time to write a personal letter of protest to the president of the Soviet writers' union, imploring them to reinstate Pasternak's membership.

In 1960 Merton dedicated a collection of his essays, *Disputed Questions*, to Pasternak. In the volume's opening, in his lengthy essay, "The Pasternak Affair," Merton said the Russian writer "stands first of all for the great spiritual values that are under attack in our materialistic world. He stands for the freedom and nobility of the individual person, for man in the image of God, for man in whom God dwells. For Pasternak, the person is and must always remain prior to the collectivity."

"One of the more important judgments made by this book," Merton observed, "is a condemnation of the chaotic meaninglessness of all twentieth century political life, and the assertion that politics has practically ceased to be a really vital and significant force in man's society."

By the time Olga Andreyev Carlisle visited Pasternak, it was January 1960 and most of the international debate over the Nobel Prize, and his refusal to accept it, had subsided. She would later recount her meetings with him and other writers in two books—*Voices in the Snow* (1962) and *Poets on Street Corners* (1968). She wrote with much affection about her meetings with him and the poignancy of Pasternak's remarks.

Through Andreyev Carlisle, I learned how intimate and urgent Russia's relationship was to its poets. As Yevgeny Yevtushenko pointed out, unlike the West, the best Russian poets were never hermetically sealed off from the public.

"Scholars interpret my novel in theological terms," Pasternak explained to Andreyev Carlisle. "Nothing is further removed from my understanding of the world. One must live and write restlessly, with the help of the new reserves that life offers. I am weary of this notice of faithfulness to a point of view at all cost."

Pasternak died of lung cancer at his dacha at the writers' colony on May 30, 1960 at the age of seventy, a few months after 29-year old Olga Andreyev Carlisle had traveled there from the U.S. to interview him.

Only a short notice about his death appeared in the local papers, yet four thousand mourners attended his funeral. The poet, who had been silenced by the Soviet government and whose real-life mistress had been imprisoned, never saw his novel appear in print on Russian bookshelves, even though at the time the book was completed, it had represented Pasternak's first major creative work after twenty-five years of non-publishing.

It took thirty years—until 1988—before *Doctor Zhivago* was finally authorized to appear in Russian bookshops. American filmgoers had long ago stopped talking about the movie, and two generations came and went without hearing much about Boris Pasternak's literary legacy and of the moral courage it took to write his novel.

I am standing outside of Pasternak's dacha in Peredelkino with my close friend Igor and his sister, Olga. Pasternak's former home has been operated as a state museum since 1990 under government approval. The brown and white country home sits behind a green iron fence, nestled under tall firs and evergreens. Twelve symmetrical bay windows wrap around the dacha's curvy structure on the first and second floors, giving the building a slight nautical flair.

The museum's atmosphere is more subdued than I expected—no commercial signage to mark it, no concrete parking lot, no glass ticket window, no multi-media kiosks or balalaika folk music piped in for background. Most of the writer's home remains exactly as he left it when he died. We pass through the kitchen door, which today serves as the museum's entrance. On Sundays when he held open house—as was the literary custom of the day—the poet greeted his guests through this same kitchen door.

I follow Igor through the first floor, admiring the framed charcoal drawings that Pasternak's father made of Tolstoy, Rachmaninoff, Scriabin, and other artistic celebrities. Fresh pink roses, cover the crisp white duvet on the bed where the writer slept. Olga says museum visitors often bring remembrance flowers.

The matronly interpreter speaks to a guests in drone-like tones about the poet's life, reeling off historical facts. Igor signals to me that we should sneak out of the docent's mini lecture, and we hurry upstairs to the second floor. Olga nods gently and smiles when she sees us skirt the tour group and quietly leave the room.

The second floor is also open to the public, and when we arrive via the narrow, wooden staircase. We are alone in Pasternak's study. Igor points to a desk and tells me it's where the poet sat while writing *Doctor Zhivago*. He wants to snap a photo of me at Pasternak's desk before any meddling tour guide catches us. I stop for a second to peek out the study's window. The writer must have spent half his life staring out this window toward the empty field across the narrow lane.

From this desk, perhaps, Boris Leonidovich wrote his letters to Anna Akhmatova. Pasternak, while still on the board of the Union of Soviet Writers, had refused to attend a meeting in which Akhmatova was to be officially renounced. For this, Pasternak was expelled from the board, according to Elaine Feinstein, Akhmatova's biographer, and in spite of the obvious danger to himself, Pasternak generously gave the her 1,000 rubles which she desperately needed. He also wrote to Stalin on behalf of his fellow poet asking him to release her son Lev from imprisonment in a labor camp.

A few books are displayed on Pasternak's bookcase, the *Collected Poetry of Robert Frost*, poetry by Dylan Thomas, and plays by Shakespeare. In *Voices in the Snow*, Andreyev Carlisle writes that after several meals and walks, Boris Leonidovich mentioned his admiration for the work of American writers, especially William Faulkner. Like Thomas Merton, he also confessed something else—how much he missed his privacy. Pasternak said, "Everyday life has grown very complicated for me. It must be so everywhere for a well-known writer, but I am unprepared for this role. I don't like a life deprived of secrecy and quiet."

"I love my life and am happy with it," Pasternak continued. "I do not need extra gilding for it. I cannot conceive of a life that has no secrecy, no privacy, a life lived in the crystalline glitter of a display window."

I'm reminded of a scene from *Doctor Zhivago*, in which Yurii talks about Pushkin, reminiscing about how proud the beloved Pushkin was about being of the middle class.

Yurii complains about the pompous, high-flown rhetoric being spoken during the present revolutionary fervor, "the building of the new world" and the "torch-bearers for mankind." Yurii paraphrases Pushkin, "My greatest wish—a quiet life, and a big bowl of cabbage soup."

As a famous writer, Pasternak desired to live a more monk-like existence, like his literary friend Thomas Merton. But, he died before he found that solitude.

Igor smiles and directs me once more, "*Katya, pozhaluista*—please sit for a moment at Pasternak's desk."

"Maybe he will send you good inspiration," Igor says. And so I nervously follow his wishes. The oak desk is bare except for a small lamp with a very yellowing, cracked shade. I move the heavy wooden chair and then carefully lower myself to sit at Pasternak's desk with my red leather journal opened and with a pen in my trembling hand. I whisper his name, *Boris Leonidovich Pasternak*. The great poet lived here and wrote here, in this study, in *this* place. He is buried in the village cemetery, a kilometer or two down the road. At his grave two simple words appear under his name: *Ne zabud*—don't forget!

I hear the *click-click* of Igor's camera as my mind flashes back to my Pittsburgh birthplace and to my Russian experiences in Alaska. I recall the gold and blue onion-domed churches I'd visited and photographed around the state—St. Michael's in Sitka, the Russian Orthodox church in the Old Town part of Kenai—the small, white, church on top of a hill in Ninilchik, and the little wooden church at Eklutna, the same one Thomas Merton visited and photographed near Eagle River.

I am an American sitting at Pasternak's desk and I have cherished Russian friends with me. We are freely and openly enjoying this moment in one another's company. No one is spying on us, and we have nothing to be frightened about.

This is *life*, as Pasternak saw it, life streaming forward, life streaming back, past lives redefining new ones. The Cold War is over. The Soviet Union is gone. The spirit behind *Doctor Zhivago* lives. I became an Alaskan but then after a time, I also became something of a Russian—inside.

We are all poets here caught in the wild enchantment of life.

Igor quickly snaps another photograph, but the museum guide senses we're up to mischief. A heavy-set docent enters the study to check on our whereabouts and finds me seated at Pasternak's desk holding a pen. "*Nyet, nyet!*" she shouts with her fingers pointed, her face turning red, her black pumps hitting the wooden floor with brute force.

I jump to my feet as if this woman is some kind of 1930s prison guard shouting an order to us behind the bars. Without a pause, Igor apologizes in Russian for my inappropriate behavior, my poor foreign manners, and assures her I am a "sister from the north," a harmless tourist from old Russian-America. My face turns red. This is Russia. What gives me, the careless American, the right to blatantly break the rules? How dare I think I can take a seat at the great writer's desk with my red leather journal in-hand.

We dash into another room, where we find a grand piano, hand-embroidered pillows, and an oval mirror before moving into the room in which Pasternak spent his last days and where he died. Near the exit door, stacks of coffee table books are for sale—Pasternak biographies, souvenir poetry collections, and plenty of editions of *Doctor Zhivago*.

We exit the museum the same way we entered, through Pasternak's kitchen door and start walking down the driveway toward the unpaved country lane where Igor parked his car.

As soon as we're outdoors, Olga lights up a Virginia Slim. After chiding me for almost getting us thrown in the gulag, Igor suddenly bends down and stoops low to the ground. Olga and I cast confused looks at him kneeling over the damp grass. Igor carefully moves clumps of soil, pushes grass blades apart, inspecting it as if he might have dropped a small object and needed to find it.

Digging fingers down into the damp earth, he continues searching without saying a word. Olga looks at me and shrugs her shoulders as we patiently wait until he's ready to tell us what he's doing.

"Katya, here, you must take this," Igor says.

He gently cups a seedling, no more than four inches tall, in the palm of his hand.

"It's a little Russian birch tree," Igor says smiling. "Our mother, Lydia, will keep it in water for you until you are ready to leave Moscow. Think of it, Katya! You will plant this in your Alaskan yard, and someday you will have a Pasternak tree. And you will remember Russia this way."

I promise him I will plant my Pasternak birch tree under Alaska's long July sun.

Pasternak's Tree

...I went to bed like a good little monk at eight o'clock but could not sleep. Arm hurting, back hurting, heart empty and desolate. I lay there thinking. And thinking some more. Obsessed with the idea that M. might conceivably find her way out here though she has never seen the place and could not possibly find it in the dark, etc. If only there were a soft knock at the door and I opened it and she was standing on the porch...

—Thomas Merton's journal, June 19, 1966

...I cannot regard this as 'just an episode.' It is a profound event in my life and one that I will have entered deeply into my heart to alter and transform my whole climate of thought and experience. In her, I now realize I had found something, someone, that I had been looking for all my life. I know that she feels the same about me...

—Thomas Merton's journal, June 22, 1966

13 Prelude to Merton's Alaska Journey

After I ran off to Kentucky—while Michael took that much-needed break from the cold, snow, and winter darkness—my obsession with Merton continued. Michael and I weren't communicating much beyond day-to-day routines, mainly because it was the monk who was eating away my time and whatever mental focus and concentration I had. The synchronicities started to add up. Internally, I was getting somewhere with Merton and I didn't want to quit.

Life was not arbitrary and haphazard, nor could it be reduced to science. If humans might be inclined to long for an essence of the Divine, then that longing had to originate from something other than chemical reactions, hallucinatory drugs, or wishful thinking.

Every heart hungers. And wants to feel there are real and intrinsic forces that can help us combat the indifferent universe. That we are more than the proverbial sum of our parts—blood, bone, flesh.

So I stuck with Merton. Not because I hoped for some sort of mystical experience or a religious epiphany. I clung to him because he made a lot of sense to me.

He defied the image of the soft spoken, scraggly-bearded monk in a tattered robe, frayed leather sandals and dirty toenails. Thomas Merton was more like a spiritual torpedo.

He became my alter-ego, the mirror to my own hang-ups and imperfections. In the wild goose chase to know my own soul, I made false starts and took wrong turns. It was easy to blame my inner malaise and confusion on the world today. The twenty-first century was not giving any respite from political lies and violence. In Merton, I heard a friendly, lyrical voice, but also a voice full of compassion and insight about life's complexities and paradoxes in knowing one's true self in relation to God.

Writing became more urgent in my life. It seemed something similar happened to Merton after his Columbia days—the growing need to return to writing. Merton sat down in the Abbey of Gethsemani with pen and paper, and strongly encouraged by his Abbot, began a dialogue with his past, which became the *The Seven Storey Mountain*. He described his prideful youth and young adulthood and the all the "stupid" phases he passed through. It was his past, in all its conflicts and tensions, that laid the foundation for his writing.

He didn't want to wall off his past. He confronted it and asked the big questions.

I had questions of my own. Who was I? Why did it seem I was paying more attention to Thomas Merton than to my husband? What kind of interior life did I really have?

Our inner nature is formed by those memories, images, experiences, landscapes, environments, words read, words spoken, all the reactions and intonations we've accumulated about where we've gone, what smells we've detected, what bells we've heard, what verses uttered—what cold rain has fallen hard on our arms.

Rhymes, songs, tones, connect our personal narratives to something greater. Maybe there *was* a Holy Spirit leading me to a sense of liberty and inner freedom. Mary Oliver's "Wild Geese" gave me hope.

> You do not have to be good.
> You do not have to walk on your knees for a
> hundred miles through the desert repenting.
> You only have to let the soft animal of your body
> love what it loves.
> Tell me about despair, and I will tell you mine.

> Meanwhile the world goes on.
> Meanwhile the sun and the clear pebbles of the rain are moving across the landscapes, over the prairies and the deep trees, the mountains and the rivers.
> Meanwhile the wild geese, high in the clean blue air, are heading home again.
> Whoever you are, no matter how lonely, the world offers itself to your imagination, calls to you like the wild geese, harsh and exciting— over and over announcing your place in the family of things.

Merton's politically active friends tried to persuade him to be more engaged in the political goings on of the day. Thomas Merton, known in the monastery as Father Louis, could not participate in peace marches or other demonstrations. But through his writings he protested. He criticized and bemoaned the growing barbarism of the times. In his book *Disputed Questions* (1960), Father Louis confronted Christianity and totalitarianism. *Peace In the Post Christian Era* (1962) was banned by the Church for calling into question the Church's weak moral code on war. *Contemplation in a World of Action* (1964) attempted to reconcile monastic silence with the need to be in the public sphere. *Gandhi on Non-Violence* (1965) contextualized Gandhi through a contemporary lens. *Raids on the Unspeakable* (1966) explored Merton's nearly militant concern with the critical situation of man in the world. *Conjectures of a Guilty Bystander* (1966) shared reflections on diverse authors— from Dietrich Bonhoeffer to Gandhi and Karl Barth.

Despite the censorship of his work, and the trouble he had with his superiors, he did occasionally send controversial excerpts of mimeographed letters to his inner circle. As the poet and writer Kathleen Norris said, "poets and monastics are nice to have around until they're asked to be taken seriously."

The more words Merton set down, the more he realized that one day, there would be *no more words*. The constant questioning and hyper-intellectualizing that brought him satisfaction, and kept him in touch with so many diverse individuals, also took its toll. He craved a more ideal solitude—to be a real hermit rather than the half hermit he was. If he were to enter into a deeper state of solitude and contemplation, the incessant writing would have to stop. And so would the trifles and talking and distractions.

Over the course of his 27 years at the monastery, he was rarely able to participate in sanctioned overnight trips outside the monastery's walls. Most trips were for various medical appointments in Louisville, and a few brief meetings, including one in New York to meet the famous Zen master, D.T. Suzuki when Suzuki was in his nineties. As a Trappist in the strict and austere Cistercian Order, it's not as if Merton could ask his superiors for special permission to travel to Cincinnati for the weekend. And without any money of his own, all travel would have to be sponsored. He did little traveling outside of Kentucky until the later years of his life.

Merton continued to struggle with balancing his public literary identity with his monastic and spiritual life. As far back as 1949, only one year after his autobiography became a smash hit, he wrote, "Maybe I am finished as a writer. Far from disturbing me, the thought made me glad. Nothing seems so foolish as to go on writing merely because people expect you to write. Not that I have nothing to say, but fame makes me inarticulate. Anyway, I certainly find it extremely difficult to believe in myself as a poet."

"I realize more and more," he said, "that what really matters to me is meditation—and whatever creative work really springs from it."

He often found himself running to the infirmary for various ailments such as intestinal problems, bursitis, bad skin, the flu. He admitted in his journals that he liked to break away from his responsibilities, which meant he was grateful to be sent to the infirmary for much-needed serenity. He had lots of trouble settling his mind and was a chronic insomniac. On this, we were identical twins.

But in the years that followed, either by correspondence or in personal meetings and gatherings, he became like a tourist attraction, a commodity, a product, a cottage industry. And as one of America's famous religious celebrities, everybody wanted a piece of him.

"How much precious time and energy I have wasted," he complained, "in the last three years, doing things that have nothing whatever to do with my real purposes and which only frustrate and confuse me. It is a wonder I haven't lost my vocation to solitude by trifling and evasion."

Part of Father Louis' wishes for more solitary time came true. He was allowed to spend a few hours in an abandoned tool shed on the monastery's property. And he later stole some moments of solitude to write poetry in a trailer left behind by a construction crew. But the real difference came in 1965 when the extroverted monk became an "official" Cistercian hermit at the Abbey of Gethsemani.

Merton received special permission from his Abbot to live in a small cinder block house with a covered, concrete porch—a cottage he affectionately called Our Lady of Carmel.

This structure would be referred to as his hermitage.

Father Louis moved full time into the somewhat crude cottage on August 25, 1965. It still lacked running water, electricity, and an indoor bathroom and had few pieces of furniture. He walked to the Abbey for water, which he carried back in jugs to his hermitage. He took his noonday meals at the monastery where he also retrieved his fan mail. His *hermit-hood* was eventually eased by the addition of modern conveniences—electricity, a bathroom, and an added small room that served as a mini-chapel with a cedar altar where Merton could pray and offer sacraments. Though furnished sparsely with a twin bed and a small table near the fireplace used as a desk, Merton was nonetheless ecstatic to enter into his new, blessed sanctuary.

Instead of moving toward more asceticism, however, the increased dose of solitude meant he only added to his social network and over stimulated his fertile yet overtaxed mind by writing more. As a secluded monk, he still retained strong outgoing tendencies. His need to be loved and to maintain real human contact continually caught him in social snares.

In other words, he wanted to be a hermit and eat his hermit's cake, too.

At his little house in the woods, Merton received many visitors from far and wide and went on short picnics with Kentucky friends and admirers. Friend Tommie O'Callahan whose husband and brood considered Merton a member of their "Louisville" family were among his visitors, and helped arrange the logistics when Merton needed to leave the abbey. He hosted daytime visits from Joan Baez and the poet Denise Levertov. Kentucky poet-farmer, Wendell Berry, whom he greatly admired, also visited. Merton's fans affectionately described him as the "relentless woodpecker" for how many typewriter ribbons he went through. He corresponded with professors, theologians, rabbis, Jacques Maritain, Thich Nhat Hanh the young Vietnamese Buddhist monk, Eric Fromm, Dorothy Day, Rachel Carson, students and teachers.

People close to him showered him with goodies—tea, rolls of film for his 35-mm camera, and more free books he was running out of room to store. Occasionally, he was driven into town to do a little shopping to buy a John Coltrane album or beer.

Besides Boris Pasternak, he wrote Henry Miller, James Baldwin, Czeslaw Milosz, Walker Percy, Louis Zukovsky, and William Carlos Williams. He felt a special closeness to Hispanic poets. Merton wrote a "Message to Poets," which he mailed to a 1964 gathering of "new" Latin-American poets in Mexico City for an informal international conference. Most of the Latino poets were poor and could hardly afford to be in Mexico City. Someone read the message on the monk's behalf. It was later included in *Raids on the Unspeakable*.

Merton, the poet, knew the time had come to dispense with so many words.

> It is the businessman, the propagandist, the politician, and not the poet, who devoutly believes in the 'magic of words'. For the poet, there is no magic," Merton said, echoing Pasternak.
>
> There is only life in all its unpredictability and all its freedom. All magic is a ruthless venture in manipulation, a vicious circle, a self-fulfilling prophecy...."

As he approached age 50, and because of his international fame, he enjoyed the liberties of excursions to nearby Bardstown or Louisville. He was a rock star among monks, one with his own New York City literary agent, who had single-handedly created a new and steady revenue stream for the Abbey of Gethsemani.

Every week, as Master of Scholastics, the monk prepared lectures for whomever in the community wanted to attend. Sometimes he gave retreat talks to the nuns at the nearby Sisters of Loreto convent twelve miles from the Abbey.

He was the founding editor for a small circulation literary journal called *Monk's Pond*. The hermit of Gethsemani had already solicited poetry and essays from Mark Van Doren, Charles Simic, Czeslaw Milosz, Hayden Carruth and Carlos Reyes. In one editor's note, Merton stated, "The purpose of this magazine is to publish a few issues devoted to poetry and to some unusual prose and then to go out of business."

The years immediately preceding his Alaska journey proved to be more emotionally trying and heart-wrenching for Father Louis than all his previous years at the monastery.

A story unfolded which shed a different light on the events and context leading up to his 1968 world trek and Alaska sojourn.

Merton, the man—the man stripped of his monastic identity, his international reputation as an intellectual and writer, his pedagogical duties and responsibilities, the man who stood truly naked before God, in the flesh as well as in the spirit, exposed with all his weaknesses, fears, and human desires—this imperfect man at age 51 fell in love.

> ...I cannot regard this as 'just an episode.' It is a profound event in my life and one that I will have entered deeply into my heart to alter and transform my whole climate of thought and experience. In her, I now realize I had found something, someone, that I had been looking for all my life. I know that she feels the same about me...
>
> —Thomas Merton's journal, June 22, 1966

Celibate monks were supposed to strictly adhere to their vows, foregoing sexual relations with the opposite sex or with other men. Talking openly about sex was also taboo. The way I thought of it, monks were used to hiding their manliness and physiques under their monastic garb. Without all the sexual distractions and desires that "ordinary" people experience, a lot of journals can be filled and verses written.

Merton became a Catholic convert at age 23 and by age 26 was avowed to being a Trappist monk precisely when testosterone and sexual thoughts were more a driving force in a young man's life, when sexual impulses and fantasies raced through masculine minds multiple times a day.

How much dogged discipline, how much self-sacrifice in suppressing the body's biological and erotic desires, must it have taken, to do that?

And what about all those bespectacled nuns with their strange, metaphorical language about being "brides of God" who enter convents and supposedly stop dreaming or thinking about sex for the rest of their lives? How were these women able to suppress their desires for intimate male companionship and to deny their biological urges for motherhood?

As I delved into Merton's life story, the rules about celibacy, especially for men and women in their twenties, was beyond my understanding.

In 1966, two years before arriving in Alaska, after some major back problems involving a damaged disc, Father Louis was sent to a Louisville hospital for surgery. While convalescing after surgery, Merton fell passionately in love with a 24-year-old student nurse who tended to him at the hospital.

He was not an "old" wounded, hurting, and balding man of 51, but a man who still attracted female attention. The student nurse was bright and talkative. She enjoyed innocently flirting with him. Merton had spent time with female friends, had corresponded with many females—academics, and editors—and conversed regularly with the Sisters of Loreto nuns. It must have been a breath of fresh air for Merton to offer seminars and talks to nuns, as the student body at St. Bonaventure's, where he taught immediately before becoming a monk, was all-male, as was the Abbey.

The student nurse, less than half his age, was described by Merton as having long dark hair and gray eyes. The patient was caught completely off-guard by his sudden affections for "M." When Merton first made notations about this twenty-something on the pages of his journal in 1966 and 1967, he referred to her only as "M." Years later it was publicly revealed that "M" was for Margie—Margie and Fr. Louis.

She saw past his age, his aches, pains, weak muscles, medications, and plain clothes, and relished any chance she had to talk with him. She understood that his confined, restricted lifestyle made him appear a bit "out of it" when it came to popular culture, but still, for a monk she admired how much he knew. Merton knew who Bob Dylan and the Beatles were, and wasn't that far behind the times.

The emotional involvement and sexual arousal Margie caused astonished the monk. It was like a long-neglected and frozen side of his basic humanity rapidly thawed.

As his feelings developed for this young nurse, he forgot about being the acclaimed teacher, monk, scholar, writer, and religious intellectual—he was simply a man.

I imagined that Merton, and surely any monk supposedly living an obedient, pure, chaste existence had at times been awakened in the middle of the night by vivid sexual dreams. Merton must have had memories about girls of long ago he and Robert Lax knew at Columbia, or the girls they might have met in Bradford, Pennsylvania and Olean, New York when they hung out at the Lax family cottage there in the summers of 1939 and 1940 trying to write the Next Great American novel. If he had any sexual dreams while living as a monk in a Trappist community of up to 200 men, he might have recalled a former sweetheart, a woman whose breasts and lips he once touched on a date in New York. There must have been moments like these when Merton, the studious one working alone under the lamp at his hermitage, glanced up from his French philosophy book because his mind drifted off to a tender moment with a woman. Or maybe he had an innocent thought or two about some young nun he recently met who, unknowingly to the nun, had made a strong and cherished impression on him.

Then as quickly as these memories entered his mind under the lamplight, he willfully banished them. He picked up his pencil again and went back to jotting reams of notes on a book about Buddhism he was reading. Merton (and many men I imagined) could not, or chose not to vocalize such personal thoughts about how much the female touch was missed.

Ironically, the pretty nurse-in-training who captured his heart had once considered becoming a nun. Margie was a former member of the Sisters of Charity of Nazareth community located 14 miles from the Abbey of Gethsemani. I spoke to a member of the Sisters of Charity of Nazareth, a woman who entered her religious life there at age 18 and who is now retired from her work as a hospital chaplain. She verified that when she was a novice in 1960, Margie was in her class, and she was a serious-minded young woman. Sometime around 1963, she guessed, Margie left the convent to pursue nursing as a vocation. She remembered Margie as being "petite, under five feet two inches, very bright, with beautiful features, like China doll." She further described her as "vivacious, and a quick learner, able to catch things, to pick up on things about other people."

As an apostolic mission, the Sisters of Charity perform community and ministry work outside the convent. The very active, work-oriented order was founded by pioneer women of Kentucky in 1812, before the Abbey of Gethsemani was established in 1848. The Sisters started teaching, established schools for girls, cared for the sick, and helped immigrant children who arrived as orphans at Louisville's river ports. Once the Vatican II reforms got underway, the Sisters moved into fuller roles in the church by renewing the charisms of their community. The Sisters of Charity of Nazareth "promote the dignity and equality of women and other oppressed peoples in church and in society," as their website stated.

Margie, intelligent and much younger than Merton, was clearly smitten with her new patient whose warmth, charm and garrulous nature made and instant and lasting connection.

Margie detected something profound in him, an intangible quality unlike other men she had known. For Merton, her warm smile, and the barrage of questions she sincerely asked him about his work, his teaching, the books he read, brought a spark of vigor to the bed-ridden monk—something that chopping piles of wood or finishing another poetry manuscript simply could not match.

The monk appreciated Margie's spiritual depth as well as her femininity. A quarter century has passed in his monastic life, but he didn't have it all worked out with the feminine, or with who women really were in his life. If any female could break through the emotional and physical walls, challenge him and be a revelation to him, it was Margie. She awakened the divine feminine as something beyond a concept or abstraction. Perhaps for the first time, Thomas Merton, the man, felt the special dimension of the divine feminine as something tangible, forceful, and sacred.

My fantasies took over. I put myself in that hospital room imagining how he responded to the lightness of Margie's fingers on his forehead as she dabbed him with a warm wash cloth, how he felt himself tremble inside when she came close and massaged his lower back or propped him up slightly with more pillows. She purposely arranged her hospital schedule to snatch any extra minutes she could with him, just as I would have done for the opportunity to converse with such a learned man. I envisioned her leaning over him and reaching across his chest, how the hairs on his arm caught a tingle from her skin. How his hands grew warmer and more blood rushed to his groin, while he tried hard to hide the perspiration increasing on his temple and palms, the red color flushing his face. How he enjoyed her calming, non-anxious demeanor, the frequency of her smiles, and the whiff of lavender or jasmine he smelled in her shiny, shampooed hair.

In his erotic attraction, he couldn't help but turn his eyes to the curve of her hips, to her small firm breasts under her crisp uniform, and to the white lace of her slip that might have accidentally hung a bit below the hemline. When Margie moved a certain way, he heard the soft swoosh of her uniform brushing against her white nylon stockings, and he probably closed his eyes for a second or two as he listened to her softly humming while she performed her basic medical duties. Or when she was asking him questions about one of his latest books, I'm sure he tried as hard as he could to remember the precise details about the inflections of her voice. He wanted to make a sonic imprint of her quick movements, her stride, her spirited nature.

I imagined Margie sidling into his room, upbeat and happy, saying, "Good morning Father Louis, how are you today? May I do anything for you?" Margie might have straightened the bed linens, and on her way out, glanced at his chart. "I'll be back to check in on you a little later, maybe bring you today's paper."

As her eyes locked with his blue eyes, "M," too, could feel herself grow weak and light-headed and moist. She felt his gaze upon her, how he could not stop following her graceful, feminine shapeliness. Fr. Louis blushed. She looked his way and innocently smiled back. And they both knew how much they wanted one another.

It had been almost three decades since he had had the chance to look at a woman as intensely and as vulnerably. In my fantasy, she brought him extra glasses of water and more daily newspapers and towels than were necessary, one excuse after another to remain star-struck by his formidable, superior mind, but more so, to be embraced by the warmth and aura he naturally exuded with men and women of all backgrounds. She wanted to listen to his voice, too, as much as possible, a voice that turned excitable, sometimes too professorial, and often passionate, and one that sounded like none other. Any chance to feel his eyes move up and down and over her body drew out long-dormant feelings, or maybe certain feelings that had for the first time in her womanhood been expressed. Her whole body was alive with new sensations and energy, as if to tell her that yes, this is what a woman was supposed to feel like when right, loving emotions and physical joy combined in one union. She responded completely, as if every minute that passed with him was another sun-drenched, spring day.

In "M's" nervousness, her hands shook slightly as she flitted about the room tidying up the magazines and rearranging the tissue boxes, when there was no real mess to worry about. She enjoyed Merton's good humor and laughter, the way he genuinely emitted affection and interest as if she were the only woman in the world, and the two of them could pretend they were truly alone.

I pictured them comfortable with one another, appreciative, and confident that in the erotic tension they both intuitively felt, and without needing to speak a word about it, that something life-changing was happening between them.

An ordinary event—a medical problem for a bad back and a trip to the hospital brought them together. But it wasn't accidental; it was fate, perhaps. Age mattered not. Through some mystery and grace they found and challenged each other.

The experience of the complicated, short-lived, but very powerful liaison deeply moved Thomas Merton. Once he recovered from back surgery, he and Margie made clandestine phone calls, which monastic rules forbade him to do. He had the trusted confidence of friends who helped him and "M" meet at the Louisville airport or at borrowed private offices, or whenever he had another medical check-up. They sneaked away for picnics in the woods and they wrote letters to one another. Their affair wasn't anything tawdry or salacious; it was real.

Margie rekindled the poet in Merton. He had always written poetry but now instead of experimenting with surrealism and veering off into over-intellectualization in his verse, he began composing love poems. Over the course of their encounters, which lasted for about six months, Merton composed a cycle of 18 poems, most of them dedicated to or inspired by Margie. He shared a few of his love poems with Joan Baez when she came to visit. To protect his privacy, he sent copies of his poems to James Laughlin for safekeeping. At Merton's request, Laughlin, maintained the "Margie" poems in a confidential folder at New Directions dubbed "The Menendez File." This way, superiors would think the poems were translations he was working on, and it was also part of a private joke between Merton and Laughlin that the file was labeled Menendez.

I found this stanza from one of the poems he wrote. It comes from "For M. on a Cold Grey Morning:"

> A grey good morning and rain and melting snow
> Far from any help. Or love, I am warmer
> At least wanting you…

In another poem, "Aubade on a Cloudy Morning," he mentioned being at war with his own heart. (An aubade is a musical composition or love song to be played or sung early in the morning.)

Margie filled an emotional chasm, one he didn't recognize in himself even though he had always been enthusiastic about women. In *Day of a Stranger*, Merton wrote,

> "All monks, as is well known, are unmarried, and hermits more unmarried than the rest of them. Not that I have anything against women. I see no reason why a man can't love God and a woman at the same time. If God was going to regard women with a jealous eye, why did he go and make them in the first place? There is a lot of talk about married clergy. Interesting. So far there has not been a great deal said about married hermits. Well, anyway, I have a place full of ikons of the Holy Virgin."

Learning about his love affair stopped me in my tracks. How could he have let things get so out of hand? It further showed me that monks did not live quiet, undisturbed, and "simple" lives. A monk was not immune to the heart's struggles. With his open mindedness, vitality, and infinite curiosity about all people, he willingly allowed himself to be vulnerable with Margie.

The monk who had heretofore spoken so eloquently about finding one's truest nature, connecting to one's deepest, most authentic core, the self that society doesn't paint on, was the monk who still hadn't gotten down to the essence of it—what *love* is.

When he spent time or thoughts on Margie, he no longer fought against fundamental physical impulses and desires, but allowed those biological urges to be expressed. The sexual attraction greatly energized his fatigued self. As the relationship blossomed, he knew it beheld something special beyond carnal knowledge. It was as if a new life force and sensation breathed into him. And from what I could determine, he did not use the word "sin" when writing about his conflicted feelings over the student nurse and the attendant physical aspects of love she suddenly stirred up.

As a scholarly monk, with a number of ailments—vows or no vows—her presence and interest alone flattered him tremendously. The romantic in him begged for metaphorical and physical expression. And the emotions he started to feel after such a long absence both re-ignited and rattled him.

Merton did not keep the affair entirely hush-hush. Eventually he confessed his romantic feelings to his Reverend Father Dom James Fox, the administrative head of Gethsemani. The Abbot showed Merton great empathy and compassion over the stress-filled dilemma. He was aware of Merton's conflicted feelings, that he might be questioning his vocation to remain a monk, and he knew how emotionally torn and despondent he was over his feelings for "M."

Though he fell in love, Merton ended it with Margie before everything got too messy and out of control. Speculation remains to this day about whether or not they engaged in intercourse. Maybe they did; maybe they didn't. What did all this mean to me, though? It told me Merton might have been the most mixed-up monk to have ever walked the grounds of the abbey of Our Lady of Gethsemani since its founding in 1848.

It also added an important and overlooked dimension about his mental state of mind as he undertook his world travels in 1968 to Alaska and points beyond.

And the spiritual bond I felt with Merton only grew stronger when I learned about "M" and the special person she was.

He was definitely and as humanly confused as everybody else. His love affair told me that his fasting, disciplined, sleep-deprived body confined so frequently under the guise of his monk's habit and scapular, was still partly a stranger to him, even when he had the luxury of wearing his denim shirts and baggy jeans.

After all his autobiographical reflecting and journaling and writing he did in the monastery, he was still side-swiped by his own vulnerabilities and the impulses of his own physical being. The experience between Merton and the nurse made me reconsider the spiritual connotations of such inhuman abstinence, and led me to more questions about the "Godliness" of physical self-denial.

Before he met and fell in love with Margie, the know-it-all Merton still answered to a false self. Hadn't he purposefully separated his sexual being from his true self, pared it off psychologically, as if the physical body and its sexual feelings no longer existed within himself, the innermost core of who he was before God?

I spent entirely too much time dreaming about Merton and the cycle of poems he wrote for her.

Maybe a part of me projected myself onto Margie. Would I have wanted to picnic with him somewhere in the woods near the Abbey of Gethsemani? Would I have lain with him on a blanket to share a bottle of ice cold Chablis on a hot, stuffy day? Yes, I know I would have. The poet, the romantic, the lover in Merton, had pulled me aside, whispered in my ear, and devastated me.

Up until this time, 1966, Merton believed he had reached the deepest truths about himself. And that was that. But then along came Margie. It was as if Merton had discovered he didn't really know *love* at all.

The effect she had on his heart, psyche, and body—it was all so perplexing. The great intellectual, the world sophisticate, the spiritual guru, and big-time author who lived without the need for a woman's real affection and touch had learned a more important lesson about life and love than he had from all the books crammed into his bookcase at the hermitage.

I admired that Merton gave himself the power and permission to move in this highly personal direction. He emotionally shared a part of himself he'd never really shared with any woman before, except in dismissive, superficial ways. This was something different than the fun and games he had with the women from his past, the parties, the drinking, the laughter, the sexual advancements and diversions, the ways he might have toyed with women before in his New York City college days which he wasn't proud of.

Perhaps this being with Margie and whatever spirit drove him to explore it, was something new, an echo of something holy even, after decades of being wracked with guilt over his past mistakes with other women.

Merton did feel some spirit driving him toward Margie not in the sense that he was necessarily ready to cave in to all the erotic impulses he felt for her, and she for him, or that he could easily and nonchalantly break his vows.

First and foremost, for always, he was called to be a Trappist monk and priest and not a family man. He lamented "What will I be without her? What will she be without me? First of all, we cannot really be without each other anymore. There is something completely permanent and irrevocable in our lives: the love that we have known in each other, that has changed us, that will remain with us in a hidden and transfigured—transfiguring—presence…" (June 23, 1966)

It was Merton who broke it off. A short time before he flew to Alaska, in August 1968, he burned all of M's letters after agonizing and soul-searching about it. He noted in his journal how stupid he had been in 1966. It was time once more to face the important truths and facts about himself and his vocation. There was no doubt the whole experience impacted his monastic life. But he would re-dedicate himself to God with renewed acceptance.

His new clarity was emotionally painful and a great emotional relief all at the same time. Not even the pure and profound love of a woman could cause him to leave his religious order and to stop being a monk whose life was clearly devoted to loving and living alone for God.

The relationship caused Merton to reaffirm his true destiny. He was not meant to be anyone's husband or lover. The life of a solitary and future hermit was the life for him.

He loved her, no doubt. And this love, he ultimately concluded, wasn't something to be sinfully ashamed of. It was not something to hide from or to deny. He didn't journal about the seductive, evil powers of women and blame "M" for leading him on. It was real love, not a casual erotic fling in the Kentucky grass. One human being loving another. One open heart made more aware of the beauty in the world by another experiencing the same.

Their relationship, though they never spent an entire day and night together, reoriented Merton in ways he never expected.

The way I started to think of it, his relationship was a gift from God that taught him to no longer question or doubt his purpose. It gave him pause to think more about the silliness and trivial nonsense of his past, his wanting to be widely admired by people as a great novelist or poet, his wanting to build a vast fan club and be thought of as someone important.

In a moment of deep reflection, on November 1, 1966, he sorted out his thoughts:

> How evident it becomes now that this whole thing with M. was, in fact, an attempt to escape the demands of my vocation. Not consciously, certainly, but a substitution of human love (and erotic love after all) for a special covenant with loneliness and solitude, which is the very heart of my vocation.
>
> I did not stand the test at all but allowed the whole essence to be questioned and tried to change it. I could not see that I was doing this. Fortunately, God's grace protected me from the worst errors…I think I am gradually getting back.

Beginning December 10, 1941, the day he first crossed the monastery's threshold, he had chosen the right course all along. All roads led him to Gethsemani monastery and to his inner journey dedicated to loving God.

But the irony was because of an "outside of the monastery" relationship, through a woman's genuine love and affection, that he could now be most true to himself.

> I know our love affair is over and there is no point trying to keep it alive. Certainly, I miss her, but one has to face facts," he wrote. "I am humbled

and confused by my weakness, my vulnerability, my passion. After all these years, so little sense and so little discipline. Yet I know there was good in it somewhere, nevertheless." (March 5, 1967)

He knew Margie loved him. She was tragically full of passion, wide-open, he said. She wasn't teasing him, trying to see how far she could use her feminine wiles to tempt a religious man. She did not want him to stray from or abandon his work. Most importantly, she wasn't, in any kind of tabloid fashion, trying to capitalize on his fame and reputation and hasn't to this day.

Thomas Merton would go on being a monk. As he readied for his Alaska journey and all the other unique places he planned to see, more than ever before, he was ready to be a pilgrim and a seeker. The brief, intense love they shared better prepared him to do so. It gave him fresher insights about what it means to be human. As a human being, as a man, as a thinker, and as a writer, he grew.

To this day, no one knows how crushed Margie was after their prohibited phone calls, meetings, correspondences, and poems written for her stopped. She moved away and took a job in Ohio, and supposedly married well, and bore children. I have tried imagining her life now. I wonder, did she keep Merton books on her shelf? Whatever feelings she still possessed, out of respect for her husband and family, she kept them close to her heart. She refused to say much about her youthful encounters with the religious celebrity. She might have burned all Merton's letters and poems, too. If alive, she must be approaching eighty years old. To my knowledge, she has remained unwilling to officially go on record about the affair. In today's celebrity obsessed culture when it's standard practice to cash in and sell life stories as media products, to her credit, this shy, mysterious woman has maintained personal integrity. She's never written a single book, gone on a talk show, or tried to profit in any way. Supposedly, she's granted only one interview since Merton's death and was so very disappointed by the reporter's account she's not been seen nor heard in the media again.

How much was Merton still dreaming about "M" once his plans for global adventuring fell into place? There must have been plenty of moments when the memory of her, the experience of knowing her and maturely loving her, invigorated him. The world was chaotic and falling apart in 1968, all the more reason why he'd want to keep her close, not purposely try and erase the whole interlude from his mind. How could he pretend it was nothing, that as a monk, he had temporarily lost his way? For Merton, it was a real and true love, given freely and without any other expectation, wants, or needs than to give and to receive love.

In the silence of the hermitage, his thoughts must have naturally turned to Margie, the memory of how passionately they kissed in the sun on that mossy bank next to the trickling brook. How closely they held one another and perfectly entwined their arms. How they made each hurried, flashing moment in Kentucky feel like an eternity.

And when Thomas Merton finally got to Alaska in September 1968, Margie's spirit went with him through the distant rains and tallest mountains of his heart.

…The monks work hard to earn a meager living. Wars, revolutions, and iron curtains have cut off their supply of vocations as well as their revenues. And if life in the monasteries themselves is austere, it is all the more so out in the cells and hermitages where men live on the rugged mountainsides in conditions on a level with the those of the poorest of the poor in the Balkan countries.

—Thomas Merton essay,
"Mount Athos," *Disputed Questions*

14 Igor and the Holy Mountain

In Thomas Merton's day, the rest of America understood the intricacies of the 49th State about as much as they understood the Soviet Union. Alaska was a good place to be sent if you were a member of the U.S. military and had a hankering for a more adventurous assignment, one that provided a chance to catch enormous salmon and halibut and hunt moose.

Alaska was typically seen as a remote and frozen wasteland, on par with Murmansk, a costly place to live, a land of transients and misfits, a cultural backwater, and no place for a Lower 48 woman unless you were searching for a burly man. Besides its staggering mountains and its minerals and fisheries wealth, Alaska didn't have much to recommend it.

But it did have a unique connection to Russia, unlike any other part of America. At an Anchorage downtown bar a few years ago, I laughed to see this Russian proverb printed on the back of the menu, "The church is near, but the road is icy. The tavern is far, but we will walk carefully."

I have in my possession a torn and yellowed copy of the *Moscow News*, vintage November 3, 1962, a gift from a friend and an artifact from the Cold War. Blazing across the front page in bold, red type the Russians proclaimed the 'USSR was a bastion of peace, a bulwark of human happiness." It was shortly after the Cuban Missile Crisis. Two world superpowers, on the brink of a possible nuclear confrontation, had achieved a miraculous resolution without combat and weapons. The Soviets took complete political credit for thwarting the potential nuclear disaster.

According to the *Moscow News*, the world could breathe a sigh of relief "mainly due to the wise action of the Soviet government....The colossal, arrogant military machine of the United States, put in readiness to attack Cuba, had been stopped."

The *Moscow News* also reported on the ongoing celebrations honoring the 45th anniversary of the October Revolution which gave Soviet Russia ample opportunities to tout their latest economic statistics—the millions of tons of steel being produced, the 140 million tons of oil, the new and widespread electric power grids installed in the hinterlands. And there was another important measure of progress: Over 1,600,000 televisions had rolled hot off the Soviet assembly line!

The Russians vocally criticized the U.S. and Western capitalism, believing our rampant materialism had gone too far while they often relied on bloated economic figures to service their propaganda machine. Who was winning the ideological race? Well, the Communists! Their system was truly progressive, a marvel of social and factory engineering. Consumer goods were flowing like the Don!

I hold this 1962 edition of the *Moscow News* dear because it contained another bold proclamation. One Soviet journalist wryly noted, "The erstwhile Russian soul, so popular among literary snobs, was now declared dead."

The mythological, mystical Russian soul, as understood by anachronistic poets and the rest of the "literary snobs" (Merton was one of those literary snobs) was snuffed out of existence. Writers and artists, trapped in pre-Revolutionary nostalgia, had promoted cultural beliefs and historical ideas about *Russian-ness*. In the "Russian soul" was a passionate closeness to Mother Earth and an abiding reverence for God. As an official atheistic state, this type of thinking was dismissed as passé. It was peasant-like and it was politically and socially irrelevant.

"We must go to the Village of Old Believers," my Russian friend Igor insisted one Sunday afternoon while sitting on the couch in my Alaska living room. We were drinking mugs of strong black coffee and trying to figure out how to spend our afternoon.

"Really, Igor? You would rather do this," I said, "than look for mushrooms or fish for kings on the Kenai?" I felt certain he'd prefer another nature outing.

We last saw one another in 2003 on a visit to Moscow when he surprised me with that special excursion to the writer's village of Peredelkino to see Pasternak's country home, and to pay our respects at the nearby cemetery where he was buried in May 1960. I reciprocated his kindness by inviting Igor, his sister Olga and her husband Misha to come to Alaska.

Though the village of Old Believers was about a two-hour drive away from the small town of Soldotna where we lived at the time, I had never been. Unless you were a public school teacher or had other personal ties, most residents had no reason to veer off the main highway to the mysterious religious community of Nikolaevsk (*neek-o-LIE-a-vesk*) located on the southern end of the Kenai Peninsula, not far from Homer, Alaska.

"It's been difficult for Russian Old Believers to keep their identity, culture and traditions alive while migrating around so much," Igor said in his perfect English.

"Nikolaevsk—it symbolizes Russia's deep spiritual roots, and Katya, it is time you learned about this, too."

I'm recalling these memories now, years later, because back then, in the early 2000s, and pre-Thomas Merton, I didn't fully grasp what lay behind Igor's strange request. I was basically agreeing to go to make my friend happy and because I considered myself a student of Russian history.

Listening to Igor that day, it struck me how much had changed in Russia and in the relations between our countries. During the heyday of *perestroika* and *glasnost*, when we were more or less business associates, I fondly recalled the how we often drank chilled shots of *Pshenichnaya* vodka with one another. There was much to discuss—the logistics and plans for the next big trade exhibition, Siberian mining prospects, and inevitably, the Great Patriotic War. His father, Boris Alexandrovich, now in his eighties, was a decorated Hero of the Soviet Union, a World War II army officer. Once on a trip to Moscow, I attended an obligatory Victory Day celebration. I stood on the sidelines blending in as I watched Boris Alexandrovich, tall and proud, walk through Red Square with groups of other aging but distinguished patriots whose long rumpled coats and lapels were covered over with medals and ribbons. Igor often reminded me about the incredible losses and suffering endured by the Russian people, the over 27 million who perished in the war years. He dragged me to every museum in Moscow on his mission to teach me more about this history and to encourage me with my Russian language skills. He passed onto me the Old Russian custom to sit for a moment of silence with comrades and family before embarking on any journey as a kind of prayer and protection.

We never spoke about private religious beliefs. The talk in my living room that day felt completely out-of-character for both of us, drifting, as we were, into new interior territory.

He, as a former member of the Communist Party, now a moustached man in his early 50s, tried explaining where he stood philosophically since 1991 when the USSR had nonviolently dismantled. He said it all boiled down to finding the right way to build the rest of his life.

In post-Cold War Russia, with the introduction of capitalism, Russians were struggling with a drastic drop in wages and living standards as the economy took a severe downward spiral. Much personal and economic chaos ensued. People like Igor were reaching back into the past, trying to combat the despair and malaise. He openly acknowledged the horrible mistakes and miscalculations our governments made. The stereotypes, lies, propaganda, and the war-mongering voices on both sides of the Cold War that had burned into our brains.

I recalled the biting satire of Stanley Kubrick's *Dr. Strangelove* (1966), starring Peter Sellers and George C. Scott. The film mocked burly, vodka-drinking Russians as stupid and dysfunctional. Nikita Khrushchev was portrayed as Premiere "Kiss-off."

American military leaders were rendered as caricatures of rough-riding cowboys eager to deploy nuclear weapons. The film ends with a terrifying scene. Due to a series of military miscommunications and technical mishaps, a sole U.S. Air Force bomber flies under mistaken military orders. The American plane drops a nuclear bomb over its enemy and evil rival. The screen fills with the nightmarish image of the explosion in the form of a giant mushroom cloud. All dialogue stops.

The movie and the "jokes" are over.

"Through prayer and meditation, I hope to feel a *real* part of the world, Katya," Igor said. "I want simple rules, not dogma or collective commandments. These simple rules will give me internal structure to fight exterior instability."

"Well, you're Russian," I said, "so I can certainly understand your problems with stability."

But his face turned rueful and his voice grew serious. "*Simple rules*, Katya. I think there is such a thing to search for. A trip to Nikolaevsk, this may be the only chance to see something of our deep spiritual history in Alaska," he said with some sense of urgency. It was as if the village itself would vanish into the abyss of time if we didn't hurry and experience the remnants of Old Russian culture, alive and well and on display down the road from my home.

"*Ladno, konechno*, okay, of course, we can go to Nikolaevsk," I said without a second thought. His sister Olga followed me into the garage to locate a cooler, retrieve some bottled waters and load up the car."

Yevgeny Yevtushenko (1932-2017), a poet of the Soviet era who visited Alaska in 1966, once described the massive regions of Alaska and Siberia as "unjustly divided twins." For generations, indigenous peoples engaged in cross-border travel, but as the Cold War intensified, those friendly social exchanges were abruptly halted and legally forbidden by J. Edgar Hoover as FBI director in 1948. As the accepted political argument of the day went, borders must be closed to stop the communist menace and to prevent any possible communist infiltration. This was no time for Yup'ik Eskimos to paddle across the

Bering Strait to dance and to drum with their Russky brothers. The stark reality, we were told, was that if the U.S. military didn't try and stop those "God-less commies" from ruling the free world, it would be a terrible mistake, one from which we'd possibly never recover. Our free market economy would be doomed and we'd live like robots on black bread and beets.

With Gorbachev, a new era of grassroots diplomacy and cultural cooperation opened between the Soviet Union and the West, but none more pervasive on a per capita basis than in Alaska. The "Ice Curtain" between Alaska and the Russian Far East had not only thawed, it had melted and disappeared forever into the Bering Sea. I imagine Merton would have been delighted to see those changes. When Aeroflot made its historic first landing in Anchorage in 1989, I worked on the organizing team to help plan the official welcome and itinerary. A planeload of over 200 exuberant Soviets, many of them Soviet dignitaries, arrived in black leather coats and heavy mink hats eager to start business joint ventures with their arctic comrades. I remember business and cultural events surrounding our *Soviet-American Reunion Week* as a time of supreme optimism and hope with boisterous singing and toasting every night, until we were all nauseous and hung over.

Later, I helped organize business trade missions to Russia in the early 1990s as a staffer at the Alaska State Chamber of Commerce, which is how I first met Igor. He held a high level post with a Moscow trade organization, our administrative and logistical partner on the Russian side. Over the years, we stayed in close communication as I continued for personal reasons to travel to Russia. I befriended Igor's family and visited the Moscow flat where his parents, Boris and Lydia, Olga, and her husband Misha lived together.

All my new international experiences led me to examine my own cultural values and assumptions.

Igor and the Holy Mountain

As most people of his generation, Igor was brought up to believe in the brotherly, egalitarian ideals of communism as the one, true salvation of humankind. His family's Party affiliations provided many coveted career opportunities and postings, and chances for foreign travel (the family once lived in Canada where his father worked as an agricultural attaché for the Soviet government). As a young professional, Igor had obediently clung to bureaucratic rules and regulations, had maintained a great deference to titles and central authority. As a functionary, he seemed a master of government paperwork and official speechmaking, a model of success and worldly sophistication. In his current job he was once again fostering international business cooperation. In short, Igor was one of the New Russian muckety-mucks.

But my initial impressions of him, as I came to know, were far from accurate. On the day Igor asked me to go to the Village of Old Believers, I began to see him differently.

In their desire to live closer to God, and away from the corrupting influences of American popular culture, the reclusive Russian Orthodox community, population approximately 300, intentionally shunned the outside world and discouraged any curiosity seekers. For most of Nikolaevsk's forty-plus years of history, the road leading into it was unpaved with a simple hand-painted sign that said "Private Property, Road Closed."

I sometimes encountered Old Believers when out shopping for groceries at Fred Meyer during the 12 years we lived in Soldotna. In winter, Old Believers were easy to spot in a crowd. They didn't look anything like me, a typical, no-frills woman, layered in a Polar fleece vest and hooded jacket, wearing off-the-rack jeans, old Sorel boots.

Old Believer women adhered to strict religious customs—they never wore pants in public, not even in the dead of the spiritually-challenging subarctic winters. In summer, they were not permitted to bare their arms. They wore dainty white anklet socks, long skirts or matronly smocks, mostly handmade, loose fitting, frumpy clothes—clothes that a 19th century farmer's wife might have worn with a type of jumper, called a *sarafan* used as an outer layer. Hairstyles were old European, mostly plaited into two thick braids and pinned up and twisted onto the head, or tucked beneath a *platok*, or head scarf.

As a woman, and putting God's divine mercy aside, I couldn't imagine it. I wouldn't follow any religious dictates about how to style, wear, or cover my hair. I wouldn't let anyone tell me how long or short my skirt should be, how far I should walk behind any man, how many children I ought to bear, or how much skin I was allowed to show a man on a hot, sunny day.

Out-of-state visitors who drove 160 miles from Anchorage to the Kenai River for to sport fish for king salmon weren't quite sure what to make of these costumed people they saw in the produce aisles. They often mistook Old Believers as members of a Slavic dance troupe.

In public places, Old Believers tried not to call attention to themselves. They murmured Russian, as if they felt self-conscious simply by being out shopping for bread and hamburger meat like the rest of us.

I remember seeing a young woman, maybe in her early 20s, walk into the grocery store with two or three small children in tow. With an infant swaddled in one arm, she unloaded her cart in front of me and placed four gallons of milk and various canned goods on the counter while her toddler boy clung to her dress, eyeing the many rows of candy and chewing gum with great temptation. The little boy could no longer resist. He reached for a chocolate bar.

"Nyet, Sasha," his mother said, without raising her voice or slapping his hand as she returned the Snickers Bar to the rack. Children of Old Believers did not throw temper tantrums in the big box grocery stores.

Old Believers bewildered and fascinated me. I saw them as a touchstone, a portal to another dimension of time or reality.

In the eyes of self-righteous Old Believers, I was another lost person living in the midst of a spiritually bankrupt culture.

Igor and the Holy Mountain

In my lukewarm version of Christianity, I was spiritually inert, without a pious or devotional bone in my twenty-first century body.

In the "Summer of Love" in 1967, five Old Believer families from the Willamette Valley in Oregon purchased 640 acres on the Kenai Peninsula. Old Believers worried about the negative effects the volatile 1960s counterculture was having on their children. To help protect their families from the climate of drugs, the sexual messages of the new rock music, the increasing immorality, and the wanton revelry surrounding them, they migrated to Alaska.

Eventually, by the 1980s, the new settlement grew as more Old Believers, many of them skilled craftsmen, arrived to fell trees and hew wood, building permanent dwellings including a small white church and workable commercial fishing boats to catch salmon in Cook Inlet.

Old Believers have a history of taking escape routes. Their origins began as a breakaway sect within Orthodoxy. The religious controversy began centuries before with the Great Schism in the 1600s. Patriarch Nikon sat at the top of the Russian Orthodox Church. As the leading church authority on doctrinal matters, the patriarch began forcefully instituting changes to the liturgical services. Nikon was actually harkening back to the earliest religious traditions, calling for a return to the older, original Greek liturgical practices that had been transmitted from the Greeks to the Russians as far back as the tenth and eleventh centuries.

But many of the current Russian faithful, particularly from the peasant class, steadfastly objected to the proposed religious reforms, preferring to keep things the way they were, opposing even minor textual changes and practices proposed by the patriarch. They became known as the Old Ritualists, or Old Believers. In the centuries of disobedience that followed, bands of Old Believers were forced to scatter to the forests of Siberia, Brazil, Canada, and even to Oregon in the US.

By the time Merton arrived in Alaska, four lonely, raw cabins in a vast spruce forest, had been built in Nikalaevesk, as one old timer described it. The sure-footed Old Believers came to the last frontier for more solitude and mental renewal. And to live in deeper union with God's divine energies. Had fate ever brought him back to the state for a second visit, Merton might have begged to be driven to the Village of Old Believers. He would have wanted to see their hermitage carved out in the middle of a Kenai forest of cottonwoods, aspen and spruce.

Seeing Old Believers in public as I often did, I had to admit that something inside me stirred. A part of myself stopped cold in those brief moments, the same part of myself that did so when I first heard Russian monastery bells ring on the Volga River. And when as a child, I had caught a glimpse of those shimmering cupolas reflected in the haze over the river in Pittsburgh.

My Russian comrades and I sped south to Nikolaevsk in my Ford Explorer on a day that was cool and overcast. Misha needed a rest stop to light up a cigarette. I pulled off the Sterling Highway momentarily and Olga went with her husband to have a smoke.

"Katya, when the time comes," Igor said, "I will travel to Mount Athos in Greece for my Christian rites, and this seems—"

"Wait a minute! What?" I said as I leaned over the steering wheel shaking my head.

"Igor, did you say *Christian? And what mountain in Greece?* Hold on. I have no clue what you're talking about."

"I plan to go to the Holy Mountain," he said. "My future journey must be there."

Instead of seeing an Orthodox priest in one of Moscow's newly restored and reopened churches, Igor wanted to skip the standard baptismal rites in favor of becoming a true pilgrim at Mount Athos. Mount Athos, located on a rocky peninsula in the Aegean Sea, was the greatest monastic center in all of Christendom, he explained, a site reeling with cenobitic hermits, and a place, I learned years later, that Merton had fondly read about.

Igor informed me that his mother, Lydia, to whom he was greatly devoted, had taken seriously ill. He had been desperately praying for her recovery, but he needed to try something else. He would go to Mount Athos and meet some of the Orthodox monks for spiritual counseling and recite more prayers from one of its many monasteries. From this mystical place, he believed, perhaps God might answer his pleas.

Arranging such travel to northern Greece required a lot of money, bureaucratic red-tape, special entry passes, visas, and complicated travel arrangements, something Igor had vast career experience handling.

"No female pilgrims are allowed on Athos," he reminded me.

"What? Not even in the twenty-first century?" I said with indignation.

I began forming a mental picture of Igor at Mount Athos as he told me about it. I easily imagined him trekking with a few unshaven and malnourished monks to the top of the Holy Mountain, a peak of roughly 6,000 feet, or challenging himself to walk to each of the peninsula's twenty monasteries, his rucksack and water bottle flung over his shoulder, an Orthodox cross and a medal of St. Panteleimon (The Healer) hanging around his neck.

Ever since I met Igor, he's been a world traveler engaged in one pilgrimage after another. Before embarking on any trip, Igor studies every facet of the country or region's geography, its longest rivers, its highest elevation. On any occasion anywhere as my host, he plots every basilica, art gallery, and museum for me to see. He buys stacks of road atlases, memorizes arcane economic facts, reads ten pounds of guidebooks, and immerses himself in enough history to deliver a lecture to the Politburo. He satisfied his sense of wanderlust by traveling to Kazakhstan and Kirgiziya where he rode skinny Mongolian horses in the Tyan-Shan Mountains. He explored much of the Old Silk Road in Central Asia for another diplomatic project he masterminded to help revitalize ancient trading routes. He drove the entire perimeter of Turkey. He hiked on the Appalachian Trail, and traipsed around Italy and Norway. It was no surprise he knew of the Village of the Old Believers.

His current job with an international transportation consortium involves the United Nations, which regularly takes him to Geneva, London, and New York City. On rare moments at home at his flat in Moscow, he likes to drive alone for over ten hours to retreat to his *dacha*—his family cabin. It's 600 kilometers away in the Republic of Chuvashia and is his mother's ancestral village. The village of Shimkusy is tiny with muddy, pot-holed roads, wandering ducks, and shepherds with goats in a region surrounded by fields of rye and hops. Igor likes to pick mushrooms in the birch forest and tend to his apple trees.

As we approached the turnoff to the village, I noticed a hand-painted sign I'd not seen before: *Russian Gifts, Books, Music.* For another ten miles, we passed through undeveloped country, grassy fields with patches of hot pink fireweed, and acres of beetle-damaged spruce trees, and I was thankful we saw no newly installed billboards or flashing neon arrows reminding us "This way to Russian City for *suveniry!*"

We kept going another thirty minutes until we found the small bright blue and white onion dome of its one church, St. Nikolas. "Katya, park the car," Igor said. "Maybe it is possible we can take a look inside."

Except for the single dome, the small white church looked bland and un-picturesque by normal Russian standards, and the smattering of plain ranch houses surrounding it seemed deserted. As this was August, in the waning days of summer, villagers had most likely fled to their favorite recreational hideouts in the Caribou Hills or to Kachemak Bay as locals do.

"Too bad, but the church door is locked," Igor said with disappointment.

"Looks like worship services ended hours ago and we missed it," I said.

Two young boys pedaling bikes appeared, dressed in white tunic-type shirts, *rubashkas*, with hand embroidery in red and blue around their collars. Misha looked up and called out in Russian. The blonde-haired boys mumbled something back, smiled, and darted off on their bikes. We gladly followed them to the Samovar Café, part of the Fefelov Mercantile, the settlement's only year-round storefront business. A totem pole about 20-feet high, painted in garish, nontraditional motifs and colors—lilac, lime green, all shades of red and orange mixed with purple, yellow, and black—welcomed customers. A cartoonish rendering of a woman's round, smiling face with extra thick, black eyelashes and comical, red ruby lips occupied the center of the tacky wood totem.

"Only in Alaska would you see such a thing as this," Igor said, "faces of *matryoshka* dolls painted all the way to the top of a totem! Who else in the world would think to blend Native tribal culture with Russian folk designs? You see, Alaskans and Russians are still linked in history!"

The Fefelov Mercantile was closed, but while Olga was snapping a few photos of us in front of the totem, a portly, middle-aged woman, her hair half-fallen out from her barrette, came running towards us through the high grass in a nearby yard. She fumbled for the café's front door keys in her apron pocket, tried to catch her breath through heavy breathing, and spoke in choppy English.

"Welcome, welcome. Please, I will open for you," the Old Believer woman said while wiping her hands on the sleeve of her smock.

Igor greeted the Old Believer woman, Nina, in Russian. Nina beamed through the redness of her face, pleased that three out of four of her rare Sunday afternoon customers were real, flesh-in-the-blood, Muskovites. As soon as we stepped closer to the six stools along the luncheon counter, the flustered woman, popped in a cassette tape of Slavic folk guitar and balalaika and threw open the café's lace curtains. I understood her to ask if we'd like to order some borscht or *pelmeni*, but none of us had much of an appetite.

"*Pozhaluista, chai*," Igor said. Out of politeness, he ordered some stale looking meringue cookies to go along with our cups of tea, and they began chatting, which seemed to further please the woman, to be talking to Russians who had financial means and political freedom to vacation in America. People who might gladly spend some money.

The Samovar Café overflowed with typical Russian imports: fringed woolen scarves in bright floral patterns, cheap versions of matryoshka dolls, birch barrettes, imitation amber necklaces, and the gold, red and black painted wooden spoons and bowls you can find in every Moscow or Saint Petersburg gift shop.

"Please, you like *knigi*—books?" she said turning to me.

"*Nyet, spasibo*," I said. "I already have many Russian souvenirs," I answered in a curt tone that I quickly regretted. Maybe Nikolaevsk wasn't a good idea. A café stop was a far cry from the more subdued and holy atmosphere I imagined we'd find with a chance to see some beautiful icons in the church.

The Old Believer woman hastened over to another crammed shelf and pulled down a few more books. Again, I shook my head *no*, but this time with a half-smile, she reached into her apron pocket and handed me a piece of flimsy photocopied paper, folded over into the shape of a business card: *Russian Gifts, Books, Tapes, Samovar, Café, Giftshop, 2 Apartments for Night*.

"*Muzyka?*" Nina asked as she held up a cassette tape of folk songs.

"*Nyet, nyet*," I said more softly, trying to remain as courteous as possible, and hoping Igor would intervene and the awkwardness and tension would be slightly lessened.

Old Believers had lived in a time warp for decades, purposely distancing themselves from mainstream society to live more closely with God, in body and soul, with less compartmentalization. But the outside world with its economic pressures had begun to interfere. Their tranquil, less-tainted lives were rapidly changing.

I finally agreed to buy one of the publications. *How We Escaped from Russia* cost five dollars and was held together with a blue plastic comb-binding. Each of its fifteen photocopied pages included the original language with an English translation describing how one Old Believer family had escaped religious persecution by ruthless Communists.

Over the next few minutes, we sat and sipped our *chai* in the stuffy Samovar Café and each of us thanked Nina for her kindness in opening her business.

Igor left a generous tip, and since there was nothing left for us to do in the Village of Old Believers, we headed to my car.

"Well, Igor, it wasn't exactly the kind of visit we hoped for, was it? " I said. "People have to lose some of their old customs to fit the economics of the times, I guess. Even Alaska isn't what it used to be."

"It's okay, Katya," he said. "You know the Russians. They will always find a way to survive. They are like blades of grass in a field. They know how to bend when the winds blow."

A few years passed before I saw *moy droog*, my friend, Igor, again. This time he returned to do some backcountry hiking with his Chicago friend Viktor. Before dropping the men off at the Resurrection Pass trailhead, I invited Igor to the Anchorage Museum of History & Art for tea and conversation. Lots of noisy, summer visitors filled the museum lobby, atrium and café, making it difficult to talk above the shuffle.

Igor looked relax and content. He was dressed in his new, favorite clothing, like a poster boy for Patagonia—in beige, nylon hiking pants with lots of pockets, perfect for global trekking, a short-sleeved T-shirt, a vest with many zippered pockets, fanny pack, and white tennis shoes— the only un-Alaskan part of his outerwear. As we settled into a table in the museum's café, I was ready to hear reports about his latest escapades to Geneva or

Paris, or his take and analysis about Russia's improving economic conditions due to rising oil prices.

"Well, Katya. I did it," Igor said smiling while he pulled sheets of paper out of a large envelope he had carried and placed on the table. "I finally wrote it all down because of you."

"Katya, see what you've done? Somehow, I wasn't able to stop and a few pages turned into something much larger. I even wrote about my first travels abroad to England and America during *perestroika*. And my time in the Ministry of Foreign Trade. And how we met. And the wild freedom that came when the New Russia was born in travail. The chaos…the wrong decisions…."

He kept talking with barely a breath. "…and the political divides…how it led me to more of a spiritually-centered life, at least to start thinking about it anyway. And all of that led to my pilgrimage to Mount Athos, of course!"

For months, through email, I had nagged him about his Orthodox Christian baptism, hoping he would one day share the more personal, intimate details about this strange place called Mount Athos.

"Igorchik," I said with tenderness, "You didn't need to do that—to write it all down. I only pestered you so that you wouldn't forget to tell me more of the story, that's all. Hundreds of monks and hermits living in caves on rocky cliffs with no women around? It's so bizarre. These men are praying for our salvation, you say. In some kind of penance for the world?"

"*Da, da, da, pravda*," he said, "My beautiful sojourn is now written down, *droog moi*."

I lifted the stack of papers. He had paid a translator a lot of money to have his twenty-page essay, "The Rock," put together in English for my benefit.

In a slow, half-whisper, he revealed the details about the sacraments of his Christian baptism. And again, I sat mesmerized to hear him talk in such personal terms. He sounded as if he were repeating a religious parable, giving me a kind of confession or speaking of some sublime experience in the wilderness. I wondered where all this holy talk and study was going. Every time Igor spoke with such conviction, it reminded me how out-of-balance I felt. I'd been piecing things together intellectually, trying to educate myself about the world's great religions in general, especially my scant knowledge of Islam. The historical statement about Moscow being the Third Rome had always intrigued me.

"Of all people, I want you to know this," he said. "Legend has it that the Blessed Virgin later in her life, in answer to a sign from On High, spent several years on Athos, spreading the teachings of Christ. She is the official protectorate of Athos. The monks and pilgrims revere sites associated with the Virgin. She is the Patron Saint of the Holy Mountain, Katya!"

"Well, that's a pretty big claim about Jesus's mother," I said, "incredible, really."

"On Athos they showed me the spot at the foot of the mountain where the Virgin's boat was moored," he said. "A stream of pure spring water flows there. It is five meters from the salty breakers of the Aegean Sea."

I didn't know whether to sit in silence or to start arguing with him that this whole story sounded preposterous.

"And Katya, I *saw* this spring and drank from it!"

I chose to keep quiet, still clutching the pages, and he went on.

"Pilgrims attempting to climb the summit always stop to rest and pray at the Panagaia Chapel," Igor said, "only 15 meters square. It is where the Virgin Mary spent the night during her climb to the summit."

"Uh-huh....Really, Igor? So you believe in this far-fetched Mary, Mother-of-God legend, do you? That she journeyed by boat to Athos?"

"*Da, da, da.*"

Listening to him, I thought about a Russian word I came across once—*istina*—though I can't remember the exact source or if I translated it correctly. *Istina,* an inner light, a verity.

Could this be what Igor was talking about in himself?

At Mount Athos, he had engaged in the reenactment of Christian baptismal rites carried out for over a millennium and following these sacraments and ancient traditions had brought him a sense of inner tranquility, as if the bodily connection to something revered and honored since the earliest days of Christianity had transformed him. He had distanced a part of himself from market fluctuations, the onslaught of technology, and dry, rational political theory. He had found something else, an inner light of joy, a communion in spirit with others, an enduring *love*.

"I will never forget the gentle Aegean Sea in the rays of the setting sun which closed over my head three times at the culmination of the wonderful service. I breathed in the scents of wax and incense, caught the reflections of the candles on the beautiful faces of the saints. *But oh, how can I really explain this?*" he said.

"Katya, I gave myself the freedom to dissolve into the darkness and mystery of the church and in the sounds of the monastic chanting which came and went…"

And with this, his voice trailed off. I could sense some frustration as he earnestly searched for the perfect words.

The baptismal ceremony required him to take a long walk in the black night, from the chapel to the seashore, approximately 300 meters, all alone, dressed in a white robe and carrying a burning candle.

A Holy Mountain. A windy sea. A white robe. A solitary flame of light. These elements had combined in a profoundly symbolic moment, a divine union of body and spirit, in a memory and feeling he would carry with him the rest of his life. The choices he made were nothing less than a pure calling of his heart; he acted on his inmost desires to seek more spiritual wholeness. It was time he realigned his interior self. Not that my Russian friend had found all the right answers, but that he had gotten somewhere in his searching. Like the stubborn and still struggling Old Believers, he found some right rules to guide him. Through prayer, he felt more connected to God in the holiness of community.

My friend rose above the propaganda drone to the mystical voices of poets and dreamers and wanderers. He dismissed the pronouncements and decrees promulgated by the social engineers, commissars, Communist party members, and self-aggrandizing political operatives.

Igor no longer wanted lies; he wanted truth. The *direct* truth and insights from his own life, first of all. But he wanted also to know the real truth about Russia, the other side of Russia that today seemed impenetrable. The Russian government was still tampering with the truth. He wanted to know the facts about its Communist history. For political reasons history was disappearing from memory again. What were the real impacts of Stalin's political purges and drastic agricultural policies? What was the extent of the terror and starvation in Ukraine under Stalin's misguided decisions in the wretched 1930s? Though he hadn't lived through Stalin's dictatorship, Igor somehow hoped for a feeling of repentance in his country, an open acknowledgement of the atrocities, in the way Germany had faced and apologized for its Nazi past.

I could see a new passion in his eyes. I knew it was true that the Orthodox faith meant something to his life now. Igor felt an internal light of joy, a communion and liberty *in spirit* with others.

Whether on the sun-filled cliffs of Mount Athos or in the green hills of rural Kentucky, monks—marginalized and misunderstood—continued to pray for the world's salvation as they have done for centuries on end, seven days a week. Through wars, the build-up of nuclear arsenals, hypocrisies, abuses of power, radical religious extremism, and terrorist bombings, they prayed. Through endless sorrows, the monks prayed.

Igor became a faith explorer, a new Russian pilgrim. Times were changing. Igor pushed forward and questioned everything. He allowed his false self to crumble on that holy mountain.

The example of his life gave me hope that I would find some right answers, too.

...I have never had such a feeling of the strange madness that possesses this country. And yet there is still some hope—based not on reason but on a basic good will and a luck that might still hold. Or *is* there a basic good will? Has it all been mortgaged to a police state? Are we already *there*? We may be!...

—Thomas Merton's journal, March 20, 1968

...More sorrow. I went down to the monastery with my laundry—saw the flag at half-mast and asked someone if Robert Kennedy were dead. Of course he was! The news was very depressing: there seemed to have been so much hope he would survive. I sent a telegram to Ethel...

—Thomas Merton, *The Intimate Merton*, June 6, 1968

...No despair of ours can alter the reality of things, or stain the joy of the cosmic dance which is always there...

—Thomas Merton, *New Seeds of Contemplation*

15 Retracing Merton's Journey—1968

On California's rugged, northern coast waves crashed below me onto rocks and boulders.

Ocean swells—turquoise and thick with kelp—rolled past rocky cliffs and into the small bay. Ferns and scrub brush stood dried and scorched by the burning sun. A few clumps of white sweet alyssum and low-growing yellow daisies offered spurts of color along the sandy trails about fifty miles north from where Merton first saw the Pacific. Merton traveled to northern California in search of a new hermitage, and to begin a trek of interfaith exploration.

It's no longer the desolate shore he saw and described in 1968 prior to his arrival in Alaska. I don't know what he'd say about the place now. Mendocino and its surrounding area is congested with Victorian-style hotels and B&Bs, organic wineries, restaurants serving fair-trade certified coffees, eclectic art galleries, naturally-grown foodstuffs to satisfy any *locavores*. Hordes of campers, cyclists, and high-spending tourists drive north from the San Francisco Bay area. They come for the ocean views, and to pay homage to the magical groves of 2,000-year-old giant redwoods. "Who can bear to be away from them?" Merton asked. "I must go back. It is not right I should die under lesser trees."

In summer of 2008, Michael visited me at the end of my residency in Marin County. We drove north in an old Ford Bronco we borrowed from a friend. I insisted we go to the Monastery of the Redwoods in tiny Whitethorn. I sat in the chapel with the Flemish nuns and listened to the afternoon prayer service while Michael waited in the car. After the prayer service, Sister Veronique served us a simple lunch of soup and homemade bread.

After a few hours, Michael drove us onward through the mountainous terrain along a treacherous narrow road with more S-curves and switchbacks than we'd ever seen. I was never so close to being car sick as I was that day we parked at Shelter Cove and walked on the rocky beach. Shelter Cove, with its warning sign, "Never turn your back on the Pacific," was closer to the kind of solitude Merton dreamed he could steal for himself.

I was retracing Merton's travels. When Father Merton was on that swath of coast in 1968, Sister Veronique was one of the young nuns who met with him. He took a side trip to stay several nights in a guesthouse on a private property in tiny Bear Harbor not far from Whitethorn. There, he roamed about its seascape in solitude with no people for miles. But even then, he could foresee that future development would encroach upon the quiet and solitude the hippies had been enjoying.

I shared his attachment to "this Asian Ocean" as he referred to it. Both of us dreamt and meandered to the sounds of its tumbling surf. The Pacific filled us with a sense of being utterly happy whenever we were near its shores.

He wondered if the Pacific was where his true destiny lay.

In the Mendocino headlands, I sat down on a large, hand-hewn driftwood bench, journal on my lap, and ran my fingers across the pairs of initials in heart symbols indelibly carved into the wood. While looking at how young lovers had declared their affections captured in time, I thought about Michael. He wrote poetry, yet I couldn't recall a single one ever written for me. How was he sleeping in our B&B? Had he even realized I took my journal and went for an early morning walk? I envied M with the complete surrender of Merton's affection, the poetry he'd written for her. I questioned my youth, my decisions, my marriage. My past haunted me.

In the spring of 1967, the conflicted monk admitted that some of the same feelings, which had plagued him in his youth, continued troubling him.

"This persistent desire to be somebody," he said, "which is really so stupid. I know I don't really need it or want it, yet I keep going after it. Not that I should stop writing or publishing, but I should not let myself be flattered and cajoled into the business, letting myself be used, making statements and declarations, 'being there,' 'appearing.' Pictures appear (without any desire of mine, to tell the truth) and I am ashamed of myself."

Merton needed to go on a fast—a fast from his own fame. As 1968 came into view, it was time that Radio Free Merton shut down and stop broadcasting.

Even as a long-time Trappist of Gethsemani who took a vow of stability, poverty, chastity, silence, and obedience, nothing was completely settled for him. The way he looked at it, his real home might never be found, and if he were to be a homeless pilgrim, that was alright with him.

With Merton, my spiritual search seemed well underway. But it was still subject to heavy wave action and slippery footing. If it was answers I wanted, I knew I had come to the wrong priest. He didn't claim to have any. He didn't prescribe. He didn't pontificate or proselytize. He didn't offer any 12-step plans to spiritual wholeness. His books weren't found in the feel-good Christian self-help books section.

In the non-conformist times, even monks went a little stir-crazy and started questioning the religious Establishment. As a Catholic trailblazer and bridge-builder between East and West, Merton wanted to learn from Buddhists, Hindus, the Orthodox, Islam and Sufi mysticism, and Judaism. What could Catholicism gain from a deeper study of these other religions? Thomas Merton, for one, was not in the least bit interested in maintaining the status quo.

Long after our Shelter Cove excursion and back in Alaska, as I sat at my desk and considered how I retraced his steps, I felt like a Merton groupie. I once took a taxi to Columbia University Campus and walked to the Corpus Christi Church on 121st street in New York City. Without appointment, I tracked down and spoke to the newly assigned priest. The priest walked me over to the baptismal font used for Merton's baptism in 1938.

While in California, I lingered at City Lights Bookstore in San Francisco.

I remembered how I stood in snow flurries on a December afternoon in New Mexico after asking a man whom I barely knew to take me on a scenic drive outside Santa Fe in search of the road leading to Christ in the Desert Monastery, another one of Merton's stops in 1968. I wanted him to drive another fourteen miles down the road, but it was snowing and we were out of time. I never made it to that monastery. And there were all those off-the-beaten path places in Alaska, like Dillingham, Cordova, and Yakutat. What was it about Thomas Merton that kept me interested and curious?

I liked Merton's honesty, his sense of spiritual glasnost, his open attitude, his willingness to embrace aspects of popular culture. Merton admired the lyrics and music of Bob Dylan and Joan Baez, the jazz artistry of John Coltrane and Duke Ellington. He liked the Beatles and owned a copy of their album, "Revolver." In the book of letters, *Hidden Ground of Love*, he wrote to a professor of Christian culture at St. Mary's College in Indiana in 1967.

> "To me," Merton wrote, "one of the most amusing things that has happened lately is this: The progressive and activist Catholics began hailing the Beatles as very hip people (which of course they are). Then all of a sudden, the Beatles start going to a yogi to learn contemplation – which is anathema to the progressive etc. Catholics. Hmmm. My feeling is that our progressives don't know what they are talking about, in their declarations about modern man, the modern world, etc." Merton said, "Perhaps they are dealing with some private myth or other. That is their affair…

Oddly, Merton was far more in touch with popular culture than one might expect given that he lived in some unknown monastery in the back hills and woods of Kentucky—not exactly the center of 1960s counterculture. It was in stark contrast to the picture-perfect Cistercian Abbey in the wine region of Bordeaux or under the olive trees and dangling grape vines of Mount Athos off the coast of Greece.

For God's sake, Merton was in the folksy bluegrass state with hillbillies, and coal miners like my grandfather and his poor immigrant family. Thomas Merton left the comfortable path of his Ivy League education and the beginnings of what was bound to be a stellar academic career as a literature professor to be an undistinguished, obedient, and celibate monk without need for an RCA television.

For America, 1968 was either the year of the poet or the year of hell, depending upon how you looked at it.

The writer Mark Kurlansky observed in his chronicle about 1968 that it was one of those rare times when poetry mattered and everyone aspired to be a poet.

In either case, whether it was good for poetry, or a hell-hole of misery, it was an unforgettable time—culturally, politically, musically, and socially. Sixty-eight was a year that stood out from all the others in my childhood for the tragic events and explosion of creativity.

In 1968, the Pope issued an encyclical reiterating the Catholic Church's ban on the use of birth control pills. Andy Warhol was shot and wounded by a mentally-ill self-proclaimed feminist. Nixon became the president. Demonstrations escalated in lock-step with the Vietnam War and Civil Rights Movement, punctuated by the death of Martin Luther King. British rock band, Led Zeppelin, made its American debut. Meanwhile, the rock music of The Rolling Stones and Beatles drew criticism or was outright banned by both religious conservatives in the US and Communist Cuba alike.

People wanted to tap into their subconscious, to attain feelings of transcendence, to dispense with the rigid conformities and social conventions that repressed them politically, artistically and sexually. Merton was immersed in Eastern thought about the same time as the West Coast poets—Gary Snyder, Kenneth Rexroth, Gregory Corso—were also coming under the influence of Zen Buddhism, and making names for themselves in the literati.

As the year dawned, Merton ominously foretold the year's madness and tragedy in his journal. "It is already a hard year," the worried monk said, "and I don't know what else is coming but I have a feeling it is going to be hard all the way and for everybody. Never has the world been torn up with so much violence and conflict." The year also began with terrible news that one of his close friends from his New York days died in a house fire. Merton was overworked and over scheduled with social and intellectual activity.

Merton "the hermit" reported that once on a particularly hot evening at his cottage when he was sitting in his underwear, two uninvited admirers peeked in at him through the windows. He frequently struggled with unwanted visitors, who hoped to catch a glimpse of him strolling under the linden trees. He'd often leave in the afternoons to walk in the woods and would hide in the nearby bushes until the coast was clear if he spotted any one near his hermitage.

I recognized his angst, and wrestled with it many times myself. I wanted to be more like a solitary water droplet resting on a single leaf. With my own Loud Girl tendencies, I could relate to Merton's need for more silence. It's not that I wanted to check myself into a convent or become a Desert Mother, or live for years on Knight Island like the Pavliks did. But I did want to stop the chattering, the trifles, the constant activity of being yanked from one thing to another. I was living in the center of a land mass of 486,000 square miles, with more unpopulated corners to meditate and lose yourself in than any other state. Still, I seemed unable to live more contemplatively.

Sometimes, I talked to Michael about it.

"We should move to a dead-end dirt road on the Kenai Peninsula surrounded by woods," I'd say to Michael. He never liked urban life anyway and still considered Yakutat his spiritual home.

"Let's get out of suburbia," I said. "Or wait for a public land sale on a remote parcel somewhere. Or how about we try living on a sailboat?"

"A sailboat, are you serious?" Michael replied. "I get terrible seasickness, remember? Besides, you're kidding yourself. You'd never be able to leave the city permanently anyway."

In the next breath, after I made my "We ought to escape from the subdivision" speech, I went back to planning another theme dinner party. Like Merton at his hermitage, I was getting by with a lot of help from my friends.

In a 1949 journal entry, and in response to a letter from the Carthusians in Rome, Merton wrote, "…It (reminded me of my own longing for solitude, interior purity, perfect silence, a life for God alone. I haven't prayed in months as I have been praying since I read that letter: not praying to be anywhere but here (except of course heaven) but burning up with desire of God and with shame at my unmitigated interior activity and the futility of so much that I do."

Merton admitted, "I am content that these journal pages show me to be what I am: noisy, full of the racket and imperfections and passions and the wide-open wounds left by sin, full of faults and envies and miseries, full of my own intolerable emptiness."

Bemoaning the sound of his own voice lecturing and conversing, the sounds of his banging typewriter keys, the idea of finding a penultimate, silent, utopian kind of hermitage remained his monastic fantasy.

Preferably, he'd turn himself into a solitary person surrounded by nature. He loved being in the outdoors, though it sometimes proved a distraction from serious mediation when he tried learning the names of plants and birds.

Merton confessed the April air made it hard to say the Psalms because his attention would get carried away by trees, hills, grass, and the vast blue arc of the sky. How many times had I packed my journal on a hike through Anchorage's parks and trails to record whatever I saw—a bull moose tearing into willows, gulls zooming over Cook Inlet, the silhouette of Sandhill cranes elegantly stepping across the mudflats? How often had I stuffed the wildflower guide into my daypack and checked off shooting stars and alpine arnica?

Random observations in *Conjectures of a Guilty Bystander* (1966), were a marvelous journey through his wandering mind, and interspersed with his sometimes harsh sarcasms. There were fragments about the muskrats he watched paddling in the water, the sweet spring air, and "the alleluias that came back by themselves."

"How absolutely central is the truth that we are first of all part of nature, though we are a very special part, that which is conscious of God," he said. In another turn, he commented on the musical rules of monastery.

"Music is being played to the cows in the milking barn. Rules have been made and confirmed: only sacred music is to be played to the cows, not 'classical' music. The music is to make the cows give more milk. The sacred music is to keep the brothers who work in the cow barn recollected." Merton continued, "For some time now, sacred music has been played to the cows in the milking barn. They have not given more milk. The brothers have not been any more recollected than usual. I believe the cows will soon be hearing Beethoven. Then we shall have classical, perhaps worldly milk and the monastery will prosper. (Later: it was true. The hills resounded with Beethoven. The monastery has prospered. The brother mainly concerned with the music, however, departed.)" I imagined Merton sitting in his hermitage pondering the details of his not-so-solitary life among the brothers, nature and of course, the music for the cows. It seemed like he was not really living a hermit's existence, despite his official designation as a hermit.

Many of the scholars, historians and Merton acolytes I came across were quick to point out that in the last few years of the monk's life he lived as a hermit—the first monk officially allowed to do so within the Cistercians of the Strict Observance religious order since the Middle Ages.

But as an Alaskan, I couldn't buy this. Merton wasn't even close to being a hermit after he moved into his private cinderblock cottage. Real hermits—as bush dwellers along the Kuskokwim River or any of the Pavliks could tell you—didn't live on the road system surrounded by people the way Merton did.

If he needed medical treatment, doctors and nurses lived a short car drive away and he didn't even have to drive himself. Louisville was less than two hours north of his hermitage and it had plenty of shopping plazas, Dairy Queens, gas stations, convenience stores, and a modern airport with more than a sprinkling of commercial jet planes per day and in far more cooperative weather than Yakutat.

It was less than a twenty-minute, pleasant walk, or a short bicycle ride—never by snow machine—to the monastery's enclosure. Though lacking some basic amenities at first, he did not need to use a honey-bucket for his toilet, though he did use an outhouse until a fully plumbed private bathroom was installed in 1968.

The Abbey's coffers supplied most of his basic foodstuffs, mainly boring canned goods, tea and cereals since daily diets were spare, practically vegan, and mostly excluded meat, fish and eggs. No subsistence hunting or fishing were required. He didn't have to tolerate long cold

Alaskan or Canadian winters, the likes of which he'd never seen before. In the Bluegrass State, Merton needn't worry about avalanches that could block the main supply road in or out for weeks at a time as it happens in Valdez where average snowfalls exceed 300 inches in one season and where 47 inches of snow can fall in a single day. His mail wasn't dropped off by bush plane once a month. With his precious book in-hand, he could saunter into the silence of the woods without the worry of running into a sow and cubs and pissing his down his leg in mortal fear. There were plenty of people nearby to help if he needed it.

As a former, somewhat pampered city boy from New York City, Merton liked physical work, especially if it involved planting or cutting trees on the Abbey's property. He sometimes got annoyed at how crowded the monastery had become with over 175 monks and novices. When he needed a break from his brother monks and from his own mind, he trudged through hills and fields.

Writing to the extreme, as he was prone to do, was also a therapeutic mechanism. Writing was a shield to keep his mind from the invading truth that, despite his brother monks, he was alone and without family in the world by 1968. His only sibling, his younger brother, died in World War II in a military plane crash while serving in the Royal Air Force. Merton's parents and grandparents, and his one living relative in New Zealand, his Aunt Kit, were all dead. And he and nurse Margie no longer communicated.

Though he dreamed of being a more serious kind of hermit, Merton also loved and needed people, warmed to their company and attention. He would probably not last long in Alaska or anywhere else for weeks or months on end without real human contact. A psychiatrist who met with Merton in 1956 described the monk's dualistic personality quite well, saying he displayed traits of megalomania and narcissism, calling him the "Times Square hermit."

Merton's latest book *Zen and the Birds of Appetite* was published earlier in the year, and by the time he headed to Alaska, he was predictably working on a host of other projects. He was editing issue number four of the new literary journal he founded, *Monk's Pond*, was occupied writing book reviews for the *Sewanee Review* and prefaces he promised to supply, plus he kept up with voluminous correspondence.

Upon receipt of an invitation to participate in a conference of Asian abbots and the religious in Bangkok, Merton persuaded his abbot, Dom Flavian Burns, to approve his participation. After 27 years in the monastery, it might be a good time to hit the road again under the pretense that he was using his religious travels to search for a future, more remote hermitage, one that might even be used by other Trappists.

After accepting the invitation to Bangkok, Merton created an ambitious itinerary, a pilgrimage of sorts, for spring and summer before the Bangkok conference. The pilgrimage included several stops around the world. His plans included Christ in the Desert Monastery near Abiquiu, New Mexico, a visit to what is now the Georgia O'Keeffe ranch, various places in California, Alaska, Ceylon, India, and Tibet where he met with His Holiness the Dalai Lama. After the Bangkok conference, Merton tentatively planned to fly to Malaysia.

Merton wanted to let the winds and currents carry him where "the face of God" could be seen most clearly.

"I really expect little or nothing from the future," Merton reflected. "Certainly not great 'experiences' or a lot of interesting new things. Maybe, but so what? What really intrigues me is the idea of starting out into something unknown, demanding and expecting nothing very special, hoping only to do what God asks of me, whatever it may be." (July 29, 1968)

The more I studied Merton's life, the more I thought about Merton's vagabond self. I was a spiritual bindlestiff. He relished the idea of bopping around, the chance to return to his wanderlust past, and to the excitement of waking up in a new piece of country, meeting strangers and other seekers on the road. At age 53, the monk looked forward to spending time near seascapes again, as he had done in his youth in Bermuda and Cuba in 1940. He was coming full circle, back to the years when his artist-father, Owen Merton, dragged him between New York, France, and England.

After his father's untimely death, the young Tom traveled unencumbered around Europe with his rucksack. The kind of Bohemian existence he enjoyed as a college student living off his maternal grandfather's generosity was something I could only dream about. My desire to see European and Asian landscapes was a latent, and so far, unfulfilled dream.

Still at my desk, I realized how much I needed the salt air. As a landlocked monk, I believe Merton, too, needed a strong dose of that Pacific breeze—the golden plovers that darted in and out of the tides, the shiver of angry seas.

Like William Blake, Merton hoped to access the human imagination with or without any future listeners or readers. "I look through the eye," Blake said, "not with it."

In one of his mimeographed circular letters to friends in 1968, Merton said, "Our real journey in life is interior: it is a matter of growth, deepening, and of an ever-greater surrender to the creative action of love and grace in our hearts."

What was my problem? Hadn't I learned anything from Merton's example? I was hung up on the nuts and bolts of the writing business, looking for recognition, searching for New York literary agents to vindicate my vocation, worrying about "making it" and "lookin' good" as I chased the signposts of success. I remembered my time in California, the most self-aggrandizing, celebrity-crazed state in America, a place once called in the 1960s, the spiritual guru capital of the world. It was opposite of everything in Alaska.

As Merton prepared to embark on his global travels, he recognized the motivations for his future journeys entailed more than a search for more purifying solitude or finding the best possible locations for a possible hermit colony.

Stepping across another threshold was, perhaps, what he sensed. As he moved physically closer to the Pacific, he was ready to strip away his identity, his status, and his routines. He wanted to forget his writer-self, his monastic-self, and his teacher-self.

"Are monks and hippies and poets relevant?" he asked. "No, we are deliberately irrelevant. We live with an ingrained irrelevance which is proper to every human being. The marginal person accepts the basic irrelevance of the human condition…The marginal person, the monk, the displaced person, the prisoner, all these people live in the presence of death, and the office of the monk or the marginal person, the meditative person or the poet is to go beyond death, even in this life, to go beyond the dichotomy of life and death and to be, therefore, a witness to life."

He was ready to exit the mainstream of monastic expectations. In his next passage into uncertainty, he wanted to be less noticed—and in Buddhist fashion, to awaken into the ten-thousand things.

...Whatever else I may say—it is clear I like Alaska much better than Kentucky and it seems to me that if I am to be a hermit in the U.S., Alaska is probably the place for it. The Southeast is good—rain and all.

...I have still to go out to Western Alaska—and missed Kodiak where there is, I hear, an old Russian hermit.

(Last week I saw the Russian church in the Indian village of Eklutna, up the road from the convent.)

—Thomas Merton's Alaska journal,
September 27, 1968

16 The Monk Flies North

Merton departed Kentucky for America's icebox via Northwestern Airlines in Chicago. He flew in gray, cloud-covered skies. Flight attendants wore matching hats and skirts and served passengers hot meals on real plates. People traveled without electronic devices, laptops, and bags of chargers, cables, cords, ear buds, and noise cancelling headphones. The date was September 17, 1968, approximately one month after the massive protests and demonstrations at the Democratic National Convention in Chicago.

With its vast wilderness, thin population, unnamed mountains, the Last Frontier could calm any high-strung soul. Alaska represented a soothing antidote to a country rotten with violence, controversy and political chaos.

On the way, while maybe enjoying a Bloody Mary, he was reading *The Tibetan Book of the Dead* and scribbling notes about Herman Hesse. There he went again, compulsively filling journals and studying everything around him, including noting a few details about his flight—a Japanese mother and her beautiful baby, a man in the Peace Corps, the perfumed ginger ale and hot towels.

Alaska was a young state—statehood was granted in 1959—and generally perceived as economically and culturally backward. It was geographically isolated from national politics, fashion trends, music and pop culture. People who lived in its remote towns and villages, like Bethel or McGrath, hovered over radios listening to shows like "Tundra Tom-Tom" and "Trapline Chatter." Communities depended on radio stations to freely transmit messages and information to outlying towns. "To Bob at Trapper Creek—it's a boy." Or, "Winchester .308 rifle for sale. Call Sam." National news lagged behind the rest of the country because tapes had to be flown up from Seattle for rebroadcasting on Alaskan-run television stations.

Though times seemed darkly disturbing, Merton felt the opposite. He was full of excitement, optimism, and joy about his big travel year ahead.

While the nation was besieged by turmoil, the 49th state was rejoicing over its good financial fortunes. The giant North Slope gusher had been publicly announced on June 26, 1968, the largest oil deposit ever found in North America, an "elephant field" they called it, and now everything appeared up for grabs, and subject to great social change in the hinterlands, too.

The politics heated up, tempers flared, and the economic battle lines were being drawn as the monumental land conveyance issues concerning the Trans- Alaska Pipeline project had to be solved. Federal and state government, private oil companies, and Alaska's Native people debated and fought over shares of royalty and tax payments, engineering and environmental issues, and who really owned Alaska? Land claims for Alaska's Native people had been in limbo since the Alaska Purchase of 1867, when the mostly unexplored land of Russia's fur-trading colony was sold to the United States for two cents per acre, or $7.2 million. By the late 1960s, a slew of controversial legal issues broke out over indigenous land claims and what choice parcels the State of Alaska would be entitled to select in the federal land transfer.

Merton wasn't much interested in oil pipeline construction. What drew his attention was Alaska's unspoiled nature, its inviolate solitude, and all-encompassing beauty that no rural location in the Appalachians could possibly match. He was right. There were more square miles of silence in Alaska to last any hermit until judgment day, he said.

The giant territory had always attracted loners, alpine adventurers, fortune-seekers, Siberian explorers, Russian *promlysheniki* (fur traders), and Japanese enthralled by the aurora borealis and its imagined mystical powers. The eternally restless ones, people who longed to break free from their ordinary, lackluster lives, and to escape their troubled pasts, as I had done.

People looked to the north as a kind of medicine for whatever ailed them.

This need to go it alone in longer periods of isolation was a common trait among artists and landscape painters, as Merton, the son of a painter, well knew. His father, Owen, didn't work regular day jobs to support his two young sons, but tried to make it on his artistic talents alone after his wife died. And though his son, Thomas, never became a painter, he had a keen eye for landscapes and light. Father Louis closely studied light through his forays into black and white photography after he entered monastic life.

A painting by famous Alaskan artist, Fred Machetanz, hung on our living room wall. It was a painting Merton would have been fond of. The painting showed an Iñupiat (Eskimo) hunter, his body heavy with furs, standing at the edge of arctic sea ice gazing from under his fur-trimmed hood somewhere off in the vast distance. Machetanz rendered the hunter and his five Siberian huskies bathed in the deep turquoise lights of the aurora borealis. The scene evoked mystery. Machetanz was an Outsider who hailed from Kenton, Ohio. He came under the spell of the north, as so many did, after having served in the U.S. military in the Aleutians. Later, as a visual artist, Machetanz traveled throughout the arctic enthralled by its unusual light and peculiar hues of blue.

But by the time Merton got to Southcentral Alaska it was during the narrow window of time when summer abruptly ends and the shortest of seasons—autumn—begins. When days are crisp and Alaskans are starting to wind down like the foraging bears, physically transitioning to survive the long winter ahead. This was the off-season, not the middle of July, when almost every Outsider visits, when the Father Merton might have roamed about in his Levis and hiking boots in the "white-nights" of summer.

Meanwhile, back at the ranch—at the Abbey of Gethsemani—his fellow monks might have been found toiling under warm and sunny skies on a bright September day, cutting hay in the fields, or spreading cow manure over the monastery's gardens.

Thomas Merton ventured to communities along the Southeast Alaska coast—places such as Juneau and Yakutat—which can be at their worst in autumn. From the incessant gloom above, rain dumps by the barge load. The sun seems to disappear into the folds of a giant Chilkat blanket that's stored away in another galaxy. In Yakutat, the average monthly rainfall for September alone can reach 30 or 40 inches.

Alaskans would have been busy putting up moose from their early fall hunts, picking and freezing the last of the blueberries, emptying flower pots, dragging out last year's snow tires, checking over furnaces and woodstoves, adding more logs to their woodpiles, and scurrying to winterize their homes and cabins.

The long, dark winter was coming. Termination dust—the early seasonal snows—had already capped the Chugach Mountains surrounding the city.

Steady rains and gusty, easterly winds stripped the golden leaves from the stands of birch and tall cottonwoods in Southcentral Alaska. Birch leaves lay flattened and stuck to the asphalt like slippery wet paper. Currants and high-bush cranberries were tinged in fluorescent shades of coral and scarlet. Tarp-sized leaves of devil's club, thick throughout the forested area, curled into tissue-like sheets of sepia and yellow. Plump rosehips dangled from wild prickly roses like pink beads. Gangs of magpies and ravens hung close in neighborhood yards and chickadees raced through the trees.

Few of these details from the natural world would have escaped Merton's keen eyes.

Anchorage was noticeably losing daylight. One day, five minutes, 39 seconds of it—gone. The next day, another five minutes, 43 seconds—gone. The transient birds knew it as well as anyone. Merton would have seen and heard flocks of Canada geese flying overhead on their migrations south to warmer climes honking like practicing wind ensembles over the city. Under the right conditions—in dusk's fading sun—chances were good he viewed masses of noisy Sandhill cranes flying south in loose V-formations, as many as 600 at a time, dotting the sky like spots of black ink. Trumpeter swans stopped to refuel in the local marshes and lakes before heading south along the Gulf of Alaska coast, from Cordova to Yakutat, and along the rest of the Pacific Flyway. They were the avian reminders that locals might have chagrined to see.

Merton saw heaps of heavy clouds hanging in mountain passes, and over the Old Glenn Highway, leading north to the small community of Eagle River and the Precious Blood convent. He was assigned to stay in a chaplain's trailer during the first four days of his journey.

The brainchild behind Merton's northern trek was the Most Reverend Joseph T. Ryan, first Archbishop of the brand new Alaska Diocese. The Diocese, based in downtown Anchorage, had only been in existence since 1966. In 1915 the city of Anchorage and its first Catholic Church, Holy Family, were founded. Half a world away, in Prades, France, Thomas Merton was also born in 1915.

The church was elevated to its "cathedral" status in 1966, when an archbishop was sent north to create the diocese to institute its parish mission of outreach. Father Ryan, a former U.S. Navy chaplain, gambled that Merton's presence would breathe life and purpose into the fledgling diocese. Besides, the bishop was also from New York.

Following adoption of the major reforms of the Second Vatican Council (1962-65), Archbishop Ryan put out a call to priests and nuns in the Lower 48 appealing to their sense of adventure, inviting them to come north to help him grow the new archdiocese. Some of the changes implemented by Vatican II within the Roman Catholic Church included offering Mass in English as well as in Latin, and a movement was underway for the "people of God," whether Jews, Muslims, Orthodox, or Protestants, to be more openly welcomed by the Church.

A group of six contemplative nuns heeded Father Ryan's call and departed from their motherhouse in Portland, Oregon. They belonged to the Sister Adorers of the Precious Blood Order founded in 1861 in French-speaking Quebec. Nuns of their order wore ankle-length white tunics covered by red scapulars with a red sash. I remember the first time I heard the name— Sister Adorers of the Precious Blood—and how jarring I found the combination of words. At first, I didn't understand the Christian meaning, that the "precious blood" was Christ's redeeming blood from the Resurrection. The nuns who established the Precious Blood convent looked forward to a life of purer contemplation.

Besides the chance to look for a possible future hermitage, Alaska provided another, but unexpected, benefit to Merton— more female companionship. Upon arrival, Merton's first order of duty was to meet these intrepid nuns known by locals as the Fire Lake Nuns. A small floatplane basin, where de Havilland Otters and Super Cubs took off and landed daily, Fire Lake was located a few short miles down the road from the Precious Blood convent.

The contemplative nuns lived in a plain brown, two-story, very modest home in the woods. Merton was placed under their special care and charge and was given private quarters in the chaplain's trailer located on the same property as the small convent. Reforms adopted from Vatican II created a more liberal dress code for women in religious orders. The nuns could "throw off" some of their stiff and restrictive clothing, which was especially important for nuns in the far north who needed the warmth of pants and mukluk type boots.

Owned by the archdiocese, the property and 1961 house, built originally as a family home, sounded idyllic. The Sisters were nestled in thick woods of spruce, cottonwood, aspen and birch, and without a lawn to mow. During the clearest days of winter with the foliage long gone, the convent offered views of the Talkeetna Mountains and of Denali (formerly Mt. McKinley) about 170 air miles north through its row of eight large windows.

The Monk Flies North

With enough bedrooms to comfortably accommodate them, the house came equipped with a communal kitchen and large living room, a room that is basically unchanged to this day with an imposing floor-to-ceiling rock fireplace. Merton gave his informal workshops to the Sisters of the Precious Blood Order in this space.

The Sisters imagined Alaska would offer them a more perfect and solemn place for solitude and prayer, contemplation and quiet labor. Part of their order's mission was to pray for the sanctification of nations, to pray for the holiness of the clergy, to "labor in the tempest tossed vessel of the Church," and to "pour out the balm of their prayer on her deep wounds."

But the gung-ho Anchorage Archbishop, someone whom Merton personally liked, was busy trying to raise the profile of the local Catholic community. Father Joseph T. Ryan insisted on using their Precious Blood Convent as a temporary retreat house. He filled it with out-of-town guests and retreatants until a more permanent center could be built in Anchorage.

Their convent lacked a dependable source of running water. During Merton's visit the water problem was still unsolved and was attributed possibly shifting water table caused by the enormous 9.2 earthquake of 1964. All the water the six sisters needed for their subsistence had to be trucked in. The physical caregiving and ongoing water supply issues wore the nuns out. The kind of serene and quiet life they had aspired to eroded as the months wore on.

Father Joseph bet that Merton would offer words of encouragement to the women about their chosen vocation in the far-flung diocese. The Archbishop had shown great concern for the welfare of the Alaska based priests and Sisters. He feared that during severe winter months, and with a shortage of light, that they'd suffer "cabin fever."

Thomas Merton definitely raised the spirits of the Alaskan nuns. "You can imagine our feelings when we learned that he (Father Louis) would be in the archdiocese for about two weeks and the first four days spent with us," the Sisters wrote. "Archbishop Ryan told us repeatedly he wanted us to study under this renowned monk but we hardly believed it was possible."

The *nunnies*, as Merton sometimes affectionately called them in his personal letters to friends, could hardly believe they were to study with him for a Day of Recollection, along with the invited priests from across the state. Simply put, the *nunnies* were aglow and soon forgot about their water supply problems. They could barely contain their excitement about having such a celebrity, a true *homme d'esprit*, under their wings.

The star-struck Fire Lake nuns took their assignment of caring for Merton very seriously as they went about hosting and feeding him. The women later reported having "achieved the maximum output of victuals when serving lunch to 48 and dinner to 42 priests and chaplains who came from all parts of the state."

As the story goes, Merton's arrival, however, did raise some hackles. Mary Alice Cook—historian and author of author of *A Community of Grace: An Orthodox Christian Year in Alaska*, said Merton wasn't revered by everyone.

"Merton might have been treated and considered a Catholic treasure, but to the more conservative Catholics around here," Cook said, "he had evolved into a thorn in their sides." Cook, a long-time Eagle River resident, met me on a Saturday morning at the Jitters coffee shop not far from the convent.

"One man who wasn't at all interested in meeting or hearing from Merton when he was visiting was Claire Shirey," Cook said. "Claire lived in Eagle River at the time, was Catholic and his brother was a local priest. But Shirey was not a Merton worshipper and he was quite open about his disapproval.

Cook continued while I listened, "Shirey described him as 'a monk on a junket,' and said that for a monk who had taken a vow of silence, Merton sure had a hard time keeping his mouth shut."

Though the Merton fan club reached across a wide variety of people in the nonreligious world, within the Catholic rank and file, Shirey and others like him didn't endorse

Merton's inter-faith explorations. The Trappist monk had strayed too far outside standard Catholic boundaries and was speaking in too many new tongues and languages. As for Merton's interest in Muslims, Orthodoxy, Jewish and Eastern mysticism, opinions were voiced that a "good Catholic" doesn't need to go exploring outside of the faith.

In his correspondences with Czeslaw Milosz, Merton wrote, "Even as a Catholic, I am a complete lone wolf, and not as independent as I might seem to be, yet not integrated in anything else either." This "lone wolf" always raised questions and sometimes he stirred the Catholic pot and hierarchy.

The more nuns he could hang out with on the ground in Alaska, the better. Merton said that one of God's greatest creations were women. Throughout his monastic life, he often spoke and showed great warmth towards nuns he'd befriended such as Sister Miriam Dardenne, the Abbess of the Cistercian Abbey, Our Lady of the Redwoods monastery, and Sister Mary Luke Tobin of the nearby Sisters of Loreto in Kentucky.

And there were other professorial nuns with whom he regularly corresponded. He might have appreciated hearing about the feminist revolution, which continued brewing in the early 1970s, had he lived to see it. With his liberal views towards women, it's possible he would have expressed public support for passage of the Equal Rights Amendment. He would have delighted witnessing more women CEOs and elected public officials or a woman president.

If he had picked up the Anchorage newspaper during the week of his arrival, and chances are he did knowing how inquisitive he was, he might have glanced through some of the offerings on the pages of Alaska's largest newspaper, the *Anchorage Daily News*. Of note was its women's section, which featured a very important story for its female readership on how to cook hush puppies and make fish dinners more special. Next to the hush puppy advice column appeared a brief article reporting on the bold proclamations being touted by the Chinese dictator, Mao Tse-tung. The dictator proudly announced that under

Chinese Communism their society and their women were "free from the shackles of femininity." His Chinese women had more important things to think about than the sublime perfection of hush puppies.

I can imagine how alien it was for Merton to adapt to the Alaskan way of travel…to take his chances flying around by bush plane, after waiting for the right weather conditions, if a person wasn't used to it. The numbers of independent travelers who visited the state in the late 1960s, especially its more remote communities was miniscule. The more remote and primitive locations were often a deterrent for regular travelers. Alaska hadn't yet been heavily promoted and advertised on television and in magazine ads by the cruise ship lines. Its "Last Frontier" description had not yet become a hackneyed cliché. Alaska was still the mystical frontier, the giant, unfathomable nature reserve, the home of polar bears and icefields.

Merton was whisked from place to place without complaint. As it was, he hardly had time to understand what the actual logistics were in arranging his travel throughout the state.

During those blustery and damp, forty-degree days, I bet Merton would have heard Cessnas and Super Cubs buzzing through Anchorage skies, one after another, a sight we hear and see in all seasons. Small aircraft were kept busy traveling to and from well-known hunting and fishing sites across Cook Inlet near Mt. Redoubt—more private aviation traffic in one week than Kentucky probably experienced annually.

On the surface, Merton would have found the state's largest urban area—it's population in 1968 estimated at 45,000—to be a quiet, uneventful city without massive political demonstrations or cops resorting to using tear gas. Overall, the state's political scene, at least on its surface, appeared calm compared to the unrest in Louisville, Detroit, Atlanta and other big cities.

During his Eagle River remarks, Father Louis reminded the freezing faithful that as Alaskans, they didn't have the luxury to talk about any possible identity crisis.

"You have enough to worry about with all the Kodiak brown bears running around," he said. The room erupted in laughter.

But widespread racism did exist in the Last Frontier just as it did throughout United States. Alaska Natives were not integrated economically or culturally and were treated as second-class citizens. They were restricted to "Native-only" areas in public establishments. Until schools were built in the villages, many students were forced to attend government-sponsored (BIA) boarding schools in other parts of the state far away from their homes and families. Those schools were a tool to assimilate Native people into American society and undermine Native culture.

Had Merton stayed on the ground longer, he would have undoubtedly learned more truths about Alaska's public image. With his abiding interest in indigenous peoples, he might have met some of the up-and-coming Native leaders and spokespersons like the young and good-looking Willie Hensley, an Iñupiat who clerked for a prominent Alaskan judge around the time of Merton's visit. Hensley, now a recognized, well-respected statesmen in Alaska, was in his twenties and writing a critical paper about land rights for Natives which eventually helped to formulate the historic Alaska Native Claims Settlement Act of 1971.

"The spiritual-ceremonial world was falling apart, family units were being destroyed," Hensley told me when we were talking about the cultural atmosphere of Alaska in 1968. Hensley had just published his memoir, *Fifty Miles from Tomorrow*, about his life growing up in Kotzebue, above the Arctic Circle, and not far from the international date line.

"Then there was the welfare and educational strategies that came at people, and the state and institutional changes, the cities, the government policies, the introduction of the white system, and all that was piled on top of people, and when you do that, there's bound to be repercussions.

"No wonder during those times you could see a poor Native man stumbling around; he was a lost, fucking soul," Hensley said.

"There was a new language and new values, new skills required and it was their world, not *his* world, and he was trying to make adjustments."

It's raining hard today in Alaska, same as it was the day Thomas Merton first saw Southeast Alaska. Water gurgles down from the gutter; it thumps the deck and is no doubt flooding my sunflowers.

It's damper and drearier than usual. If Merton were in Anchorage or Southcentral today, I bet that even the nature lover in him would moan and curse the deluge.

In the slim notebook he began keeping of his far north travels, rain references abound. The monk spoke of the torrent, the driving rains and how the rich undergrowth of the forest smelled of life and rot, full of wet grass, decaying weeds and shrubs, fallen trees. On his excursions out of the city flying in bush planes to Dillingham in the Bristol Bay region of southwestern Alaska, and south along the foggy, rainy coastline to Cordova, Yakutat and Juneau, he encountered foul weather that often grounded the plane. He covered thousands of miles of territory in his short stay.

"I never saw such torrential rains as what met us when we got out of the plane," he said after his pilot finally landed in Juneau. In Alaska's capital he observed "green walls of mountains in the rain."

Back home in the Kentucky countryside, the monk had made it a habit to saunter through the hills in his dungarees and listen to the "festival of rain," as he called it. In *Raids on the Unspeakable* he observed, "The rain I am in is not like the rain of cities, it fills the woods with an immense, confused sound…"

He often prayed for rain, even if Kentuckians didn't need another drop.

He said that many do not appreciate "its gratuity, thinking that since rain has no price, it's free, not sold on the market, it has no value.

"Nobody started it and nobody is going to stop it. It will talk as long as it wants, this rain. As long as it talks, I am going to listen."

Merton missed experiencing a full-bore, Alaska winter, but he started to get a small taste of it as the seasons changed. Termination dust topped peaks in the Chugach Range before the end of September.

In between the great amount of religious commitments and obligations he had to honor in giving seminars and Days of Recollection talks to the nuns and priests, the busy monk vowed to try and take in as much as he could of Alaska's grand alpine landscape. Whatever the Great Land, with its wildness, birds, and highest mountains told him, he was eager to listen.

As I listened to the pounding rain, my heart felt it was in and out of dark, sad places. Michael's words came back to me, "Why so much fuss about Merton? What is he to you? Why should you or anybody care so much?" And on that trip to northern California, I couldn't adequately answer him.

…There is no question this place is full of ideal solitude in every form. So far I have seen the Anchorage area which is not so good—relatively crowded, big army bases, etc. Southeast of here there is a wild coast going for thousands of miles down to Vancouver, with literally thousands of little islands, most of which would be too remote or savage to live on…

…I have also seen the Chugach mountains which are extremely wild and probably too wild to live in mostly. Some of the central area which would be too cold. I am interested in the coast and expect to see a lot more of it in the next few days. The Bishop and clergy here are extremely generous and encouraging, and the people are simple, frontier types.

"I think Alaska would be the best place in the U.S. for a hermitage."

—Letter from Thomas Merton
to Fr. Flavian Burns,
Anchorage, September 25, 1968
The School of Charity

17 Merton's Alaska Journal

The authorized biography of Thomas Merton, *The Seven Mountains of Thomas Merton*, appeared in 1984, written by Michael Mott, a poet and novelist from Williamsburg, Virginia. Officially sanctioned by the Merton Legacy Trust, Mott's impressive biography ran 579 pages. It spent several weeks on the New York Times bestseller list and garnered Mott a well-deserved nomination for the Pulitzer Prize.

Alaska was left out of the book's index. The story about the monk's 17-day Alaska sojourn (September 17 to October 2, 1968) warranted a mere two pages in the entire biography due to the overwhelming amount of material the biographer needed to sift through and synthesize.

Michael Mott devoted more pages to the other exotic locales Merton visited in 1968 such as the details surrounding his meeting near the tea plantation with His Holiness the Dalai Lama, a meeting that took place a short time after Merton's scouting trip to Alaska.

Previous biographies, for example, Monica Furlong's, *Thomas Merton: A Biography* (1980) and Sister Elena Malits' *The Solitary Explorer* (1980), don't discuss Merton's Alaska connection. Despite the significance and length of time Merton spent in Alaska, the lack of mention in Merton biographies puzzled me.

Merton was obsessive about keeping journals and Alaska was no exception. But according to his explicit wishes, none of his many personal journals dating back to his days at Columbia could be mass-published until twenty-five years after his death. Perhaps it was for that reason that Alaska was largely overlooked.

In 1988, a very limited, fine-press edition (140 copies at $175 each) of his northern journal was published by a tiny California publisher called Turkey Press, four years after Mott's biography. The publisher of Merton's poetry, New Directions, in 1989 released the more comprehensive trade paperback, *Thomas Merton in Alaska: The Alaskan Conferences, Journals, and Letters* and included the added bonus of letters and notes from the talks and conferences he delivered in Alaska.

From what I could tell, outside of the Mertonites, the people who followed anything by or about Merton—the scholars, historians, and members of the International Thomas Merton Society—*Thomas Merton in Alaska* received scant attention.

If the Alaska journal appeared at all in bookstores, it wasn't something I never saw or stumbled upon in Alaska. Few beyond the Catholic crowd knew about it. The name Thomas Merton made little to impact upon the state's literary community its general readers. It was understandable that a collection of random recordings made by a Catholic thinker arrived with a bit of a thud, for less than twenty percent of the state's Christian population identified themselves as Catholic.

When I found the slender journal, it was instantly compelling. As a writer, I related to how a hasty, working notebook from a fellow writer looked and sounded—a bit scatter-brained and stuffed with a lot of useless facts and disjointed information. The ever-industrious monk made notes about all he saw and heard, the news headlines of the day, the graffiti he spotted on Alaskan bathroom walls.

"A Russian spaceship returns from moon...Helicopter shot down in Vietnam. Students rioting in Mexico City (for days)..."

Merton tuned into KHAR radio one Sunday morning and poked fun at the radio announcement originating from the agricultural heartland of Palmer, Alaska:

> Alaskan Golden Nugget Potatoes respectfully suggest that we worship God since we are a nation under God and want to build a stronger America. Nugget potatoes are glad of this opportunity to 'voice this thinking.' A good thought from a respectful potato.

On a day-trip to the Kenai Peninsula, though his notebook didn't record exactly where he went, he noted that many people were wearing "George Wallace for President" buttons.

As others have pointed out, the journal's start-stop nature signified the intensity of his mind. While trying to experience the rich outdoors, he felt he couldn't waste one quiet minute simply gazing at mountain goats on the rocky cliffs of the Chugach. He constantly wrote notes about the books he read while traveling, or composed letters to his brother monks back in Kentucky and to his personal secretary, Brother Patrick Hart. (Br. Patrick is still a monk at the Abbey of Gethsemani today and is in his 90s.)

Merton scholar, Lawrence S. Cunningham, described the fragmentary journal as "starkly impressionistic" and "aphoristic" and replete with "un-self-conscious entries." Cunningham said what struck him first and foremost was the alertness of Merton's eye and ear. Merton's writings reflected a certain spontaneity, he said. "We learn from Merton not doctrine or systematic teaching but a way of being and seeing."

A librarian and writer, Marjorie K. Cole, now deceased, was living in Fairbanks in 1989. She wrote a book review for the *Fairbanks Daily News-Miner* with the headline, "Wandering Hermit Hears Call to Solitude in Alaska." Alaska thrilled Thomas Merton to the core, the reviewer said.

But Alaska's strong and growing military presence greatly disturbed him. The military's visibility in the 49th state unnerved him. He noted that several of the religious he addressed were chaplains from various missile-launching sites in the Aleutians.

Eagle River, where Merton stayed during his first four days, was about an hour's drive north from Anchorage along the Old Glenn Highway. In those resplendent snow topped peaks of the Chugach Mountains, at the 4,000-foot level right above him, stood one of three Nike Hercules Missile sites. (Across the nation at that time stood 145 Nike Hercules Missile sites.)

Given Merton's disdain for war and military build-ups, his travels to Cordova and Yakutat gave him a different perspective.

I imagine, toward of the end of his Alaska trip, that Merton had more serious conversations with the diocese about the possibility of being a hermit in the secluded coastal town of Cordova. It was just far enough away from Anchorage's military installation, yet close enough to have support. "…I have no hesitation in saying Eyak Lake seemed perfect in many ways—for a place to live. The quiet end of it is several miles back in the mountains completely isolated, silent. Wild geese were feeding there," Merton wrote about Cordova, September 23, 1968.

The U.S. Military's first nuclear capable anti-aircraft missiles were designed to destroy any close formation of Soviet bombers at ranges in excess of 87 miles. Site Summit was one of only two Nike Hercules missile sites in the nation to conduct live fire exercises. If the Russians had aggressively advanced into American air space from across the Bering or Chukchi Seas, nuclear-capable anti-aircraft missiles with speeds over 2,700 mph, were stored on metal tracks, poised and ready to fire above Anchorage. Besides the missiles and launch control facility, the military had installed sentry stations, barracks, and other necessary administrative and storage facilities for the 200 or so U.S. Army personnel based year around on the mountaintop.

Merton, who had written extensively about the dangers of nuclear war, was probably told about the 244-acre missile site, Mt. Gordon Lyon, part of the U.S. Army Base of Fort Richardson, established in the year of statehood, 1959. And the adjacent U.S. Air Force Base, Elmendorf. Today they are referred as the J-BER (Joint Bases Elmendorf-Richardson).

"The shortest distance between the United States and the Soviet Union was over the North Pole, placing Alaska at the front lines," one military history pamphlet attested. "Alaska's strategic military importance helped cement its bid for statehood. The economic, social and political impacts of the Cold War on Alaska continue to be felt today."

Shortly after Thomas Merton struck up a correspondence with Boris Pasternak, the monk frequently addressed the precarious political landscape between the two world superpowers—the United States and the Union of Soviet Socialist Republics. Merton first spoke up about the dangers of nuclear proliferation back in 1961-62.

Merton hurled sharp criticisms about the build-up of more nuclear-capable weapons, which happened on both sides. He lambasted the political rhetoric instigating unrelenting fears about communism.

On June 8, 1962, the Trappist monk wrote a personal letter to one of his correspondents, a British schoolteacher named John Harris in which he stated, "I have just been instructed to shut my trap and behave, which I can do since these are orders that must be obeyed and I have said what I had to say."

In the manuscript for *Peace in the Post-Christian Era*, Merton called for a revolution of man's spirit and a full return to the God who, in the modern world, is singularly and terrifyingly "absent."

> How easily we assume that all negotiation has become futile, that the Russians are simply crooks, that war cannot be prevented except by threats. Obviously, there is some element of truth in all this, but perhaps we ourselves are not honest either, and perhaps we are looking for excuses to justify the use of violence. This could be a very grave matter indeed.

> As to proportion between the evil of war and the good achieved by it: it is true that one can and should sacrifice material things for spiritual values. But the sophistry about being *better dead than Red* conceals a dangerous fallacy.

> In war, particularly nuclear war, the awful physical destruction is only one aspect of the evil. The spread of demoralization and crime, the tragic corruption and decadence of society, even the

destruction of all social order, can follow from conventional war. How much more for nuclear war? There is every likelihood that a nuclear war would mean the total collapse of the social structure we are trying to defend. Would such a war be rational or just?

Merton vocalized these warnings in 1962. It took another 42 years, until 2004, before *Peace in the Post-Christian Era* was publicly printed.

What would the outspoken monk have to say today about the world we live in? When military budgets still grow exponentially and drones kill so many innocents? What would Merton say about the pockets of radicalized, violent, religious extremists, both domestic and abroad? Had Merton lived to see them, what would he say about Al-Qaeda and Daesh (Islamic State in Syria, or ISIS) or Timothy McVeigh's bombing of the Oklahoma City Federal Building, and David Koresh, of the Branch Davidians in Waco, Texas, or more recently, the destruction of the World Trade Center and loss of 2,996 lives, and more than 6,000 injuries—all in the name of someone's God? And the military coalitions, and anti-terrorist groups who use weapons and bombs to retaliate against acts of terror, killing innocent people in the process? What would he have to say?

I doubt Merton could keep his trap shut about policies of using terrorist tactics to fight terrorism. Surely, he would have criticized the individual acts of violence alongside the blanket condemnation of entire religions. Could he be still and silent knowing ISIS resorts to barbarism and uses the Internet to brainwash youth around the world and spread its hatred? Could he remain complacent when a sitting U.S. President bans people of a single religion from entering the country?

What would Merton say about the absurdities of the human family in the twenty-first century? The way lies are spun to look like Truth? How words are blatantly misused? He taught the younger monks to think for themselves, and verbalized about the dangers and "moral seduction of the collective" as Riehold Niebuhr cautioned.

The Fairbanks book reviewer was right. Alaska overwhelmed the Kentucky monk once he rested his busy mind. He knew beforehand about the High One, Denali, and he knew the territory was overrun with frightening bears and too many fighter jets on high alert. But once he really got a good, first-hand look at the land, rain and all, the experiences of Alaska's nature left deep impressions in him.

Merton said Alaska's mountains were the finest he had seen anywhere.

In Merton's letters back home to Brother Patrick Hart (September 24 & 26, 1968), he noted, "…have finished a workshop with the nuns—pretty good—and have seen some fabulous wild country. No question that this is the place for solitude—plus earthquakes, bears, etc.—and long dark winters….Anyway, everyone here is very nice and I have been all over the place in bush planes, really wild country and just terrific from every point of view…"

He concluded by saying the "mountains have got the Alps beat by a mile. This is utterly unique. Lots of live volcanoes too."

Merton viewed the beautiful Sangre de Cristo mountains of New Mexico for the first time in 1968. But Alaska's peaks surpassed those, too.

On his flightseeing trip toward Valdez, Merton said they were the most impressive mountains he had ever seen.

> Mt. Drumm (sic) & Wrangell and the third great massive one whose name I forget rising out of the vast birchy plain of Copper [River] Valley.
>
> They are sacred and majestic mountains, ominous, enormous, noble, stirring.

> You want to attend to them…I could not keep my
> eyes off them. Beauty and terror of the Chugach.
> Dangerous valleys. Points. Saws. Snowy nails.

The manifest for his northern program was jam-packed leaving little time for dreamy alpine meditations. In the course of roughly two weeks, he traveled to Eagle River, Cordova, Juneau, Yakutat, and Dillingham and wherever else the Bishop kindly thought to send him.

With boyish optimism, Merton was determined to take in as much as he could of the state's grand and pristine landscape, as long as it wasn't near any bears. Most of Merton's direct encounters with wild animals involved Kentucky's birds, possums, rabbits, squirrels, and weasels.

Up and down Eagle River (the town and river share the name) not far from where the small group of contemplative nuns resided, and where Father Louis stayed in his borrowed trailer, bears were probably in close proximity, only he didn't know it. At the higher elevations within the city boundary, it wasn't uncommon for brown and black bears to wander into yards and onto people's porches and decks. Bears could be seen on biking and hiking trails close to human populations.

Like a true artist, Merton sensed the landscape's unlimited potential. Its panoramas created a gold mine of inner rewards and treasures for anyone who paid attention. At the end of his questioning and global searching, if he could really lessen the cerebral activity and transform himself from a half-time hermit into a true-blue hermit, the miles of stark silence Alaska provided was worth more than a cursory look.

Alaskan men and women hold strong beliefs about the mystical powers of the wilderness. A chance to commune with the Most High does not require recognized gurus, priests, ministers, nuns, or any other intermediaries. You must go into the wilderness and experience it for yourself. Float down that cold river, trek across that ice field, hike into that rain forest, scamper up that mountainside trail. Witness the handiwork from the Divine.

The windswept Aleutians, the Interior's lonely rivers, towers of overlapping alpine cathedrals reach all the way to heaven. As the Russian expression goes, "Better to see it once than to hear about it many times."

As Merton circled about the 49th state, he continued making nature observations.

His journal entry of September 18, 1968 spoke about the "...woods of Alaska, marvelous—deep in wet grass, fern, rotten fallen trees, and big-leaved thorn scrub, yellowish birch, stunted fir, aspens."

He said the air in Anchorage was as cool and as sharp as late November in the "'Outside'—the Lower 48..."

September 19, 1968. "I am now here on a bright cold morning and the first thin dust of snow is on the lower hills. Mt. McKinley is visible in the distance from the Precious Blood Convent. Next to which I live in a trailer (very comfortable)."

The Alaskan *nunnies* would have gladly arranged for more nature hikes and kept their distinguished guest under their charge and care for months, if they could. But they understood Merton had a lot of important domestic and international places ahead of him.

Father Merton made promises to the Fire Lake nuns that one day, he would return. The nuns, the bishop, Frank Ryman in Yakutat and everybody else Merton ever casually met in Alaska also knew that a *second* trip was absolutely mandatory. The place was too big to comprehend in an initial visit, no matter how many bush planes he was to jump in and out of.
Without being on the ground for very long, he sensed the Great Land's potential for a purer solitude.

In another letter to Kentucky dated September 26, 1968—a letter Merton somehow managed to compose while juggling his social and religious schedule—he could have been describing Mike Pavlik when he said, "My feeling at present is that Alaska is certainly the ideal place for solitude and the hermit life. In fact, it is full of people who are in reality living as hermits. Men who have gone far out into the wilderness with a stack of books and who get themselves a homestead, cut wood, read, and stay away from everyone, living on moose, fish, caribou etc. "I don't plan it that way. But it gives you a good idea of the character of the place…"

But he only got a whiff of Alaska's more penetrating solitude, the sort of solitude that soaks to your bones, the kind of wilderness solitude that people like John Haines and the Pavlik family had known.

Another quick observation made the day he arrived, "…Fine snow covered mountains that lift their knowledge into a gap of clouds and I am exhilarated with them…first sight of mountains of Alaska, strongly ribbed, through cloud. Superb blue of the Gulf, indescribable ice patterns. Bird wings, vast, mottled, long black streamers, curves, scimitars, lyre bird tails (September 17, 1968)."

During that chilly, damp week, in a fleeting moment of self-reflection and dialogue, with his ever-present notebook close at-hand, Merton wondered why God had called him so far north, to such wild and unfamiliar terrain.

And on the pages of his thin, half-forgotten, Alaskan journal, in that turbulent, soul-cleansing time, he scribbled these hurried, yet prescient words:

"I'm here in answer to someone's prayers," he said.

And as I came to believe, those prayers were mine.

...Flew to Dillingham in a Piper Aztec (two engines), a fast plane that goes high. Bristol Bay area—like Siberia! Miles of tundra. Big winding rivers. At times, lakes are crowded together and shine like bits of broken glass. Or are untidy and complex like the pieces of a jigsaw puzzle.

...Two volcanoes: Iliamna—graceful, mysterious, feminine, akin to the great Mexican volcanoes. A volcano to which one speaks with reverence, lovely in the distance, standing above the sea of clouds...

...Redoubt...ugly and sinister as you get near it. A brute of a dirty busted mountain that has exploded too often. A bear of a mountain. A dog mountain with steam curling up out of the snow crater. As the plane drew near there was turbulence and we felt the plane might at any moment be suddenly pulled out of its course and hurled against the mountain..."

—Thomas Merton's Alaska journal,
September 30, 1968

18 Dillingham

I must be the only person in Alaska who ventured to Bristol Bay in the peak of summer for non-fishing related reasons. The Alaska Airlines flight southwest from Anchorage took 54 minutes and covered 330 air miles. With fewer-than-normal inbound passengers to Dillingham, and with its light cargo load, the first eighteen rows of the cabin remained empty for weight balancing purposes. Homeland Security confiscated my good pocketknife—one that Michael had given me—which was accidentally left inside my carryon. Merton never had to worry about any Homeland Security when he flew to Dillingham accompanied by an older Alaskan priest on his chartered Piper Aztec.

I was anxious to step outside the jet and onto the tarmac, my first trip to Dillingham. I walked into a scene immediately reminiscent of Cordova and Yakutat. Pallets of identical fish boxes marked "Wild Alaska Salmon" were stacked outside the sheet metal terminal for shipment to Lower 48 markets. The late July day was a cool 57 degrees with clouds like piles of snow accumulating in the sky.

The sheet metal terminal, partially caved in on one side, was stuffed wall-to-wall with people of all color—fishing crews, mostly men. Everyone squeezed next to the baggage claim corner. Loud thumps of blue plastic totes, ice coolers, and duct-taped boxes tossed through the chute could be heard throughout the room. Deck hands and cannery workers clamored to vacate town as quickly as possible, taking their hard-earned cash with them to Anchorage, Astoria, Seattle, or wherever they came from.

Merton would have learned about Bristol Bay's abundant fish. It remains the largest, richest wild sockeye salmon fishery in the world with average recent harvests of 25 million fish. Well-to-do sport fishermen and celebrities, who can spend more than $10,000 per week per person for a taste of anonymity and solitude, fly out to one of the exclusive, more remote fishing lodges in Wood-Tikchik State Park, 30 miles north of Dillingham. At 1.6 million acres, Wood-Tikchik is largest state park in the nation established ten years after Merton's visit. When the Kentucky monk slipped into town, and was introduced by air to Lake Aleknagik, the region was lesser known, and infrequently visited by recreation enthusiasts.

I wanted to retrace Merton's brief steps in southwestern Alaska. It was a good excuse for me to put timelines, meetings, reports, data, and family worries aside for a while. My first order of business was to try and find a pilot who could take me flightseeing over Lake Aleknagik. Dillingham wasn't set up to accommodate individual tourists. Pilots made their livelihoods by hauling employees, adventurers, and groups of fishermen to outlying lodges and by delivering supplies, gear, and luggage in the fast and furious summer and early fall seasons. For about $400 I could take a 40-minute flightseeing excursion, but my chances of finding an available pilot over the next four days was probably nil.

My cell phone went dead upon arrival. Only one telecommunications carrier served the region and it wasn't mine. I was off-the-grid completely and would have no Internet access for the next five days. Standing in the over-crowded terminal waiting for my checked bag to be thrown in, and with barely enough room to turn around, I wondered how I would find the woman with whom I had made prior arrangements to rent a vehicle.

I looked out of place in my pink-purple jacket and new Kelty daypack among the tattooed young men in rolled down rubber boots and soiled T-shirts and hoodies. I had no choice but to ask a kind local couple near the exit door to help me call the car rental woman. They instantly knew who I was talking about and agreed to call Connie. A few minutes later Connie showed up in her small car, rolled down the window, and told me to hop in. She was dressed in a baggy red T-shirt and black sweat pants, a woman in her 50s or 60s with curly salt-and-pepper hair, talkative and friendly. Her car was crammed full, she explained, with items she bought at a Saturday rummage sale, including an electric skillet she wanted to give to Sherol Mershon, the owner of the seasonal Silver Fin B&B where I'd be staying on Lake Aleknagik.

"Sherol and I go way back," Connie said. "Friends since we were teenagers. Everyone in Dillingham knows Sherol. She's the number one net-hanger in the whole region. She's been doin' it since she was sixteen. You'll be well taken care of at the Silver Fin B&B. The drive out to Lake Aleknagik is nice too, only the winding road is kind of dippy."

We drove into a gravel lot and walked into Connie's office where she took my payment on a manual credit card machine. Walls were covered over floor to ceiling in dusty, old license plates from every state. Nobody else was around. Connie's rental fleet consisted of two vehicles and I was taking one of them. She handed me the keys to a white, road-weary, 12-passenger van.

"Hey I'm sorry about the driver's side mirror," Connie said. "It was blown off from the forces of a helicopter. But don't worry, the other mirrors are undamaged as you can see."

Since there were no traffic lights or many roads in Dillingham, and it's impossible to drive to Dillingham from Anchorage, a driving map wasn't necessary. She pointed off in the distance a little way. "Take a right and follow that dippy road straight for 25 miles until you get to Lake Aleknagik."

Traditionally, Dillingham's Catholic priests hold private pilot licenses in order to serve as occasional pastors in over 13 outlying mission villages in the 33,000 square-mile Bristol Bay Region. This must have been an interesting curiosity to Merton when he met with his fellow priests, that priests and even a few archbishops do their pastoral work in Alaska by flying their own planes.

The latest pilot-priest, Fr. Scott, just arrived for his second assignment at Holy Rosary Church. He flew a Piper Cherokee to minister to the 500 or so Catholics scattered in places like King Salmon, Egegik, Port Alsworth and Iliamna. Another pilot-priest, Fr. James Kelly, crashed into a mountainside during a snowstorm in 2002 and died in his single-engine Piper Cherokee. In 2010, Alaska's longest-serving U.S. Senator, Ted Stevens, died in a plane crash along with four others about six miles from Lake Aleknagik in mountainous terrain.

I thanked Connie for the van and drove around Dillingham for a few minutes to get my bearings. On Wood River Road, I passed a shack with these spray-painted words, "Know your history, it will give you strength."

Next stop was to buy food at Alaska Commercial Company store, which 150 years prior, was the Russian American Company. I bought canned chicken noodle soup, an avocado for $5, and a small block of cheddar cheese and Pilot Bread. I got on the two-lane road and bounced my way to Lake Aleknagik.

The owner of the Silver Fin, Sherol Marshon, showed me to my room in the backside of her shop adjacent to her family's boat yard. Her two private cabins were full but led me to a private room with a shared bath next to where Silver Fin's deck hands often slept. Everywhere I looked around the grounds, neat piles of pale green fishing nets were loosely stacked up, three feet deep, and their buoys looked like candied almonds.

"Those mukluks on the wall belonged to my grandfather," Sherol said. "So did the antique snowshoes."

"You might want to know how the lake got its name. When Eskimos traveling in fog wrongly paddled up Wood River instead of arriving at Nushagak they yelled "Aleknagik!"—which meant *wrong way home*!

I interrupted, "Sherol, excuse me, but I really need to find a pilot who can fly me around Lake Aleknagik. Can you possibly assist me? I don't have a cell phone, laptop or anything."

"Oh, sure I can try and help. Let me make a few calls. It's weather dependent, you know. And it's iffy today, thick clouds, broken visibility. But be patient."

Sherol grew up on the lake. Her grandparents came to Alaska from a Washington State logging area to homestead in the 1930s. Her grandmother, Mabel, had many children, and was expecting another by the time she and her husband, Ray arrived in the tiny village of Lake Aleknagik.

"My grandmother took care of her eight children while living in a tent," Sherol said. "A tent was about the only thing they could bring north, plus a small cook stove. And that's how they lived for a long time—in a tent. She eked out an existence by taking in laundry and baking bread for fishermen."

Sherol never spoke on a real phone until she was 14 and didn't see a television until 1968.

"I remember when I first saw an apple tree, too. I thought all the red in the trees was because someone had strung up red ribbons. The only apples I had ever seen were the ones that came in weekly on our mail planes."

The book, *They Came the Wrong Way Home*, was published in 1961, which partly related the story of Sherol's pioneering ancestors, who very much reminded me of the Pavliks of Yakutat. It was left in my room as reading material. The author described Alaska's colorful history. "As long as there were minerals and mines, fish and furs, and men with imagination and a stiff backbone, hard times could be licked in the north."

I settled into my quarters and took out the two bottles of red wine from my luggage. While hanging around waiting for any available pilot, I planned to re-read Merton's Alaska journal and maybe use my time off-the-grid to write in my journal.

A few hours later, I found Sherol's daughter, Heidi, at the back of the main house. She was gutting and rinsing salmon at the fish cleaning station when I asked if she could kindly heat up some water for me. I had a pouch of freeze-dried beef stroganoff, expiration date of 2027. Heidi's sister Sally was occupied with her little girl, Bristol. Every summer Sherol's three grown daughters, their husbands, and kids leave Walla Walla, Washington to help their father Phil gill net and to help Sherol run the Silver Fin B&B.

Sherol and her family were Seventh Day Adventists. I didn't exactly know how to translate that, but it did explain why I was the only one sneaking glasses of red wine in my room every night behind the net-hanging shop. And why I never saw a cigarette, a television, or heard a single cuss word spoken around Silver Fin. And maybe why Sherol seemed to take each day as it came, living her daily life as if all was right with the world, that there was no reason to look out across America's political landscape and feel any kind of malaise had befallen the country.

"As Christians, it was about endless hope," Sherol said, "not a hopeless end. I don't pay much attention to the elections in Washington."

Merton flew mostly under the radar when he came to Anchorage, leaving little chance that anyone could make much of a fuss over him, outside of the clergy and nuns he met. Hardly any of the lay Catholics knew he was on the ground in 1968, certainly no one in the outlying villages and I'm guessing those were Merton's wishes. He didn't want to give any auditorium talks or reporter interviews.

I talked with Sherol's daughter, Heidi, about what it might have been like had the archdiocese announced Merton's arrival through some kind of publicity campaign. She was sympathetic to the monk's desire to slip quietly into Alaska.

"Everywhere you go, there would be people following you, taking pictures, asking to sign this or that," Heidi said. "Or they'd be saying they want to be photographed with him. But he's a man of God, not a movie star. He's representing God, but he couldn't just say to any possible fans, 'please go away, I want to be left alone and don't want to talk to you right now.' He had to be a kind Christian. No wonder he didn't want many people to know he was here," Heidi said.

The sky over the Silver Fin B&B on Lake Aleknagik was furrowed with clouds. Merton said he saw winding rivers, endless lakes, estuaries, vague, snow-covered peaks he could not name, no real towns per se, nothing below but brown and green puzzle-like pieces of the Earth. "Desolation like Siberia," he wrote.

Day two and there was still no pilot for me. I roamed around the lakefront kicking up rocks and gravel along the shore. The placid lake was breathtaking in its beauty, but without going up in a small plane, I couldn't begin to understand the vast scale of this wilderness the way Merton was given the opportunity to do so.

Merton wrote in his Alaska Journal, September 30, 1968, "Dillingham—gray sky, smelling of snow. Cold wind. Freezing. Brown tundra. Low hemlocks. In the distance, interesting mountains. We flew to them, between them. Brown vacant slopes. A distance somewhat like New Mexico (flat, dark blue line). Another distance with snow covered mountains vanishing into low clouds."

A hermit and his dog were rumored to live close to the end of the 20-mile lake, in a place called Sunshine Valley with no electricity or running water or an income. This hermit bought the land sight-unseen and likely subsisted on porcupine, huckleberries, beans and rice. A cup of coffee with sugar would be as luxurious to him as a plate of caviar to someone from Outside.

"What would it take to live here as a hermit-survivalist back in the 1960s?" I asked Heidi, a young mother in her twenties.

"This man, Tom Merton, you described...It's possible he might have died out here. Was he a person of bad health?"

"Well, yes," I said. "Back problems, bad teeth, stomach issues, bursitis. And people said he was a bit of a klutz."

"No, Dillingham area was probably not for him. He'd need a dog sled team, too, at the lake. And like my mother would say, he'd have to trust in God's protecting hands when he faced the elements."

"You'd have to know about everything," Heidi's sister, Sally, said.

"You have to know how to gather all your own food, fix motors and engines, and drive a snow machine. If you accidentally cut yourself or needed any kind of medical help, you'd have to have people around. People who could help you if got an infection. Or if you disappeared for two months in the back woods, somebody who would even know you were missing."

I appreciated their interest and curiosity about my personal mission to fly over the lake. When I absentmindedly walked around killing time in the yard of fishing nets, we had the chance to speak more.

"From what you have told me about Merton" Heidi said, "he inadvertently converted people through his writing. He never preached, right? That's interesting."

"No, he was a priest who didn't preach," I said while taking another swap at my forehead quickly getting chewed up by no-see-ums. "He was more of a working writer monk. And a great teacher. A bit frenzied and manic. Tried to do too much. Sort of like your mother in that respect."

"Work is her middle name," Heidi said.

"Your family is lucky to have such a long history and connection here, a place to always return to," I said. "Merton needed and was searching for the life-giving silence of such a place.

His Alaska journal mentions another lake that impressed him—Eyak Lake in Cordova."

Was there anything more Alaskan than watching brawny, smart men, like Phil Marshon and his sons-in-laws, pulling their 32-foot aluminum work horse—the "Knot to Scale"—with the 3208 Turbo Cat engine out of the waters of Lake Aleknagik to be dry-docked for the season right behind their large shop?

And was there anything more Alaskan than watching Sherol, 61, the master net hanger? With all my years living in and around fishing communities, such as Sitka and Yakutat, I never witnessed anything like what Sherol did to supplement her family's income hanging and mending nets of fifty fathoms or more.

Working inside her large shop, one side completely without walls and open to the air, Sherol stood in socks only over pieces of lead line strewn over the floor. It massaged her feet as she worked standing for 11-hour days hanging nets like a machine—efficient, precise, and with a sense of rhythm that only comes from forty-five years of practice. Her eighteen-year old helper, Shelby, re-spooled the needle with nylon twine, as Sherol worked non-stop with the lead lines, the cork lines, sometimes hanging over 200 nets for her customers in one fast-moving, intense, sleepless season.

She wielded her needle, black tape, and small knife with the finesse of a sushi chef. She did one knot…And one *more* knot, and one *more* knot. All at once, she carried on a conversation with me, answered her Bluetooth device, took a reservation, and listened to religious program on her CD player. She hung net, waved at people driving by, and kept track of two fishermen who helped lift stuff sacks full of nets weighing close to 200 pounds. Sherol never lost her concentration.

"You only need three things to fish," she told me while she was moving her hands swiftly down another line of net. "A boat, an oar, and a net."

For all boats and fisherman she ever worked for, she kept a log book and history of every net, noting the specifications of whatever she used on it. On some of the corks, she used a waterproof marker and affixed what she called "love notes" to the fishers and their crew onto the plastic floats. They sometimes read, "Here fishy, fishy, fishy" and "Get set for a great set" and "If you don't stand for something, you'll fall for everything."

And what was more Alaskan than the buzz of floatplanes taking off and landing all afternoon from the shores of Lake Aleknagik. I wished one of those planes on pontoons would have room for me.

Day three arrived, and no pilot. After another excursion into town. I visited the Russian Orthodox Church and cemetery, and watched arctic terns and cliff swallows on Kanakkanak beach. By the time I drove 25 miles back to the Silver Fin, Shelby and Sherol were still in the shop hanging nets.

Rain fell hard after a few minutes of sun and drifting clouds, fickle weather all day long. The shop clock sounded an alarm reminding Sherol it was time to pull her three loaves of bread out of the oven. She invited me to walk over to the kitchen in her private home. The mountains were visible, though flecks of blue existed, massive pearly white puffs of clouds dominated the skies.

"Now don't you give up on finding a pilot," Sherol said, "because I'm not gonna give up on it. I've made a few phone calls and know one real nice pilot, a young wilderness outfitter named Mark who lives close by. He'll call me if it can be worked out."

I sat at the table next to a bouquet of watermelon berry mixed with wild cucumber and dug into a serving of double-crusted homemade rhubarb pie.

As she placed a plate of fresh raspberries from her yard that had been "kissed by the rain" in front of me, I told her how many fond memories I had of living in the bush.

"I still don't know how to run a skiff by myself," I admitted, "and I can't load or unload firearms properly. I don't quilt, sew, bead, do pottery and I'm a terrible mechanic."

I held back from relaying any more of my survivalist shortcomings and domestic deficiencies. After hearing Sherol's stories about growing up on the lake, I felt as I did long ago when I first got to Yakutat and met the Pavliks.

Wouldn't I feel more useful to the world as a nurse, radiologist, engineer, geologist, carpenter, fishermen, or net-hanger? What kind of ridiculous vocation is this that brings in zero financial returns for years of effort when I could work on a fishing boat as a deck hand and have cash to take to the bank?

Merton was tiring out from his vocation, all the words he scratched and bled out for decades. Merton wanted to fell trees, study clouds, learn to hunt spruce grouse, grow plumper carrots.

Sherol went about her business in the kitchen while I took another big gulp of black coffee she poured from her French press.

"Merton wasn't here very long," I said. "But he made an interesting notation in his journal which I should read to you. Sherol, you especially will appreciate his words." She stacked a few dishes as I pulled out Merton's Alaska journal.

What Merton said was this, "Lake Aleknagik speaks to me."

"That's nice to know," Sherol said. "Kind of gives me chills."

"And he also mentioned seeing a chain of lakes far from

everything," I said. "And he asked, 'Is this it?' Meaning is this the place where he should be a future hermit?"

"Oh, yes. God did a masterful job here," Sherol said. "He had lots of fun and delighted to share it with his children as he's doing with you."

"Merton made a few other notes about the area which I'll read to you verbatim. 'On September 30, 1968,' he said, 'In Dillingham, some time ago (a year or two) the sister of the Orthodox priest went berserk and tore through the Catholic mission with an axe, breaking down one door after another as the Catholic Father retired before her from room to room, calling the State Troopers on various telephones....'"

"Hmm. I don't know a thing about that," Sherol said.

"Merton was searching for a pretty special place," I said. "He wanted to go to the farthest margins of society for more purifying silence, but wasn't very realistic about what geographic isolation can do to a person. Maybe it brings out the worst in us sometimes. Can turn us into animals. Dillingham in the 1960s was probably no place for a French-born intellectual and spiritual writer who didn't own a boat."

Sherol smiled and donned oven mitts to pull three loaves of mixed grain and flax seed bread out of the oven. She sprinkled a few tablespoons of water over her hands to run over the hot crusts, a technique she said her father showed her many moons ago to soften the crusts.

"On the other hand, that might be exactly what that monk was searching for," Sherol said.

"Maybe he needed to cross another threshold."

"It's like this," she continued, "if you have a good captain and a lousy boat, you'll get to where you're going. But if you have an idiot at the helm on a good boat, you'll run aground in no time. Seems to me that Merton was steering his boat toward the horizon."

Confirmation finally came. Sherol located an available pilot with a small three-seater, a Piper Pacer A-20. I needed to be ready to go in 20 minutes. I was going to finally see something of the "Siberia" Merton was in awe of.

The Russians have this idea of *sobornost*, a more intimate term of collegiality, and they have always had this idea of the Church as a real communion of souls and thought and consciousness, much more than we have until recently... Russian way of prayer is maybe one of the best for us. Russian spirituality would probably be the most helpful thing to really start contemplatives grooving in this country.

—Thomas Merton's lecture in Alaska on "Prayer and Conscience"

19 The Russian Icon

Two years before Thomas Merton arrived in the land of Old Russian America, during Easter week of 1966, Jack Ford, a philosophy teacher at Bellarmine University, came to the hermitage to present his monastic friend with a small, but very special gift.

Merton's book of meditations and essays, *Conjectures of a Guilty Bystander*, published in 1965, included a piece called "The Madman Runs to the East." In it, he mentioned that he was studying the Russian mystics, specifically Theophane the Recluse (1815-94). Theophane, a bishop and monk, resigned at age 51 to live in solitude eventually becoming a complete recluse. For 22 years, Theophane received no one but his abbot, his confessor, and a brother who saw to some of his basic survival needs.

Merton said the Russian monk did quite a lot of translating and literary work and carried on an immense correspondence with the people he was directing. "Theophane was a man who was quite above the vicissitudes of life, who lived in a rare atmosphere and yet remained fully human," Merton observed. "He stands out like Isaiah among the prophets. Here is a man I deeply admire because he was able to see what to do and then do it. He could walk straight forward and follow God."

The life of Theophane was an apparent oddity that went against reasonable norms and made no sense. Merton felt the presence of real greatness, nobility, and wholeness in the example of this impressive Russian recluse and mystic.

The gift presented to Merton that day was a replica of a Russian icon. Merton treasured it instantly. He placed the icon with great affection on the cottage's east wall. "What a thing to have in the room. It transfigures everything," he said.

Merton chose his words carefully in saying it *transfigured* everything—because the icon was none other than a depiction of the Holy Prophet Elijah in Hebrew Scriptures, translated in the Greek and Orthodox Biblical traditions as *Elias*.

"It's fabulously beautiful, delicate and strong," the monk said, "A great red globe of fiery light and glory, with an angelic horse rearing up in unison inside it, drawing a simple Russian peasant's cart with the prophet standing in it, looking toward the great globe of the divine darkness to which he ascends—the blackness of the divine mystery. Darker curve and shelves of mountains below…"

The icon must have also pleased Merton because it conjured up many ideas and memories, reminding him of a poem he wrote in 1955, one of his most well-known verses, "Elias: Variations on a Theme."

Merton remembered when he was sixteen years old, and visited his father, Owen, who was in long-term care at a hospital in Middlesex, England, suffering from a brain tumor. Owen showed his sketches of the icons he was working on to his teenage son.

Merton recounted his deep love for his father in *The Seven Storey Mountain*. As an artist of some reputation who was definitely selling more of his work and hoping to rise internationally, Owen taught his son to regard art not merely as a means to more sensual pleasure, but that "art was contemplation," involving "the highest faculty of man."

The religious art form of iconography took hold of his father's imagination, and it was something Tom never forgot. During the last few visits to the hospital, Merton recalled how his father worked from his sickbed on a series of drawings. They were unlike any of his father's previous drawings. Merton later described the sketches of icons as being closer to the earlier Byzantine style. Owen traced figures with elongated faces and saints with great beards and halos.

The death of his father left him sad and depressed. "But that eventually wore away," Merton recalled, "and when it did, I found myself completely stripped of everything that impeded the movement of my own will to do as it pleased. I imagined that I was free. And it would take me five or six years to discover what a frightful captivity I had got myself into."

"It was in this year, too," Merton wrote, "that the hard crust of my dry soul was finally squeezed out of all the last traces of religion that had ever been in it. There was no room for any God in that empty temple full of dust and rubbish which I was now jealously to guard against from all intruders, in order to devote it to the worship of my own stupid will."

Tom Merton became the complete twentieth-century man, lamenting that he now belonged to the world in which he lived. "I became a true citizen of my own disgusting century: the century of poison gas and atomic bombs…"

His father's death was also the catalyst to take many rucksack trips around Europe, studying French and Latin, immersing himself in history and art wherever he went.

If he found himself admiring a cathedral in France, or some little church somewhere, whether it was Protestant or Catholic, and especially when he was in Rome, he noticed something about those places that took hold of his imagination. It was purely sensory, as he wasn't yet reading theology or Scripture, nor did he consider who Jesus was, or what defined a Catholic sensibility or imagination.

But something *did* tug at his subconscious, though he couldn't label it or point to anything specific. The architecture drew him in. He remembered while growing up how his father often expressed artistic thoughts to him about the way a particular French village looked, whether or not it beheld panache and flair. If a location didn't register any artistic nuances, if it didn't emit any mystical, artistic energy, or symbolize some unlocked vital essence in its light or scenery, then Owen Merton informed his son it was time they pulled up stakes and moved on.

While wandering around Rome as a college student, Tom Merton visited ancient churches with bright, mosaic tiles, and icons with bejeweled frames. The attraction and curiosity with Byzantine art and icons stayed with him the rest of his life.

Many years later, in the 1960s, Merton composed an essay titled "Sacred Art in the Spiritual Life" where he wrote that sacred art is not meant "merely to provide an accurate representation of material forms. Sacred art conveys a hidden and invisible spiritual reality…"

He said the Byzantine tradition of mosaics is the "taproot of the great tree of Christian art." Merton eventually moved the Elias icon from the mantle to the wall of a small room, which was later added to the hermitage, a space he used as a chapel.

Having no formal religious education, I was acquainted with Elias only because my beloved mountain in Yakutat was so named. The Russians named the mountain when Vitus Bering and his sailors first spotted the unknown, magnificent snowy peak from their ships off the coast of Yakutat on July 17, 1741. Consulting their Orthodox Christian calendars, the sailors saw that it was near the Feast Day of Elias, and thus bestowed the name accordingly.

In all the years since I first got to Yakutat, I never bothered to find out what a Feast Day was nor who this Elias was in the Biblical story—not until I discovered Merton's Elias icon.

The Elias of Hebrew Scriptures, I learned, was a penniless cave dweller. Elias means the Lord's strength. Elias was often depicted traveling to the heavens in a blazing chariot because of his fiery zeal for the glory of God. A rendition of this scene was pictured in the icon Merton cherished—the prophet Elias returning to the Lord in a chariot.

Merton composed his lengthy poem, "Elias: Variations on a Theme," ten years before moving into his hut in the woods. In the spare quality of its lines, the poem affirms how a "free man" is a man of spiritual freedom, comfortable in his own solitude—never lonely—a man who can metaphorically wander free into the desert.

Under the blunt pine
I who am not sent
Remain. The pathway dies,
The journey has begun.
Here the bird abides
And sings on top of the forgotten
Storm. The ground is warm.
He sings no particular message.
His hymn has one pattern, no more planned,
No less perfectly planned
And no more arbitrary
Than the pattern in the seed, the salt,
The snow, the cell, the drop of rain.

(Snow says: I have my own pattern:
Rain says: no arbitrary plan!
River says: I go my own way.
Bird says: I am the same.
The pine tree says also:
Not compulsion plants me in my place,
No, not compulsion!)

Elias – Variations on a theme, (part IV)
—Thomas Merton

When Merton received the Elias icon, he had no way of knowing that two years later, he would fly down the cloudy Gulf Coast of Alaska, past Cordova to spend time near the foot of Mt. Saint Elias.

What was Merton thinking when he arrived in the "ramshackle fishing village," of Yakutat? It was as if the prophet Elias had been following the monk around.

When Frank Ryman, Sr. hosted Thomas Merton at the Airport Lodge, he put on his best public relations pitch in an effort to lure Merton to choose Yakutat for his future hermitage site. The lodge owner and World War II veteran bragged about the alpine splendor of the peak. Locals often boasted about the region's most important visual marker—Mount Saint Elias.

"Too bad, you can't see Elias today," the locals would say. "Sure hope, you get to see it before you leave." I remembered how Michael's first boss, Jim Jensen, had done the same thing on that night he first showed Michael and I, the two newlyweds, to our government apartment.

Jim repeated several times that we'd enjoy spectacular views of the mountain, *if* and *when* days were clear enough.

In the years that followed, I prided myself that I could easily rattle off dates about the peak's history, could cite a few details about Vitus Bering's voyages, and could name his ships.

But I didn't try and locate a Bible to read any references to Elias. It was the synchronicity with Merton's icon that led me to know more about the prophet.

God spoke through the prophets, as I found out. And it wasn't that prophets told the future, but that they, being a special breed of people, spoke the truth about God in the here and now. Prophets didn't win popularity contests with the people because the people often didn't want to hear God's word.

In a letter Merton wrote to Lawrence Ferlenghetti he said, "Old Testament prophets hit hard in the right places, and the chief reason was they were not speaking for themselves." (August 2, 1961)

The Holy Prophet Elias was a pivotal figure in the Old Testament, which referred to Elias as Elijah, as were Moses, Isaiah, and Jeremiah. In the Jewish tradition and feast of the Seder, an extra cup of wine is always poured for Elijah at the family's sacred meal, or left by the door, in the event that if Elijah should appear it would signal the coming of the Messiah.

I read the Old Testament books of Exodus and Kings, specifically to learn more about Elias. I then cross referenced the Catholic Encyclopedia. The Biblical story bears repeating with a few asides.

…And there, an Angel of the Lord visits him and tells him to go on a journey, and he wanders for 40 days and 40 nights in the desert and arrives at Mount Horeb to take protection in a cave where he waited to hear the voice of God.

A terrible storm arises, and then a big earthquake, and a burst of flame, and Elias still waits in his cave to hear the voice of God. But it is in the quiet wind, that the prophet finally hears God's voice…

On Mt. Carmel (also the name Merton gave to his hermitage) Elias overcame the pagan-priests of Baal by challenging them to a kind of spiritual duel—their false god against the one, true God.

…An altar was erected by the Baal-worshippers and the victim laid upon it; but their cries, their wild dances and mad self-mutilations all the day long availed nothing: 'There was no voice heard, nor did any one answer, nor regard them as they prayed.' Heaven was silent.

Towards evening, the holy Prophet Elias, having built his sacrificial alter of 12 stones, one for each of the 12 tribes of Israel, placed the sacrifice upon the firewood.

…Through the prayer of the prophet, there came down a fire from the heavens and it fell upon the sacrifice, the wood, the stones, and even the water.

The people fell down to the ground crying out: 'In truth the Lord is the One God and there is no other besides Him!'

…Through his prayer the heavens opened and there came down an abundant rain, watering the parched earth."

I had to let the Biblical story about my mountain's namesake sink in. The Old Testament prophet was a wandering solitary, the lone voice crying out in the desert wilderness for the Israelites to keep their faith. He showed those pagan worshippers who was in charge. And after all the fiery showmanship was over, *God then sent down a huge rainfall to soak the lands* and to wake the people up as the Holy Prophet had hoped.

Elias became the patron saint of droughts and earthquakes.

Elias received God's revelation directly and he showed up in the Bible again in the New Testament when he stood with Jesus, Moses, and the three disciples on another mountain—Mt. Tabor. On Mount Tabor, Christ's raiment, his clothes, start to shine in the "uncreated light," the Divine light of God's essence. In Christianity, this story is the famous moment of Transfiguration.

Had he made it back to Alaska, Merton would have come back to Yakutat to gaze at Mount Saint Elias again, to search for God in the mountain breezes and in all that alpine whiteness up there.

With great feelings of personal relief in 1968, as he began his world trek, Merton admitted, "I have needed the experience of this journey."

I dreamt about how perfect it would have been if he could have come back to live as a real hermit underneath Mount Saint Elias, the prophet's mountain.

329

…We are not hungry but neither are we happy. We are in search of *meaning* and the search is consistently frustrated, not only by the fact that ancient and traditional symbols seem to have lost their efficacy, but by the fact that artists, *poets*, and so on have suddenly become hostile and uncommunicative, frustrating the desire for meaning by declaring that there are no meanings left and that one has to get along without them…

—Thomas Merton,
Conjectures of a Guilty Bystander

20 In the Land of Russian America

The time had come to make a pilgrimage to the former home of the Sister Adorers of the Precious Blood Convent. Eagle River is no longer considered rural. As a bustling part of the Municipality of Anchorage, it's currently home to over 30,000. On weekdays, steady streams of cars line up along the Glenn Highway as daily commuters merge with the mass of other commuters driving into Anchorage from the Matanuska-Susitna Borough. Small businesses and strip malls, auto-parts stores, coffee shops, banks, pizzerias, gift shops, gas stations, a small nursery on a hill, and a few big box stores span the main thoroughfare. A short distance from its core shopping district, in America's second largest state park, Chugach State Park (500,000 acres), beavers build dams, bears freely roam the same trails as the walkers and hikers, and runs of wild salmon still migrate from the ocean through the silty waters of Cook Inlet and into Eagle River's estuaries.

On a September day, I turned onto the aptly-named, Monastery Drive in my green Honda SUV caked with grime and dirt. The road to the former Precious Blood convent and to the brown, single-domed Saint John Orthodox Cathedral that now stands next it, is bordered by well-kept single family homes. Their big picture windows face the surrounding wooded acreage and the Talkeetna Mountains. (At the time of Merton's visit only two structures existed on the site: the chaplain's trailer where he slept and the two-story convent, the Big House.)

The door to the Big House was left open and I didn't see anyone around except for a few children kicking a ball in the yard in front of Saint John Cathedral.

Inside the Cathedral, the walls were graced with luminous, translucent colors—and bearded faces and robed figures in golds and blues. On another wall, a wood map of Alaska and icons of Alaska saints—St. Herman, the Wonder Worker, St. Juvenaly, and St. Peter the Aleut Martyr. I imagined Merton would be amazed and pleased to find so many icons—theology in color and art melded into something beautiful, as they've been described—were mostly painted by a woman iconographer, Robin Armstrong.

A few months prior to Merton's visit, in a March 1968 newsletter, the Precious Blood nuns reported that their driveway was a sheet of ice and that the 18-inches of snow they had enjoyed was almost gone. Their chaplain, Father Grady, slid all the way down the icy hill after offering Mass. "We have suggested many times that there should be a rope between our Monastery and his trailer," the nuns reported.

One of the green-carpeted bedrooms in the Big House is now a guest room, affectionately known as the Thomas Merton Room. A framed black and white picture of the famous monk at the Abbey smiling cheek to cheek in his denim jacket hangs on the wood-paneled wall. Two hand-sewn pillows decorated with images of black bears, something Merton would be amused by, lay on top of the quilt-covered bed. On the wall near the fireplace, hangs a framed watercolor of a golden eagle in what could be Denali Park where they famously migrate.

I recognized a framed black and white photograph of Merton's grave taken at the Abbey of Gethsemani. I remembered the rows of plainly-marked, identical white crosses uniformly marking the graves of deceased monks, including Merton's.

On the shelves of the built-in bookcase, was an eclectic selection of books, *The Philokalia*, *The Silver Chalice*, *Daily Vitamins for Spiritual Growth*, assorted other religious texts, plus a copy of *Boundaries in Dating*. But oddly, there were no books by Merton.

After seeing the coast was clear, I made my way upstairs and sat in the large living room with the massive, floor-to-ceiling rock fireplace where Merton gave his Days of Recollection talks.

It was strange and a bit unsettling to be sitting in that room, more than forty years after Merton stood there. My imagination drifted to what the scene might have been. The monk zoomed into action, donned his glasses, and rifled through a few folders of notes. He walked over to the row of tall windows a dozen times. How could he not? He checked the sky and shifting clouds, hoping the drizzle would stop, and enable him to catch another partial glimpse of the High One, Denali. He wasn't overly serious and philosophical when he gave his pep talk to the Alaskan nuns and priests. They could count on him to show warmth and humor.

If I had been in the room with Merton that day, I would have been as gleeful and as happy as those nuns. I'm sure I would have blushed a few times, too, had he looked my way when he uttered these timely words of advice to his many admirers, "Our life demands breakthroughs to go beyond where we are, to get out of the woods somewhere."

And I was imagining that after his experience of being in love with Margie, that those words echoed in the depth of his heart, lending a stronger dose of conviction to these words as well, "Be men and women of prayer for whom God is everything, He's enough. Sufficient. Be content to live close to Him," he advised the Alaskans.

No one disturbed me in the living room of the Big House. I was in silence staring up at the antique wood snowshoes that adorned one part of the wall, and the replica icons grouped to the right of the fireplace. A pile of assorted pillows in all shapes and sizes covered one of the corners. On the mantle, a plain wood cross and a thick, Orthodox study Bible sat near two red votive candles.

Merton's spirit, was it still present in this room?

His bridging ability between the Roman Catholic tradition and the Orthodox tradition was decades ahead of his time, as the Canadian scholar, Ron Dart pointed out.

Catholic clergy and Protestant missionaries who ventured to Alaska at the start of the 20th century acknowledged the long lasting cultural legacy and profound impacts Russian missionaries and monks had. Russian Orthodoxy is still today the most widespread Christian faith among Alaska Natives.

However, Russian influence began long before the first mission of ten Russian monks outside Russia arrived in Kodiak in 1794 to establish orthodoxy. Early Russian seafarers and fur traders began exploring the Alaska coast and islands at least 50 years earlier.

The Russian American Company conducted business in Alaska under a special license secured from the Russian Empire. During the early fur trading days, in the worst historical estimates I heard, Russian *promyshlenniki* (fur traders) decimated almost 80 percent of the Aleut population by the mid-1700s. Natives were murdered, subjugated and enslaved. The introduction of new diseases further harmed the Native population.

By the time the group of eight Orthodox monks and two priests arrived, they must have recognized the pain and suffering of the Native population, for reports of atrocities being committed were relayed to the Czarist government. They came to convert the indigenous people, not with the sword, but by personal example of their faith and monasticism. They also served as moral buffers in their emissary role for the Imperial leadership. The Russian monks tried to mediate the overall conduct of the Russian trading companies and often differed and clashed with them over their mistreatment of Natives.

In addition to establishing schools, orphanages and caring for the orphans, it was the Russian Orthodox monks who were credited with translating Alaska Native languages into written form.

Herman, one of the original monks sent from Imperial Russia to Alaska in 1794, later became the legendary Saint Herman. Herman, as an elder, built a log hermitage on Spruce Island off Kodiak in the early 1800s where he intended to live in seclusion and remain a hermit for the rest of his days.

But Fr. Herman was unable to completely separate himself from Aleut culture and the Aleuts he befriended. He felt an obligation and duty to remain attentive and compassionate to the needs of local people. The hermit-monk had advised high Russian officials in 1822, that he founded a school and orphanage for Native children and started Russian America's first agricultural program.

Innocent Veniaminov, a priest, and a humane and learned man, as historians have described him, arrived first in Unalaska in 1824 and later transferred to New Archangelsk (Sitka) where he became Bishop Innocent of Alaska. He wrote Aleut cultural histories, designed and built churches and the landmark Cathedral of the Archangel Michael in Sitka, promoted literacy and education, expanded Orthodoxy across Alaska and empowered Native leadership of the Orthodox missions. (After his service in the Russian colony, Veniaminov eventually returned to Russia and became the top leader, or Metropolitan of Russian Orthodoxy, in Imperial Russia.)

Russia's greatest poets and novelists enthralled Father Merton, but he was also captivated by Russia's Christian heritage and the great monastic traditions kept alive by the Eastern Church.

While in Alaska, Merton was casually told about Fr. Gerasim, a spiritual man, or *starets*, who lived in seclusion on Spruce Island. Merton made a note of it in his Alaska journal. Merton hoped to meet Fr. Gerasim. The Orthodox monk also wrote poetry, however, Merton likely did not know it. But the Russian monk, nearly 80 years old, who sewed his own vestments and embroidered his own altar clothes, lived too far away. Travel logistics from Anchorage to Spruce Island—approximately 8 miles long and 4 miles wide were challenging. The old Russian Orthodox monk was originally from Kazan, Russia. He had been in Alaska since 1927, and in the last decades of his life, chose to be the "caretaker of the flame," to keep Fr. Herman's memory alive on Spruce Island.

The Soviet Union banned organized religion and closed most of its Orthodox Churches and monasteries and whitewashed over many centuries-old church frescoes. Following the religious persecution and tumult of the Communist Revolution, many Orthodox, such as the Old Believers, fled Russia for Europe, North and South America.

In the 20th century the Orthodox faith was preserved in Russia's former colony. The Russian monks and priests learned to address the native people in their own languages. The National Register of Historic Places lists 36 Orthodox churches from Unalaska to the Pribilofs to Kodiak, and to small villages like Russian Mission and Ninilchik, as well as in Anchorage, Kenai and Sitka.

Father Gerasim died one year after Merton's visit to Alaska. Two years later, in 1970, Fr. Herman was canonized, or glorified, as the Orthodox refer to it, as the first Russian Orthodox saint named in all of North America, Saint Herman. Today, Saint Herman, the "wonderworker" icons hang in churches throughout Alaska.

Monasticism, Merton recognized, is an old and respected tradition among the Orthodox, and Alaska, evangelized by the venerable St. Herman and other monks from the Valaam Monastery, was no exception. Like the monastics, both then and now, Orthodox faithful participate in the Church's liturgical schedule of worship, and keep their own daily prayer rule. Monastics, along with the Orthodox laity, observe the Church's fasting rules on Wednesdays and Fridays and before designated feast days.

The blushing Fire Lake Nuns, the nuns of the Sister Adorers of the Precious Blood Order, are long gone, having been finally forced to vacate the property sometime around 1971 over the terrible water supply conditions. All of the Sisters who once lived in Eagle River have since died.

The former convent is now known as the Saint James House, and is used as a community education center. College kids who come for spiritual instruction are expected to fast from media, computers, and cell phones under a prescribed schedule. The young people willingly do it.

A few weeks after Merton's September visit, the autumn days faded, and the lights of the aurora borealis danced across the November skies.

The Sister Adorers of the Precious Blood compiled an Advent newsletter which they forwarded to their religious superiors in the Lower 48. The mimeographed newsletter opened with some of the nuns' observations about their first full winter in Alaska, the way they personally experienced it:

> The past months have been eventful and packed with the unexpected and unprecedented. Perhaps when we have been in Alaska longer we will be surprised at nothing, but 17 months has not conditioned us to expect the sight of the tremendous mountains tinged in early morning pink, the glory of the moon rising at three in the afternoon and setting in the darkness of nine in the morning, a large moose grazing by the hour in our front yard, winter beginning the 13th of October with a foot of snow, weeks of subzero weather, the awesome vision of the northern lights…

> So often we are asked about the northern lights. We have seen them a few times, but this month they were visible for about one hour on a cold, clear night. They were all over the sky but were not vivid colors, rather rainbow hues. It was a thrilling experience.

> We were happy.…

The report concluded with a lament about the poor water supply and how the water for their convent had to be hauled in by truck. "Please pray for us that our community will be a vital witness of Christ's presence in Alaska," it said, and was signed, "Devotedly in the Precious Blood, Sister Rosemary, Secretary."

I exited the Big House and walked across the grassy yard and down toward the small cemetery where a winding dirt footpath bordered with wet ferns and high-bush cranberries began.

Harold and Barbara Dunaway, the founders of the current St. John Orthodox intentional community, were buried in the cemetery.

In the same year of Merton's visit, the Dunaways arrived in Anchorage, also from Kentucky. The husband and wife were members of the Campus Crusade for Christ ministry. They were on an evangelical mission to help spread the word of the Gospel to military personnel based in the region's army and air force bases.

Father Harold eventually left the Campus Crusades organization to begin his own ministry where people could gather for serious discussion and Bible studies. The Dunaways purchased the Big House from the Anchorage Archdiocese and five acres of land surrounding it in 1972.

After a decade of continued faith work, deeper questioning, and a search for the right church of the New Testament, the Dunaways felt a strong spiritual pull toward Eastern Orthodoxy, which led them to be formally received into the church, along with their children. To them, Orthodoxy provided more of what they were looking for—a more fully integrated and disciplined Christian way of life. Rather than follow a religious ritual or practice relegated to carved-up pockets of time on Sundays only, and rather than battle the constant interferences from society, media, politics, and material pressures, they sought a more *living* tradition.

They envisioned the establishment of an "intentional community," where many Christian members of their future parish could live in proximity to one another, as in those Russian villages of long ago. It took lots of private funds to finance the construction of St. John Orthodox Cathedral. People pulled their resources and donated their annual State of Alaska oil royalty dividends, their Permanent Fund Dividends, and the building began.

Sister Kathleen O'Hara arrived in Anchorage in 1971, three years after Merton. I met her in 2006 at St. Benedict's Rectory in my "early Merton days," when Merton was only the spiritual spackling—not the wall. I hoped she'd be able to fill in some details about his Alaska activities. A nun in the Sisters of Mercy, Sr.

Kathleen wore a plain navy skirt, white turtleneck, with a black and silver cross around her neck, a silver band on her left ring finger, and no earrings. As she remembered, the nuns who were fortunate enough to meet Father Louis in Eagle River talked about him constantly. She heard nuns tell stories about Merton having dined at the Marion House in 1968. The excitement over Merton's visit had not yet subsided—it went on for years after. Five nuns who belonged to the Sisters of Mercy from the Diocese of Providence Hospital, the hospital where both of my sons were born in Anchorage, were elated to be sharing a meal with Fr. Louis.

One of the exuberant Sisters asked Merton "What should we call you?"

Merton gently patted the nun's knee and said, "Just call me Uncle Louie."

"He had a real *human-ness*," Sr. Kathleen said. "He was outgoing and could move in and out of all worlds comfortably, with people from all walks of life. He had reached a new depth in his own spiritual life by the time he got to Alaska."

"He was urged from the grace he had been given to do something with it. He wanted to be more of a recluse, but people would have still invaded his life. I think he needed to recharge his batteries.

"He impressed everyone with his great simplicity and complete freedom to be himself. I think we learned a great deal from his person as well as his lectures and the discussions which gave a much deeper and more realistic concept of the contemplative life in this century," Sister Kathleen said.

Sr. Kathleen believed that Baby Boomers missed having much of a spiritual life and that some kind of spiritual dryness set in. "People are hungering and are grabbing for spiritual entities now, but the church let them down," she said. The Boomers were sucked into materialism. On the other end, there's greed, injustice, insensitivity, and corruption.

"But people, all people, are made in the image and likeness of God," she added, "and whoever he is for you. We can't disclaim others' profession of faith." At that, she stood up and excused herself to take a phone call and left me sitting alone in the office waiting area. I felt a little out-of-place sitting in St. Benedict's office talking to a nun about Thomas Merton because I *was* one of those people, I thought, a Baby Boomer yearning for what, I didn't quite know, but certainly trying to stay balanced. I didn't know where any of my probing was leading but this nun was highly entertaining, genuinely warm, and a good listener.

I learned that for many years, she taught kindergarten, before switching to a full schedule helping the sick and divorced, visiting people who were homebound, and working at the assisted living house at Providence Hospital.

I glanced down at my list of questions but she didn't wait.

"This is the little poem I used to tell the kids, she said. "Surprise! Surprise! God is a surprise! Surprise! Surprise! God is right before your eyes!"

"Sister Kathleen, thanks for sharing that. It's not something I heard as a kid."

"It's a good one, alright," she said as we both smiled at one another.

"Oh, and here's something else I just remembered. Thomas Merton gave a Day of Recollection retreat to our Sister of Mercy nuns in Anchorage. He kept telling them how much he would love to see snow. And by golly, on September 24th, on the Feast of Our Lady of Mercy, it snowed! And Fr. Louis was ecstatic."

After about an hour when our conversation came to a close, I confessed that my knowledge about Merton was still so limited and that I had a lot of studying to do. As a writer, I was full of doubt.

"Maybe you should pray to Thomas Merton for his help," she said. And as I stood up to leave she hugged me and kissed me on the cheek. "Now, see, you've been kissed by a nun!"

Another nun, Sister Mary Catherine, who dined with Fr. Merton at Marian Housem wrote that, "Meeting Thomas Merton was one of the most grace-full experiences of my life. I will never forget his eyes: clear blue, sincere and interested. His handclasp was firm and his warm laughter a soft chuckle that came quickly and was definitely contagious.

"I can remember being surprised at the humor of one who had spent [27] years in a Trappist monastery. He was real, totally relevant, yet completely simple. He spoke as one who was entirely free and his whole manner conveyed a message of this Freedom of Spirit."

The letter continued, "We were the first group of Sisters to whom he had preached a retreat and, providentially, someone thought of taping it. We have often remarked that every time we play that tape we hear something we had missed previously.

"Merton loved Alaska!..."

"He left promising us that he would return. We were shocked at his death but there is a certain comfort in remembering him, his interest in the Alaskan Sisterhood, and his promise to remember us in prayer."

By the time the Dunaways came to purchase the Big House and the surrounding Eagle River property, the nuns from the Sister Adorers of the Precious Blood had been forced to return to their Mother House and were scattered to other convents across the Lower 48.

Sister Rita Mary Lang, the Mother of the Precious Blood nuns, later moved to a convent in Brooklyn where she died in 2008. Mary Alice Cook, who resides in the intentional community, conducted as many interviews as she could to track down those who might have met Merton for articles she wrote for the Saint John Orthodox newsletter.

Cook found Sister Rita Mary, former "Mother" of the Eagle River sisters, by phone a few months before she died. The nun told her that Archbishop Joseph T. Ryan was always concerned about the welfare of the priests and sisters working in his diocese, fearing that some of them might suffer cabin fever in the cold and isolation. For this reason, the archbishop invited Merton to come and give them encouragement through his charismatic presence and teaching.

Mary Alice Cook said the nuns who met Father Louis were delighted by his sense of humor, how totally relevant, yet completely simple and down-to-earth the acclaimed religious writer and teacher was.

Cook converted to Eastern Orthodoxy from Southern Baptist. On the day we met at the Jitters Coffee Shop in Eagle River, she confessed she had formed some of her own prejudices about Thomas Merton when she first learned the story about him.

"With my strict Baptist upbringing," Cook admitted, "I learned the only way to God was through Jesus Christ, and not through Buddha or Krishna or any other spiritual guru."

As I walked past the cemetery, I heard, but could not see chickadees zipping through the trees. At the end of the short trail covered with broken and bent spruce trees, bunchberries, and thorny devil's club, I came to a small knoll and stood for a moment in the soft rain, with the Chugach Mountains semi-covered in clouds. Termination dust lightly covered the gold and blue peaks. In times like that, the mountains surrounding Anchorage were like an iconostasis between earth and heaven.

I made my way up the small hill less than a quarter-mile and found the picture-perfect Saint Sergius chapel surrounded by spruce and birch—its two gold onion domes gleaming through the grays and browns of the woods. The small structure was designed by a Moscow artist whose family immigrated to the States and lived in the St. John's community from 1990-94.

The small Russian chapel was built near the property where the contemplative nuns once lived. The one-room chapel, with its blue roof and keyhole-shaped windows, was consecrated in 2009 and paid for entirely by the people of St. John as a tribute to the famous, but humble monk, St. Sergius of Rodonezh. And the sight of this would have sent chills up Merton's spine for he knew all about the history of Eastern theology and monasticism.

Saint Sergius founded the Holy Trinity Chapel in the deep forests outside Moscow in the 1300s. The Mongols' conquest of Russia lasted more than 200 years. When it ended, St. Sergius was credited with the renewal of monastic life.

As a visitor to St. John's, they gave me a large metal key dangling from a block of wood to unlock the chapel door. As I stood before an icon of the beloved St. Herman, I turned over the square of wood. Lacquered onto the backside, was a passage from Thomas Merton's book, *New Seeds of Contemplation*.

"Let there always be quiet," it began, "where men can take refuge. Places where they can kneel in silence. Houses of God filled with his silent presence. There, even when they do not know how to pray, at least they can be still and breathe easily.

"Let there be a place somewhere in which you can breathe naturally, quietly, and not have to take your breath in continued short gasps. A place where your mind can be idle, and forget its concerns, descend into silence, and worship the Father in secret."

During another meeting at Jitters Coffeeshop, Mary Alice Cook shared a historical anecdote about the Eagle River nuns and Merton. In her research, Cook found out it was Sister Rita Mary who, after being kindly asked by Father Louis to mend a pair of his socks, decided instead to keep them for herself as a relic, and never gave them back.

…Basically one who is obsessed with his own inner unity is failing to face his disunion with God and with other men. For it is in union with others that our own inner unity is naturally and easily established. To be preoccupied with achieving inner unity *first* and then going on to love others is to follow a logic of disruption which is contrary to life.

—Thomas Merton,
"The Madman Runs to the East,"
in *Conjectures of a Guilty Bystander*

21 The Madwoman Runs to the Dark

I have seen the closing line of Pasternak's famous poem "Hamlet" in various English translations. One translator rendered it as "To live life to the end is not a childish task."

But my ear much prefers this translation, "To live a life is not to cross a field."

"Poetry is a direct product and consequence of our life. The artist does not *think* up his images—he gathers them from the street."

Pasternak's words about life, and what he ultimately believed about poetry resonated.

Things have to fall apart several times over before they start to make any sense. We get squeezed and squeezed until we are stripped empty inside from the conflicts and troubles and dramas that come our way when we least expect them—serious family illnesses, sudden job losses, heroin addictions, skin cancer, domestic violence, deaths of loved ones.

On my interior journey, when I thought the spiritual thirst was being partially quenched, when I thought I weathered enough personal storms for the time being, when I felt certain the roughest patches must be behind me, and when I accepted, for once, that my soul molted and made it into calm, that's precisely when God sent a Chinook wind barreling over the mountains and into the very core of my "new" being, and the force and shock of it knocked me over.

The ugly truth. When I was back in Merton's old Kentucky home, attending my first ever spiritual retreat, being introduced to the concept of contemplative living, making my first pilgrimage to Merton's grave at the Abbey of Gethsemani, my husband was in Hawaii. He was making love to a married woman.

It wasn't the solo vacation Michael told me he was taking to relieve his winter blues. And he didn't happen to meet her at the pool in Hawaii. He and the married woman plotted all along to secretly travel together from Alaska, and the irony was she was a practicing Catholic.

I didn't know a thing about it, that he had been having an affair with this woman for several months. But he was wracked with guilt and finally confessed the relationship to me a few days before Mothers' Day.

I broke out into tears and turned into a raging madwoman who couldn't stop choking and wheezing. I screamed and cursed. And I came close to a mental breakdown. I could not see out of my swollen eyes. I started losing control at the top of my lungs. I had no idea what to do.

"Why didn't I see this? It was right in front of me! Right here," I yelled between tears, "right under my nose in *my* own town!"

My voice grew louder and angrier from the spare bedroom where I ran to get away from him. I sprawled across the bed, tightly gripped a pillow over my stomach with a box of tissues next to me. I was not done yelling, except my speech was incoherent, punctuated by unstoppable sobbing. I sounded as if I should be put in a straightjacket and sedated. I couldn't focus; my eyelids had tripled in size from the puffiness.

Michael's affair was more than a fling; it was something quite serious, and I was more than distraught. I was afraid. The facts behind the betrayal, the relationship and intimacies that developed with the woman left me with an acute sense of abandonment.

Was a broken family to be the pattern God decided for my life? What kind of cruel lesson was he trying to teach me?

I confronted Michael again. "What is it about her? She strokes your ego, right? And all I do is tear it apart with my nagging and my criticisms. She's easy. I'm hard. She's smiling all the time. I'm lost in stupid thoughts about monks and monasteries and acting like a weirdo." Michael stepped into the bedroom to try and calm me down.

"Is it because she is more on the subservient side than me, quieter, sweeter, gentler…?"

I gasped for another shallow breath, "And men prefer that, don't they?"

He stood and rocked back and forth but didn't answer. Michael often practiced the Rule of Silence in our thirty years of marriage, but he was more silent than usual. His hands were trembling. His face turned completely white. He looked as if he'd burst into tears at any moment. He placed his hands in the pocket of his green Polarfleece vest. I knew he wanted to hug me and tell me we'd get through this mess, but it was a personal struggle he didn't quite know how to deal with.

He mentioned another detail about his betrayal. "You probably don't want to hear this," he said, "but she is a Catholic. And she feels the guilt, believe me, she does."

I violently pushed him away and reached for more tissues. Through the bedroom window, over the birch trees on our neat and clean subdivision street, I caught a glimpse of the Anchorage sky. Clouds scudded across the reddening western horizon. Beautiful spring clouds moved swiftly and gracefully, and I moved in the opposite direction. Down into a cold, dark pit.

"I can't explain what happened," he said. "Some kind of chemical imbalance in my brain. And seeing her was like an addiction of sorts. But I have thought long and hard about it. I know how much I've hurt you. But I choose you. I want to stay with *you*," he said.

I was blind and didn't pick up the signs or symptoms of all that went wrong between us besides our growing intellectual disagreements and typical spats.

But the domestic divide and marital vacuum were things I equally created.

All the days I locked myself away and said I couldn't spend time with him because I had to write. Like Merton, I had to neurotically jot more notes in my journal. I had to write more letters and emails. I had to keep sending my drafts out to prospective literary agents. I had to try and publish another article. I had to start another scrap of an essay or poem that would never bring in a dime or go anywhere.

The past few years I was cranky and irritable on a daily basis juggling too much. *Jesus Christ! How could I be so stupid and so naïve?* I put my misdirected literary ambitions first and now I was paying the price for all I took for granted.

All the years of writing and grappling, what had it gotten me? A storage box of rejection notes? More annotated books on the shelf? A lot of facts about Russian writers and Trappist monks? And a husband who fell in love with somebody else.

Since I was a young woman, the self-doubt was always there, lurking underneath the surface. I didn't want to admit it out loud, but I was still chased the life-long dream *to be somebody*, as Merton had done. All the frustrations I harbored since I was sixteen to break out of the familial patterns, our undistinguished lineage as coal miners, garbage truck drivers, meat-wrappers, secretaries, and bartenders.

The weeks after Michael confessed were awful. I vacillated between telling him he should get the hell out and go away—run to her. If that's what he truly wanted for his happiness, I didn't need him, didn't need anybody because I was done. Our sons were grown, and I could.....*I could*.....I could do anything.

But now that my world was unrecognizable, I didn't know what I could really do. How would I get out of bed and face the next morning? A few weeks earlier, I was standing before a Jesus statue in the meadows across from the Abbey of Gethsemani muttering prayers, and now I was home and my marriage, disintegrated.

In that moment of utter humiliation and heartbreak, with the hatred I felt for the other woman, I felt somehow that I deserved what I got.

After moving to the couch downstairs, I stayed up all night and balled my eyes out until my head ached. I felt as if my brain would burst and my head would detach from my body. By morning, I could not see, could not drink coffee, could not talk. We had made a commitment to attend a fancy and very expensive Mothers' Day brunch at the Alyeska ski resort south of Anchorage with dear friends who pre-paid for our tickets.

"Michael, I'm going to try and pull myself together," I said in my stubbornness and looking more hung over, red-faced and ragged than a drunk. "We need to make an appearance, at least. I don't want to lie and say I'm sick, though really, I guess I am sick. Maybe thick make-up can disguise all the redness."

"I don't think we should go at all" Michael said. "Look at you. You're in no shape to be around people, and neither am I."

"This is between you and me, and we have a lot of talking to do," I said. "You were the one who said we should go to a counselor, and it was me who was always against it."

"I still think we should try it," he said.

"Okay, maybe a counselor, I don't know…okay, yes….but I do not want to drag any of our friends or family into this mess. I am not going to breathe a word about your affair to anybody, especially not to our kids. I think it's best if we keep it completely private. Let's pretend things are fine, and go to the Mothers' Day brunch. It won't take long, and we can drive and talk."

Once we got to the ski resort's restaurant, my energy at an ultimate, life-time low, was spent. Everyone around the table knew I wasn't myself, though the sunglasses helped. I pretended that I'd been up half the night due to my typical literary insomnia.

I was bereft, shocked, completely disoriented and in emotional chaos. I lost my appetite and couldn't pick up a book nor watch a moment of television. We talked about his betrayal for days on end. It circled back to chemistry and brain waves and male weakness. For over six months, he enjoyed her company, that she was Filipino, and she made him feel good about himself.

The interloper claimed she liked being with my husband. It boosted her ego, too, to spend time in his quiet, calming company. Things progressed as they did. Mr. Rationality admitted there was nothing logical or rational about it.

We agreed it was best to remain private about it, believing we'd get through it somehow. If only we could alleviate the pain we caused one another. We needed to focus on the future. We were empty-nesters, after all, and I already spent three academic years away at the University of Pittsburgh and we survived that. It was too many years to throw away. We built our lives together in Alaska, beginning with our early years in Yakutat, and we made it. Only one marriage between us. Though it was more than a simple indiscretion, we could survive.

He made his decision to stay with me, and I with him, and that was the end of it—we both emphatically agreed. He was over her and said so time and time again. He made a terrible mistake. He said, "Let's stay close to home as summer is coming. We'll power ahead. Cope with it one day at a time. This happens in lots of marriages."

I tried to let the whole subject die, to stop obsessing about the black-haired, petite woman, imagining how it must have been for my husband to be strolling on Hawaiian beaches with her, a woman so obviously accustomed and comfortable in the tropics when I could rarely show my pale, freckled skin uncovered in full sun. I thought about all the provocative emails and gifts they exchanged.

I thought of the love poems he might have written for her.

As the months ticked by, as much as I tried to reset my emotions, again I'd bring up Hawaii, then deeply regret it.

Hawaii is the number one winter tourist destination for sun-starved Alaskans, yet in our whole marriage, in all the years we spent in Alaska, we never went there together as a couple or family to escape the cold and wrath of winter. And this fact only gnawed at my insides.

There was a pack of jackals inside me. They gnarled their teeth and were ready to pounce. How could I let everything that came between us quietly slip into oblivion, as if his affair never happened?

How could I switch off and simply turn my focus back to the churning of spiritual ideas and feelings?

"I chose you, remember?" he said, "and that's all that matters. You told me you'd stop obsessing over her, but you can't let it go, can you? You have to stop bringing it up in my face every day."

He was right. I took some comfort knowing that I took the high moral road, and never contacted the other woman to tell her exactly what I thought. I wanted to show up at her workplace to cause a scene. Or follow her into a restaurant to do the same. I mulled over the possibility of telling her husband. I did none of these things though the hurt ran deeper than I realized. It opened up all sorts of other emotional wounds from my past. We were on the verge of creating another broken family. And this was something I could not bear.

In the middle of everything, I was out looking for a job in academia, and needed to concentrate on that as much as I could.

Every morning, as a kind of meditation to prop myself up, I pulled out *The Sign of Jonas*. I'd choose some soothing, lyrical passages to read. Merton's words helped connect me to the self without ego. Without pretenses. My God-centered self.

In this double-whammy—marital chaos and spiritual confusion—I floundered for a long time. My innermost self was the real frontier—the last frontier, the place I understood so little. And I wasn't very good at explaining this last frontier of me.

"Michael, I know I've been difficult to be around the last few years," I said. "Maybe you don't really understand what's been going on with me because it's so hard to talk about. But I really have tried to live as a more spiritually whole human being and not as some flickering light that will probably burn out at any moment."

"I'm not sure what a spiritually whole human being looks like," he said. "We each have to do what we have to do, I guess. You know me, I don't choose or like to talk in those terms."

"I know that, and I understand where you're coming from. But now that this has happened in our marriage," I said, "it's all so jarring and unbelievable and completely one hundred percent devastating…Oh, my God, are we really having these kinds of conversations?"

I continued, "Let's see, how does this story go again? Oh, right. I was in the Holy Land of Kentucky learning about contemplative living, and reading Mary Oliver poetry with my fellow retreatants, and I was standing before a Jesus statue attempting to say some prayers, and you were in Maui romping around in the fun and sun with your lover?"

The paradox was that contemplation after the retreat on contemplative living proved impossible.

My domestic foundation was jerked away. I couldn't seem to heal from the deepest, freshest wounds. Me, the super-energetic woman, the most "educated" and most "together" and most "successful" one from my side of the family, now despondent and weak. The tears came indiscriminately at all hours of the day, whether driving or in the spaghetti aisle of the grocery store.

And then there were the unrealistic expectations I put on Michael. How sometimes I wished he'd learn to tango, my metaphor for tapping into passion. Or write love poems for me, the way Merton did for the nurse, Margie.

I wanted *my* "M" to rush out the door breathless and happy and ask me to chase down a view of the northern lights with him, even if it was three degrees outside and we had to drive far out of the city to catch the best views.

I wanted *my* "M" to amplify his voice, not in anger, and not in a cool, matter-of-fact, managerial tone, but in pure, unadulterated joy, laughing, talkative, excitable, like he was a college student again letting loose after finals. On our college graduation night together in Pensacola, Florida, we climbed a chain link fence after midnight and skinny-dipped in the university pool. I wanted him to be more like that again, exuberant, ready to plunge into the next adventure.

"Don't be a jar full of water, whose rim is always dry," the poet, Rumi had said. "Don't be the rider who gallops all night and never sees the horse that is beneath him."

Michael didn't read Rumi, but this is the poetry I should have recited to him. Now that we were middle-aged, where was his spontaneous verbal expression of awe? Why did he rarely show it to me? Why didn't I share more with him? Why did I criticize? Why let intellectualizing interfere with personal relationships?

The bright star I followed—the blued-eyed Thomas Merton—was no mere exercise in literary curiosity. He was real, a spiritual guide, and apparently, I needed a mentor now more than ever. Merton's religious conversion and life story spoke to me. *I'm sorry. I know I gave him too much time and attention. No doubt God knows, I needed some spiritual straightening out.*

Serious questions and reflections about faith came and went again, thwarted and botched by the next emotional crisis.

I was a half-wife and a half-writer and both were mentally incapacitated.

If my true vocation was to be a writer, then God had a strange and painful way of showing it all those years. Conversely, by the time Merton wanted to renounce writing he had long been a big literary success.

John Howard Griffin studied Merton's private journals soon after the monk's death and said they were particularly fascinating to read during the point in Merton's life when he had achieved fame and celebrity "because everyone was pushing him to speak, to use his influence while he was moving toward a deeper solitude. He felt an internal connection with the great Zen poet Chuang Tzu, who wrote poems that hit Merton very deeply.

"The Chinese Master writes that a sense of achievement was the beginning of failure and that fame was the beginning of disgrace."

Griffin went on, "Merton already believed this. Chuang Tzu, in Merton's translation, says that the authentic search for truth is to become a nobody. Only a nobody can be universal. Merton said he disappeared into the monastery, not to get away from the world but to become a nobody."

Michael's love affair confirmed it was damn time I put away all the pens, paper, and flash-drives. I was a would-be writer without an agent, without a book contract, without a regional or national reputation, and was full of impossible self-contradictions.

Look at me! As a writer, I sat dressed in thick brown socks, a ten-year old athletic bra, ragged black sweats, and a with a cheap, Walmart nightgown layered on top. I didn't have a drop of make-up on my ruddy cheeks, no pearl studded earrings, no pink lipstick to moisten cracked lips. I had stale, coffee breath and hadn't brushed my teeth since the night before. What man wants to see his wife like this at 5:30 a.m. busy at her precious work?

That other woman, well, she had nothing to lose. She had an ex-husband, a current husband, and now she had mine.

My skin was peachy-pink. How could I make myself more riveting, more exotic and enticing? I have red hair and freckles. How can I be more alluring and attractive, more submissively feminine? How can I hold a husband's interest if all I talk about are obscure literary journals I want to write for, and essays that don't generate a penny of revenue and can't be turned into film scripts?

A Day of Recollection for me evolved into weeks, then months. I already lived more years than I had years left. Why didn't I stop all the stupid charades of trying to quench the spiritual thirst? This was the twenty-first century. Churches were practically obsolete given we're all trying our best to manage our practical needs of staying alive, working our jobs, keeping our families fed and safe. Who cared about spiritual conversion stories from dead Christian monks and what they said or wrote decades ago?

Why didn't I get back to the real business of being a better partner and wife? Seek a higher-paying job? Study yoga to create more feelings of spiritual wholeness? Take on an exciting new home project to distract me? Write a poem about my mother's death? Stick a bandage on the inner emptiness and call it good?

Could I give up the writer-self who shadowed me around since childhood? The little scholarship girl who escaped her family's arguments and abuse by running to the Carnegie Library? The one who wrote a short story on a used piece of construction paper and gave it as a present to her third-grade teacher?

The writer-self who followed me with Michael into Yakutat long ago and absorbed as much as she could about her new home where she didn't belong. The one who demanded I shut up and start paying real attention to the world right in front of me, in the here and now, in the middle of the rain forest in the middle of nowhere, regardless of social status. The one who immersed herself in Tlingit history and Russian poets to learn more about life and how to live it.

Since stumbling upon *The Seven Storey Mountain*, I immersed myself in Merton-style monasticism, and learned about how monks prayed the Liturgy of the Hours and recited all 150 Psalms of the Bible every few weeks. I moved in new directions, right into the no-man's land of me.

But so far, I didn't like what I found there. Sometimes that pack of jackals would show up growling to keep me out.

The writer-self got scared; she needed to vanish again. She was a sorry excuse for an artist, financially non-producing, a problem as a wife, and didn't deserve any more creative energy.

After the rebellious talk, the literary fire and life started to flame out. There was no more fire left. I was the piece of soap dropped at the bottom of the shower stall.

In a quiet moment alone that spring, I took out a pen and paper. I didn't know what for. I would draft whatever popped into my head. And when I read it over, tears trickled down again.

My words came out sounding like a Psalm:

> Lord, I am aloft in snowy, nameless mountains.
> In the snowy, nameless mountains,
> mountains of no mercy,
> my soul longs to know thy will. Lord, I long to
> know thy will without obstruction, in the wide-
> open field.

This morning, we flew in bad weather to Yakutat, came down out of the thick clouds onto a shore full of surf and hemlock and muskeg. Desolate airstrip. Frank Ryman drove us into the village.

Broken down homes, mostly inhabited by Tlingit Indians, and old fish cannery, and a small dock with a few fishing boats on a lovely broad bay with islands. Everything seemed covered with hemlock…

Driving rain, mountains invisible…

We left Yakutat after dinner (at Ryman's "Lodge" out at the airstrip), flew in rain to Juneau which turns out to be a fascinating place clinging to the feet of several mountains at the edge of a sort of fjord. I never saw such torrential rains as met us when we got out of the plane!

—Thomas Merton
Alaska Journal, September 27, 1968

22 Contemplations from a Cabin

Lord, how manifold is thy rain in Yakutat!

I hunkered down in my little *obidtil*—hermitage—in the rain forest by the sea, and it was pouring, as usual. *O beata solitudo!* Whenever Michael and I made it back to Yakutat, this was where we liked to stay—at Skip and Rose Mary Ryman's cabin on Monti Bay. The cabin was only a few paces from Jennie Pavlik's water-front house, and a short walk down the dirt road to the place where her father died.

I let myself go there, let silence wash over me and then… subside. I *did* subside. Breathed. Listened. I had nowhere to go. There was no one I had to talk to. Even the lapping surf ran out of energy, as if the water, too, took a rest from itself.

Whether or not I would end my days in Alaska, I couldn't know. But I couldn't give up being Alaskan no matter where I went. I set my anchor well. It was this place that gave me clarity, silence, and peace.

Yakutat's landscape was my novena, same as it was for Mr. Pavlik, same as it was for his children and grandchildren. An occasional small aircraft hummed by. A pair of bald eagles, nested on top of a spruce tree next to the cabin, carried on a ruckus early in the morning, feeding their eaglets, but otherwise, it was peaceful. Sailboat quiet. Sleepy quiet. Rain forest quiet. Only the rain fell, baby. Only the rain that never quite disappeared.

I was always lonely for this view and had to tear myself away from it whenever it was time to return to city life. It was good to get away from the flood of language in media and politics that sucked dry the juices of real solitude.

We Are All Poets Here

Michael left me all alone that morning but I didn't mind. He went exploring with our friend, Robert, hiking around the Harlequin Lake area. Robert enthusiastically explained this was their chance as men to trek across virgin land where possibly no man had trod before.

While they readied their gear, Robert said, "After about 10,000 years, the Yakutat Glacier has started receding." He continued, "Think of it, Kathy. We could possibly be the very first humans to set our boots down on newly exposed rocks and to step into glacial mud no one else has stepped on before!"

Robert had longevity with glacial moraines and fjords. He relocated to Yakutat around 1981, about two years after we moved there, to work as a sport fishery biologist with the Alaska Department of Fish and Game. Besides keeping track of salmon escapements on the Situk River and filing biological surveys and reports, his duties over the years involved a lot of wildlife interventions. If a great white shark or whale washed up on the beach, he was the authority who got the call. And when errant brown bears wandered too close to people's houses and kids in the village, as they often did, it was "Clam-Bear," as some of the children nicknamed him, who came to their rescue. Most times, he sedated the bruins, but sometimes, as a last resort, was forced to kill bears in defense of life and property.

Though I knew I was going to miss seeing Michael for the rest of the day, especially considering our marital problems, I thought it best to let the men have their manly adventures without me. Hiking into new territory might prove to be an all day, overnight ordeal involving complicated logistics, walking for long distances with heavy packs, bushwhacking through Devil's club and alder, sleeping in a cramped tent, dining on power bars, and smoking cigars by the campfire. I was content to read Merton and do some bird watching, except all I had were a pair of cheap binoculars I found on the dusty window ledge.

Last time I stood on this cabin's porch and looked out across Monti Bay, Jennie stood next to me. A bright silver flash streaked across the dark, blue-gray sky. She pointed to the horizon and broke into a wide smile.

"Look, Kathy, the swans are welcoming you!" she said, for she knew trumpeters were some of my favorite birds. "God did that just for you. You're blessed today. Thirty trumpeter swans came talking to you."

A gleaming white cruise ship suddenly crossed the empty horizon. From the wide mouth of Yakutat Bay, it was a straight dash to the open sea—into the Gulf of Alaska.

The Pacific breathed on you and on all the mountains and glaciers, a reminder of its immense power and how many lives the ocean claimed.

And Mount Saint Elias, though practically invisible that day, guarded over the larger Yakutat Bay announcing its own strength and permanence. Skip said Mount Saint Elias was Yakutat's mountain and all the rest were mere rocks.

> If you were to ask me why I dwell among green mountains,
> I should laugh silently; my soul is serene,
> The peach blossom follows the moving water;
> There is another heaven and earth beyond the world of men.
>
> —Chinese poet, Li Po

To enjoy that maritime existence, you needed to love gray shifting skies, and temperatures forever stuck between 40 and 50 degrees, with only 30 rain-free days in a year. If there existed a Holy Spirit of the Sea, surely it seeped and flowed across the porous terrain. A place mostly left the way God made it. A fisherman's dream. A writer's dream. And a monk's dream.

Skip believed Yakutat confounded the well-ordered world, and he was right.

"Everything is fleeting here," he said. "To the outside world, Yakutat has no real history, and no defined future. We live in the constant charge of the present."

Skip served as the manager of the City and Borough of Yakutat. When we met him, Skip was the Alaska Airlines station manager, where he worked for over thirty years.

"It was really a man's place back then, in the 1960s, when Merton dropped into town," Skip said, "much worse than when you came to live here. Yakutat was no easy place for regular women."

"Yeah, well Jim Jensen told me the same exact thing in 1979 the night we arrived." I said, "He told me that it would eat women alive. I don't think it had really changed much by the time I got here."

Yakutat had no television, no radio, no daily newspaper, and no school in town beyond the 8th grade in Merton's time. Until recently, it lacked regular, reliable cell service, had one school up to 12th grade, and is still minus a traffic light or a single street connecting it to the road system.

"As a philosopher and a thinker, Merton would have had little in common with a blue collar Yakutat," Skip added, "much less with a population barely a half generation away from a total subsistence lifestyle. In fact, I would say, and I am sure he would agree, that Merton the Monk had more to learn than he had to teach in Alaska, which is probably one of the forces that brought him here."

If Merton arrived on a commercial plane, Skip speculated, he would have most likely come in on a four-engine, turbo prop Lockheed Electra, operated by Cordova Airlines. But then again, maybe he flew on a private charter, courtesy of the Alaska Archbishop. There were probably only two people in town who had ever heard of Merton—Skip's father and mother. And that would have been a great relief to Father Louis.

Skip's father was a World War II vet and a Catholic convert. He served on the *USS Arthur Middleton* in the Pacific. Before the ship engaged in combat, helping to support the 3rd U.S. Marine Division, a priest or chaplain listened to spontaneous confessions on deck. Frank Ryman was afraid of dying in battle, and when he saw the more accepting faces of his fellow shipmates who were Catholic, he converted right on the spot.

"Most of the soldiers in World War II weren't the big heroes Hollywood propaganda created them to be," Skip said. "They were like my father, and your father, too. Youngsters serving in

Contemplations from a Cabin

the U.S. Navy. Frightened to death. A lot of them crammed into foxholes and shot randomly up in the air, shitting their pants. That's why the vets didn't come home and brag about it. They couldn't live up to the war's hype."

In his Alaska journal, Merton described the local "Cathliks" he met as being good and simple people not yet caught up in the mess of problems of the Lower 48 states.

"Dad offered him a free parcel of land not far from the one paved road, but Father Louis didn't bite at the offer," Skip explained. "Maybe he would have accepted the property had he returned to the state before he died."

Merton had no concept of how rare private land was in a state as big as Alaska—486,000 square miles, and 375 million acres. The majority of the state was tied up by the federal and state governments, and the twelve regional, native corporations which came into existence after 1971. Under three percent of Alaska was held privately, as opposed to Kentucky's eighty-eight percent.

Ryman's free quarter-acre parcel wasn't enough to entirely persuade Merton. He wasn't at all interested in spending time ministering to the Pavliks, the Rymans, and the smattering of other Catholics in Yakutat, Dillingham, Cordova, or anywhere else for that matter, and he made that clear, much to the dismay of Skip's father.

The piece of land sat less than two miles from the Rymans' cabin and Jennie's house on the road locals simply call, "the road to Ocean Cape." Further along the same dirt road lay Ankau Lagoon and the cemetery where Mr. Pavlik was buried, not far from where the Russians once maintained their small fort and trading post.

If Thomas Merton made it all the way to the end of Ocean Cape road—he would have traveled on a very narrow, almost undrivable road, full of nasty potholes, thick with brambles of alder and devil's club. He would have passed bogs and small lakes full of yellow skunk cabbage, and the woods where a small group of Russians once lived, until he reached the bluffs of Ocean Cape where a White Alice radar site existed. If he were on those windy, high bluffs and gazed down at the icy cold waters of the North Pacific rushing in with huge swells and dangerous breakers, Ocean Cape's mystical beauty would have done him in.

When Merton traveled to the village, it didn't yet have a building dedicated or used as a Catholic church. (The two-story house that served as St. Anne's wasn't constructed until 1972.)

While growing up, Skip watched his father serve as a kind of unofficial church deacon, entrusted with the Catholic Mass kit supplied by a Juneau church. It contained the chalice, altar wine, candelabras, cruets, and unconsecrated hosts (wafers) for Holy Communion. It always bothered Frank Ryman to see any symbols of animism in the tiny Yakutat parish—Tlingit motifs of eagles or ravens shouldn't be anywhere inside a church, even near makeshift altars, he believed. The elder Ryman was conservative in his views and probably didn't support most of the changes and liberties brought about by Vatican II. Lay people needed special dispensation from a bishop to touch the chalice. The Mass kit could only be used by a visiting priest, and he was 225 air miles away in Juneau.

Skip was at college in Idaho in September 1968, but he remembered how ecstatic his family was to be hosting such a renowned Catholic as Thomas Merton.

Merton joined the Ryman family at their small Airport Lodge. Their cook prepared a country style meal, which the monk greatly enjoyed. After a few minutes, Merton inquired what it was. The cook beamed as she looked at Merton and innocently replied, "Well it's a little bit of this, and a little bit of that. We call it shit on a shingle."

Merton broke into laughter and Mrs. Ryman was horrified.

I missed the sun like anyone else after a spell of endless rain, but that's why we invented airplanes and California, as Skip liked to remind me. If you grew up in a place like this, you paid close attention to the terminal forecasts, to where the fronts and squalls came from, and what the weather might do in the next five minutes. The definition of a drought in Yakutat is ten minutes without precipitation. For long-timers like the Rymans and the Pavliks, it was more than having reserves of local knowledge; it was local knowledge of *exceptional country*.

The phrase *driving rains* appeared several times on the pages of Merton's Alaska journal. After he came in contact with Southeast Alaska's torrential rains, combined with frequent winds and fog, he found out how terrible the weather was. He saw how many aircraft were grounded on a regular basis, including a few of his own chartered flights.

Had he stayed in Southeast Alaska for any length of time, I bet he would have waxed less rhapsodically about precipitation. There would be no more "festivals of rain" metaphors coming from his poetic lips.

Suddenly, the rain quit as it often did, before it began to cycle all over again. But for a moment, there was no more thumping rain hitting the cabin's metal roof.

What I heard were waves turning, what I felt was moisture; what I hoped to see was Mount Saint Elias.

When we first came to settle here, I felt I was no longer "of the world," that I had withdrawn from it. Just when every bone and nerve in my body was primed to strut down the runway, I wound up in a dreary fishing village in America's largest rain forest.

But it was in the middle of this soggy solitude that ravens and eagles and trumpeter swans became my therapists, and I began to respond, as if a part of me, long suppressed and shielded, started breaking free.

In the quiet of the Ryman's cabin, I peered outside. Someone had been fishing their set-net in front of the cabin. Another boat came into view. A man in a rain jacket and rubber boots rode alone in a skiff to retrieve whatever fish he caught in his net. A large fishing trawler moved beyond Khantak Island on its way past the promontory of Ocean Cape, and into the Gulf of Alaska.

Jennie told me the story about how for centuries, Tlingit women dragged their husbands out to Khantak Island. Men helped them collect long roots from spruce trees, which they needed for weaving baskets. Collecting spruce roots, laborious and painstaking, took physical strength and more hours than most women would ever want to give. But it was an ancient spring ritual Jennie still engaged in.

Tlingit women dug into loose, sandy soil with their bare hands to find the best, most uniform roots 30-to-50 feet long. After digging the roots, each piece of pale, yellow fiber had to be split and peeled, dried over a fire, and tied and coiled into bundles. In olden times, dyes came from the juice of wild blueberries.

One evening standing outside Jennie's place, she led me to a piece of lumber staked in the ground and notched with two deep grooves on the top. She pulled long spruce roots through the V-shaped notch to strip off the bark layer. Still very much her father's daughter, inventive and crafty, she liked working with her hands.

"You can't harvest the roots in summer," Jennie said, "because they grow pitch pockets and then get too bumpy to strip. They need to be pliable. And each fiber has to be hand-dyed."

It takes her four to six months to weave one, three-inch basket, lots of long hours sitting still in saintly patience.

In the late evening, the sun set behind Mount Saint Elias, but the mountain didn't show itself in any hour of any day that week. It was socked in by thick clouds. I was sure it was equally so for Robert and Michael on their trek to the glacier.

The entire top half of Mount Saint Elias' pyramid summit was cloaked; only faint outlines of its bottom half were visible, but still I hoped. The monk who loved metaphors, made a few notes in his Asian journal shortly after he visited Alaska, "… The full beauty of the mountain is not seen until you too consent to the impossible paradox: it is, and it is not. When nothing more needs to be said, the smoke of ideas clears, the mountain is SEEN." (November 1968)

The Atlantic Ocean had its own special *dramatis personae*, too, from what I saw of it along the crowded eastern seaboard, packed with tourists, beach goers and large congested hotels. But the Atlantic beaches couldn't compare to the lonely North Pacific coast between Icy Bay and Yakutat, and south to Lituya Bay.

Alaska's Lonely Coast encompassed the most pristine wilderness, and least populated waterfront I'd ever seen. It attracted no hordes of tourists to beachcomb for shells and sea glass. You couldn't do lazy surf-fishing by sitting in shorts and flip-flops on plastic chairs sunbathing with a cooler of beer. Hubbard Glacier calved house size blocks of ice, that melted into bergy bits and drifted through Yakutat Bay. Alaskans fished glacial ice out of the water to chill their gin and tonics. Along the borders of Yakutat bay, killer whales have been known to hunt deer wandering too close to shore; brown bears frequently roamed the tidelines poking around for tasty morsels.

A single loon called from the water's edge. Its sound was like no other bird and that's why people stopped cold when they heard them. A loon's call touched a certain melancholy part of the soul that a caged parrot or a whole tree of singing mockingbirds could never quite penetrate.

This solitude was glorious! I didn't have to clean the kitchen or empty the dishwasher. I didn't have to go grocery shopping or meet anyone at my office. I didn't have to wash and condition my hair, apply another layer of eye shadow or mascara, fill in the eyebrows, moisturize or sanitize. I didn't have to listen to any loud lawn mowers, sirens, garbage trucks or roofing contractors disturbing the neighborhood. I didn't *have* to be *anywhere*. There was gloom above, but I was not gloomy. Rain, but who cared? Eagles screeched as they soared through speckled light.

Had Merton trekked around Latitude 59 or 61 a little longer, especially in those other worldly surroundings, would he have liked being a rain-soaked hermit?

He was 53 years old, had lived in the Abbey of Gethsemani for most of his adult life and was bursting with desire to satisfy his latent wanderlust. He looked forward to a spiritual quest that didn't involve reading every theological treatise in the

Abbey's scriptorium. He was not interested in a phony "hermit-mystique," as he said, but a calling by God into silence and solitude.

Skip seemed to think the odds were good that Merton would have seriously considered the Tlingit community or maybe Cordova, especially since their winters were considered almost non-existent by Interior or Arctic standards.

In his hurried northern sightseeing, Merton made a few other observations:

> Bay with small islands. Driving rain on the docks. A few fishing boats. Beat-up motorboats, very poor....it is a village of Indians with an FAA station nearby.
>
> Battered houses...cannery building falling down....the woods are full of moose, and black bear and brown bear, and even a special bear found only at Yakutat, the glacier bear (or blue bear). Frank Ryman had in his lodge the skin of a wolf as big as a small bear. Yakutat has plenty of wolves and coyotes, besides bears...
>
> And in the village are many murders...Tlingit Indians..."

How Merton came up with the comment about village murders, I didn't know. Historically, the only "murder" I ever heard about involved the Tlingits' attack on the Russians in the early 1800s. Throughout his far north wanderings, as Merton's ears stayed closely tuned to the state's Russian history, he recorded a few details about Yakutat's Russian history, though he was a bit mixed up about the facts. Merton wrote, "...Here there was once a Russian penal colony. It was wiped out by the Indians..."

It wasn't a penal colony; it was the Russian fort and small trading post established somewhere between Ankau Lagoon and

Ocean Cape which the Russians occupied from 1796 to 1805 under the name of "The New Russia." Not a trace of the wooden barracks, storage sheds, or other Russian-made structures remain, but the story of what happened is forever embedded in the minds and memories of the Yakutat Tlingits.

I often heard the story of how Russian traders blatantly mistreated Tlingits by cruelly blocking access to some of their traditional fishing resources. The invaders may have even robbed graves, and Russians were also accused of appropriating Native women for their pleasure. Speculation also ran high that Tlingit children under the guise and promise of giving them a better life with more education, were in truth, shipped to Russia and forced into servitude.

As the story went, Yakutat Tlingits eventually lost all patience and trust with the Russian traders in 1805 and retaliated in a brutal sneak attack during the middle of night. An estimated 40 unarmed Russians were stabbed to death; Tlingits allowed fewer than five Russians to live.

After the killings, the Russians never tried to re-establish any kind of trading post or agricultural station in the area again. For well over a hundred years, a kind of historical silence befell the event, and a few generations refused to openly talk about "the great shame."

But today, the story was no longer whispered—it took on a different connotation. Tlingits exuded much pride about defeating the Russians in Yakutat. They mentioned how cunning their ancestors were in standing up to the Russians. In Yakutat, a sign at Raven's Table, a local fish business owned by a Native family read, "Homeland Security—Fighting Terrorism since 1802."

Neither the Russian fur traders, nor the Tlingits, nor the Protestant missionaries, could have predicted what Mother Russia's real legacy in Alaska would be—namely the introduction of the Russian Orthodox faith and its Russian Orthodox churches. The stockades, the trading posts, the ship-building sites, the iron cannons, the three-mast sailing ships, and the cobalt blue trading beads disappeared in time. But the golden cupolas, the onion domes that still dot the Alaskan landscape remained.

As I glanced toward Point Carew, the sky moved from bright to ominous, from calm to stormy, and my mind did *not* stay at rest for long. I thought about the thick clouds and the loon's call piercing my heart and the unfinished projects on my desk at work and how I should really check in on my brother, Richy, to see how he was faring after his stroke. And I was thinking about all I was observing!

That was *not* what Thomas Merton was talking about when he spoke about contemplation. Contemplation was not a frame of mind you casually slipped into because you put down the pen and tablet, shut off the cabin's overhead light, burned some incense.

Contemplation was more of an ongoing, integrated spiritual existence, which involved the soul and the body, divinely aligned, as the pious Old Believers also understood. It wasn't a concrete concept. It was not a "count me out" contemplation to escape or to avoid, and hence, to ultimately focus on yourself. It was quite the opposite of self-centered thinking.

Like the wind we couldn't see, but felt pass by, contemplation meant being fully present in the epicenter of who you were. The more neglected part of me was found in that epicenter, only I had been wrestling with too many contradictions, torn between conflicting roles as wife, mother, writer, family member, and being a "good citizen." The irony was, that if I could come in closer contact with my non-cerebral self, I might also realize, in 1960s terms, a more universal consciousness. If I lived more contemplatively, my engagement with what was going on *outside* with the larger world I lived in, would deepen on an entirely different level. And as Merton believed, if more of us tried doing that, we might create *real* communication—not superficial, egregious lies, manipulation, and empty pop slogans.

Merton wrote about poetry and contemplation in *Commonweal* magazine on October 24, 1958, in which he said,

Contemplations from a Cabin

>...Contemplation itself takes on the appearance of a safe and rather 'bourgeois "cause"—the refuge of a few well-meaning Christians who are willing to acquaint themselves with St. Thomas and St. John of the Cross and to disport themselves thereafter in Edens of passivity and fervor as cannot be disapproved by the so-called "Masters of the Spiritual Life." For others, contemplation means nothing more than a life of leisure and of study: in many cases, more a fond hope than an accomplished fact...
>
> The contemplative is not just a man who sits under a tree with his legs crossed, or one who edifies himself with the answer to ultimate and spiritual problems. He is one who seeks to know the meaning of life not only with his head but with his whole being, by living it in the depth and in purity, and thus united himself to the very Source of Life—a Source which is infinitely actual and therefore too real to be contained satisfactorily inside any word or concept or name assigned by man: for the words of man tend to limit the realities which they express, in order to express them.

This was not the hidden self. It was the self that God knew you as, but maybe the true self you hadn't yet discovered.

Contemplation was not a pain-killer you popped for physical or mental comfort. It was not an act of forgetting the world and all your struggles in it, but rather to be more deeply connected with it in all its grief, unfairness, and absurdity. Contemplation meant to love the world more.

Merton, in *New Seeds of Contemplation*, said contemplation was the highest expression of man's intellectual and spiritual life. Contemplation was life itself: being fully awake, fully active, being fully aware one was alive and connected to the world and to others.

Contemplation was spiritual wonder. It was spontaneous awe of the sacredness of life, of being. It was the vivid realization of the fact that life proceeded from an invisible, transcendent, and infinitely abundant source.

And that if you journeyed inward, and lost diversions and distractions that blocked your interior journey, you would come in contact with a contemplative realm.

If I understood it, what the great monk and thinker was saying was that to be contemplative, whether as an obedient, sequestered monk or as a regular, secular, non-religious person, was to find what always existed inside you—the profound life-force, the oneness—and to enter a new reality that was closer to God. Merton believed this, that each of us was meant to travel there on our own unique spiritual quests, but few made the attempt, and even fewer arrived because our own falsehoods, illusions, and insecurities stood in the way.

Contemplation—a loaded word—as it was to me when I made that first trip to Kentucky, implied something I had to procure, plan, or strive for. It meant I went into contemplation to work on *me*, my frazzled self, my personal wants, needs, and concerns.

But that wasn't it at all. As my admiration for Merton grew, contemplation, as I came to think of it with his guidance, was not to satisfy myself, or to quell my bad nerves, or to get my slice of the solitude pie after gut-wrenching marriage problems.

And to Merton, it was an illusion for monastics themselves to believe they were somehow above the spiritual fray, religiously superior, more self-sacrificing in their separate, holy existence.

Contemplation was to be in attention to God or the Divine Presence, without words, concepts, doctrines, legalisms, terminology, prescriptions, catechisms, definitions, exact rituals and behaviors to which one must conform and adhere.

But there in Ryman's cabin all alone, listening to the squawking bald eagles, it was difficult not to think of another interpretation.

Merton attached a more mystical interpretation to it. Contemplation was "Divine dialogue," day-to-day spiritual existing. It was not what you were trying to attain, as if you were trying hard to memorize a poem.

Merton admitted he was really "getting into" the poet, William Carlos Williams. Yet, Merton wasn't talking about the Zen idea of "empty-mind" or "empty-self" exactly, either, in the same way as William Carlos Williams' famous and spare "Imagist" poem.

> so much depends
> upon
>
> a red wheel
> barrow
>
> glazed with rain
> water
>
> beside the white
> chickens.
>
> —William Carlos Williams
> "The Red Wheelbarrow"

With the poem, readers opened their eyes to see the image, as if through a pure mirror, but not to judge or impose meaning, analyze or glue down concepts. The red wheelbarrow was what it was, nothing more—an unadulterated moment of pure observation.

Merton believed it was one thing to merely observe, and something else to seek higher spiritual connection.

Very few people felt a calling to be true solitaries and true religious contemplatives, like those Mt. Athos hermits, the Cistercians of the Strict Observance from the Middle Ages, and the Carthusians have.

Merton craved to be more of a contemplative. "...Meanwhile, for myself, I have only one desire and this is the desire for solitude—to disappear into God, to be submerged in His peace, to be lost in the secret of his Face," (December 13, 1946).

In my decade-long odyssey with Merton, it was as if I arrived at a great intersection of past and present. Writing brought me to Vespers, to Russian monastery bells, to poetry, to Trumpeter swans, and Trappist monks, and to the idea that the soul, like water, must find a place to go. It must move like water, flowing and filling all the holes and emptiness within.

Contemplation couldn't be defined in terms of greater or lesser amounts of perfect solitude and silence. Was it possible, then, to lead a more contemplative life while I still showed up at my stuffy office cubicle five days a week? Or when I had a family to cook for, a house to clean, and a stack of bills to pay? When my brother suffered a second stroke? When national politics was fraught with lies and no longer made any sense? When my husband betrayed me?

Merton wasn't talking about compartmentalizing contemplation as I had compartmentalized my life.

Merton's great irony was to be a Cistercian monk in a strict and austere religious order where monks spoke in sign language and bemoaned the inner and external noise. He was a monk who admitted he never found what he was looking for—ideal solitude in a truly contemplative existence. Merton concluded he needed to rid himself of old and new diversions. And as much grounding and security the Abbey provided, as much of a home as the monastery gave him, by the mid-1960s, Thomas Merton was restless for another kind of existence.

Merton was full paradoxes. He was the mirror image of me, and the more I realized he was, the more he became a beacon, an alter-ego to my confused and jittery self. The voice in his writings was confident, yet self-effacing, bold, yet questioning, philosophically serious, and passionate.

One line from his autobiography made me grin every time I read it. "If this book does not prove anything else, it will certainly show that I was nobody's dream-child."

The older Merton looked back at his youth and admitted:

> What did I care about monks and monasteries? The world was going to open out before me, with all its entertainments, and everything would be mine and with my intelligence and my five sharp senses I would rob all its treasures and rifle its coffers and empty them all.
>
> And I would take what pleased me, and the rest I would throw away. And if I merely felt like spoiling the luxuries I did not want to use, I would spoil them and misuse them, to suit myself, because I was the master of everything.

Merton laid bare his soul in *The Seven Storey Mountain*. He didn't come across as a haughty intellectual or as a lofty, obtuse theologian. He was a humble and confused member of the human race, a person who had to confront and reconcile his own sins, misery, emptiness, and selfishness.

Consider Muriel Rukeyser's words. "Breathe in experience, breathe out poetry." That's how I saw Merton. That's what he did with his life. He inhaled experience, and exhaled poetry.

Merton wanted to be contemplative where the "active" part did not involve spreading the fruits of contemplation through the acts of writing and lecturing to novices and religious groups. That would have been the antithesis of contemplation as he meant it. He wanted to step away from his monastic day job.

He did not want to be the subject of his own writing any longer; he wanted to disappear so that the writing should mean nothing special to him. Its end results should not concern him, he said.

> In the same way, the true philosopher and the true poet become what they are and 'go beyond' philosophy and poetry, and cease to be 'philosophers' or to 'be poets'. It is at this point that their whole lives become philosophy and poetry—in other words, there is no longer any philosophy or poetry separable from the unity of their existence.
>
> Philosophy and poetry have disappeared. The ordinary acts of everyday life— eating, sleeping, walking, etc., become philosophical acts which grasp the ultimate principles of life in life itself and not in abstraction.
>
> —*The Madman Runs to the East*, Thomas Merton

The work was the prayer. All work, whatever the chosen vocation, if thought about in this way, was prayer.

In moments of desperation and frustration that he was not really living the kind of contemplative life he dreamed of for years, he addressed God, "You have got me kneeling behind the pillar with my mind as noisy as a bank! Is that contemplation?" In the *Sign of Jonas*, he wrote:

> Nevertheless, work in the fields helps contemplation. Yesterday we were out in the middle bottom spreading manure all over the gray mud of the cornfields. I was so happy I almost laughed out loud. It was such relief to get away from a typewriter.

Alaska would have answered his call to be aloft in the silence of nowhere.

It took me going back to Yakutat to really contemplate Merton's genius.

All I had were my books and coffee gone cold in the pot. It had been twenty-four hours and no personal human contact. How did Rudy Pavlik go for weeks or months on end wandering all over the country, around the Upper Situk Lakes, even in winter, without a companion?

I wondered how long I could last as a hermit without conversing with anyone in person, as those extreme recluses in France, the Carthusians, did. They only saw their fellow monks once a day for communal meals, otherwise they lived in total silence alone in their cells. My guess is that I'd have lasted five days, tops. Then I'd need to see someone, would need to start talking.

In no way was I cut out for the ultimate solitary life or to enter a convent to be closer to God. I agreed with Billy Joel. "The Catholic girls start much too late…and I'd rather laugh with the sinners than cry with the saints…the sinners are much more fun."

Learning how to sit in zazen for meditation or merely delving into the next Merton book, though interesting and satisfying in many ways, was not enough if I were to undergo a real conversion of heart and mind.

For that, I had to reorient my whole being, to learn to live with myself and my mistakes, doubts and contradictions. My salvation depended on reaching a new understanding about my innermost self.

I had to leave more about my life up to God's will with acceptance and humility and love.

With the men away from the cabin, I planned to walk over to Jennie's place. I wanted to catch up on what life had been like since her father's death. I thought about going over to Mr. Pavlik's cabin for old time's sake, but decided I couldn't. Four straight days in Yakutat, the men were out of my sight, and I had yet to pay Jennie a visit. I knew she was a bit sore at me that I didn't call in advance to tell her we were flying down from Anchorage. The truth was, I had been acting like a hermit ever since I got there.

...Under the blunt pine
Elias becomes his own geography
(Supposing geography to be necessary at all),
Elias becomes his own wild bird, with God in the Center,
His own wide field which nobody owns, His own pattern, surrounding the Spirit by which he is himself surrounded:

For the free man's road has neither beginning nor end...

—Thomas Merton's poem,
"Elias: Variations on a Theme"
from *The Strange Islands*

The man of Tao
Remains unknown
Perfect virtue
Produces nothing
'No-Self'
Is 'True-Self.'
And the greatest man
Is Nobody.

—Chuang Tzu (as translated by Thomas Merton)

23 Ocean Cape

Alaska was one of the last places on earth that Thomas Merton saw.

The date of Thomas Merton's death, or of his "repose" as the Orthodox prefer to say it, was December 10, 1968, less than two months after his northern sojourn when one of the unhappiest years in American history drew to a close.

After his travels in Alaska, and the Lower 48, Merton went to India and later met with His Holiness the Dalai Lama. He then flew to Thailand as part of his long-awaited Asian journey, where he attended a conference on the outskirts of Bangkok. Everything in the second half of 1968 seemed personally to be going his way. He was out of the monastery traveling extensively to broaden his understanding of Buddhism and Eastern monasticism, and thinking about all the changes that might lie ahead in his monastic future. As the conference's most celebrated guest and speaker, he gave a midday talk to a group of Asian monastics, predominately priests and abbots—a talk which happened to be recorded by a foreign film crew. After his brief remarks, Merton encouraged his audience to go grab a Coke and to take a short break. From the podium, with his spectacles across his nose and shuffling some papers, he joked, "So, I will disappear from view now…"

The monk returned to Cottage Number 2 for a short rest on the grounds of the Red Cross' compound. A few hours later, around 4:00 p.m., a fellow priest, discovered Merton lying on his back on the terrazzo tile floor with a standing fan, about five-feet tall, toppled diagonally over his body. His biographer, Michael Mott, described the details from the handful of witnesses who were present. The presiding abbot allowed only a few photographs to be taken, out of respect for the dead.

Burn marks appeared on the right side of Father Merton's body, but none on his hands. Blood showed on his head from striking the hard floor. A small pool of urine was found, caused by the body's release from the strong electric shock. Merton's mouth and eyes were partially open. When one of the priests quickly moved the fan, when he too, received a 220-volt jolt before it was unplugged.

Who could have foreseen the preposterous way in which Thomas Merton died—accidental electrocution from touching a fan with faulty wires while barefoot and in his underwear, right after he took a shower? I suppose it was conceivable I could have startled a moose with a calf, and been stomped to death, dead and gone in a split second, no long drawn out suffering. Death surprised Father Merton at age 53.

His death occurred exactly 27 years to the day after he first arrived at the Abbey of Gethsemani the night of December 10, 1941. Within a week after his death, and without an autopsy, his corpse was flown in the bay of an SAC Bomber, alongside the bodies of fallen soldiers from Vietnam, across the Pacific Ocean and back to Kentucky where he was buried in a simple grave marked with a plain white cross. There has never been any evidence supporting a conspiracy theory about his death or being anything other than an accident.

Dan L. Thrapp, a writer for the LA Times/Washing Post Service discussed Merton's final weeks and his death in an article that appeared in the *Huntsville Times* newspaper dated December 21, 1968. In it, Thrapp wrote, "Society's deep sickness has developed from the fact that it is 'too cerebral' and neglects the rest of man, Father Thomas Merton, renowned Trappist monk and writer, believed toward the end of his life.

"He felt open to such manifestations of renewal as 'pop spirituality,' but he believed it fell far short of restoring man to the wholeness he experienced in the 12th century, and even in Neolithic times, when the early Old Testament was being lived.

Thrapp went on to quote Merton directly, "…The whole business of hippies and LSD and everything else is an outcry of protest against this imbalance.

"And Christianity connived with this. Official Christianity has gone along with this kind of repressive and partial fragmented view of man, and now we have to face the consequences."

The story Merton was born into, the story he set down through his lyrical prose, was a story I paid attention to and learned from. My manic temperament was undeniably tempered by Merton's thoughts and writings. Toward the end of his life, Merton's moral duty as a writer was not to critique the world as a high-and-mighty religious man, but to "praise the mutilated world" as Polish poet Adam Zagajewski, wrote in one of his poems.

In the end, Merton's message was one of hope, unity, and necessity for the inner journey. He never gave up on the world as it was. Even during the worst of times post-World War II, and during the tumultuous 1960s with the threat of nuclear annihilation, he didn't resort to sinister pessimism. He did not believe we were inevitably laden with hopelessness and catastrophe. Nor that we were destined to suffocate in the continuum of our spiritual poverty.

How could Father Louis deny his God-given talents, give up writing in order to sit quietly as a hermit, adoring and praising God and praying in his glorious solitude each and every day?

In reality, Thomas Merton wanted to give up writing so he could live more wholly as a hermit in solitude. However, being true to self, writing was his way to honor his Maker, the Supreme Lyricist. How long would God have put up with it before throwing him out of his sterile cloister and back into the sea of humanity again as the writer he truly was?

I imagined that God abhorred complacency and absolutism, self-righteousness, and dogma. Women and men were called to

God's graces by whatever way their unique spiritual pathways guided them to be seekers and pilgrims.

Being the monk that he was, he could never confine the competing parts of himself and his contradictions into leak-proof compartments. Merton never stopped being a sojourner and an explorer, and he never entered into the bona fide hermitude he desired. To be a writer and poet were Merton's greatest vocation. I seriously doubt he could have lived without publishing his work. He might have gone into a period of literary silence, but given his curiosity, and his desire to connect with people, chances were good, he would have return to publish again. God planted the desire in him to be a writer. Writing nourished and drained him in every way.

He was an imperfect monk in an imperfect world and he died carrying his angst and frustrations with him, still seeking that perfect tranquility in God.

Had he lived, Merton would have spent the rest of his life searching for the perfect setting, the perfect monastic cell, the perfect mountain to ascend, the perfect piece of frontier darkness from which to see light, the perfect unity and solitude with God, but all the *Alaskas* on earth would never have fulfilled it. He might have moved from cell to cave to skete or to a homestead on Knight Island such as the brawny Pavliks did, or to the end of the road in Cordova near Eyak Lake.

But sooner or later, he'd draw visitors. He was too famous to hide out anywhere for long; his many admirers and friends would have tracked him down, even in rural Alaska.

Had he been given the chance, I believe Merton would have returned; Alaska's dizzying mountains would have called him back. In the closing pages of *The Seven Storey Mountain* he wrote, "Oh, America, how I began to love your country! What miles of silences God has made in you for contemplation! If only people realized what all your mountains and forests are really for!"

Lawrence Cunningham, Notre Dame theology professor, said, "There was, obviously, no anchored solitude in his brief stay in Alaska. The journal is an almost breathless catalogue of trips, conferences, visits to possible sites for a hermitage, and letters to the monastery requesting books to be sent to this or that person. In the background of that was the anticipation of the journey to Asia. Yet, and the point deserves emphasis, there was Merton the hermit who affirmed his desire for greater solitude either in Alaska or, perhaps, in Asia."

Alaska touched Merton in such a way, that it was the only state he wrote about for which an entire notebook could solely be dedicated.

Things definitely moved forward in the conversations between the renowned monk and the energetic Anchorage Archbishop about the best spot for a future hermitage. Discussions were well under way for Merton to return to the far north and to see more of the country around Cordova and Eyak Lake—a remote but not-too-distant place from Anchorage—after he completed his Asia travels.

In general, local priests and nuns, the "freezing faithful," would have been the only ones thrilled with this tentative plan. Most Alaskans at the time didn't have much of an understanding about Merton's real reputation. My experience told me that it wasn't the "Alaskan way" then or now to be awestruck about any big shots who showed up, even religious ones.

In 1968, many Americans still considered Alaska a gigantic snow prison, but after ten years of immersing myself in Merton's life and writings, I believed he would come back.

Merton made many entries about the landscape in his Alaska notebook. Through conversations he had on-the-ground with locals whom he personally met, he frequently expressed his awe. The great spiritual writer and thinker was wowed by the lakes lost amid tundra, and the beautiful islands he found everywhere. Though he did convey that its churches looked "poverty-stricken."

It was more than rumors and hearsay. Once, I spoke to a priest affiliated with the Archdiocese. He confirmed that Merton was on-track to return to Alaska one day, with much-needed and promised logistical support. Merton clearly favored the option of undergoing a kind of monastic experiment by remaining a monk of the Abbey of Gethsemani while somehow living as a distant hermit in Alaska.

In a letter to his good friend Wilbur Hugh "Ping" Ferry he sent from Anchorage to Santa Barbara, California on September 26, 1968, Merton wrote, "It is quite possible that if and whenever I get back from Asia I may end up here. Local Bishop extremely generous and everybody very helpful…"

But this has never been brought to the forefront; the Alaska detail was never emphasized by the biographers, scholars, filmmakers, the Abbey, or the Archdiocese, because Merton died suddenly. It was probably decided by the religious leaders involved that it was best to drop the whole subject once the news was received that the most famous monk in American history was accidentally electrocuted.

With the perspective of time, I sorted out more details about Merton's journey. Alaska not only provided miles upon miles of snowy all pervading silence, it also symbolized Merton's desire to bridge East and West while still remaining in America.

What better place than Alaska, with its indigenous peoples and culture, its historical ties to Russia and to Orthodoxy, and its geographic position on the Pacific Rim, to contemplate and pray for more profound East-West understanding?

Summer came around again and Michael and I decided to celebrate the Memorial Day holiday on a quick getaway to Yakutat with long-time friends, Steve and Lisa, a married couple from the Kenai Peninsula. They both liked deep sea fishing for halibut and flying to the more remote parts of Alaska regular tourists didn't visit. On any trip back to Yakutat, I insisted we drive out to Ocean Cape.

It was late in the day when we collected food and decided to have an impromptu cookout on the beach at the cape. Green-winged teals floated on a pond near a mansion sized beaver dam. At the next curve, we were surprised by a bright yellow

"Hazardous Work Area" sign because the access road rarely had any maintenance. Ocean Cape road existed for one reason—for locals to get out to the point and bluffs. There were many palpitating views in Alaska, but I couldn't think of any that matched the spectacular views of Ocean Cape on a clear day.

Once you left town, there wasn't a cabin or structure of any kind along the road whose tricky surface was known for beating up vehicles. People out walking alongside the road this far from town were also a rare sight.

"What's so hazardous?" I asked.

"A work crew has been in trying to remove old fuel tanks left over from World War II," Robert said. "Don't you remember seeing the U.S. Army Quonset huts out here?"

"Oh, that's right, but I forgot about them," I said. "But now that you mention it, I do remember how some dilapidated old huts were practically covered over in the brush."

The weather turned out to be extraordinarily rare for that particular late May evening, as I remember it now, almost perfectly clear with temperatures in the 60s. How elated we were to arrive at our favorite beach, none of us shivering in rain gear, or wearing thick socks and XTRATUF boots. Lisa, a life-long Alaskan wore flip flops and Michael had on a short-sleeved tee-shirt, without his usual dark green Polar fleece vest. Robert stood rosy-cheeked in his tawny nylon hiking pants, sturdy Keen sandals, with a neck-knife hanging over his chest. Content to be the designated grill master, he was eager to try out his new, stainless steel barbecue Alaska Airlines delivered to him via air-freight.

It was summer in Alaska and almost 8:00 p.m. We didn't need to worry at all about the sun going anywhere until closer to midnight.

"Lisa, let's go for a walk," I said. "Let's see if we can find some coyote or wolf tracks in the sand."

We gladly left the men behind to build and tend the fire. Heading north down the deserted shore toward the spot where the North Pacific meets the inshore waters at the entrance to

Yakutat Bay. We crossed through the dark, coarse and pebbly sand and over large pieces of twisted bull kelp that looked like circus whips. Quartz-veined rocks and boulders, exposed by the low tide, lined much of the beach, and when the waves splashed on them, the rocks turned black and shimmered like a seal's skin.

For a more panoramic view, I stopped and craned my head in all directions as far as I could see along the coastline. I couldn't believe my eyes. The weather gods were doing more than cooperating. It was pure magic, that moment. I entwined my arm in hers, and we both stood still and sighed. Her legs were tanned from playing a lot of golf in the land of the midnight sun, and her hair was peppered with the first few streaks of gray. She was as relaxed as I was, which said a lot. She hardly had the chance to experience that kind of soothing relaxation anymore since taking on one demanding job after another. Neither of us felt compelled to ruin the solitude and beauty by chitchatting.

A slight breeze came up and blew my copper hair under my baseball cap. I felt an energy surge through me. I paused to stare at the sea and the rocks without so much as even a sweater on. A glaucous gull into a decaying ling cod while a few other gulls landed and lined up on a nearby boulder.

I turned to Lisa and started mumbled, "Lisa, I don't know, but I think it's….it's more than a spectacular view this evening in absolutely perfect conditions. I don't know…it's something else…You know I've been here before….but I am never going to forget it, this feeling, this sensation, this *now*, whatever it is, whatever is happening." I stopped talking. Merton's Elias poem floated through my mind.

"*O, listen Elias, to the sound of these waves crashing in and to me who abides in the flickering light. I am here with you*"

Mount Saint Elias was out in full force, and this was shocking enough. But it looked softer than usual. The mountain's countenance changed from a stark, all white front to a peak backlit in a golden nimbus, creating an even grander appearance than I remembered.

Years ago, as a new wife and before motherhood, I lugged my 35-mm camera around as did Merton when he got to Alaska, as if I were a female version of Henri Cartier Bresson.

Mount Saint Elias looked beautiful in summer, but especially in the dead of winter with an opalescent moon hanging next to it, the mountain awash in the palest, calmest rose hip pinks. As the mid-afternoon winter sky darkened into swaths and billows of mauves and blue-grays, and the moon moved higher, the peak would be lost to the shadows becoming a mere outline against the sky. No matter what I did, or what new technique or filter I tried, I could never record the almost surreal December scene in the alpenglow the way my eyes saw it.

After about thirty minutes of stretching our legs, and taking in the view of golden light that bathed Mount Saint Elias, Lisa and I walked back to the picnic site encircled by piles of driftwood the size of full-grown trees. Michael helped Robert carry armfuls of sticks to drop in the fire pit they had dug into the sand. Steve's pony tail flapped in the breeze while he tossed a football with one of the Tlingit teenagers we brought along.

Before we could all gather on top of the washed-up logs, Robert abruptly lifted his spatula from the grill and perked up his ears.

"What's up, Bob?" Lisa teased, "One of your ex-girlfriends find you?"

A vehicle bumped and clanked its way through the rutted road and moved toward our secluded spot.

"Uh-oh, looks like we have company," Bob said with disappointment.

A thin, young man clad in a black wetsuit and sporting a head full of grayish-blonde dreadlocks jumped out of a rusty van. Bob shot him a scowl for disrupting our peace, but the guy glanced our way and didn't wave or say a word. With his surfboard tucked under his arm, he walked straight past our parked cars and across the open, gravel-filled beach into the water. The young man lay down on his surf board, paddled out, and with the ease of a cormorant merely resting on the water, he bobbed up and down with each passing swell. The breakers, smaller than normal, meant he had to simply paddle around for a while before there were any sizeable waves to catch.

"Renegade surfers have discovered us over the past ten years," Robert said as he went back to flipping over the ribeyes. "Stragglers hang out in town for a few weeks, surf in Ankau, Cannon Beach, or Ocean Cape and then they disappear back to wherever they came from, and hopefully taking their squatter's garbage with them. These surfer dudes drift in and out of town the way cannery workers used to."

Merton worried about increasing populations and noise when he wandered around the beaches of northern California near Shelter Cove, south of Mendocino. He witnessed the signs of encroaching bulldozers and cement trucks and commented on it in his travelogue. Alaskans were testy about their special places of solitude in the backcountry, their secret spots that sometimes required years of tromping in mosquito-filled brush or anchoring in many Prince William Sound coves to find the best places to be left alone.

But even with the occasional surfer, Yakutat remained mostly undisturbed by outside influences. And I believe that would have pleased Merton.

Robert promised to show us something new in Yakutat a short hike from our picnic spot.

"Keep going up that hill," Robert shouted from behind. "That's where you'll see it—the Coast Guard lookout tower. It's kind of hidden, but it has a beacon on top. Pretty cool, huh?"

One by one, Robert directed us to ascend the steel ladder, straight up for about 40 feet, until we got to a small viewing platform made out of metal grating.

"The beacon's a signal, a navigation device for cruise ships," Robert said, "and for merchant cargo vessels."

We filed onto the small space and stood in the breeze on the highest level of the tower and gazed at the ocean. His words about *merchant cargo vessels* struck a nerve.

Ocean Cape

I remembered my father's service on the *USS Wisconsin*, and much later the merchant marines. Louis J. Witkowski received a Victory Medal for his service in the US Liberation of the Philippines, but not even his three sisters ever mentioned it.

December of 1944, the *Wisconsin* was caught in a severe typhoon. The US lost three destroyers in Typhoon Cobra, all of them capsized and sank. A total of 790 American servicemen were lost. Nine other warships were damaged and over 100 aircraft were wrecked or washed overboard in the storm. But the *USS Wisconsin* proved its mettle and seaworthiness. It pulled through. When my dad told my mother about surviving a typhoon, he told the truth, though she didn't believe him. Just over a month after the typhoon, on February 19, 1945, his battleship repelled night enemy aircraft while making strikes against Iwo Jima.

At the top of the Coast Guard tower, two bald eagles snapped me out of my memory. They soared close over the trees behind us then locked their talons and cartwheeled through the air.

As I watched the two birds glide in a courtship ritual, the story of Father Louis' love affair with Margie entered my mind. It was interesting how Margie the nurse once wanted to become a nun. My mother Margie, who worked as a hospital clerk always wanted to be a nurse, but never was able to afford it.

While I was gathering history on Father Louis, the monk, I was also seeking truth about my father, Louis. They were both men I knew so little about. In the wake of learning about how my father died, it donned on me, both men died similarly. One from striking his head on a hard tile floor, and the other from striking his head on a barroom floor—one man rooted in service of God, the other rooted in service of country. I learned about the father I met and loved, but never really knew through the spiritual journey I took with the father I knew, but never met.

The Polish writer, Stanislav Brzozowski, wrote against the scientism of the age, the scientific image of nature. "Poetry must be seen as the creative self-definition of man," he wrote in 1910.

"...We can't reject our epoch, we can't reject history—human history is the final and deepest work, because we don't have anything with which to replace it. It is all man has...the reality of man is relative, provisional, unfinished; there is no ready, finished and closed reality."

Merton epitomized the idea that there was no finished enclosed reality. We were caught in transitions, evolutions, movements, and go-go-go; trapped in the fleeting, ephemeral—a glimpse, a blink, a puff, a moment blending into another moment, impermanence. Life was alive and moving.

Everything we did was bound up in everybody else's life. Prayers I didn't know I was making were answered in community. Total strangers, poets from foreign lands, Russian Orthodox pilgrims like Igor, testy old men like Mike Pavlik, and loving women like Jennie, filled me with stories and tales of spiritual survival. These unexpected, unpredictable, unconventional characters and literature entered my life and became part of me. They healed the undefined something that ailed me.

In the sweet failure of words, there were still signs of spring on the other side of the mountain, *if only you looked*. If you were attentive.

"The way to find the real world is not merely to measure and observe what is outside us, but to discover our own inner ground," Merton's said. "For that is where the world is, first of all: in my deepest self."

"Seclude the mind, not the movements, remain living in the world of man," Zen poet, Ch'iao-jan (734-c.792) said. "Lack a tree? Plant a sapling. Without a mountain? Look at a picture. Living amidst clamor I am not flustered; true meaning is found in this."

Once, in talking to the novices at Gethsemani, Merton advised them to thank God even for their past faults, for they were past and they were, in God's wondrous providence, occasions for moving us forward on our inner journey. He added that had it not been for the sins of his youth, he might well have ended up a second-rate diplomat off in some corner of the British Empire rather than a monk at Gethsemani.

Thinking of my own mistakes, I might have ended up as a droning Washington, D.C. press aide obsessed with political circles of power rather than being a wife and struggling writer hanging out with poets in Alaska.

I always came back to Pasternak. It was good to recall how Pasternak expressed the sacredness of life amidst the revolutionary clamor in *Doctor Zhivago*.

In the novel, Yurii—also called by his more intimate and affectionate family name of *Yura*—grew up to become a young doctor. In the early part of the novel, one scene unfolded in which Yurii sat at the bedside of the dying Anna Ivanova, the woman who was so dear to him, the woman who brought him up after his mother's untimely death when he was a little boy. Anna Ivanova lay drenched in sweat, her lips parched. Yurii was quiet.

"Surely, Yura, you know something to say," Anna said, as tears streamed down her cheeks.

"You are clever and smart and therefore different."

Yurii searched for the right words and began a long, rambling monologue to offer Anna Ivanova some comfort, knowing she was close to death.

Yura spoke, "What is it about you that you have always known as yourself? What are you conscious of as yourself? Your kidneys? Your liver? Your blood vessels? *No.*

"However far back you go in your memory, it is always some external, active manifestation of yourself that you come across your identity—in the work of your hands, in your family, in other people.

"And now listen carefully. *You in others—this is your soul. This is what you are,*" Yura told her gently. "This is what your consciousness has breathed and lived on and enjoyed through your life—your soul, your immortality, *your life to others.* And what now? You have always been in others and you will remain in others. What does it matter to you if later on that is called your memory? This will be you—*the you* that enters the future and becomes part of it."

We are not drunkards here, carousers immune to the sufferings of the world. We are all poets here, bound to one another through the inner spirit, one beating heart to another.

This was the silent prayer I muttered, "God, thank you for all you have given me, though I did not always see, and I did not always understand what you were trying to tell me."

Merton said the Spirit breathed where it willed and you didn't know where it came from or where it was going. The journey inward was long, and getting there was not pleasantly sacred and serene—it was damn noisy. Full of anger against God, and anger against the ones you love, full of grief, loss, guilt, self-doubts—the emotions that needed to be shouted out in the middle of sleepless nights. The very idea that I had been making a prayer I didn't know, and that a Trappist monk I couldn't have met was answering my prayer before I even made it—this was my definition of something mystical and Divine.

I recalled the sequence of events, and remembered where and when I first possessed momentary sparks of spiritual clarity. In those first brief sparks, where was I, exactly—in what place on the planet?

Merton experienced his epiphany in 1958 on the corner of Fourth Street & Walnut in downtown Louisville where he happened to be for a few brief hours. The monk looked astoundingly at the faces of all the city workers rushing by, black and white faces, haggard and handsome faces, richly dressed, and farmers in dungarees, and in that sea of humanity, he realized he loved all those people, those perfect strangers, the "others" who surrounded him. His glorious destiny was to be a member of the human race and that God himself, Merton said, had gloried in becoming part of human history. There was no such thing as a separate holy existence for monks, priests, nuns or any religious, Merton believed. We were all walking around shining like the sun.

Ocean Cape

Where was I when I had my epiphany? I was there, right in that water-sodden place just as I was long ago, standing at Ocean Cape, eyes wide open, perhaps, for the first time in my life.

I gazed at the stormy, desolate Pacific, at the ravens playing along the shore. I saw the faint outline of the Malaspina Glacier off in the distance. All the best scenic views Alaska offered converged in that one spot. What I once thought of as essential, the externals in my life—status, money, jobs—were no more. Something stripped off, peeled away like a salmon skin.

Somehow, I stood there naked before God in the pouring rain, with the winds and water beating against my face. And with conviction I said, "I am nothing. Here, in this place, I am nothing."

Ocean Cape, made by God, is all and all, and my petty thoughts and inadequacies and doubts dissolved into the sea. Though my ancestry was mostly ill-defined, unremarkable, and untraceable, I felt connected in community.

I was not alone on that lonely coast. It was in the solitude and contemplation of Yakutat, and through Merton's legacy, that I realized God took me here to that faraway place to quiet me, to give me time to scrape off the hardened crust of my false self.

The mountain, like God's icon, was robed in iridescent white, backlit by the fading sunlight of a long summer day.

I was no longer adrift. I found the solid deck beneath my feet. I understood that it was good for me to be there again surrounded by so much quiet beauty, to be huddled happy in the sun or in the pouring rain with those I loved.

I had to lose myself to find myself. If was unable to cope I remembered Elias was there. I yearned to be nearer to it, even when my mind and heart were far away and my vision was blocked.

I found my footing in Mother Alaska. With Merton, I understood what a centering was, what a real prayer was, what contemplation was. My Faith in God was confirmed under the Prophet Mountain.

When all you knew disintegrated—when you fell on your knees and cried in despair—at those dark, dark moments of feeling forgotten and forsaken, there was comfort to be found on the other side of the mountain.

When it comes time, I want my ashes tossed into the sea at Ocean Cape to circulate among the halibut bones and humpback whales, to settle on the ocean's bottom until Japanese currents or an underwater quake moves me on. It's for the Earth and its waterways to decide where my remains will scatter.

As Steel Town Girl, I detested the idea of being placed in a metal crypt or a metal casket, buried on cemetery land, fenced-in, organized and marked plot-by-plot. I didn't want my body to be draped and enclosed in blackness where direct physical contact with Alaska and the sea would be severed forever.

Once my ashes are scattered in the Pacific, what's left—molecules, bone particles, dust—will, in a sense be reconfigured and renewed in God's mystery.

Earth, the fragile blue dot—blue as glaciers are blue—it's into this big blueness I want to go.

Thomas Merton's 1968 Alaska Itinerary

Alaska journey as published in *Thomas Merton in Alaska* (New Directions Publishing Corporation).

Tuesday, September 17
Chicago to Anchorage

Wednesday, September 18
Eagle River (Convent of the Precious Blood)

Thursday, September 19
Eagle River

Friday, September 20
Eagle River

Saturday, September 21
Eagle River—Ft. Richardson
Elmendorf Air Force Base

Sunday, September 22
Eagle River

Monday, September 23
Cordova

Tuesday, September 24
Valdez—Copper Valley
Matanuska Valley—Anchorage

Wednesday, September 25
Anchorage

Thursday, September 26
Anchorage—Palmer

Friday, September 27
Anchorage—Yakutat—Juneau

Saturday, September 28
Juneau—Anchorage

Sunday, September 29
Anchorage

Monday, September 30
Anchorage—Dillingham

Tuesday, October 1
Dillingham—Anchorage

Wednesday, October 2
Anchorage to San Francisco

Thursday, October 3
San Francisco to Santa Barbara

Bibliography

Furlong, Monica. *Merton: A Biography.* San Francisco: Harper & Row, 1985.

Griffin, John H. *Follow the Ecstasy: Thomas Merton, The Hermitage Years 1965-1968.* Latitude Press. 1981

Echoing Silence: Thomas Merton on the Vocation of Writing, Robert Inchausti, editor. Boston: New Seeds Books, 2007.

The Intimate Merton, Patrick Hart and Jonathan Montaldo, editors. San Francisco: HarperCollins Publishers, 1996.

Matlits, Elena. *The Solitary Explorer: Thomas Merton's Transforming Journey.* New York: Harper & Row, 1980.

Mott, Michael. *The Seven Mountains of Thomas Merton.* Boston: Houghton-Mifflin, 1984.

Shannon, William H. *Thomas Merton: An Introduction.* Cincinnati: St. Anthony Messenger Press, 1997.

Shannon, William H. (editor) *Thomas Merton: The Hidden Ground of Love.* New York: Farrar, Straus & Giroux, 1985.

A Thomas Merton Reader (revised edition), Thomas P. McDonnell, editor. New York: Doubleday, 1989.

Thomas Merton in Alaska, Prelude to The Asian Journal, the Alaskan Conferences, Journals, and Letters. New York: New Directions, 1988

Woodcock, George. *Thomas Merton—Monk & Poet: A Critical Study*. New York: Farrar, Straus & Giroux, 1978.

Films
Merton: A Film Biography, Produced by Paul Wilkes, 1984.
Soul Searching: The Journey of Thomas Merton. Producer: Duckworks, Inc., 2007.
The Many Storeys and Last Days of Thomas Merton, Duckworks, Inc, 2014. Produced by Morgan Atkinson.

Electronic Media
Thomas Merton, The Seven Storey Mountain and the Rest of the Story, Dr. Michael W. Higgins, Ph.D., NowYouKnowMedia, 2014.

Thomas Merton: A Spiritual Guide for the Twenty-First Century, by Fr. Anthony Ciorra, Ph.D., NowYouKnowMedia, 2011.

Thomas Merton on Contemplation, by Fr. Anthony Ciorra, Ph.D., NowYouKnowMedia, 2012

Articles/Essays

Dart, Ron. "In the Footsteps of Thomas Merton: Alaska" *The Merton Seasonal*, Vol. 33, No. 4, Winter 2008.

(*Author's note*: This bibliography is *not* meant to provide a complete list of all the books, articles, and other media consulted in my spiritual journey with Thomas Merton. I've highlighted a few references and sources I found especially valuable.)

Acknowledgments

In Thomas Merton's life-long passion for writing, he believed that the courage for truth was the special gift of writers. Truth is, this book would not exist if it were not for the friends, family, and colleagues who took a genuine interest in the story I was trying to tell. To everyone who shared a part of this meandering, often paradoxical journey, thank you. There are far too many individuals to thank here by name, however I am grateful just the same.

I am forever indebted to Jessica Mesman Griffith. She has been my beacon of light since day one. Besides her treasured friendship, I have learned from her literary brilliance. Jonathan Montaldo, scholar, writer, editor, helped set my compass toward Thomas Merton over a decade ago. Jonathan's supportive feedback has been immensely helpful. It was through his skillful eye, expertise, and compassionate wisdom that this book finally became a reality. I owe much to my friend Andromeda Romano-Lax, novelist, teacher, and world traveler for wholeheartedly believing in this work and for offering valuable input on messy, early drafts. Mary Alice Cook, historian and writer, shared her knowledge and freely gave her time whenever I needed it. Mary Alice's friendship and energy kept my pen moving and my spirits up—and all the coffees we shared helped, too. I thank Olga Livshin for who she is—a lyrical dynamo and a creative force with whom I shared many inspired exchanges. In my formation as a writer, Igor Runov has been nothing less than instrumental. Without his loyal friendship, and keen historical and literary

Acknowledgments

perspectives, I would have been lost. He is a one-of-a-kind human being who never stops guiding me in the right direction. And I especially thank Mikhail Pokrovsky, and Olga and Lida Pokrovskaya for taking care of me on so many levels, emotionally and logistically. I will remember their kindness and love.

It's difficult to find adequate words to properly thank Wayne Pichon, fellow Alaskan and long-time Thomas Merton admirer. Wayne kept the literary dream alive. He pushed me to never, ever give up. He exuded the enthusiasm and spark needed to carry on. I can't thank him enough for all the support he's given me.

With heartfelt appreciation and many smiles, I thank my friends, writing groups, and writing circles from years past and present: Joan Wilson, Doug O'Hara, Lee Goodman, Bill Sherwonit, Amanda Coyne, Scott Banks, David Ramseur, Linda Ketchum, Barbara Hood, and Shehla Anjum. For always listening and offering a positive outlook, I thank Lisa Tarr, Diane Pennington, Tony and Sylvia Logar, , Kim Sylvis and Dorothy Sylvis, Kathy Beeck, Robin Richardson Matthews, Cindy Premo, and Peggy Rogers. From the University of Alaska Anchorage, for their never-ending moral support and invaluable literary mentorship, I acknowledge my former colleagues and extraordinary writers Sherry Simpson, Dr. David Stevenson, and Anne Caston. And I say thank you to Rachel Epstein from the University of Alaska Anchorage Campus Bookstore. George Core, former editor of the *Sewanee Review* for over three decades, provided important literary momentum and validation just when I needed it most. Gary Freeburg, art professor, photographer, and sailor, I thank for listening to me yammer on about "the book" for years. I also thank Barry Lopez for his correspondences with me on Thomas Merton and the writing life. I must express special appreciation to Joe Durepos of Loyola Press, Chicago, for his wise advice and many consultations that gave me hope.

From my days at University of Pittsburgh where, for over three years, I was fortunate to cross paths with so many talented people. I acknowledge Julie Wan, Kristin Cosby, Julie Hannon, Amy Andrews Alznauer, Cassandra Soars, Hattie Fletcher,

Courtney Bray, Elaine Vitone, Sharon McDermott, Jeff Oaks, Jennifer Lee, and my former professors Lee Gutkind, Jeanne Marie Laskas, Bruce Dobler, and Mary Briscoe. All of them have been extremely important in teaching me to hone my skills, but more importantly, to dare.

I especially thank these organizations for providing time, space, inspiration and opportunities to write in solitude throughout the years: Virginia Center for the Creative Arts in Amherst, Virginia; Mesa Refuge Writers' Residency, Point Reyes Station, California; 49 Writers and the 49 Alaska Writing Center; and Kachemak Bay Writers' Conference, Homer, Alaska.

For their interest, scholarship, and wide-ranging research assistance, I will always be grateful to Dr. Paul Pearson and Mark Meade of the Thomas Merton Studies Center, Bellarmine University, Louisville, Kentucky. I extend a heartfelt thank you to the trustees of the Merton Legacy Trust.

I thank Fr. Tom Connery of Glenville, New York, Sister Adelajda Sielepin, Krakow, Poland, and Krystyna Lenkowska of Rzeszow, Poland for the many spirited conversations and discussions. Early research efforts led me to the bookshop at Holy Family Cathedral in downtown Anchorage. There Christine Reichman, fellow Merton aficionado, piled on the Merton titles for me to read nearly a decade ago. Thank you.

I owe a big round of applause to my colleagues at University of Southern California's Institute for Advanced Catholic Studies, Los Angeles, where I was lucky to be a designated "Mullin Fellow" from 2013-2015. I thank the following cohort of writers and mentors with whom I had the great pleasure of conversing and studying: Fr. James Heft, Gregory Wolfe (founding editor of *Image Journal*), Dr. Gary Adler, Dr. Brian Volck, Dave Griffith, Jenny Shank, Lisa Ampelman, and Samuel Martin. And many thanks to Peter Mullin for his philanthropic gifts.

To the co-editors of *Cirque: A Literary Journal for the North Pacific Rim*, Michael Burwell and Sandra Kleven—thank you for sharing your astute editorial insights, for all the good work you do, but most of all, thank you for your dedication to art and literature. To my publisher, Vered R. Mares, founder of VP&D House whose mission of bringing good and much-needed stories to the world is something she passionately lives and breathes, I say thank you. I am honored beyond my wildest Alaskan dreams that we have trudged this crazy path together from Alaska to Cuba and back.

Finally, to my family—especially my sisters Patricia Holmes, Beth Ann Burmaster, Donna Summerlin, and to my niece Kelsey and nephews Kyle and Sam—for everything they've bravely endured while I was writing this book.

A loving thanks to my sons, Banan and Derek, and to their father, Michael Tarr, for the critical, life-affirming foundation provided for so long.

The people who stand quietly and humbly in the background are those who often matter most.

> ...I would say that for me most of the hardship has come in connection with writing. It is possible to doubt whether I have become a monk (a doubt I have to live with), but it is not possible to doubt that I am a writer, that I was born one and will most probably die as one. Disconcerting, dis-edifying as it is, this seems to be my lot and my vocation. It is what God has given me in order that I might give it back to Him.
>
> —Thomas Merton,
> *A Thomas Merton Reader*, 1962

Publisher's Note:

Wherever possible, traditional or historically used place name spellings or names of people (fictitious or real) were favored over modern spellings—for example, Yurii from *Doctor Zhivago*, has been spelled using that which was used in our original source material showing the double "i" at the end, and not the more modern or westernized spellings of Yuri or Yury. This is true for the Russian language and Native language words as well.

In a few cases where there were multiple acceptable spellings available, we chose the most commonly used version. Womens Bay, although often incorrectly written as "Women's Bay" is shown on maps of Alaska as "Womens Bay" without the apostrophe. We used the correct map version despite its appearance of being incorrect.

Transliteration of Russian phrases use spelling that most accurately helps with reading and pronunciation, or are the most commonly used transliterated versions.

The peak shown on the cover of Thomas Merton's Alaska Journal, which came from one of Thomas Merton's photos, was identified as O'Malley Peak with the help of a geologist here in Alaska, among other mountains from his photos such as Mount Redoubt and Mount Augustine. Thomas Merton's photo of the Mendenhall Glacier near Juneau was also identified through a comparison of USGS images of the glacier from 1968 against Merton's photo, though the glacier looks very different today.